A CONCISE INTRODUCTION TO PHILOSOPHY

Fourth Edition

WILLIAM H. HALVERSON
The Ohio State University

McGraw-Hill, Inc.

New York St. Louis San Francisco Auckland Bogotá
Caracas Lisbon London Madrid Mexico Milan
Montreal New Delhi Paris San Juan Singapore
Sydney Tokyo Toronto

This book is printed on recycled, acid-free paper containing a minimum of 50% recycled de-inked fiber.

A CONCISE INTRODUCTION TO PHILOSOPHY
Fourth Edition

18 17 16 15 14 13 12 11

Library of Congress Cataloging in Publication Data

Halverson, William H.
   A concise introduction to philosophy
   Bibliography: p.
   Includes index.
   1. Philosophy—Introductions. I. Title.
BD21.H23   1981   100   80-21178
ISBN 0-07-554307-9

To Bernhard M. Christensen,
who first introduced me to philosophy

PREFACE

Henry David Thoreau, in a memorable aphorism, once recommended to his contemporaries that they "read not the *Times,* read the eternities." Now it may be somewhat pretentious to suggest that the problems philosophy deals with have to do with "the eternities," but they clearly do concern matters that are of more enduring interest than the latest dispatches from London or Tokyo or Wall Street. Indeed, to the extent that philosophy succeeds in clarifying our understanding of the human situation—some would say the human predicament—it provides a context and a perspective within and from which the events of our time may be more fully understood.

The relevance of philosophy for an understanding of current issues and events is, however, indirect rather than direct. Questions such as "Should marijuana be legalized?" or "Should abortion be freely available to any woman upon request?" are important and timely questions, but they are not *philosophical* questions. Philosophy cannot provide a direct answer to such questions, nor should it attempt to do so. What philosophy can and should do, however, is to clarify the kind of reasoning that is involved in our thinking about ethical issues with the hope of raising the discussion of these issues to a higher level of rationality than would otherwise be likely to occur. To represent philosophy as being *directly* concerned with such timely student concerns as abortion, drugs, homosexuality, the draft, and the like is, in my opinion, to trivialize philosophy and to defraud the students toward whom such pseudophilosophy is directed. Students have a right to expect that the insights gained from a serious study of philosophy will be relevant to the problems of tomorrow as well as to those of today.

This edition of *A Concise Introduction to Philosophy,* like its predecessors, examines a number of fundamental philosophical problems the answers to which are held to be relevant to the development of a coherent world view and philosophy of life. The introductory section has been totally rewritten and shortened to two chapters in order to get students more quickly into a discussion of the substantive problems with which the book is chiefly concerned. This edition also restores, at the request of many instructors, a discussion of the problem of induction, and includes a new section on aesthetic judgment as well. The sequence of topics has been altered somewhat in order to accommodate these changes, and every chapter has been reviewed and revised with a view to achieving the maximum possible clarity of exposition. A companion volume, *Concise Readings in Philosophy,* has also been prepared, thus providing a convenient opportunity for students to supplement the discussions in this book with appropriate readings in the primary sources.

The *dialogue form* that is used throughout this book calls for a few words of explanation. Each topic is introduced in an introductory chapter in which I attempt to clarify the problem that is to be discussed, define the principal alternatives, and introduce any technical terms that may be necessary for the discussion that is to follow. Each succeeding chapter on that topic is then written *from the point of view of a convinced advocate of the view in question.* Only in Part I (Chapters 1–2) and in the introductory chapters of each succeeding part do I write, so to speak, "in my own name." The remaining chapters should read as if they had been written by many different authors.

What is gained by this somewhat unusual format is a combination of the principal advantages of an anthology and of a single-author text. Like an anthology, *A Concise Introduction to Philosophy* keeps the discussion in the first person. The various writers are not merely talking *about* something: they are advocating a point of view, trying to secure agreement. Also like an anthology, *A Concise Introduction to Philosophy* is able to give a fair hearing to a variety of philosophical views: it does not bias the argument in favor of any one philosophical tendency or school. But it is also like a single-author text in certain respects: it has the coherence and, most important, the terminological consistency that cannot be expected in a book that is the product of many different authors.

Thanks are due to many individuals who have helped in countless ways to make this a better book than it would otherwise have been: to the users of previous editions, who made numerous suggestions for improvement; to the Ohio State students in Philosophy 101 who, by their questions and comments, helped to identify some of the places where further clarification was needed; to my colleagues at Ohio State who graciously accepted added duties in order that I might have time to bring this project to completion; to Jane Cullen and her associates at McGraw-Hill, Inc. for many helpful suggestions; and to Doris Coon, who supervised the typing of the final manuscript. Finally, for the critical role that he played in introducing me to philosophy, and for the inspiring example that he has been to me and to others for so many years, I express my deep and heartfelt thanks to Dr. Bernhard M. Christensen, President Emeritus of Augsburg College, to whom this book is affectionately dedicated.

W.H.H.
Columbus, Ohio

CONTENTS

PART I

A PROLOGUE
TO PHILOSOPHY

1

PHILOSOPHY

The curiosity of a child is a wonderful thing. It begins to appear in an observable way when the child is but a few days old. An infant boy, for example, attempts to focus his eyes on a nearby object, tries to touch the patch of light or color within his field of vision. At first—before he learns to move about—the only available objects for his curiosity are those bits of the world that happen to lie in the vicinity of the particular location where he is placed. Soon, however, he is moving about. He finds things to open, take apart, throw, jump on, shake, swallow, strew about, and, in general, treat in ways that bear little resemblance to the uses for which those objects were originally intended. The boy, we say, is playing. True. But he is also exploring his world, finding out how things work, testing his ability to make things happen in the world. He is, in short, satisfying his curiosity.

Curiosity—the desire to understand and to know—lies at the root of all science and philosophy. Man, as Aristotle said long ago, by nature desires to know.[1] The desire of the scientist or the philosopher to expand the horizons of our understanding is but the mature result of that original curiosity with which every human life begins.

Science

Absolutely anything that falls within the field of human awareness may, theoretically, become an object of study, an object upon which

---

[1]Aristotle, *Metaphysics,* I, i, in Richard McKeon (ed.), *The Basic Works of Aristotle* (New York: Random House, 1941), p. 689.

we may vent our curiosity, our desire to know. When that study takes the form of a disciplined inquiry concerning the physical universe, the result is what we call science.

What do we mean by "disciplined inquiry"? We mean the systematic search for general laws governing some class of phenomena by methods appropriate to the phenomena being studied. We mean gathering data, advancing a generalization (hypothesis) that may be supported by those data, testing that generalization, perhaps reviewing it, then testing it again, until finally a generalization is achieved that appears to be consistent with all the known facts. We mean, in short, what is commonly called the scientific method.

It is a grave mistake to think of science as having to do primarily with test tubes, microscopes, cyclotrons, and the like. One should not confuse the gadgets of science with science itself. "Science" is simply the collective name for the totality of human efforts to achieve a systematic understanding of the physical universe through disciplined inquiry. The purpose of the gadgets is merely to assist in these efforts.

Why, then, do we not have only one science? Why do we have physics and chemistry and astronomy and biology and all the other sciences? Why is there not one all-embracing science that attempts to understand the whole physical universe? Surely, the answer is obvious. It is more efficient to divide up the labor of inquiry among specialists who are then able to give their full attention to the study of some manageable range of natural phenomena. If the physical universe were not so incredibly complex, a single, all-inclusive science would suffice. Specialization among scientists is a matter of efficiency and convenience, not one of principle.

The ultimate goal of science—that is, of all the sciences together—is to produce a description of the universe so complete that everything that occurs can be understood as an instance or instances of regularities that we call laws. If this theoretical goal were to be reached, science, in the sense of disciplined inquiry, would come to an end. Each generation would, of course, have to master this voluminous knowledge anew, but—if we assume that the laws of nature do not change—there would be no *new* truths to discover. New generations would have no further use for the "gadgets" of scientific inquiry, except perhaps to satisfy themselves that the findings of their predecessors were absolutely accurate. A complete account of the universe—its origin, its laws, its predictable future—could be written down in books for all to read. If someone were able to master the contents of all those books, he or she would know everything there is to know about the physical universe.

Beyond Science

If we could know everything there is to know about the physical universe, would we know *everything* there is to know? Is there any true knowledge—knowledge of anything—other than the knowledge that comes through scientific inquiry? Is the physical universe the only reality there is, and is it thus the only possible object of knowledge? Indeed, is scientific knowledge itself as secure as we usually consider it to be?

To ask such questions is to leave the domain of science and to enter that of philosophy. To answer such questions—no matter what answer we may give—is to take a philosophical position, to affirm a philosophical theory. One theory may be true and another false. Our present views on these matters may be right or they may be wrong. It may be that by careful study of these and related questions, we can determine what is true and what is false. Such is the path by which our inborn curiosity—our natural desire to know—leads us from the gaping wonderment of childhood to science and ultimately to philosophy.

The intellectual quest that leads us beyond science leads us also beyond art, beyond historical inquiry, beyond political science, beyond every field in which the search for knowledge is pursued. When one asks about the nature of beauty, or searches for meaning in history, or attempts to discover a foundation or rationale for the authority of government, one is no longer doing art or history or political science: one is doing philosophy. Whatever may be the focal point of one's interest—natural science, art, history, political science, psychology, or business—one cannot think seriously about it for long before one finds oneself asking questions that are essentially philosophical in nature.

Philosophical questions typically exhibit some or all of the following characteristics: (a) they do not fall within the competence of any of the sciences, (b) it is genuinely difficult to determine what kind of evidence, if any, is relevant to answering them, (c) they are logically fundamental, and (d) they are questions of broad generality, questions whose answers have far-reaching consequences for our understanding of ourselves and our world. Scientists and other specialists have as much right as anyone else to ask and attempt to answer such questions—but when they do so, they leave the realm of science and enter that of philosophy.

Make no mistake about it: the acquisition of knowledge is not an easy task. Humankind's present fund of knowledge is the hard-won product of the efforts of countless millions of human beings who, in their desire to know, have succeeded in discovering some new truth. Countless other human beings have spent a lifetime attempting to expand our fund of knowledge, but have failed to do so.

Why is the achievement of knowledge so difficult? In part, it is because the world is genuinely complex and yields its secrets only to those who inquire with infinite care. But there is another reason, too, and that is that what is believed to be the truth at any given time is almost certainly a mixture of truth and error, and the error prevents us from making further progress until we go back and correct it. The science of astronomy, for example, was held back for many years because it was attempting to go forward on the mistaken beliefs that the earth is at rest in the center of the universe and that the sun and the planets revolve around it. Only when these mistaken beliefs were corrected—only when the error was discovered and what we now believe to be the truth was substituted in its place—could the science of astronomy move forward.

Philosophy: The Critical Task

In the unending quest for knowledge, philosophy has two important tasks to perform. Let us call them, respectively, the *critical* task and the *constructive* task.

The critical task of philosophy is to *question truth claims* whenever they may be put forth—to ask, so to speak, by what right this or that belief is to be accorded a place in the fund of human knowledge. The purpose of such questioning is not, of course, to destroy or tear down the truth but rather to purge it of error. It is assumed that truth is stronger than error, that under the critical questioning of philosophy the truth will survive and, hopefully, the error will not. To the extent that it performs this task effectively, philosophy contributes to the advancement of human knowledge by locating errors that might otherwise retard its progress.

This side of the philosophical task is beautifully exemplified by Socrates, the great Greek philosopher of the fifth century B.C. whose life and works are largely known through the writings of his friend and pupil Plato. Socrates was regarded as such a menace by the "establishment" of his day that he was eventually haled into court on charges of "impiety" and "corrupting the youth" and, after a brief trial, was condemned to die.[2]

What led to the charges against Socrates? According to Plato's *Apology,* which is considered to be a fairly accurate account, the facts are these. A friend of Socrates, Chairephon, inquired of the oracle at Delphi whether anyone was wiser than Socrates and received the reply that no one was. Hearing this, Socrates—who, as he says, knew in his conscience that he was *not* wise—proceeded to test the oracle's statement by interrogating some of his fellow citizens who were generally regarded to be wise and learned. Socrates comments on his interrogation as follows:

> I approached one of those who had the reputation of being wise for there, I thought, if anywhere, I should test the revelation and prove that the oracle was wrong . . . But when I examined him . . . and when I conversed with him, I thought this man *seemed* [italics added] to be wise both to many others and especially to himself, but that he was not . . . After that

---

[2]A moving description of Socrates' death is given in Plato's *Phaedo.*

> I tried another, one of those reputed to be wiser than that man, and I
> thought just the same; then he and many others took a dislike to me.[3]

Socrates took it to be his unique task to interrogate his fellow citizens
to see whether or not their opinions could stand up under close scrutiny. Whenever he found people holding opinions, or making truth
claims, he went to work. Does Meno claim to know whether or not
virtue can be taught? "Meno," asks Socrates, "What *is* virtue? Do you
really know what virtue is? And if you do not know what virtue is, how
can you possibly know whether or not it can be taught?" Does Euthyphro claim to know that his father is guilty of impiety? "Euthyphro,"
says Socrates, "I do not even know for sure what piety and impiety are.
Could you instruct me in this?"

This picture of Socrates going about questioning the men of Athens
to test the soundness of their opinions represents what we have called
the *critical* side of the philosophical enterprise. We all take many
things for granted; indeed, everything we do is determined by, or at
least affected by, our assumptions, even though very often, perhaps
most of the time, we are scarcely aware of them. It is in the assumptions that underlie supposed knowledge that the philosopher is chiefly
interested. He wants to know what those assumptions are and whether
or not they are reasonable; thus, like Socrates, he examines them.

Socrates, of course, went about his business in an informal and
personal way. Since his time, however, philosophy has become more
or less institutionalized. The questions that philosophers raise today
are directed not so much at individuals as at fields of learning. The
philosopher questions not the scientist but the assumptions and the
truth claims of science; not the religious person but the assumptions
and the truth claims of religion; and so on. Philosophy is, so to speak,
the gadfly in the curriculum of a modern college or university, just as
Socrates was a gadfly to his fellow citizens in ancient Athens.

Philosophy: The Constructive Task

The second task of philosophy—the constructive task—is to develop a
picture of the whole of reality, in which every element of man's knowledge and every aspect of human experience will find its proper place.
Philosophy, in short, is man's quest for the unity of knowledge, a
perpetual struggle to create the concepts that allow the universe to be
seen as unified rather than as fragmented. The history of philosophy
is the history of this attempt. The problems of philosophy are the
problems that arise when one attempts to grasp this total unity.

Consider, once again, that hypothetical state of affairs in which

---

[3]Plato, *Apology,* in W. H. D. Rouse (ed.), *Great Dialogues of Plato* (New York: New
American Library, 1956), p. 427.

everything there is to know about the physical universe has been discovered. We would still want to ask certain questions. What are good and evil? What is their place in a universe whose physical workings we now understand so completely? Does this complete description of the universe describe the universe as it is, or is it, wholly or in part, merely a description of the universe as we perceive it? Is beauty a quality in objects that we call beautiful? Is it something "in the eye of the beholder"? Or is it something else? Does the physical universe exist as a self-subsistent entity, or is it dependent for its being on some reality beyond itself? Is the consciousness that we ourselves experience merely a physical phenomenon, or is it something else? The fact is that our awareness of suffering, of tragedy, of injustice, of good and evil, of beauty and ugliness, of meanness and nobility, leaves us dissatisfied with only a physical description of the universe. We cannot be content until the truths about these and other dimensions of our experience have also been understood and brought into some coherent relationship with what we know about the universe as a system of purely physical phenomena.

The attempt to achieve this total understanding stands without rival as the most audacious enterprise in which the human mind has ever engaged. Just reflect for a moment: we are surrounded by the vastness of a universe in which we are only a tiny, and perhaps insignificant, part. Yet we want to *understand* it, to conceive the whole thing in our minds, in such a way that no reality that confronts us, no event that occurs, no fact that we discover, nothing that we experience, is beyond the categories of our understanding. Audacious indeed; but what are the alternatives?

One alternative would be to attempt no understanding at all. Perhaps, if one tried hard enough, one could learn to accept the world unquestioningly, responding to it in terms of self-preservation only. Apparently other species do no more and survive rather well in the struggle for life.

In all seriousness, however, it does not appear likely that human beings ever could or would do this, even if it were desirable. Aristotle was right: man, by his very nature, desires to know. Not only do we seek to know in order that we may more effectively manipulate our environment, we also seek to know purely for the sake of knowing. The total abandonment of the quest for understanding, then, is not a promising alternative to constructive philosophy.

Another alternative would be to be content with piecemeal knowledge—to establish what we can in each of the special sciences and to make no attempt to see the "total picture," of which each of these fragments is presumably a part. Such an approach is expressed in statements like "It is better to know one thing well than to know a little bit about everything" or "It is better to be a good chemist than a poor philosopher."

But here, too, there is a problem, one that makes it impossible to hold such a view except in the half-jesting mood reflected above. For as we focus our attention on first one area and then another, we are sometimes driven to conclusions that appear to be in conflict with one another. How, we insist on asking, can a person be free in the sense that ethics seems to require if, as appears to be the case, the whole universe is subject, without exception, to causal law? If all knowledge comes to us through experience, and if experience yields only probability, how is it that in mathematics we appear to be able to establish our conclusions with absolute certainty? These and other questions thrust themselves upon us, almost in spite of ourselves. It is out of such tension among the various elements of our piecemeal knowledge that much philosophical thinking arises. For to ask such questions is precisely to ask for the wider concept, the total picture, in which what is legitimate in each of these competing truth claims can be given its due.

The truth is that all human beings—philosophers and nonphilosophers alike—carry on their thinking in terms of some comprehensive view of the whole of reality. We do not intentionally or knowingly hold views that are inconsistent with each other—for example, that all people are free in certain respects and also are not free in those same respects, or that God exists and also does not exist. We try, successfully or unsuccessfully, to "put it all together," to assent only to those well-supported truth claims that are consistent with the other truth claims to which we have already given our assent. Constructive philosophy is simply the search for the comprehensive view—the "big picture," as it is sometimes called—that is most adequate to all the known facts.

World Views

A particular view of the whole of reality, through which one attempts to understand everything that comes before one's consciousness, is called a world view. The constructive task of philosophy, then, can be described as the quest for an adequate world view. The problems of philosophy are the problems that arise as one pursues this quest.

Much later in this introduction to philosophy—when we have dealt with enough philosophical problems to make the effort meaningful—we will look in some detail at several alternative world views. It may be helpful to bear in mind from the beginning, however, that one theme that underlies nearly all philosophical discussion is the perpetual conflict between *naturalistic* and *nonnaturalistic* world views. A *naturalistic* world view is one in which it is affirmed that (a) there is only one order of reality, (b) this one order of reality consists entirely of objects and events occurring in space and time, and (c) this one order of reality is completely self-dependent and self-operating. According to philosophical naturalism, a complete knowledge of the physical universe would constitute a complete knowledge of the whole of reality. Any world view that denies any of the above-stated tenets of naturalism, then, may be termed *nonnaturalistic.* Thus a world view affirming that human beings possess a mind or soul that is something other than a physical entity, or affirming that the entire physical universe is dependent for its existence on a God who is not Himself a part of that universe, is nonnaturalistic.

The perpetual conflict between naturalistic and nonnaturalistic world views explains in part why philosophers sometimes defend so vehemently their views on what may appear to be relatively trivial matters. Indeed, because every philosophical question is related in one way or another to the quest for an adequate world view, no philosophical question is ultimately trivial. Every philosophical problem is, so to speak, a test case. Our whole world view—the entire system of beliefs by which we attempt to understand the complex array of data coming before our consciousness—is always at stake.

Philosophies of Life

Closely related to the quest for an adequate world view—a counter-theme, one might say, that runs through much philosophical discussion—is the quest for an adequate philosophy of life. What is humanity's place in the scheme of things? Does human life have any purpose, and if so, from whence does it derive that purpose? Are there some things in this world that are worth living for, striving for, and, if so, what are they? One's answers to such questions constitute what is called a philosophy of life. And, as we shall see, the answers that it is possible for us to give to these questions depend to a significant degree on the world view that we have adopted. Thus, the philosophical journey, however circuitous it may at times appear to be, issues ultimately in beliefs and commitments of profound importance for the conduct of our daily lives.

STUDY QUESTIONS

1. Is it true that man by nature desires to know? What evidence is there either for or against this proposition?
2. What, exactly, is the ultimate goal of science? Do you think this goal will ever be reached? Support your answer.
3. Consider the following question: "Does the physical universe constitute the whole of reality, or is there some reality that is not a part of the physical universe?" Is science competent to answer this question? Explain.
4. A college president once said to a graduating class, "About half of what you have learned at this college is true, and the other half is false. Your job now is to try to figure out which is which—and don't ask us to tell you, because we don't know." Do you think this is an accurate description of the state of human knowledge today? Explain your answer.

5. What, exactly, is the "critical" task of philosophy? What are some of the questions that a philosopher might ask in attempting to pursue this task?
6. "We cannot avoid doing constructive philosophy. We can only decide whether to do it carelessly and haphazardly, or carefully and well." Do you agree or disagree? Why?
7. What, exactly, is a world view? What determines whether a world view is naturalistic or nonnaturalistic?
8. How would you describe your present world view? Is it naturalistic or nonnaturalistic? How have you come to hold this world view? How confident are you that in its main outlines, it is correct?
9. What do you understand to be the elements of a philosophy of life? How does this relate to either the critical or the constructive tasks of philosophy?

2

THE STUDY OF PHILOSOPHY

This book proceeds on the assumption that you, the reader, are a beginning student in philosophy. You do not claim to know very much about what the so-called great philosophers thought or said. More than likely you have never taken a philosophy course in your life. Yet the fundamental issues of philosophy are issues that all of us think about at one time or another. Undoubtedly, you have been "doing" philosophy for some time—that is, asking philosophical questions, engaging in philosophical arguments, and adopting philosophical views.

The new element in the picture for you, then, is that you are now going to *study* philosophy. You are going to try to get a handle on it, to find out what it is all about, and possibly even find the answers to some important questions that have been puzzling you lately. The philosophizing that you have done up to this point has probably been fairly tentative and unsystematic. You know that the questions you have been asking are important ones, but you have not quite known how to go about finding the answers. The study of philosophy, you have been told, will help you in your search.

Perhaps it will. But in order for your study of philosophy to achieve this result, you must employ a methodology appropriate to such study. The purpose of this chapter is to suggest what that methodology should be.

Two Approaches to Philosophy

Introductory courses in philosophy typically employ either an *historical* or a *systematic* approach. In the former, one studies, in chronological sequence, the thought and writings of selected philosophers from ancient times to the present (or perhaps from some more limited time span). A principal objective in such study is to acquire historical information—to find out what Plato, Aristotle, Descartes, Kant, and others thought about whatever topics they happen to have dealt with. The truth that one is seeking in such a study is historical truth, that is, an accurate account of the thought of this or that philosopher or group of philosophers. The methodology appropriate to such an approach is the methodology appropriate to any historical study: authentication of the primary sources, careful interpretation of selected texts, and the like. A good student of the history of philosophy exercises the learning skills needed to acquire a correct and thorough knowledge of the philosophical views of the particular philosophers whom he or she elects to study.

The approach to philosophy employed in this book, however, is not historical but *systematic.* The understanding that we are seeking is an understanding of a series of philosophical problems, and of the possible solutions to these problems. The truth that we are seeking is the truth with respect to each of these problems, and the relation of this truth to that adequate world view and philosophy of life that are the ultimate aims of the philosophical quest. If in the course of our study we learn something about what this or that philosopher had to say with respect to our problem, all well and good: then our historical knowledge will have been incidentally enriched in the process of our systematic study. The acquisition of historical knowledge, however, is quite incidental to the learning tasks required by a systematic introduction to philosophy. In fact, they may divert one's attention from those tasks. The skills and techniques of the historian will not take us far toward mastery of the problems with which we shall be dealing in the succeeding chapters of this book.

What, then, *are* the techniques appropriate to the systematic approach to philosophy?

Three Steps Toward Understanding

There are three distinct steps to be mastered with respect to each philosophical problem that one encounters.

First, one must attempt to understand precisely what the problem is. It is important to remember that understanding a problem is not the same as memorizing some approved formulation of that problem. There are undoubtedly some things that must be learned by rote, but there is very little in philosophy that can profitably be learned in this way. To understand a philosophical problem is to know what question you are asking and what kind of assertion would count as an answer to the question. If you do not know this—if you cannot imagine anything that would qualify as a possible answer to your question—then, you have not really asked a question; you have only made a little interrogative noise.

Most of us, unfortunately, are so much in the habit of deceiving ourselves (and others) about what we really understand and what we understand only in a general, hazy way, that it is necessary to exercise some strict self-discipline if we are to overcome this deception in our struggles with the philosophical problems that follow. The deception is rendered all the more difficult to get rid of because there is no sure method for determining when we are guilty of it. The following may, however, be offered as a general rule: if you really understand something, it should be possible for you to vary the expression of it without altering the meaning. If you cannot express an idea in more than one way, the likelihood is that you have not understood that idea.

It is impossible to overemphasize the importance of *understanding* in philosophical learning. Facts and words can be memorized, but meanings and relations must be understood; and philosophy is concerned with meanings and relations. I know the meaning of the question "Is New York City more populous than London?" Thus, I can ask the same question in a variety of ways: "Is the population of New York City greater than that of London?" "Do more people live in New York City than in London?" "Does New York City have a greater population than the capital of England?" But I am not at all sure what people mean when they ask "What is the meaning of life?" I cannot hope to make any progress in my reflections on this question until I understand precisely what is being asked; then, and only then, can I imagine what sort of assertion might count as a possible answer to the question.

The second step is to make a conscious and determined effort to ascertain all the alternative ways of answering the question with which we are dealing. Then, and only then, can we weigh the arguments for and against the various positions and perhaps make up our minds on the matter, confident that we have not simply neglected to consider some position that, if examined carefully, might commend itself more strongly than any of those under consideration.

Some philosophical problems allow as few as two possible alternative answers. An example is the epistemological problem discussed in Chapters 3–7 of this book. More commonly a problem will allow three or four solutions. Sometimes, however, it is not possible to state with certainty that such and such are the only possible positions to take with respect to a given problem. Even in such a case, however, it is extremely important to make the attempt to define the alternatives, since in doing so we may discover why a limit to the number of possible solutions cannot be set. We may, of course, be reasonably confident that we have considered all the plausible alternatives, even though we have not surveyed all those that may be logically possible.

If we demand precision in understanding the problem, and precision and completeness in understanding the alternative possible answers, we have in hand a powerful instrument for organizing subsequent philosophical inquiry. Consider: If I have understood a given problem P, and if I have determined that positions A, B, and C are the only positions to take with respect to it, then nothing that anyone can say with respect to P can be completely novel to me. If Plato, or Aristotle, or Kant, or Bertrand Russell, or anyone else addresses himself to this problem, he must do so in behalf of (or in opposition to) position A, or position B, or position C, no matter what terminology he may employ. Hence, I can attend carefully to his arguments and can enter into the discussion with a clear understanding of what it is all about.

The third step toward philosophical understanding is a consideration of the arguments for and against the various alternative positions. Now to the making of arguments there is no end, and it is impossible to state with respect to any philosophical position that thus and so are *the* basic arguments for or against such a position. Practically all philosophical discussion consists in presenting arguments either (a) in favor of some position in an attempt to establish it or (b) in opposition to some position in an attempt to refute it. Step three, therefore, is never completed: it is the arena of philosophical discussion into which we are qualified to enter as soon as steps one and two have been mastered (with respect to any given problem).

Again, there is no great value in memorizing a list of "approved" philosophical arguments—for example, three or four arguments in favor of one theory and three or four arguments in favor of another. Rather, you should ask, what kinds of considerations would tend to support the first theory? What kinds of considerations would tend to support or refute the second theory? Then, you will be in a position to assess any arguments that you may encounter, and perhaps to devise a few of your own.

The Importance of Terminology

At each step along the route to philosophical understanding, it is important to observe one cardinal rule: maximum care must be taken at all times to establish the exact meaning of terms, and terms, once defined, must be used appropriately.

For the purposes of ordinary discourse, we can often get along without demanding absolute precision in language. We can, for example, discuss the weather, and even agree that it is a "nice day," without being too fussy about exactly what qualities a day must have before it qualifies as a "nice" day. Anyone who doubts that we operate with relatively inexact language in our everyday conversation might try giving precise definitions to such phrases as "a nice day," "a good ball game," "a boring speaker," or "a snap course."

For some purposes, however, it is important that language be used with as near-perfect precision as possible. In mathematical computation, for example, it is obviously important that the symbols employed have precise meanings, and that those meanings remain constant throughout the course of computation. The ideas of force, mass, velocity, and many others have been given similarly precise meanings in physics; calculations involving these concepts would not be possible were it not for this precision.

In philosophy it is also important to define one's terms as precisely as possible in order to avoid the confusion that would otherwise result. Indeed, the technical and semitechnical language of philosophy has been developed for the express purpose of enabling philosophers to discourse with greater precision than would otherwise be possible. The serious student of philosophy will make every effort to master this terminology as he or she goes along, for, however esoteric it may sound at first, its real and valid function is to enable us to think and speak precisely about matters that in everyday language remain obscure and imprecise.

More than this, however, we must learn to be on the lookout for ambiguities in everyday language that, if not detected, may mislead and confuse. If, knowing that Socrates died in prison, we hear someone say, "Socrates was a freer man on the day he died than those who brought about his imprisonment," the chances are that we shall find the statement confusing. In one sense of "free," Socrates clearly was not as free as his accusers. They were free to walk the streets of Athens and to spend time with their families; he was not. What, then, does the speaker mean? Is he or she talking about some "inner state," which Socrates supposedly had on the day of his death in a greater degree than did his accusers? Or is the speaker suggesting that in dying, Socrates was somehow freed from his body and, in this way, became "freer" than his accusers? Some careful analysis of the term "free" is needed if we are to dispel the bewilderment that such a statement can create. To think critically, carefully, analytically about the exact meanings of terms is to observe the rule stated above.

Qualities of Mind

Finally, it must be pointed out that the effective study of philosophy requires more than mere technique. It requires an array of intellectual qualities—habits of mind—that are both rare and priceless. Let us identify these qualities in order that we may hold them up as an ideal toward which we might aim as we pursue our quest for philosophical understanding.

The first required quality is curiosity, for without it there can be no science, no learning, no philosophy. The curious mind is ever restless, ever searching, ever asking "why?" To be curious is to preserve the wonderment of childhood, to be lured by the unanswered questions that flood in upon us if we but dare to open our minds to the infinity of the reality that surrounds us. To be curious is to wonder whether the received wisdom is wisdom or folly, to look for a truth that is deeper and more secure than that which appears on the surface of things. Albert Einstein was once asked, "How did you happen to discover the general theory of relativity"? His reply: "I challenged an axiom." Such curiosity is the driving force within all science and all philosophy.

Next, one should possess an openness; that is, a willingness to adopt a view different from the one currently held if the weight of evidence appears to be on the side of the new view. Such openness is enormously difficult to achieve. Many, perhaps most, of the beliefs that we hold at the time we undertake our initial study of philosophy are sanctioned by the authority of parents, teachers, famous people, institutions, our own peers, society, perhaps even by common sense. It is not easy to be open to ideas that contradict the received wisdom, ideas that call in question the unargued assumptions that underlie one's whole way of looking at the world. It is easier to be closed-minded, defensive, unbending, unwilling to change. Intellectual obstinacy—the attitude that says "I've already made up my mind, don't confuse me with the facts"—is without a doubt one of the major obstacles to the advancement of learning.

But intellectual openness—we could also call it intellectual humility—must be balanced by intellectual boldness. Intellectual boldness is the willingness to take a stand, to affirm a view on the basis of our best understanding of the relevant evidence. That view may or may not stand up under close scrutiny, but that should not deter us from venturing an opinion when we think we may discern the truth on this or that issue. Indeed, it is in the clash of conflicting opinions that we may hope to find the truth, and it is in risking our present opinions that we may hope, at length, to distinguish between those that are true and those that are false.

A fourth quality essential for the effective study of philosophy—one that is no less difficult to achieve than those already mentioned—is the quality of intellectual honesty. To be intellectually honest is to be perfectly candid—with ourselves and with others—about what we do and do not understand, what we do and do not believe, what we have and have not investigated with respect to whatever issue may be under discussion. Is it not true that most of us have been conditioned through long years of schooling to pretend to our parents, our peers, our professors—to pretend to understand what we do not understand, to *say* we agree when we do not agree (and may not even understand what it is that we are supposed to be agreeing with), to *claim* a thoroughness in our study that we know has not occurred? Intellectual honesty requires that we cease all such deception, that we develop, instead, the habit of professing only and always what we truly do understand and believe. It is better, as Socrates said long ago, to acknowledge your ignorance than to live with the illusion that you know what you do not know; for in acknowledging your ignorance you may be inspired to seek the truth, whereas in pretending to know when you do not know you neglect to seek the truth because you mistakenly believe that you already have it.

Learning by Doing

Thus far, we have been talking about philosophy and how to approach it as a beginning student. Such talk is appropriate when one is introducing philosophy to those who have had no previous experience with it. But now the time has come for us to stop talking *about* philosophy and to begin engaging in philosophical discussion. And here, philosophy being what it is, the student must be prepared to play his or her appropriate role.

"Philosophy being what it is"—what do we mean by this? We mean that philosophy is an activity to be engaged in, not a body of information to be committed to memory. As with any complex skill, there are some points of information that must be mastered. In learning to ski, for example, we have to find out where we should put our weight, what to do with the poles, how to use the edges of the skis, and so on, if we are to be able to execute the various maneuvers that constitute skiing. But the point of all this learning is to *do* something, not simply to acquire some information. And this is true also for philosophy. The point in studying it is to learn to philosophize, to "do" philosophy.

Thus, you should approach the discussions that follow not as a spectator but as a participant. The first chapter in each part will provide a "ticket" to the arena: a statement of the problem and a description of the alternatives. These must, of course, be carefully studied and thoroughly understood. Beyond that, it is totally a matter of arguments; each position is allowed to speak for itself, to marshal whatever arguments it can in support of itself and in refutation of all others. Some of the arguments that you will encounter in this book are powerful arguments, arguments that may convince you of the truth of the positions in whose support they are offered. Other arguments may strike you as only mildly convincing, and yet others may appear to you to be weak, perhaps even silly. Your job, in any case, is to assess these arguments as you encounter them, to be persuaded by them when you find them persuasive, to refute them when you think they miss the mark—in short, to enter as fully as you can into the living dialogue that is philosophy.

And now, to the dialogue itself.

STUDY QUESTIONS

1. What is the difference between an *historical* and a *systematic* approach to philosophy?
2. "Understanding a problem is not the same as memorizing some approved formulation of that problem." Why not? What *does* it mean, then, to understand a problem? How can one demonstrate that one understands a problem?
3. Is it ever possible to state with certainty that one has identified all the possible ways of answering a question? Consider the following examples:
   a. Is it possible to prove the existence of God?
   b. Do we have free will?
   c. What does it mean to say of some act that it is morally blameworthy?

d. Is there any reality other than the world of space, time, and matter? If so, what is that reality?

e. What is the meaning of life?

4. Define a) a nice day, b) a good ball game, c) a boring speaker, d) a snap course. Is it true that in these cases everyday language is somewhat imprecise? Why is the imprecision of language a potential problem in the study of philosophy?

5. What qualities of mind has your educational experience thus far tended to foster? Are they the qualities that are likely to be conducive to the effective study of philosophy?

6. "You should approach the discussions that follow not as a spectator but as a participant." What does this mean? Are you ready?

CORRELATED READING[1]

---

1. Plato. *Apology.* Many editions. Plato's moving account of Socrates' defense—of himself and of philosophy—before the Athenian court.

FOR FURTHER READING

Ayer, A. J. *Philosophy and Language.* New York: Oxford University Press, 1960.

Hahn, Lewis E. "Philosophy as Comprehensive Vision," *Philosophy and Phenomenological Research,* 22 (1960), 1–25.

Hamblin, Charles L. *Fallacies.* London: Methuen, 1970.

Iribadjakov, N. "Philosophy and Antiphilosophy," *Philosophy and Phenomenological Research,* 35 (1974–1975), 181–200. A Marxist account of the task of philosophy and its relation to the sciences.

Jaspers, Karl. *Way to Wisdom,* trans. by Ralph Manheim. New Haven, Conn.: Yale University Press, 1951 (paperbound). See especially Chaps. 1–3.

Körner, Stephen. *What Is Philosophy? One Philosopher's Answer.* Baltimore, Md.: Penguin Books, 1969.

Krikorian, Yervant H. (ed.). *Naturalism and the Human Spirit.* New York: Columbia University Press, 1944. See especially Chap. 15, "The Nature of Naturalism," by John Herman Randall, Jr.

Loewenberg, Jacob. *Reason and the Nature of Things.* LaSalle, Ill.: Open Court Publishing Co., 1959.

Merleau-Ponty, Maurice. *In Praise of Philosophy,* trans. by John Wild and James M. Edie. Evanston, Ill.: Northwestern University Press, 1963. See especially pages 33–64.

Nagel, Ernest. *Logic Without Metaphysics.* New York: Free Press, 1956. See Part 1, Chap 1, "Naturalism Reconsidered."

Newell, R. W. *The Concept of Philosophy.* London: Methuen, 1967.

Parsons, H. L. "The Philosopher and Mankind's Struggle for Value," *Philosophy and Phenomenological Research,* 36 (1975), 246–252. Attempts to relate the philosophical enterprise to some fundamental forms of human experience.

Passmore, John. *Philosophical Reasoning.* London: Gerald Duckworth, 1969 (paperbound). An examination of some common forms of philosophical argument.

Russell, Bertrand. *The Problems of Philosophy.* New York: Oxford University Press, 1959. See especially Chap. 15, "The Value of Philosophy."

Ryle, G. "Systematically Misleading Expressions," in Antony Flew (ed.). *Essays on Logic and Language,* First Series. New York: Philosophical Library, 1951.

Sheldon, W. H. "Critique of Naturalism," *The Journal of Philosophy,* 42 (1945), 253–270.

---

[1] *Concise Readings in Philosophy,* Part I.

Smart, J. J. C. *Philosophy and Scientific Realism.* New York: Humanities Press, 1963. See especially Chap. 1, "The Province of Philosophy."

Supek, Ivan. "The Task of Philosophy Today," *Philosophy and Phenomenological Research,* 24 (1963), 117–124.

Waismann, Friedrich. "How I see Philosophy," in H. D. Lewis (ed.). *Contemporary British Philosophy,* Third Series. New York: Macmillan, 1956.

White, Morton. *Toward Reunion in Philosophy.* Cambridge, Mass.: Harvard University Press, 1956.

Wisdom, J. O. *Philosophy and Its Place in Our Culture.* New York: Gordon and Breach Science Publishers, 1975. An interesting characterization of the philosophical enterprise by an influential contemporary philosopher.

PART II

RATIONALISTS AND EMPIRICISTS

3

THE ISSUE BETWEEN RATIONALISTS AND EMPIRICISTS

The first philosophical problem that we shall consider is, unfortunately, one that many students of philosophy find somewhat difficult to understand. It is, however, the problem with which we must begin because it logically precedes—in ways that will soon be apparent—so many other problems. We are going to face it head on here at the beginning of our study, but it is going to crop up again and again in one form or another as we move on to consider other problems. So be forewarned: the more adequately you understand what is involved in the issue between rationalists and empiricists, the better prepared you will be for what is to follow.

We begin by noting the commonplace, but nonetheless remarkable, fact that we human beings have the ability to acquire some knowledge of the world in which we live. This ability is certainly not infallible, for time and again something that we had believed to be true turns out to be false, and what we had believed to be false turns out to be true. Nonetheless, prone to error though we may be, each of us has come to know quite a few things about the world, and we would have little difficulty in writing down a long list of statements that we know, or at least think we know, to be true. Indeed, knowledge appears to be so plentiful today, and its acquisition so common an occurrence, that most of us have probably never stopped to consider that our capacity to acquire knowledge is a truly remarkable fact.

Philosophers, whose business is asking questions about certain things that many people simply take for granted, have long been interested in the phenomenon of human knowledge. There is, in fact, a division of philosophical inquiry called *epistemology* (from the

Greek, *episteme,* meaning "to know"), that is concerned with the nature and limits of human knowledge. The problem with which we shall be dealing in this section is one of the central problems in epistemology.

Knowledge

What does it mean to "know" something about the world? Suppose, for example, that we say, "Johnny knows that if you put your hand into a flame, you will get burned." Just what does this mean? It appears to mean three things: (1) it is the case that if you put your hand into a flame, you will get burned; (2) Johnny believes that if you put your hand into a flame, you will get burned; and (3) Johnny has reasonable grounds for so believing. Let p be any statement about the real world, and let A be any person whatsoever. When A knows p, then (1) what p asserts is the case, (2) A believes that p is the case, and (3) A has reasonable grounds for believing that p is the case. If any one of these conditions were not present, we would not say that A *knows p.* If (1) were absent, we would say that A mistakenly believes p. If (2) were absent, we would say that although p is true, and A ought to believe it (since he has reasonable grounds), he does not. And if (3) were absent, we would probably say that A just had a hunch or made a lucky guess.

It is important to note that the knowledge that we are talking about at the moment is knowledge about the world, knowledge about some matter of fact. That fire burns, that the sun rises in the east and sets in the west, that there are mountains in Colorado—these are facts about the world, facts the knowledge of which constitutes knowledge about the world. The statements asserting these facts are true because the world is the way it is. If the world were different—if the facts were different—these statements would be false.

Let us call any statement that asserts some matter of fact an *empirical* statement. An empirical statement, then, is a statement about the world, about reality. It is a statement that affirms that something is the case, that the facts are this way and not that way. If the facts are what an empirical statement affirms them to be, the statement is true. If the facts are not what the statement affirms them to be, the statement is false.

In principle, then, although not always in practice, the truth or falsehood of an empirical statement can always be determined by examining the relevant facts. Why only in principle? Because the facts in a given case may be difficult, or even impossible, to determine. The statement, "At the exact center of the earth there is a huge nugget of pure gold," is an empirical statement because it affirms a matter of fact. If there really is a nugget of gold at the center of the earth, the statement is true; if not, it is false. In principle, we know what would have to be the case in order for this statement to be true. But the difficulty of drilling to the center of the earth to find out what it is made of is so great that in practice we cannot determine whether this particular statement is true or false.

Empirical statements should be clearly distinguished, however, from *analytic* statements, which are statements that (a) assert nothing about the world, and (b) are true merely by virtue of the definitions of their terms. The statement, "All circles are round," for example, is an analytic statement. Its truth does not depend on any matter of fact but simply on the meanings that have been assigned to the terms "circle" and "round." If you know the meaning of the words "circle" and "round," then you know all that you need to know in order to know that all circles are round, that if anything is a circle, then it is round. No empirical facts are relevant to the truth or falsity of this statement. Indeed, the statement is true even if it should be the case that there is not a single example in the whole world of an object that fits the definition of a "circle."

The Sources of Knowledge

Let us return to our knowledge of the world—that is, knowledge expressed in empirical statements. We have, or at least we think we have, a good deal of such knowledge. How did we acquire this knowledge? What are the ways by which we come to know truths about the world?

One source of our knowledge, obviously, is our own experience. We have, in the course of our lives, seen and heard and touched and tasted many things. On this basis, we can say a good deal about the world and about ourselves—for example, that we have two arms, two legs, eyes, ears, and so on. Moreover, we know from experience that unsupported objects fall, that fire produces heat, that rain makes things wet. The list of things that each of us knows by direct experience would be very long indeed, and since every person's experience is in some ways unique, no two lists would be exactly alike.

But if each of us knew only what we ourselves had directly experienced, our knowledge would be vastly more limited than, in fact, it is. By far the greater part of what we know we have learned from others. Through listening and reading we have learned many things about history, geography, literature, and the sciences that, in all probability, we would never have been able to discover for ourselves.

In reality, however, there is not much difference between these two sources of knowledge. It is as if ten people set out together to inspect a ten-room house, and in order to save time and effort, they agreed to inspect just one room each and report to the rest. Each person, then, would know about one room by direct experience and about the other nine by indirect experience. The information that we get from teachers and from books is what we might call secondhand experience. If we trace this information to its source, we will inevitably find someone whose experience has taught him what he is now teaching us.

Rationalists and Empiricists

Apart from a minor quibble over whether or not what we have been talking about really deserves to be called knowledge (Plato, for example, called it mere opinion), most philosophers would have no quarrel with what has been stated so far. It is obvious that we have some kind of cognitive rapport with the world by means of direct and indirect experience, and it is perfectly consistent with ordinary usage to say that what we acquire in this way is knowledge of the world.

At this point there arises, however, one of the most controversial and important issues in philosophy: Are there or are there not any truths about the world—empirical truths—that can be known to be true just by thinking about them? It is clear that analytic truths are known in this way. Does this also apply to some empirical truths? Can they ever be known in the same way? Is there such a thing as "direct apprehension" of empirical truths? Is experience the whole and only source of our knowledge of the world, or is the human mind capable of grasping some truths about the world "on its own," with experience serving merely as the occasion for this insight?

Some philosophers hold that the human mind is capable of a direct apprehension of certain empirical truths, and that, in fact, we have some knowledge of the world that we have acquired in this very unique way. This view is called *rationalism,* and a person who holds this view is called a *rationalist.* Other philosophers deny this possibility and maintain that our knowledge of the world arises entirely out of experience. They are called *empiricists,* and the position that they represent is called *empiricism.* With respect to this question, rationalism and empiricism are the only alternatives, and they are mutually exclusive. You can be a rationalist or you can be an empiricist, but you cannot be both and you cannot avoid being one or the other.

In order to discuss this issue with maximum precision, however, we need a vocabulary that is somewhat more technical than the language we have been using thus far. Therefore, let us now define a few terms and then attempt to state our problem in a more precise way.

Analytic and Synthetic Statements

We have already defined an analytic statement as a statement that is true by virtue of the meanings of its terms, and offered as an example the statement, "All circles are round." In order to test the truth of such a statement, it is not necessary to examine any circles to see whether in fact they are all round. We need only analyze the subject of the statement, and there we shall find the notion of roundness. To call something a circle and to deny that it is round would be a contradiction: it would be equivalent to saying that some round things are not round.

A *synthetic* statement is one in which what is affirmed in the predicate adds something to the concept of the subject. A house, for example, may be defined as an enclosure within which human beings live and find shelter. If, then, I say, "Some houses have pink shutters," I am uttering a synthetic statement, because the idea of having pink shutters is not contained in the idea of a house. I cannot produce my statement simply by analyzing the subject (house); rather, I must make a synthesis of two different concepts (house and pink shutters) —in short, a synthetic statement.

Strictly speaking, the definitions of "analytic" and "synthetic" given here apply only to analytic and synthetic statements of the subject-predicate type. But if the distinction is understood, it can be easily generalized to apply to statements of other types. An alternative, and broader, definition of "analytic statement" would be "a statement whose truth is determined solely by the meaning of its terms"; and of "synthetic statement," "a statement whose truth or falsehood is not determined solely by the meaning of its terms." A statement whose falsehood is determined solely by the meaning of its terms is said to be analytically false.

A Priori and A Posteriori Knowledge

Two additional terms for which we shall shortly have use are *a priori* and *a posteriori.* Something is said to be known a posteriori if it is known on the basis of experience. How do we know that lemons are sour? We know it a posteriori: we have tasted them. How do we know that too long an exposure of skin to the sun causes sunburn? We know it a posteriori: we have been sunburned, or we have seen others who have been sunburned. Everything that we know by direct or by indirect experience we know a posteriori. Experience (either our own or someone else's) is the whole and only source of such knowledge, and if such knowledge is challenged, it is to experience, and experience alone, that we must appeal for confirmation. A posteriori knowledge is only as secure as the factual evidence upon which it rests.

With a priori knowledge the situation is different. Here, factual evidence is not relevant, though some philosophers would say that many a priori truths are constantly exhibited in experience. What, then, is an a priori truth? It is a statement the truth of which is evident apart from the facts of experience. To know something a priori is to know it immediately, directly, without recourse to factual evidence. In a certain sense, it is to know something prior to experience—namely, that all subsequent experience must conform to what is thus known. What is known a priori is seen, as Immanuel Kant said, to be necessary and universal. Once grasped, its untruth is inconceivable, and it is then immediately evident that it must be true at all times and in all places.[1]

Note that the terms "analytic" and "synthetic" describe two kinds

---

[1]Immanuel Kant, *Critique of Pure Reason,* Intro., II, trans. Norman Kemp Smith (New York: St. Martin's Press, 1965), pp. 43–44.

of statements, whereas the terms "a priori" and "a posteriori" describe two alternative ways of knowing that a statement is true.

The Problem Restated

It is evident that we know many synthetic truths a posteriori. No one, not even the most enthusiastic rationalist, denies this, and it is a caricature of the rationalist's position to say that he or she does.

It is equally evident that all analytic truths are known a priori. No one, not even the most incorrigible of empiricists, denies this, and it is a caricature of the empiricist's position to say that he or she does.

The question is, however (and this is where the rationalist and the empiricist part company), do we or do we not have any a priori knowledge of synthetic truths? The rationalist says we do, the empiricist says we do not. It is upon this one issue that we must focus our whole attention in the chapters that follow. The controversy might be represented as follows:

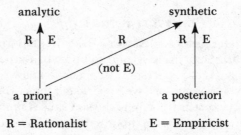

analytic   synthetic

R ↑ E   R   R ↑ E

(not E)

a priori   a posteriori

R = Rationalist   E = Empiricist

Note that we now have before us two formulations of the same problem. Our first formulation was: are there or are there not any truths about the world—empirical truths—that can be known to be true just by thinking about them? Our second formulation, which asks the same question in more technical language, is: do we or do we not have any a priori knowledge of synthetic truths? The second formulation is, however, somewhat more precise, and the language in which it is stated will be used frequently in the remainder of this section. The reader is urged, therefore, to get the key terms—analytic, synthetic, a priori, a posteriori—clearly in mind before going any further.

The Issue Behind the Issue

It may be well to say a few words at this point about what is at stake in this celebrated controversy. If empiricism is right in affirming that all knowledge of reality (as opposed to knowledge of analytic truths) is a posteriori, then it is clear that our knowledge of reality is limited to that which falls within, or can be definitely inferred from, the realm of experience. If such is the case, it seems clear to most philosophers that speculative metaphysics is impossible, for metaphysics consists precisely in the attempt to acquire knowledge of things that are beyond (the Greek *meta* means "beyond" or "behind") the world of experience. Any talk about God, or the soul, or a transcendent good, is thus ruled out as meaningless or, at the very least, beyond the scope of human knowledge.

Bear in mind, then, that when rationalists offer examples drawn from such sources as geometry and logic to build their case, what they are basically trying to do is establish the principle that an a priori knowledge of synthetic truths is possible. If they can establish this principle, then they may hope to employ it in their metaphysical inquiries; if not, their whole procedure—the very possibility of metaphysics—is highly suspect.

How the Argument Must Proceed

If we have understood the issue upon which the rationalist and the empiricist are at loggerheads, we shall not have any difficulty in seeing how they will have to go about supporting their respective positions.

Consider a simple analogy. Suppose I assert that there are some pink-tufted owls in captivity and my opponents assert that there are none. How can we proceed with our dispute? Quite obviously, in order to support my position I must produce some examples. Indeed, if I can produce just one example of a pink-tufted owl, I shall have won my case. And my opponents, what must they do? Clearly, they must attempt to show that any example I bring forth is not really a pink-tufted owl. This they may do in either of two ways. They may show that (a) although the bird I am offering as an example of a pink-tufted owl is indeed pink-tufted, it is not an owl, or that (b) although it appears to be an owl, it is not pink-tufted. If they can make good their claim to either of these points, my example ceases to be an example.

Likewise, it is up to the rationalist to bring forward examples of synthetic truths that, as he believes, we know a priori. If he can produce a single convincing example of such a truth, he will have won his case.

The empiricist, on the other hand, must show that the examples offered by the rationalist are not, after all, examples of synthetic truths known a priori. This he may do in either of two ways. He may attempt to show that although a particular example is a synthetic truth, it is not known a priori; or, alternatively, he may attempt to show that what is offered as an example of an a priori synthetic truth is not synthetic. The empiricist is convinced of two things: that all statements that are synthetic are known a posteriori, and that all statements that are known a priori are analytic. Empiricists may disagree among themselves as to which of these two categories a given statement belongs in, but they are agreed that every statement whose truth is knowable belongs in one or the other.

The empiricist, it should be noted, cannot, in all fairness, be expected to produce an independent argument to prove his contention that all synthetic truths (all truths about the world) are known a posteriori. In the very nature of the case, this is not possible. The burden of proof lies, as in a formal debate, with the party making the affirmative claim. In the present instance, therefore, the burden of proof rests with the rationalist. All that we have a right to expect of an empiricist is that he present a convincing refutation of anything that a rationalist may offer as an example of a synthetic truth known a priori.

In attempting to enter into the discussion of this issue, therefore, we must reflect carefully on the examples that are offered by the rationalist. Concerning each example that is given, we must ask ourselves two questions: Is this a synthetic truth? Is it known a priori? If, with respect to any example that is given, we answer both questions in the affirmative, then we are agreeing with the rationalist. If we find no example that, after due reflection, seems to be both synthetic and a priori, then we are agreeing with the empiricist.

STUDY QUESTIONS

1. Are you satisfied with the analysis of "knowing" suggested in this chapter? Can you think of any instance that fails to meet the criteria suggested here that you would be inclined to call an instance of knowing? or an instance that satisfies these criteria that you would not be inclined to call an instance of knowing?

2. List the several ways the issue separating rationalists and empiricists is stated in this chapter. Then check your understanding of the problem by restating it in your own words.

3. Are you convinced that rationalism and empiricism are the only possible positions to take with respect to the question of our knowledge of the world? Is it true that "you cannot be both and you cannot avoid being one or the other"? Explain.

4. What is the difference in meaning between "analytic" and "a priori"? between "synthetic" and "a posteriori"? As you understand these terms, is it correct usage to speak of a statement as being a priori or a posteriori? Is it correct to speak of a statement as being known analytically or synthetically?

5. Why must the argument between rationalists and empiricists proceed by way of considering examples brought forward by the rationalist? Why is it impossible for the empiricists to construct an independent proof of their position?

6. Do you already have an opinion on this issue? If so, where did you get that opinion? What evidence, if any, can you point to in support of your opinion?

4

THE CASE FOR RATIONALISM

The introductory chapter has presented an excellent statement of the problem about which my empiricist friends and I are in such complete disagreement.[1] It is now my turn to present what I consider to be the correct answer to the problem stated there, that is, the rationalist answer. I believe that we do have some a priori knowledge of synthetic truths, and I propose to offer a number of examples that I think will prove convincing to any fair and open-minded reader.

Before I do that, however, there is one point that I should like to clarify. The point is, I admit, somewhat subtle, but a full comprehension of it is absolutely essential to an understanding of my position.

The Two Roles of Experience

Let me state unequivocally, then, that I am not maintaining that we have knowledge of any kind (of either analytic or synthetic truths) in a way that is *totally* independent of experience. It seems obvious that if we know something, there must have been some time at which we learned it, and that the occasion on which we learned it was for us an experience of some kind. I am not, therefore, a proponent of "innate knowledge"; I do not think, as some philosophers have thought, that there are some bits of knowledge that we are born with and therefore have prior to all experience.

---

[1] The reader is reminded that the "I" of this and of subsequent chapters is, in each case, a hypothetical advocate of the view in question. See Preface, p. vi

What I wish to maintain, rather, is that experience does not always play the same role in learning. For much of our knowledge, experience is the whole *source* of what we come to know. In this case, knowledge is a posteriori. But sometimes experience functions in another way. Sometimes it is merely the *occasion* for our coming to know, and what we come to know on that occasion vastly transcends the particular learning situation. We consider some statement about the world, we ponder it, and then we "see," directly, immediately, that it is, and indeed must be, true. It is when we come to know something in this way—when experience is only, so to speak, a window through which we look—that we have a case of a priori knowledge.

Perhaps the difference can be clarified by the use of a pair of contrasting examples. Let us first consider a case of something that is known a posteriori. A teacher is talking to her class about various kinds of birds, particularly crows. "What color are crows?" she asks. The little boy in the fourth row who always likes to be the first to answer a question pipes up, "They're black." Little Suzie is not convinced, so she asks, "Is that right, Miss Twaddle? Are all crows black?" And Miss Twaddle says, "That's right, Suzie. All crows are black." But Suzie still is doubtful, so she presses a little further. "Miss Twaddle," she asks, "how do you know that? How do you know for sure that some place, some time, there may not have been a white crow? How do you know that all crows are black?"

How could our poor, hard-pressed teacher go about answering Suzie's question? One way, of course, would be to play a little trick on Suzie. She could say, "Suzie, if you come across a bird that is just like a crow except that it is white instead of black, it won't be a crow. You'll just have to invent some other name for it." But if Miss Twaddle wants to deal fairly with Suzie, she will have to proceed in a rather different way. She might ask, for example, whether anyone in class had ever seen a crow that was not black. She might report that she herself had seen thousands of crows in her lifetime, and that each and every one was black. She might send the class to the library to see if they could find any reports of nonblack crows. She might consult a bird expert and report to the class that as far as she knew there had never been an authenticated case of a nonblack crow.

The point is that the statement "All crows are black" is only as secure as the factual evidence on which it rests. The statement is a summary of the experience of many people, and if it is called into question, the only way that it can be supported is to point to that evidence. Suzie, if she is wise, will not be completely convinced. It is still possible, she may point out, that somewhere, sometime, a nonblack crow, perhaps an albino, will hatch from the egg of a normal crow. And in this, of course, Suzie would be right.

But now let us consider a second example. Our class is a few years older and has graduated from a study of birds to a study of geometry. A Mr. Twiddle is their instructor. "Class," he begins, "let us briefly review yesterday's lesson. What is a triangle?" And the young man in the fourth row, who still likes to be the first to answer any question, replies, "A triangle is a closed plane figure having three straight sides." "All triangles?" asks Mr. Twiddle. "All *Euclidean* triangles," our hero replies. "How big must the angles be?" asks Mr. Twiddle. "They can be any size you like," comes the reply, "provided only that you have a closed plane figure with just three sides. That, and that alone, is enough to make it a triangle, no matter how big it is or how big the angles are or anything else."

"Very well," says Mr. Twiddle, "but today I want to show you something else about triangles." Whereupon he demonstrates the theorem that the interior angles of a Euclidean triangle total 180 degrees. The class struggles briefly with the theorem. One by one they catch on, and by the time the hour is half over they have all apparently gotten the point and are able without difficulty to prove the theorem for themselves.

But Suzie is still with us, and she still wants to make sure that she is getting the straight information. So she asks, "Mr. Twiddle, how do you know that *all* Euclidean triangles have interior angles that total 180 degrees?" Now, in this instance, it would be pointless for Mr. Twiddle to collect evidence to show that of all the Euclidean triangles that he or anybody else had ever seen, none had ever been found to have interior angles that totaled either more or less than 180 degrees. He can only return to the proof of the theorem and try to help Suzie see that the very nature of triangularity is such that anything that is a Euclidean triangle must have interior angles totaling 180 degrees. Furthermore, once Suzie really "sees" this, once she really has hold of this truth about triangles, nothing in the world can ever dissuade her from assenting to it. To know something a priori is to know it with a directness and a certainty that experience alone can never give.

Immanuel Kant once put the matter as follows:[2] all knowledge clearly *begins* with experience—both knowledge a priori and knowledge a posteriori—but not all knowledge *arises out of* experience. It is only a posteriori knowledge (as in the example about crows) that arises out of experience. Accordingly, it is to experience alone that we can turn if a statement that is affirmed on that basis is called into question. But there is also an a priori knowledge of the world (as in the example about triangles). It is characteristic of such knowledge that if a statement whose truth is known in this way is called into question, we must turn for support not to empirical evidence but rather to an inspection of the nature of the thing about which the statement is made. You may parade before my eyes as many black crows as you like. I shall still retain some doubt about whether in fact all crows are black. But I know beyond the shadow of a doubt that if anything is a Euclidean triangle, its interior angles total 180 degrees. What is the

[2]Immanuel Kant, *Critique of Pure Reason,* Intro., II, trans. Norman Kemp Smith (New York: St. Martin's Press, 1965), p. 41.

difference? The difference is that in the one case we are dealing with a posteriori knowledge and in the other with a priori knowledge. In the former, the knowledge arises out of experience; in the latter, experience is simply the occasion for my coming to know.

I hope that these few remarks will have clarified what we rationalists mean when we talk about knowledge that is in some degree independent of experience. The point is so important to a fair appraisal of my position, and so easily and so often misunderstood, that I want to urge my readers to ponder it very carefully—until they are absolutely sure they grasp it—before considering the rest of the discussion.

Examples of Truths Known A Priori

Among the truths about the world—empirical truths, synthetic truths—that are known to all of us are many that are known a priori. I shall point out four large classes of such truths, and within each class will be found numerous examples.

One large class of such truths is *arithmetical* truths. Any true arithmetical statement will do. Let us consider the statement, $7 + 5 = 12$. This expression, of course, is simply a brief and convenient way of saying what could be said in ordinary language: seven things added to five things yield a combined total of twelve things.

The first fact to notice about this statement is that it is synthetic: it is a statement about the world. It is, of course, a very general statement about the world, applicable to apples and oranges and pennies and kittens and anything else that we might have occasion to count and add together.

Consider what would have to be the case, however, if this statement were analytic. We would then have to say that by simply analyzing the subject ("seven things added to five things") we could find the predicate ("twelve things") already present. But we cannot do this. What we find when we analyze the subject is this: (a) the concept seven, (b) the concept five, and (c) a direction to perform the intellectual operation involved in combining seven and five into a single total ("added to"). To get our predicate, we have to perform the prescribed intellectual operation. We must, therefore, leave off analysis and consider the nature of "seven" in conjunction with "five" and then perform the intellectual act of combining them. In order to do this, we must add to our subject the quite different concept "twelve" in the synthetic statement "seven things plus five things are twelve things." Arithmetical statements are one and all synthetic, empirical. They assert that something is the case.

The second fact to notice about this statement is that its truth is not known a posteriori. It is not like the examples of the crows: our confidence that seven things added to five things equal twelve things is not relative to the number of times we may have added seven and five. We know, absolutely, that any time seven things are added to five things the total will be twelve things. There is a necessity, a universality, a self-evidence, an unshakable certainty about this statement that no statement whose truth depends upon the facts of experience can ever have. The statement may be illustrated by experience, but experience can never contradict it. Its truth is known a priori. We learned it, indeed, through experience, but not by way of summarizing the facts of experience.

Here, then, are as many examples of synthetic truths that are known a priori as anyone could ever ask for. What is true of 7 + 5 is equally true of 8 + 9 and 4 − 2 and 6 × 7 and every true arithmetical statement that ever has been or will be made. Each of them, it will be seen, is a synthetic truth that, if it is to be known at all, must be known a priori.

A second large class of synthetic truths known a priori consists of the truths of *geometry*. We have already had an illustration using the triangle. Let us consider that example more closely.

Geometry is what we might call the science of physical space. Since any object that could ever appear to us must appear in space, we know a priori that it must conform to the truths of geometry. If, therefore, someone tries to tell us that one time—perhaps, say, in the jungles of Africa—he saw a Euclidean triangle whose interior angles totaled only 160 degrees, we are simply not going to believe him. We may suggest that he made an incorrect measurement, or that the sides of what he thought was a Euclidean triangle were not straight, or even that he is lying. In any case, we know that his report cannot be true, because we know a priori that Euclid's theorem is true. And because this is so, experience—wherever, whenever, and to whomever it occurs—must conform to it. Geometrical knowledge is knowledge a priori.

A third class of synthetic truths that are known a priori consists of what, for lack of a better name, we shall call *logical* truths. An example of such a truth is the statement "Anything that has shape has size." Another example would be the statement "A thing cannot both have and not have the same characteristic at the same time."

Consider, for example, the statement that anything that has shape has size. Surely it is evident that this is a synthetic statement. It asserts a fact about the world that we know to be true, namely, that in each and every instance in which there is an object that has shape there is also an object that has size. Now shape and size are not the same thing: I can know that something is round, for example, without having the slightest idea how big it is. Shape and size are diverse characteristics that an object may have. But the nature of shape is such and the nature of size is such that whenever one characteristic is present, the other must be also. There is, we might say, a necessary connection between the characteristic that we designate by the term "shape" and the characteristic that we designate by the term "size." It is this connection that we are affirming when we say that anything that has shape has size.

We do not know this on the basis of having seen a large number of examples. The proof of this is that we are not just reasonably sure about the proposition, as in the case of the crows; we are absolutely sure. We will not allow even the possibility of an exception. Why? Because in this case we "see" the connection directly, and we know without the slightest doubt that the statement concerning shape and size is universally true. We know, with a certainty that empirical evidence could never give us, that there never has been and never will be an instance of shape without size, or of size without shape. In knowing this, we know a priori a truth that no experience can contradict.

Now consider the statement "A thing cannot both have and not have the same characteristic at the same time." It is true, of course, that we have empirically observed that an object is not simultaneously hot and cold, or colored and uncolored, or big and small. But our statement goes beyond this. It affirms not merely that as a matter of observable fact things *do* not simultaneously have and not have a given characteristic: it asserts that they *cannot*. The rational mind perceives a necessity and a universality in this truth that experience could never provide, thus certifying it as a truth that is known a priori. And yet it is a truth about the world, a truth that has been exhibited in our experience countless times. It is on the basis of our certainty regarding this statement that we know with equal certainty that contradictory statements (one affirming and another denying that a certain object has a given characteristic) cannot be simultaneously true. Logical truths are synthetic truths that are known a priori.

The fourth class of synthetic truths known a priori consists of general *ethical* truths. Numerous examples come to mind, but let us confine our attention to the statement "The infliction of needless pain is evil."

There can be no question, it seems to me, that this statement is synthetic. The notion involved in the infliction of needless pain is undoubtedly highly complex, but this much at least is clear: we can analyze that notion as thoroughly as we please, but we will never find that the idea of being evil is part of it. By "the infliction of needless pain" we mean, I suppose, such things as a boy's torturing an animal "just for the fun of it," or his mauling a younger and weaker boy in order "to show how tough he is," or a parent's abusing a defenseless child. What we are saying about such instances is that, in addition to being instances of animal or human suffering willfully caused by some responsible agent, they have the additional character of being evil. In so saying, we are adding to the concept of the subject something not a part of that concept; we are connecting the subject and the predicate in our synthetic judgment "The infliction of needless pain is evil."

What evidence could possibly be adduced in support of such a statement? All kinds of evidence could, of course, heighten our awareness of how painful such acts can be, or how absurd and pointless they are, but that is beside the point. What we are affirming is not only that the infliction of needless pain is needless and painful (that *is* analytically true), but that it is also something else, namely, evil, reprehensible, morally blameworthy. Not all the evidence in the world could either confirm or disconfirm our judgment. If its truth is known at all, it is known a priori.

And its truth is known, is it not? We are not moral ignoramuses, though we may not always act in accordance with the moral truths we do perceive. We know, even if it is we ourselves who inflict needless pain, that such an act is evil. We see directly, with an immediacy and a certainty that empirical evidence could never give us, that this act has the moral quality of being evil. All ethical truths are apprehended in this direct way.

Arithmetical truths, geometrical truths, logical truths, general ethical truths—here are four classes of truths that seem to me to be clear and irrefutable examples of synthetic truths that are known a priori. But there are many others as well. Consider the following examples:

Every event has a cause.
If anything is red all over then it is not blue all over.
If anything has happened, it cannot be made to not have happened
  (that is, the past cannot be undone).
Everyone ought to do good and not evil.
Time moves ever forward.

I assume that it is evident to everyone that these are synthetic statements. If anyone is in doubt about the a priori character of our knowledge of any of these statements, however, I suggest the following question: How would you go about defending the statement if it were challenged? Would you assemble evidence? I say that you would not. Rather, you would ask the challenger to consider the statement more carefully to see exactly what is being said. You would proceed on the assumption that if the challenger really understood the statement, he or she would certainly cease to challenge it; for in the case of a truth that is known a priori, to understand it is at the same time to see that it is true. When we are dealing with truths known a priori we are involved not with empirical evidence but with direct insight. Our knowledge of the world would be much the poorer if we lacked the capacity for such insight.

Let me conclude by presenting a small but important disclaimer. In arguing as I have for the possibility and the reality of an a priori knowledge of synthetic truths, I have not meant to disparage in any way the importance of a posteriori knowledge. There are things that can be known only a posteriori, and due credit should be given to the scientists, historians, and others who, through careful observation and experimentation, have contributed so greatly to the sum of human knowledge. The point of my remarks is that however great is the quantity of knowledge gained in this way, it does not constitute the whole of our knowledge of reality. We have, as I have shown above, countless examples of truths about the real world that are known a priori. It may or may not be important for us to be aware of this; that is another matter. But important or not, it is the case, and that is all that I have tried to show.

STUDY QUESTIONS

1. What difference or differences do you see between the theory of "innate knowledge" and the theory that Rationalist attempts to defend in this chapter?
2. Is there a difference between the role that experience plays in our knowledge about crows and that which it plays in our knowledge of geometrical truths? Has Rationalist succeeded in identifying a real difference here, however one might wish to account for it?
3. List the several classes of truths that Rationalist offers as examples of synthetic truths that are known a priori. What evidence does he offer that these truths are synthetic truths? that they are known a priori?
4. Can you think of any examples in addition to those offered by Rationalist that might plausibly be considered as examples of synthetic truths that are known a priori? Which of Rationalist's own examples do you find most convincing? which least?
5. Suppose that you become convinced that arithmetical truths are not synthetic. Would this by itself make it reasonable for you to reject rationalism? Why or why not?

5

THE CASE FOR EMPIRICISM

There is some danger, I think, that readers of Rationalist's account may have come away with a view of empiricists as rather stubborn and close-minded individuals who are so enamored of empirical methods that they simply refuse to recognize that knowledge can be acquired in another way. This impression of empiricists is quite mistaken, and I shall attempt to dispel it immediately. Let me state plainly that I am an empiricist for one reason only: I have never encountered a single example of an alleged a priori synthetic truth that did not prove upon closer inspection to be either analytic (hence, not a truth about the world at all) or a posteriori. I am, however, willing to be shown, and if I ever do encounter an example of such a truth, I will concede immediately to the rationalists. Until then, I must honestly state that every synthetic truth known to me is known a posteriori, and every statement that I have ever seen that could with any degree of certainty be said to be known a priori is clearly analytic. Pending evidence to the contrary I must, therefore, continue to maintain that as far as I can make out, all our knowledge of empirical truths—truths about the world—is a posteriori.

This much, however, I will grant the rationalists: I think it would be very nice if it were possible to acquire some knowledge of the world a priori, as they believe we all can and do. The empirical method of observing, measuring, and testing one hypothesis and then another is painfully slow and laborious. It would be most pleasant if we could, by merely thinking, "see" truths about the world in the way that Rationalist says we can. But we have no right to demand that things be the way we want them to be. We have to take things the way they are.

Unfortunately, they are not the way Rationalist says they are, as I shall now attempt to show.

Arithmetical Truths

Let us begin by reconsidering Rationalist's account of arithmetical truths. Such truths have long been the rationalists' favorite examples whenever challenged to defend their position. If we are successful in refuting these examples, we may be reasonably confident that the others will prove no more difficult. If it can be shown that arithmetic truths are not a priori synthetic, then the chief citadel of rationalism will have been destroyed.

It is my belief that arithmetical truths are synthetic truths known a posteriori. I am, therefore, in agreement with Rationalist in affirming that the truths of arithmetic are synthetic truths, but I am disputing his claim that they are known a priori.

My reasons for concurring with Rationalist on the first point are the same as those given by him. It seems evident that when we know an arithmetical truth—for example, that $7 + 5 = 12$, or $4 - 2 = 2$, or $6 \times 7 = 42$—we know something about the world. We know that whenever you add seven things to five things, you will get a total of twelve things; that whenever you subtract two things from a group of four things you will have a remainder of two things; that whenever you combine six groups of seven things each, or seven groups of six things each, you will have a total of forty-two things. It also seems evident to me that, as Rationalist maintains, the notion "twelve" cannot be found by analyzing the subject term "$7 + 5$." If I know that $7 + 5 = 12$, as I do, then what I know is a synthetic truth.

The crucial question, then, is *how* do I know this arithmetical truth? My answer is that I know it by experience. I did not know it when I was born. I did not learn it in some ecstatic moment of insight, when the eternal truth of this statement suddenly flashed into my mind. I learned it in the way I have learned everything else that I know about the world: by experience and nothing else. First I learned to count. In so doing, of course, I was simply learning the meanings of the words "one," "two," "three," and so on. Then I began to notice certain relationships—for example, that I have five fingers on each hand, and that five fingers plus five fingers makes ten fingers; that I have five toes on each foot, and that five toes plus five toes makes ten toes; that if I had one penny, and my father gave me another one, I then had two pennies, and so on. Everywhere I turned, no matter what objects I had to deal with (fingers, toes, pennies, playmates, apples, kittens, everything), certain numerical relationships impressed themselves upon me. My experience, your experience, everyone's experience has been thoroughly pervaded by numerical facts since the moment we began to be aware of the world around us. It is this experience that has given us our knowledge of arithmetical truths.

What makes some people think that there must be something unique and wonderful about arithmetical truths is, I suppose, the remarkable certainty that such truths seem to have. We are, as Rationalist says, sure about these truths in a way that we are not sure about the statement "All crows are black," no matter how many crows we may have seen. So much is this the case that "mathematical certainty" is for most people, as it was for the philosopher Descartes, a model of the highest degree of certainty possible. How are we to account for this certainty?

The answer, I believe, is simple. We are supremely sure of the truth of arithmetical truths because of the overwhelming amount of supporting evidence. Every day of our lives, in thousands and thousands of different ways, experience has exhibited the truths that we express in our arithmetical equations. With all this corroborating evidence, and never a scrap to the contrary, we at length become convinced. We *know* that $7 + 5 = 12$ (and $4 - 2 = 2$, and so on); our certainty reflects the unbroken uniformity of our experience.

Why, then, are we less certain about crows, even if we have never seen a crow that was not black? There are, I think, two reasons. First, the quantity of experience upon which this inference is based is infinitesimal in comparison with that upon which our inferences regarding arithmetical truths are based. Practically everything that we experience exhibits arithmetical truths, whereas it is only on relatively rare occasions that we happen to see crows. Second, experience has taught us that in many species, color is a variable characteristic. Perhaps we have seen a black sheep in a flock of white sheep, or an albino mouse, and so we find it easy to conjecture that there might be an exception with respect to color among crows as well. Hence, it is not surprising that we are less than certain that the statement "All crows are black" will stand the test of all future experience.

It may be noted that there are other empirical truths, which everyone agrees are known a posteriori, about which we are much more certain than we are about the color of crows. We can state with a high degree of certainty, for example, that at sea-level barometric pressure, pure water freezes at a temperature of 32° Fahrenheit. We know this by experience. Countless individuals, in many different parts of the world and at many different times, have had an opportunity to observe this phenomenon, and never has a case been reported in which the stated conditions failed to bring about the same result. With all this supporting evidence, and none to the contrary, we make the statement, confident that all future cases will conform to those of the past.

If we imagine an example having even more supporting evidence, it is not difficult to see that the result would be knowledge that is so certain as to amount to "absolute certainty." The evidence in the case of freezing water is so great that it is *virtually* inconceivable that there should ever occur an exception to it. But the evidence in support of arithmetical truths is greater yet—so great, that for most of us an

exception to one of these truths is, in fact, totally inconceivable. Therefore, we can say that we know these truths with absolute certainty.

Note, however, that this inconceivability of an exception expresses
nothing more than a psychological fact about ourselves. The falsifica-
tion of an arithmetical truth is inconceivable to us in the same way
that it is inconceivable to us that an object should defy the law of
gravity, the principal difference being that in the former case the
evidence is truly overwhelming. Our inability to conceive of an exception, however, does not mean that an exception is not logically possible.

Geometrical Truths

The account that I should be inclined to give of geometrical truths is
identical to the one I have just given of arithmetical truths. They are,
as Rationalist says, synthetic truths; but like the truths of arithmetic,
they are known a posteriori, not a priori.

Consider, for example, the statement "Two straight lines cannot
enclose a space." This, presumably, would qualify as one of the truths
that Rationalist says we know a priori. I shall argue, on the contrary,
that we know it a posteriori.

In the first place (and I think Rationalist would agree with me), it
is clear that we learn the meanings of the words of this statement by
experience. We learn the meaning of "straight line" in the same way
that we learn the meanings of words like "table" and "chair." We hear
the words applied to certain kinds of objects—"straight," for example,
is applied to matches, knitting needles, a pencil, the edge of a ruler,
but "curved" describes barrel staves, the edge of a dish, a dog's nose,
or a cat's ear. If we did not have any experience of this kind to tell us
the meanings of certain words, those words would be nothing to us but
meaningless sounds.

The question, then, is this: once we know the meanings of the words
in the statement in question, how do we come to know that the statement is true? I hold that we learn this by experience.

What kind of experience is it that teaches us that two straight lines
cannot enclose a space? The question need not puzzle us long, for our
experience is replete with evidence to support this general truth. We
may have noticed that the two lines of a roof that intersect to form the
peak never (by themselves) enclose a space. We have observed the
parallel sides of a road, the parallel tracks of a railroad, the intersect-
ing lines of a leg and rung of a chair, and so on. We have *never* seen
an instance in which two straight lines have by themselves enclosed
a space. We do not, perhaps, consciously formulate the *statement* at
first, but the statement is, nonetheless, a true generalization about our
experience. Therefore, when we study geometry and come upon this
axiom (as it is called), it may strike us as being obviously or self-
evidently true. Indeed, we may be so impressed with its obviousness

that we are tempted to say, like Plato, that it is not a case of learning but rather one of "recollecting" an "eternal truth" that has been present within our soul ever since its creation. But is it really surprising that a truth so lavishly exhibited in our everyday experience should seem obvious when we see it formally stated for the first time? It does not seem so to me.

What is true of this particular example is equally true of all other geometrical truths—with one proviso. Many of the more complex and less obvious theorems of geometry are not directly exhibited in our experience, but they are deducible from those that are. If proposition p and proposition q are learned from experience, and proposition r can be validly deduced from propositions p and q, then proposition r has, ipso facto, been learned from experience as well. Geometry is a science wherein the more complex and remote truths are deduced from those that are simpler and closer at hand; the latter, as I hope I have made clear, are gathered from the vast data of our everyday experience.

The certainty of geometrical truths, as of arithmetical truths, rests upon the immense quantity of evidence that supports the foundational truths of the science of geometry. It is not necessary, therefore, to repeat what has already been said on this point in connection with arithmetical truths.

Logical Truths

If I have succeeded in showing that the truths of arithmetic and geometry are a posteriori synthetic truths, my readers should have no difficulty in seeing that the truths of logic have the same status. Rationalist's first example—the statement that anything that has shape has size—is a perfect instance of a fact about the world that has been exhibited in our experience so many times that it is now inconceivable that there could ever occur an exception to it. With all this experience upon which to base our statement, what need have we for a special theory about a remarkable human capacity that supposedly enables us to "immediately apprehend" this homely, everyday truth? The same may be said with respect to his second example, that an object cannot both have and not have the same characteristic at the same time. The "necessity" that Rationalist finds in this statement is nothing more than our psychological certainty that a truth so consistently and lavishly exhibited in our experience will continue to be exhibited without exception.

One type of logical truth, which might pardonably be taken as one that must be known a priori, would be one that states a set of circumstances in which a particular conclusion may be drawn from certain premises. Consider, for example, any statement of the form "If all A's are B's, and all B's are C's, then all A's are C's." There is, admittedly, a certain self-evidence about such a statement. We certainly cannot imagine the possibility of going wrong in asserting the conclusion if we are granted the premises, no matter what meanings may be assigned to A, B, and C.

Nonetheless, the explanation of this certainty is the same as in the previous examples. When Aristotle set about the task of formulating and systematizing the rules of logic, he did not just sit down and think, waiting for "direct apprehensions" to occur. Rather, he paid attention to the actual arguments that people used, and he noted the conditions under which arguments either succeeded or failed in establishing their conclusions. The conditions under which they did succeed he called "rules of inference"; conditions under which they failed he called "logical fallacies." But the data from which he began, and the data on the basis of which other logicians have modified and augmented his work, are the actual arguments, successful or unsuccessful, that people employ. Logical truths are derived from the data of experience. The certainty of these truths is due to the large quantity of evidence upon which they are based.

Ethical Truths

I admit that there is something unusual about ethical statements, and it is understandable that Rationalist would appeal to this class of statements in support of his position. I am not sure that I understand just what makes ethical statements so unique, but I am quite sure that it is not, as Rationalist claims, that they are synthetic truths known a priori.

For one thing, we do not know "ethical truths" with the kind of certainty that is supposedly characteristic of a priori knowledge. To affirm an ethical statement is to affirm a belief, a conviction. It is as if we were saying, "I don't know for sure what is right or wrong in this matter (perhaps no one does), but I will take my stand on this, that the infliction of needless pain is evil." What is affirmed as an ethical statement is not something that we know; it is something that we believe, something that we venture. And if it is not known at all, it is obviously not known a priori.

There are, it seems to me, two features of ethical statements that might explain their unusual character. First, they are typically affirmed in this venturing, convictional way. An ethical statement is not a report; it is a statement recording an intention to act in certain ways and encouraging others to do the same. Second, such statements, unlike all the others we have been considering, speak not of what is the case but of what ought to be the case. It may be the connotation of "oughtness" that makes ethical statements seem so different from all other statements.

There are, as a matter of fact, numerous ways in which an empiricist can construe ethical utterances without compromising his empiricism. The subject is a complex one, however, and will be discussed in detail at another time (see Chapters 45–50). For the present, we leave the status of ethical statements an open question. What is quite clear is that they are not synthetic truths known a priori; and this, so far as the refutation of rationalism is concerned, is the only point of importance.

Other Alleged Examples

As a parting gift, Rationalist offers a miscellaneous group of examples of synthetic truths that we allegedly know a priori, and he asks, "How would you go about defending (one of these statements) if it were challenged?" My answer is that I would point to the evidence upon which my confidence in the truth of these statements clearly rests. I have seen millions of examples of events having a cause, but no examples of uncaused events. I have seen tens of thousands of objects of one color, but none that were simultaneously totally another color as well. I have seen countless examples of events happening, but never an example of an event "unhappening." The point that I am urging certainly should, by now, be abundantly clear: our knowledge of the world arises out of our experience, and in no other way. The function of reason is not to invent truths to which experience must somehow conform, but to generalize from the data of experience and to refine those generalizations by testing them against further experience. Such is the origin of every truth about the world that we shall ever know.

STUDY QUESTIONS

1. Empiricist has argued that our knowledge of arithmetical truths, like our knowledge about crows, is a posteriori. How does he explain the fact that we are much more certain about the former kind of truths than about the latter? Are you satisfied with his explanation?
2. What evidence does Empiricist offer in support of the claim that geometrical truths are known a posteriori? Do you think he is right on this point?
3. Suppose that Aristotle worked out the "rules of logical inference" in the way that Empiricist says he did. Would this fact be sufficient to establish that they are truths known a posteriori? Could Rationalist allow this account and still claim that they are truths known a priori?
4. Is there something unusual about ethical statements, as Empiricist says there is? If so, does it seem plausible to you that this is because ethical truths are synthetic truths known a priori? Do you find Empiricist's explanation of this alleged uniqueness more or less persuasive than Rationalist's?

6

ANOTHER ALTERNATIVE FOR EMPIRICISTS

I wish to begin by asserting that on the main issue of the present controversy, the author of the last chapter and I are in perfect agreement: all knowledge of synthetic truths arises out of experience. We are, therefore, united in our opposition to rationalism, since we cannot allow the claim that there are some synthetic truths—some truths about the world—that are known a priori. It is our contention that whatever is known about the world has been learned from experience, and that whatever is known apart from experience (a priori) is not a truth about the world at all but merely an analytic truth.

Nevertheless, we do share a disagreement common among empiricists, that of whether certain classes of statements are to be construed as analytic a priori or as synthetic a posteriori. My colleague has argued that arithmetical, geometrical, and logical truths are all synthetic truths that are known a posteriori. I maintain, however, that arithmetical and geometrical truths are analytic truths that are known a priori, and that the so-called logical truths are, in fact, not truths at all (and thus are known neither a priori nor a posteriori). I shall also have something further to say about ethical truths, not so much in disagreement with, as in addition to, what was said about them in the last chapter.

Arithmetical Truths

Statements about the world—synthetic statements—have one distinguishing feature in common: it is always possible to specify some state of affairs that, if it were the case, would make the statement in question false. The statement "All crows are black" is made false by the supposition that there exists a white crow; hence, it is evident that in this case we have a synthetic statement. This test, carefully applied, should enable us to distinguish without difficulty between synthetic and analytic statements.

Our test, it should be noted, is not an arbitrary one. It follows from the definition of a synthetic statement as a statement about the world. A synthetic statement asserts that the world is thus and so; it asserts that something really is the case. Consequently, it must be possible to specify a state of affairs in which this would not be the case—in which, accordingly, our statement would be falsified.

Let us now apply our test to an arithmetical statement. What would have to be the case for the statement "7 + 5 = 12" to be false? Let us suppose that I put what I believe to be seven objects (oranges, for example) into a bag, and then I put in what I believe to be five more. I bring them to the grocery clerk to be priced. He counts them and finds, to my surprise, that the bag contains only eleven oranges. I count them again, he counts them again, and finally I am convinced: there are only eleven oranges in the bag.

Does this state affairs falsify the statement "7 + 5 = 12"? Obviously not. We might adopt any one of several explanations of what happened. Perhaps I miscounted the first time; perhaps one of the oranges that I counted did not get into the bag; or perhaps someone removed one of the oranges after I had put it in the bag. But note that we would not think of adopting the explanation that this was a remarkable exception to the statement "7 + 5 = 12." The case just described does not, then, falsify our arithmetical statement.

What state of affairs would falsify our statement? None. The only way the statement "7 + 5 = 12" could be rendered false would be to change the meaning of one or more of the symbols that comprise the statement. If the symbol 7 were defined to mean what is ordinarily meant by the symbol 8, the statement would, of course, become false. But then we would no longer be describing a state of affairs in the world to which the statement in question refers. We would be altering the meaning of the statement itself.

The truth about arithmetical statements is that they are, one and all, analytic truths. What tends to mislead us is the fact that a number has meaning only in the context of the whole number system. The meaning of a number consists, in part, in its relation to every other number in the system. Part of the meaning of the number 7, for example, is that it is one more than 6 and one less than 8, that it is two more than 5, and two less than 9, and so on. Hence, it is a part of the meaning of 7 that it is five less than 12. Consequently, when we affirm that 7 + 5 = 12, we are merely stating explicitly some of the meaning relations that obtain in the system between the numbers 7, 5, and 12. Were this not the case, mathematical reasoning would not have the certainty that it has.

If we look at the reasons that the previous two writers have given for holding that arithmetical truths are synthetic, it is not difficult to see where and why they have gone wrong. First, they have failed to note that the concept of a number is exceedingly complex, involving the relations of that number to every other number in the number system. If we make the mistake of thinking of 7 and 5 as simple concepts—visualizing, perhaps, 7 dots and 5 dots—then it seems natural to conclude that we cannot get the predicate 12 by analyzing the complex symbol 7 + 5. We can only get it by "performing the prescribed intellectual operation." But as soon as we realize the complexity of the concept of a number—as soon as we realize that its meaning includes its relations to the other numbers in the number system—the error becomes apparent.

Second, these writers have been misled by what I shall call the quasi-empirical character of arithmetical truths—a character they share with many analytic truths. At first glance, analytic truths often appear to be "about the world"; that is why we cannot decide on the status of a given statement simply on the basis of whether or not it "seems" to be about the world. The statement "All bachelors are unmarried," for example, seems to be a statement about real bachelors. It is only when we apply the test—when we try to specify a state of affairs that, if it were the case, would falsify the statement—that it becomes evident that the statement is not really about bachelors at all, but only about the meaning of the *word* "bachelor."

So it is with arithmetical truths. They seem, admittedly, to be about the world—about "apples and oranges and pennies and kittens and anything else that we might have occasion to count and add together," as Rationalist says. But this appearance is deceptive, as we have already shown. When the crucial test of falsifiability by empirical facts is applied, it becomes obvious that arithmetical statements are purely analytic. No state of affairs can be imagined that, if it were the case, would render an arithmetical truth untrue, for the reason that an arithmetical truth is not a statement about the world; it is a statement about the relations between numbers in a number system. Arithmetical truths are analytic truths that are known a priori by anyone who adequately understands the meanings of the symbols. Such truths have certainty because, as Rationalist asserts, they are known a priori. But because they are analytic truths, our knowledge of them does not constitute an a priori knowledge of the world.

Geometrical Truths

It is not surprising that many philosophers have believed that the truths of geometry are synthetic truths known a priori. It seems plausible to hold, as Rationalist does, that geometry is "the science of physical space" and that a geometrical statement is therefore about space, that is, about the world. If we hold this and then reflect on the peculiar

certainty with which we are able to demonstrate the theorems of
geometry, it is also natural to conclude that geometry consists of a
remarkable collection of a priori truths about the real world.

It must be said, however, that this conclusion is less tenable today
than it was in the time of Plato, or Descartes, or even Kant. Today we
know that Euclidean geometry is not the only possible geometry. We
know that what can be demonstrated in any geometry depends not on
a correspondence to the real world but on the definitions with which
we begin. We may or may not be able to use a given geometry to
explain physical space: that is an empirical question to be decided
only by trial and error. What is known, therefore, when we have demonstrated a geometrical theorem, is not anything about the world at all
but only some consequence implicit in the definitions with which the
demonstration began.

One reason so many people have been persuaded that the truths of
geometry are synthetic rather than analytic is that in studying geometry they have the impression that with each demonstration of a new
theorem, they are discovering, or "grasping", a new truth. They learn,
for example, that a triangle is a closed plane figure having three
straight sides, and subsequently they "discover" a truth that does not
seem to be contained in this definition (for example, that the interior
angles total 180 degrees). But the fact is that this latter theorem is
implicit in the definition of a triangle together with the other definitions (some of which are called axioms) of Euclid's system. If this were
not the case, it would not be possible to construct a valid proof of the
theorem. Were it not for the fact that our intellects are limited, we
would never have a sense of discovery when we first succeed in proving a complex geometrical theorem. We would immediately see all the
logical consequences of our definitions and would have no need for a
formal demonstration. But this human limitation should not be allowed to obscure the fact that geometrical reasoning always begins
with gratuitously assumed definitions and concludes with theorems
having the same gratuitous character. Geometrical truths, without
exception, are analytic.

Logical Truths

I am uncertain what Rationalist intends to include in the class of
logical truths. It may be that some of the truths he had in mind would
require one explanation, whereas others would require somewhat
different ones. I shall, however, deal briefly with his two examples and
shall add a few remarks that I hope will eliminate any possible misunderstanding on this point.

One example that Rationalist discusses in some detail is the statement "Anything that has shape has size." To me, this is rather obviously an analytic statement. The concept of a "thing" (or of an
"object," as Rationalist says later) includes both the idea of shape and

the idea of size. Shape and size are, indeed, diverse characteristics, but both are implicit in the idea of a spatial object, which is what Rationalist has in mind. Fully stated, Rationalist's statement should read, "Anything that occupies space has both shape and size." Rationalist has been misled by the elliptical character of his own statement.

Rationalist's second example is a rather confused statement of the Principle of Noncontradiction, which asserts merely that a statement and its contradictory cannot both be true. There is, to be sure, something very puzzling about the status of this principle. Let us try to make it less so.

The Principle of Noncontradiction, in my opinion, is nothing more than a linguistic convention. It plays the same role in language that rules play in a game. There are, in fact, many such rules in any language "game," one of which is that every simple proposition is either true or false. Another rule is that if a proposition is true, then it is not false; and if it is false, then it is not true—the Principle of Noncontradiction. As linguistic conventions, these rules are neither analytic nor synthetic, since they are not statements at all. They are merely rules that we must follow if we are to use language intelligibly.

Much the same can be said of rules of inference. It has been argued that rules of inference are empirical generalizations based upon analyses of the actual arguments used, successfully or unsuccessfully, to establish conclusions based on certain kinds of premises. This position contains some truth, but on the fundamental question of the logical status of the rules of inference, I think it is incorrect. It rightly asserts that these rules were determined by Aristotle and others through a process of inductive reasoning. But what Aristotle discovered by this method was not truths about the world (in any significant meaning of that phrase) but rather the rules by which we reason successfully from premises to conclusions. Aristotle might be compared to a person who, knowing nothing about the rules of baseball, figures them out by watching how the game is actually played. What would be discovered in this way, however, would be not a group of synthetic truths but a system of rules prescribing what players may and may not do in the game of baseball. Just so with the rules of inference. They are not synthetic truths, since they are not truths at all. They are merely rules governing logical inferences in our language. To know these rules is not to know some truths about the real world. It is to know how to speak intelligibly when playing the game of human discourse.

Ethical Truths

I have already indicated that I am quite in agreement with the remarks about ethical truths made by the author of the last chapter, and I have no wish to discuss, at this time, the many ways in which an empiricist might handle such utterances. I would like, however, to make just one suggestion as a kind of footnote to those remarks.

We found in the case of what are commonly called logical truths that, properly speaking, they are not "truths" at all, but simply rules, linguistic conventions governing the use of language. Once this is recognized, the question whether they are synthetic or analytic disappears: since they are not truths at all, they are neither synthetic nor analytic. Perhaps an analogous account can be given of ethical truths. Perhaps they are not "truths" at all, and hence neither analytic nor synthetic. I suggest that they might be linguistic expressions of a quite different type. Three possibilities come to mind: (a) statements of intention, (b) veiled commands, or (c) expressions of feeling. Since the logical status of ethical discourse is still a controversial issue, I do not wish to attempt a defense of any one of these options. I would suggest, however, that in view of this controversy it seems extremely hazardous to rest any part of the case for rationalism on an appeal to examples drawn from this source.

Other Truths

Of the miscellaneous statements that Rationalist offers as his final examples of synthetic truths known a priori, there is one on which I should particularly like to comment. That is the statement "If anything is red all over then it is not blue all over." I would suggest that our confidence in the truth of this statement rests on exactly the same basis as our confidence that if something is round then it is not square, that is, on our aforementioned decision not to violate the Principle of Noncontradiction. Note that it is impossible to form the concept of an object that is at one and the same time red all over and blue all over. It is clear also from this that we are dealing here not with a truth about the world but rather with a statement whose truth depends upon the definitions and the linguistic rules of our language.

Without discussing in detail Rationalist's remaining examples, let me conclude by saying that I believe that any fair-minded person who carefully considers the statements offered by rationalists as examples of synthetic truths known a priori will find that every such example can be convincingly shown to be one of the following: (a) an analytic truth, (b) an empirical generalization (a synthetic truth known a posteriori), or (c) not a statement at all (that is, a sentence that *appears* to assert something but does not in fact do so). To be sure, we may sometimes be in doubt about the correct status of a given sentence, but I believe that is only because the precise meaning of the sentence is not clear (as in the case, for example, of the sentence "Time moves ever forward," which sounds more like poetry than a straightforward assertion). Once we have settled on the exact meaning of the sentence, however, I am confident that we will find that it can always be construed in one of the three ways I have indicated. Unless and until we find an example that clearly cannot be so construed, we must remain empiricists.

STUDY QUESTIONS

1. At what point or points does the author of this chapter (Empiricist B) claim to be in agreement with the author of the previous chapter (Empiricist A), and at what point or points does he claim to be in disagreement? Would it be inconsistent for someone to agree with Empiricist A's account of some of Rationalist's examples and Empiricist B's account of others?

2. What is the "falsifiability test" that Empiricist B proposes as a method for distinguishing between analytic and synthetic truths? Does this seem to you to be a valid test? What use does Empiricist B make of this test in his subsequent discussion?

3. What account does Empiricist B give of "rules of inference"? Do you think he is right? In your judgment, would it be plausible for Rationalist to argue that these are examples of synthetic truths that are known a priori?

4. What do you think of the suggestion that what Rationalist calls "ethical truths" are not "truths" at all? Is Empiricist B right in saying that if this is the case, it is not proper to ask whether they are analytic or synthetic? Why or why not?

5. Summarize the case for empiricism as you now understand it, drawing upon both this chapter and the preceding one.

6. Is it possible in principle to finally "prove" empiricism? Why or why not?

7

A RATIONALIST REPLY

I suppose it would be excessively unkind to whisper the suggestion that our two empiricist friends, in their respective efforts to defend an embattled empiricism, rather effectively cancel each other out. Empiricist A allows that most of my examples of synthetic a priori truths (all except ethical truths) are indeed synthetic. He then attempts to show that they are known a posteriori, not a priori, and that the certainty with which we hold these truths is due to the vast amount of experience upon which they are based. Empiricist B recognizes that A's attempt is a failure, and he tries the other alternative of interpreting these statements as analytic truths that are known a priori. I cannot resist the temptation to play the role of peacemaker in the present dispute. I think each of our empiricist friends is half right: Empiricist A is right in holding that the truths in question are synthetic, and Empiricist B is right holding that they are known a priori. It is scarcely necessary to point out that in addition to being half right, each is also half wrong.

There would be little point in rehashing all the arguments in support of the view that arithmetical, geometrical, logical, and ethical truths are synthetic truths that are known a priori. I have already stated what I consider to be the most convincing reasons for regarding them so, and I have little to add to what I believe to be a strong affirmative case. Empiricists A and B have raised a number of interesting points, however, and since I have been given the last word, I propose to use the opportunity to counter their criticisms.

The Status of the Argument

There is always some danger, when arguments become numerous, that the main point at issue will become obscured. Perhaps we should begin by stating, once again, the status of the argument.

The question at issue is this: Do we or do we not have any a priori knowledge of synthetic truths? I have argued that we do and have offered several classes of examples to support my view. Our two empiricists have argued that we do not and have attempted to show that my examples can all be interpreted in a way consistent with empiricism.

Some readers may have come to the conclusion that my account of some class of truths—ethical truths, for example—is not correct. If it were not, what effect would this have on the argument? It would remove one group of examples of synthetic a priori truths, leaving the others intact. Nothing more. It would still be the case that we have some a priori knowledge of synthetic truths, and my basic thesis would remain established. Only if every plausible example of synthetic truths known a priori has been shown to have some other status has rationalism been shown to be mistaken.

I do not mean by the above to withdraw my claim that ethical truths are in fact synthetic truths known a priori. I stand by all the examples I offered earlier. My point is simply that if someone were to disagree with me about the correct interpretation of some of my examples, while agreeing with me about others, he or she would still be on my side on the fundamental issue in the rationalist-empiricist controversy. Rationalists have some differences, too, but it takes only a single example of a synthetic truth that is known a priori to clinch the case for rationalism. I turn now to a consideration of some of the points raised by my opponents.

Necessary Truths and Empirical Generalizations

Empiricist A has argued that arithmetical, geometrical, and logical truths are synthetic a posteriori, and has attempted to account for the certainty with which we hold these truths by saying that they are based on a large quantity of experiential data. I think Empiricist A is mistaken on this point, and I want to present one final argument in support of this opinion.

An empirical generalization is only as strong as the evidence on which it rests. Indeed, there seems to be a perfect parallel between the quantity of evidence upon which a generalization is based and the degree of certainty with which it is held to be true. But surely it is evident that the certainty with which we hold arithmetical, geometrical, and logical truths to be true is all out of proportion to the quantity of "evidence" upon which, if they were empirical generalizations, they would have to be based. There are, admittedly, some simple truths of this sort that are confirmed by our experience almost every day of our lives (simple combinations of numbers up to 10 or so, for example, and simple geometrical axioms such as the one about the impossibility of two straight lines enclosing a space). But consider for a moment some more complex examples. How many times in your life have you multiplied 762 by 316? Perhaps never. Yet you know, with absolute certainty, once you have done the calculation, what the answer is. How many triangles have you measured to find the sum of the interior angles? How many triangles have you inscribed in a semicircle? Yet you know, once you have understood the proofs of the relevant theorems, that the interior angles of a Euclidean triangle total 180 degrees, and that any triangle inscribed within a semicircle must be a right triangle.

There are, on the other hand, many truths that really are empirical generalizations for which there is a great deal of supporting evidence but to which we can readily conceive exceptions, though we may never, in fact, encounter an exception. I can imagine, for example, that on some occasion pure water at sea-level barometric pressure might fail to crystallize at 32° Fahrenheit, as the law says it will. I am highly confident that this will not happen, but as with even the best-documented empirical generalizations, I do not have the absolute certainty about this that I have about a priori truths. If, then, I encounter a truth that I see to be necessarily true, and therefore know to be true with absolute certainty, I know that it is an a priori truth. And if, in addition, this truth is about the world, so that in knowing it I know not just the meanings of certain terms but something about reality, then I know that it is a synthetic a priori truth. Those in doubt on this point should compare any one of the examples I have given with the best-documented empirical generalization that they can think of. I am confident that they will not fail to see the difference. There is much, very much, that we know by observation and experimentation, but we do not possess such knowledge with the absolute certainty that is the hallmark of a priori knowledge.

The Falsifiability Test

Recognizing that the truths we have been discussing cannot be accounted for by Empiricist A's approach, Empiricist B tries to account for them in another way. Contrary to what may seem to be the case, he argues, arithmetical and geometrical truths are not synthetic truths at all: they are analytic. And the proof of this, he goes on to say, is that it is not possible to describe a state of affairs that, if it were the case, would render one of these statements false. This "falsifiability test," as he calls it, is the big weapon in his attack on synthetic a priori truths. Just how lethal is it, really?

Admittedly, the falsifiability test may be of some occasional value in helping us decide whether a given statement is analytic or synthetic, but it is not the infallible test that Empiricist B thinks it is. The reason is that a logically impossible state of affairs cannot be consistently described. If, therefore, we find ourselves unable in some instance to describe a state of affairs that, if it were the case, would falsify the statement in question, there are two possible explanations. First, the statement may be, as Empiricist B says it must be, an analytic statement, or, second, it may be a synthetic truth to which there are no logically possible alternatives. It may be, in short, a necessary empirical truth.

Consider once again the statement "Anything that has shape has size." I grant that neither I nor anyone else can imagine or describe a state of affairs that, if it were the case, would falsify this statement. (I can, of course, construct a sentence that appears to contradict the statement. I can say, "Some things that have shape do not have size," but Empiricist B and I both know that in saying this I would not be describing a possible state of affairs.) The reason that I cannot describe a state of affairs that, if true, would falsify the statement in question is not, however, that my statement is analytic, but rather that there is no logically possible alternative to the synthetic truth it expresses. We can see that although size and shape are different characteristics of spatial objects, they are, nonetheless, related in such a way that where one is present the other must also be present.

Even if the falsifiability test were taken at face value, however, it would not do the job that Empiricist B wants it to do. I note with great interest that he himself does not make use of the test in his discussion of geometrical truths—and with good reason. Even by this measure, geometrical truths turn out to be synthetic truths. For it is not at all difficult to describe a state of affairs that, if true, would falsify almost any geometrical theorem we can think of. It is perfectly conceivable to a nonmathematician that the interior angles of a Euclidean triangle, for example, might have totaled 160° or 190° instead of 180°, or that a triangle inscribed within a semicircle might always have had one obtuse angle instead of one 90° angle. It just happens that Euclid's theorems with respect to these matters are true, and if we have studied a little geometry, we know they are. But to know that they are true is not, in this case, to render the alternatives inconceivable.

Even the one application that Empiricist B does make of the falsifiability test—to arithmetical truths—is not very convincing. Obviously we would not, in the example of the oranges, adopt the explanation that there were only 11 oranges in the bag due to a remarkable exception to the general rule that $7 + 5 = 12$. But surely the reason we would not adopt this explanation is that we know a priori that $7 + 5 = 12$. Because we know this, and know it with absolute certainty, we quite naturally seek some other explanation for the fact that the bag does not contain as many oranges as we expected it to; for to know something a priori is to know also that experience must conform to what is thus known.

Let us suppose, however, that (in spite of this unfortunate reliance on what has turned out to be a faulty weapon) Empiricist B were right in his interpretation of mathematical truths. What would be the consequences?

In the first place, it would remain a gigantic puzzle that we are able to use arithmetical and geometrical reasoning to draw conclusions about the world at all. It is a remarkable fact that we are able to calculate all sorts of things—budget deficits and satellite orbits and a million other things—by applying the appropriate mathematical formulas to the data with which we begin. Remarkable as this may be, it is, nonetheless, a fact. On Empiricist B's account, however, this fact is not only remarkable, it is inexplicable. According to his view, mathematical truths are not truths about the world at all. They are purely vacuous statements that do nothing more than make explicit some of the meaning relations that have, apparently quite arbitrarily, been assigned to the various symbols in our number system. It is difficult to take seriously a theory that forces us to the conclusion that the applicability of mathematical reasoning to the real world is nothing but a happy coincidence.

In the second place, if the applicability of mathematical reasoning to the real world were, as Empiricist B holds, a matter of simply "trying it out to see if it works," then we ought to question whether it will work when it is applied to phenomena with which we have had no previous experience—whether, for example, the arithmetical and geometrical truths with which we are familiar on earth will hold on the moon or on Mars. But we do not, in fact, entertain such doubts (that is not one of the things we worried about when we sent men to the moon), and the reason we do not is that we know that the truths that we express in our equations are necessarily and universally true.

Logical Truths

I am delighted that Empiricist B has seen fit to explore the status of the so-called rules of inference, because they constitute some of the most convincing examples in support of my position. I hold, of course, that the rules of inference are synthetic a priori truths. It seems to me that whatever plausibility my opponent's account of these truths has depends on the unargued assumption that speaking a language is very much like playing a game, and that the rules governing the use of language are, like the rules in a game, altogether a matter of convention. This is hardly the place for a full-length discussion of the relation of language to reality, but we should be aware that the account of logical truths with which we are now dealing presupposes an extremely implausible view of the status of language.

My own view is that language has evolved out of the encounter of the human mind with reality and, therefore, incorporates a certain logical structure that corresponds to the structure of reality. The rules of inference, in this view, are not at all a matter of convention. They are grounded in the very structure of reality. They are, in fact, universal and synthetic truths about reality. They may be ignored at the cost not simply of speaking unintelligibly, but of speaking falsely. If I were to attempt to ignore the Principle of Noncontradiction—to say, that is, that some simple propositions are both true and false—I would be guilty not merely of breaking one of the rules of the language game; I would be guilty of uttering a statement that is not true. A proposition cannot be simultaneously true and false for the reason that a given state of affairs cannot both be the case and not be the case at one and the same time. It is reality, not merely conventional rules, that determines the truth or falsity of what we say. A so-called language that did not mirror the structure of reality in its own logical structure would be no language at all.

A Word About Ethics

Perhaps it was unwise to bring ethical truths into the present discussion, since I might have anticipated that it would lead only to confusion. So much has been written of late on the status of these truths, and so many theories have been propounded, that some philosophers hesitate even to mention the matter for fear that they will be compelled to defend their position against a vast number of opposing theories.

It is interesting to note, however, that this question did not become a matter of serious controversy until early in the present century, when British and American philosophers began to rally in large numbers beneath the banner of empiricism. Since then, the question of what to do with ethical truths has remained one of the thorniest problems for an empiricist to handle. If there are, as Empiricist A has said, "numerous ways in which an empiricist can construe ethical utterances without compromising his empiricism," it is not because these various ways are all so plausible, but rather because no one of them is sufficiently plausible to win very many adherents. But this is a matter that is to be discussed elsewhere at some length (see Chapters 45–50), so we need not enter into it here.

My position, in any case, remains unchanged and, for that matter, virtually unchallenged by the few remarks that my opponents have made on the subject of ethical truths. If anyone is absolutely determined to be an empiricist, I have no doubt that he or she will be able to find among the many empiricist accounts of ethical truths one that is acceptable. If, however, I have succeeded in persuading some of my readers that we do, in fact, have some a priori knowledge of synthetic truths, I think they will have little difficulty in agreeing that ethical truths are among those known in this way.

STUDY QUESTIONS

1. Is Rationalist right in saying that "it takes only a single example of an a priori synthetic truth to clinch the case for rationalism"? Explain.

2. Is Rationalist right in saying that (a) our certainty of the truth of an empirical generalization varies according to the amount of evidence on which it rests, and that (b) the certainty with which we hold arithmetical, geometrical, and logical truths is all out of proportion to the quantity of evidence upon which, if they were empirical generalizations, they would be based? If so, how does this affect Empiricist A's position? Empiricist B's?

3. What considerations does Rationalist bring forward in his attempt to show that the falsifiability test is not capable of doing the job that Empiricist B wants it to do? How might Empiricist B answer Rationalist on this point?

4. State briefly Rationalist's attempted reductio ad absurdum of Empiricist B's account of mathematical truths. Does it succeed? Explain.

CORRELATED READINGS[1]

---

1. Plato. "On Knowing Geometrical Truths." *Meno.* Many editions. Socrates' famous demonstration that Meno's slave boy "knows" a geometrical theorem without being taught. Rationalism.
2. Hume, David. "Relations of Ideas and Matters Of Fact." *An Enquiry Concerning Human Understanding,* Section IV, Part I. Empiricism.
3. Kant, Immanuel. "Analytic And Synthetic Truths." *Prolegomena to Any Future Metaphysics,* Preamble, Section 2. Rationalism.
4. Lewis, Clarence Irving. "The A Priori and the Empirical." *Mind and the World Order.* New York: Scribner, 1929, pp. 293–308. An attempt to mediate between rationalism and empiricism.

FOR FURTHER READING

Aune, Bruce. *Rationalism, Empiricism, and Pragmatism.* New York: Random House, 1970 (paperbound).

Blanshard, Brand. *The Nature of Thought,* vol. 1. New York: Humanities Press, 1939, Chaps. 28–30.

—————. *Reason and Analysis.* LaSalle, Ill.: Open Court Publishing Co., 1962, chaps. 6, 10.

Cassirer, Ernst. *The Problem of Knowledge.* trans. by W. H. Woglom and C. W. Hendel. New Haven, Conn.: Yale University Press, 1950, Chaps. 1–4.

Hamlyn, D. W. *The Theory of Knowledge.* Garden City, N.Y.: Doubleday, 1970 (paperbound).

Harris, James F., and Richard H. Stevens (eds.). *Analyticity.* New York: Quadrangle Books, 1970.

Leibnitz, G. W. *New Essays Concerning Human Understanding.* Many editions. See especially Book I and Book IV, Chaps. 1–9.

Monsat, Stanley (ed.). *The Analytic-Synthetic Distinction.* Belmont, Calif.: Wadsworth, 1971. Both classical and contemporary selections.

Morick, H. (ed.). *Challenges to Empiricism.* Belmont, Calif.: Wadsworth, 1972. Contemporary papers.

Pap, Arthur. "Are All Necessary Propositions Analytic?" *The Philosophical Review,* 58 (1949), 229–320.

Pears, David. *What Is Knowledge?* New York: Harper & Row, 1971.

Quine, W. van Orman. *From a Logical Point of View.* 2nd ed., rev. New York: Harper & Row, 1961 (paperbound). See especially "Two Dogmas of Empiricism."

Reichenbach, Hans. *Rise of Scientific Philosophy.* Berkeley and Los Angeles: University of California Press, 1958 (paperbound).

Russell, Bertrand. *Introduction to Mathematical Philosophy.* New York: Humanities Press, 1960, Chaps. 1, 2, 13, 14.

---

[1]*Concise Readings in Philosophy,* Part II.

Ryle, G., K. Popper, and C. Lewy. "Why are the Calculuses of Logic and Mathematics Applicable to Reality?" *Proceedings of the Aristotelian Society,* Supplementary 20 (1946), 20–60.

Sleigh, R. C., Jr. (ed.). *Necessary Truth.* Englewood Cliffs, N.J.: Prentice-Hall, 1972.

Sumner, L. W., and John Woods (eds.). *Necessary Truth: A Book of Readings.* New York: Random House, 1969.

PART III

THE PROBLEM
OF INDUCTION

8

THE LEGACY OF HUME

Rationalists and empiricists agree that we have a good deal of knowledge of the world that we have gained from experience, knowledge that we could not have acquired in any other way. It is obvious to everyone concerned that we have learned many *particular facts* by experience, such as the color of the house in which we live, the name of the street on which our house is located, the color of our mother's eyes, and so on. (Note that these are particular facts, not general truths: I know the color of my house and you know the color of your house, but neither of us knows from this anything about the color of houses in general. A particular fact has to do with some particular state of affairs that obtains in some particular place at some particular time. Such particular states of affairs, we are saying, are known by experience.) It is evidently in this way that we also come to know a great many *general empirical truths.* Some of these are common everyday truths that any normal person assents to without question—for example, that fire burns, water wets, and ice is cold. Others, like the generalizations at which scientists arrive after conducting elaborate experiments, are much more abstruse and less well known.

The process by which we proceed in our thinking from the particular facts of our experience to the general truths that seem to be exhibited in experience is called *induction.* How did we come to know the general truth that fire is hot? Presumably, we tried putting our hand near a fire and discovered by our pain that it was hot. We then knew the particular truth that *that* fire was hot. On some other occasion, we tried putting our hand near another fire and discovered that it, too, was hot. After a few such experiences, we cleverly concluded that all fire is hot, and thereafter we conducted ourselves accordingly.

A general empirical truth that is arrived at in this way is called an *empirical generalization.* Induction, then, is the process by which we proceed from the facts of experience to an empirical generalization that is, as we say, supported by those facts.

This all seems simple enough, and for a long time it apparently did not occur to anyone that the phenomenon of inductive reasoning presented any special problems of a philosophical nature. Then came David Hume.

Hume's Question

The question that Hume raised concerning induction was: "What is the nature of that evidence which assures us of any real existence and matter of fact beyond the present testimony of our senses or the records of our memory?"[1] What, in other words, is the justification for affirming a general empirical truth on the basis of our knowledge of some few particular facts? By what logical right do we claim to know that some empirical generalizations are true?

It is evident, Hume argued, that we do not know a priori what properties belong to an object that comes within the range of our experience:

> Adam, though his rational faculties be supposed, at the very first, entirely perfect, could not have inferred from the fluidity and transparency of water that it would suffocate him, or from the light and warmth of fire that it would consume him. No object ever discovers, by the qualities which appear to the senses, either the causes which produced it or the effects which will arise from it; nor can our reason, unassisted by experience, ever draw any inference concerning real existence and matter of fact.[2]

It must be, then, by experience that we know these things. But what, asked Hume, are we warranted in asserting on the basis of experience? Only that *in the past,* or *in all cases thus far observed,* such and such has been the case. Hume asserted:

> These two propositions are far from being the same: *I have found that such an object has always been attended with such an effect,* and *I foresee that other objects which are in appearance similar will be attended with similar effects.* I shall allow, if you please, that the one proposition may justly be inferred. But if you insist that the inference is made by a chain of reasoning, I desire you to produce that reasoning.[3]

Hume was convinced that no acceptable answer to his question was possible. He, accordingly, adopted the position that induction is not

---

[1] David Hume, in Charles W. Hendel (Ed.), *An Inquiry Concerning Human Understanding* (New York: Liberal Arts Press, 1955), p. 41.
[2] *Ibid.,* p. 42.
[3] *Ibid.,* p. 48.

logically justifiable because every inductive generalization presupposes a proposition that can never be proved—namely, that the future will resemble the past and that "similar powers will be conjoined with similar sensible qualities." He concluded, "If there be any suspicion that the course of nature may change, and that the past may be no rule for the future, all experience becomes useless and can give rise to no inference or conclusion."[4] No doubt we cannot avoid, as a matter of habit, drawing inferences of this kind and planning our affairs as if these inferences were trustworthy; but such inferences, Hume was convinced, have no satisfactory logical warrant.

A Restatement of Hume's Question

In light of the subsequent discussion of the problem so effectively raised by Hume, it is desirable to restate the problem in a somewhat different form. It is evident that two separate but closely related questions are involved. The first question might be stated thus: Is induction a valid logical procedure, that is, have we any logical right to draw general conclusions on the basis of our limited observation of some particular facts? The second question is: If induction is a valid logical procedure, does its validity rest on any a priori principles? Thus amplified, the question becomes: Is induction a valid logical procedure and, if so, does it involve any a priori principles?

Before turning to a preliminary characterization of the alternative positions that may be taken with respect to this question, let us look briefly at two common-sense reactions to Hume's puzzle. Both of these reveal a failure to grasp the point of Hume's question.

A common reaction of people who encounter the problem for the first time goes something like this: everybody knows that inductive reasoning is warranted; this is evident from the fact that everybody does it—including philosophers who ask sophistical questions. As a matter of fact, it would not be possible to perform any of the normal activities of life if we could not assume that the empirical generalizations drawn from our past experiences are well founded and, indeed, true. It is only in this way that we know essential everyday truths, such as that bread nourishes, water quenches thirst, and so on. If we could not depend on these, all activity and all life would have to cease.

This objection, which is a very natural one, misses the point of Hume's question. As a practical matter, Hume was well aware that we all do and indeed must make inductive inferences. "As an agent," Hume said explicitly, "I am quite satisfied in the point; but as a philosopher who has some share of curiosity, I will not say skepticism, I want to learn the *foundation* of this inference."[5] After it has been acknowledged that all persons do, in fact, employ inductive reasoning, and live their lives on the assumption that the empirical generaliza-

---

[4] *Ibid.,* p. 51.
[5] *Ibid.,* p. 52.

tions thus established are well founded, the question still remains: by what logical right, if any, do we make such inferences? It was his inability to find an answer to this question that drove Hume to the conclusion that inductive reasoning has no logical warrant at all.

It has also been suggested that Hume's problem disappears if we bear in mind that all we have a right to ask of an empirical generalization is that it be more or less *probable.* Hume's error, it is sometimes said, was his failure to recognize the difference between deductive and inductive reasoning. Deductive reasoning leads to conclusions that are as certain as the premises: in a valid deductive argument, if the premises are true the conclusion must be true. But with inductive arguments, this is not the case. However many instances of a given phenomenon are observed, it is only more or less probable that the observed uniformities will hold for all phenomena of that type. Once this is recognized, it is suggested, Hume's problem disappears.

Unfortunately, Hume's problem cannot be wished away in this facile manner. Hume was well aware of the fact that empirical generalizations are not certain since, as he pointed out, "the contrary of every matter of fact is still possible."[6] His point was not the truism that inductive reasoning does not establish its conclusions with the certainty and the necessity that deductive reasoning does. His point was the far more radical one that *what we call inductive reasoning is not reasoning at all,* that we have no logical right to affirm on the basis of our past experience that it is even probable that such-and-such will be the case in the future. No doubt the most that we can ask is that inductive reasoning be allowed to establish its conclusions with varying degrees of probability. The effect of Hume's question is to raise serious doubts as to whether even this much can be allowed.

Alternatives to Skepticism

Hume's own position with respect to this question is commonly referred to as *inductive skepticism.* It consists in affirming that induction is not a valid logical procedure—that, as Hume said, "even after we have experience of the operations of cause and effect, our conclusions from that experience are *not* founded on reasoning or any process of understanding."[7] Our propensity to believe that the future will be more or less like the past, that what has been observed to be the case in the past is therefore a reliable guide to the future, is nothing more than an interesting psychological fact about ourselves. Induction itself —as a logical procedure, as a species of reasoning—remains unwarranted and unjustified.

Many philosophers, though they acknowledge the legitimacy and the importance of Hume's question, have been unwilling to accept Hume's negative and skeptical answer to that question. On the con-

---

[6] *Ibid.,* p. 40.
[7] *Ibid.,* p. 47.

trary, they have held that induction is a valid logical procedure and have attempted in various ways to show how inductive inferences are warranted. Most of these attempts may be divided into two general classes, which we shall call constructive empiricism and rationalism.

Constructive empiricism consists in the assertions that (a) induction is a valid logical procedure, and (b) its validity does not depend on an appeal to any a priori truths. The first proposition distinguishes this position from that of the inductive skeptic; the second distinguishes it from that of the rationalist. Any empiricist who wishes to maintain the logical validity of inductive reasoning must be prepared to defend both. Chapter 9 represents one such attempt to answer Hume's question along these lines.

The rationalist's solution to the problem, as has been intimated, consists in affirming that (a) induction is a valid logical procedure, but (b) its validity depends on an appeal to some truth that is known a priori. The embarrassment of empiricism with respect to the problem of induction, in the view of many rationalists, is only one more proof of the inadequacy of the empiricist epistemology. If even general empirical truths cannot be established in a way that is consistent with empiricism, they argue, then it is quite clear that empiricism leaves much to be desired. This view is developed in some detail in Chapter 10.

It should be noted that it is not absolutely incumbent on a rationalist to adopt the "rationalist" solution to the problem of induction. One might be a skeptic with respect to the problem of induction and still be a rationalist by virtue of holding that there are some other synthetic truths that we know a priori. Thus, someone could conceivably be a rationalist without accepting the "rationalist" position on this point; but one who does accept the rationalist position on this point is a rationalist, no matter what other views he might hold.

If we take Hume's problem at face value, inductive skepticism, constructive empiricism, and rationalism are the only possible positions. A number of philosophers, however, have found themselves unconvinced by the attempts of both rationalists and empiricists to solve Hume's problem on its own terms. Yet they have been unwilling to draw Hume's skeptical conclusion with respect to our supposed knowledge of general empirical truths. Therefore, various attempts have been made to discover some incorrect assumption in Hume's statement of the problem (and in its discussion since) that, if eliminated, would show the problem not to be as serious as it appears. These attempts to solve the problem by dissolving it have taken a variety of forms.

One such attempt is represented by pragmatism. What is wrong with the traditional problem, according to the pragmatist, is its presupposed view concerning the nature of truth. How the pragmatist theory of truth is supposed to be of assistance in solving the problem of induction is explained in Chapter 11.

Another way of laying this old problem to rest has been advocated by the distinguished contemporary philosopher Karl Popper. Popper's position involves two main parts: (a) an acceptance of Hume's refutation of induction together with (b) a denial that this has any serious consequences so far as our knowledge of empirical truths is concerned. This position is discussed in Chapter 12, from Popper's point of view that, once the status of scientific knowledge is understood, the traditional problem of induction will no longer be considered a problem.

A student who is considering the problem of induction for the first time should approach it with the supposition that it is a genuine and important problem to which skepticism, rationalism, and constructive empiricism are the only available solutions. In this way, he or she will be able to judge whether the other two attempts are as successful as they claim to be in solving the problem by, so to speak, circumventing it.

STUDY QUESTIONS

1. What precisely is the difference between a particular empirical fact and a general empirical truth? Give several examples of each.
2. What exactly is the problem of induction? Test your understanding of it by attempting to restate the problem in several different ways.
3. How do the two "common-sense" reactions mentioned in this chapter miss the point of Hume's question? Do they attribute to Hume some assumption that he did not make, or do they address themselves to some question other than the one Hume was asking?
4. Give two or three examples of inductive arguments that you have used or have heard used by someone else. Does it seem to you that the premises (in your examples) provide some warrant for affirming the conclusion? If so, how? Are you, or are you not, making some a priori assumption?

9

EMPIRICISM AND THE PROBLEM OF INDUCTION

It must be admitted that Hume did no favor to science, empiricism, or common sense in raising the problem of induction. Both science and common sense are outraged at the thought that the generalizations affirmed on the basis of observation should have, as Hume said, no logical foundation; and it *is* a problem that is not congenial to empiricism. Yet it is unthinkable that we should resort to ad hoc theories of a priori knowledge in order to account for such a homely thing as the belief that the sun will rise tomorrow. Hence, we may be sure that if the matter is only considered in the proper perspective, it will become clear that the problem of induction is not the stumbling stone for empiricism that it is sometimes believed to be.

I think we should be aware, particularly in view of some suggestions that have been made from time to time, that this is no mere pseudoproblem. A number of disastrous consequences would follow if it should be concluded that induction is not, after all, a valid logical procedure. It will be profitable to begin our consideration of the problem by looking at some of the consequences that we must be prepared to accept if, like Hume, we come to a skeptical conclusion.

Consequences of Inductive Skepticism

It should be apparent that our knowledge of many everyday empirical truths rests on a basis of inductive inference. We know, for example, that unsupported bodies fall toward the earth, that air-breathing animals cannot long survive under water, that bread nourishes, that water quenches thirst, and so on. If inductive reasoning is not well founded, we have no logical basis, no rational foundation, for believing these things. Then, so far as the logic of the matter is concerned, we might, with as much justification, hold the contrary view—that unsupported bodies (evidence to the contrary notwithstanding) sometimes fly upward, that some air-breathing animals flourish under water, that bread and water sometimes injure rather than nourish a hungry and thirsty person.

In the same way, many of our particular expectations with respect to the immediate future would turn out to be rationally indefensible if induction is overthrown, for these are but particular instances of, or particular deductions from, general truths. I believe that the dinner I shall eat tonight will nourish my body, not poison it. Why? Because I believe in the truth of the general proposition that food nourishes. I believe that if I were to leave my third-floor office by way of the window rather than by way of the elevator or stairs I would be, at the very least, severely injured. Why? Because I believe in the truth of such general propositions as these: that unsupported bodies fall toward the earth at an accelerating rate of speed, and that a fall of three stories is likely to cause serious injury to the human body. Yet, if induction is not a valid logical procedure, I have no rational basis for these expectations.

What is even more incredible, however, is that the whole enterprise of natural science would be without a logical foundation if induction is not defensible. All the reasoning of scientists, from Galileo and Newton and Kepler to Einstein and Heisenberg and Bohr, would have to be regarded as no reasoning at all, but simply as so many examples of the "inference-drawing propensity" of the human psyche. This, I submit, is simply absurd, and a view of induction that compels us to draw such a conclusion is similarly absurd.

A sober consideration of what is at stake in the controversy over induction makes it evident, therefore, that Humean skepticism cannot be the last word on this matter. Simply to list the consequences of the skeptical position is at the same time to construct a powerful *reductio ad absurdum* of that position. Somehow it must be possible to establish the logical validity of induction; and if we are empiricists, we will seek a way to do this consistent with empiricism.

Induction and the Principle of the Uniformity of Nature

It is hardly necessary to give an elaborate description of what we are doing when we "draw an inductive inference," since each of us is familiar with it from personal experience. We first observe some phenomenon, such as the sun rising in the east. Then, we observe another instance of that same phenomenon, then another, and another, until at length we draw our inference: that the sun always rises in the east, or whatever the inference might be. We proceed, that is, to affirm *universal* regularity on the basis of *observed* regularity. And, in the case of a true inference, our general conclusion is constantly confirmed by our subsequent experience.

It is quite evident that in reasoning in this manner we are tacitly assuming what is sometimes called the Principle of the Uniformity of Nature. This principle may be stated in a variety of ways, of which the following are representative. P_1: the universe is so constructed that everything that occurs may be viewed as an instance of some general law or laws. P_2: the universe is not a chaos of random events; some uniformities, or laws, are exhibited in phenomena widely separated in space and time. P_3: nature operates according to some uniform laws; what has occurred in the past, therefore, is a reliable guide for the future.

I do not wish to discuss in detail the differences that are evident in these three versions of the Principle of the Uniformity of Nature. P_2 and P_3 are, I think, virtually identical, the only significant difference being that the latter specifically mentions the reliability of the past as a guide for the future. P_1 differs from the other two in that it appears to affirm universal determinism. Since we do, in fact, employ inductive reasoning even though we may have serious doubts about whether or not determinism is true, it is evident that we do not necessarily assume the principle as stated in P_1 when we are reasoning inductively. I think we can safely say that *if* we had some way of knowing that P_2 is true, we would have no difficulty in understanding the logical foundation of inductive reasoning.

A brief explanation of the logical structure of inductive reasoning, *if we assume the Principle of the Uniformity of Nature* (P_2), might prove helpful at this point.

A typical instance of inductive reasoning would be the familiar one in which we infer, from the fact that all the crows we have observed are black, that all crows are black. The reasoning by which we arrive at this general conclusion is as follows:

Major premise: What is true of Crow 1, Crow 2, Crow 3, and so on is true of all crows.

Minor premise: Crow 1, Crow 2, Crow 3, and so on, are black.

Conclusion: All crows are black.

Upon what basis, then, do we affirm the major premise? It should be clear that it is the general conclusion of a higher level argument, the structure of which is as follows:

Major premise: The universe is not a chaos of random events; some uniformities are exhibited in phenomena widely separated in space and time.

Minor premise: Crows are among those phenomena that exhibit such uniformities.

Conclusion: What is true of Crow 1, Crow 2, Crow 3, and so on, is true of all crows.

It is important to note that the conclusion of our first argument—that all crows are black—is only more or less probable, and that this is exactly what we should expect if the logical structure of the argument is as I have stated. The premises from which the conclusion is drawn are known with something less than absolute certainty. This uncertainty—or, as I should prefer to say, this *varying probability*—that attaches to the premises is accordingly passed on to the conclusion.

But how do we know with any degree of certainty that the universe exhibits some uniformities? How does this ultimate major premise of all inductive reasoning get established? This is the issue that now must be addressed.

Two Kinds of Induction

We may make a beginning toward unraveling this puzzle if we make a distinction between what I shall call *informal* induction and *rigorous,* or *scientific,* induction. The former must have been practiced since the emergence of the human species upon earth, and even our prehuman ancestors must have employed something analogous to it. The latter has been practiced only within the last few hundred years.

Informal induction may well be, as Hume said, nothing more than the habit of generalizing from our experience. Every human being, including the most primitive people on earth, believes a vast number of general truths on this basis. The general truths that an Eskimo knows in this way will be on the whole quite different from those known by a person who lives in equatorial Africa or an Australian aborigine. The Eskimo will know, for example, that snow is cold, that seals are good for food, that seal oil may be used for certain purposes, and so on. A member of an African tribe will know that the midday sun is very hot, that certain sorts of animals are to be feared, that some types of berries are poisonous, and the like. And still other general truths will presumably be known by people living in other environments.

Some of the things that people believe they "know" in this way may turn out to be false. Many generations of Africans must have believed, for example, that all men are black, and the Eskimos of the far north may have believed, at one time, that all men live in houses made of snow. Informal induction, therefore, is not an entirely reliable procedure; but it is the starting point from which better things may come.

Let us now suppose a civilization in which a reasonably high level of culture has been achieved and in which there is, for some members of the society at least, sufficient leisure to cultivate intellectual pursuits. What materials would the thinkers of this culture have to work with? According to our account, they would have (a) a stock of general truths, or at any rate general beliefs, arrived at in the informal way described above and (b) as a strict correlate to this, a belief that nature exhibits some uniformities—the uniformities expressed in the particular set of beliefs that summarize the common experience of the people of that society.

In such a situation, it is natural that the following question should be asked: May there not be other, less obvious, uniformities in nature that no one has yet taken the trouble to observe? We know that nature exhibits some uniformities. Let us see if we can find others.

It is when this step is taken that we pass from the primitive to the scientific attitude toward the world, and from informal to scientific inductive reasoning. To look for uniformity is quite a different thing from simply noting the uniformity that is obvious to everyone. In the case of informal induction, we are scarcely, if at all, aware of the fact that we are drawing an inference: we simply act as if certain uniformities obtain, without consciously considering the general truth that is therein implied. With scientific induction, however, the situation is different. Here we deliberately, carefully, painstakingly attempt to find some general truth that will tie together the apparently diverse data of experience.

Scientific induction differs from informal induction in at least four ways. First, in every instance of scientific induction, we are quite consciously taking a risk. We are not simply summarizing what we have observed: we are deliberately going beyond what we have observed to affirm as a general truth a proposition that may, for all we know, be erroneous.

Second, in the case of scientific induction we actively try to disprove the generalization that is the conclusion of our inductive reasoning. When we engage in scientific inductive reasoning, we are not simply "reading off" the obvious general truths exhibited in the world. We are seriously attempting to discover uniformities that are not obvious to everyone, trying to find uniformities that hold without exception. Informal induction reveals nothing that is parallel to this.

Third, in the case of scientific induction, we continue to maintain a critical, not-quite-convinced attitude toward even those uniformities that survive our best efforts to disprove them. The conclusion of a scientific induction, however impressive the evidence upon which it rests, is always subject to modification. With informal induction, this is not the case.

Fourth, scientific induction, unlike informal induction, proceeds according to fixed rules. These rules, which were first given formal expression by John Stuart Mill (whose nomenclature is still in common use), specify the ways in which inductive reasoning can proceed with the minimum possibility of error. Mill's Methods, as they are called—the Method of Agreement, the Method of Difference, the Joint Method of Agreement and Difference, and so on—represent scientific induction fully conscious of its own procedures. It is these methods, implicit in the procedure of rigorous thinkers of every age and explicit in the work of Mill, that have produced the impressive results that make the modern era the age of science *par excellence.*

The situation, therefore, seems to be this. The Principle of the Uniformity of Nature appears to be the product of informal inductions that are themselves nothing more than the "reading off" of certain rather obvious uniformities exhibited in the everyday experience of man. The Principle of the Uniformity of Nature must, therefore, be a product of what Hume called our "habit" or "propensity" of looking for regularity among the diverse data of our experience. Once the Principle of Uniformity becomes known in this rather informal way, however, it serves as the major premise in the more rigorous forms of inductive reasoning. It, too, is subjected to the same critical appraisal to which all the conclusions of inductive reasoning are exposed. It, therefore, becomes more and more firmly established with each successful induction. Thus, the principle itself and the informal inductions upon which it was originally based are justified and rendered secure by the rigorous methods to which they have given rise.

The Security of the Principle of Uniformity

If, as we have argued, the major premise of all scientific inductive reasoning rests on merely informal inductions, then it might appear that the reasoning that proceeds from that premise must itself share in the insecurity of that foundation. This objection, which it is natural to raise at this point, has been effectively answered by Mill, who stated:

> The precariousness of the method of simple enumeration is in an inverse ratio to the largeness of the generalization. The process is delusive and insufficient, exactly in proportion as the subject-matter of the observation is special and limited in extent. As the sphere widens, this unscientific method becomes less and less liable to mislead; and the most universal class of truths, the law of causation for instance, and the principles of number and of geometry, are duly and satisfactorily proved by that method alone.[1]

In spite of the fact that the Principle of the Uniformity of Nature rests on the foundation of the informal inductions of prescientific man, it is saved from insecurity by two factors: the extreme breadth of the principle itself and the fact that it has been subsequently tested

---

[1]John Stuart Mill, *A System of Logic,* III, xxi, 8th ed. (New York and London: Longmans, Green, 1956), p. 373.

and confirmed according to the critical spirit of the scientific mind. Thus, it is able to function as a secure foundation for all subsequent inductive reasoning.

Hume's error, it appears to me, is that he failed to analyze carefully enough the logical structure of inductive reasoning. He failed to make the all-important distinction between informal and scientific induction. Hume saw, correctly enough, that inductions of the scientific type presuppose the principle of uniformity, and from this he concluded that the principle itself must simply be gratuitously assumed. It required a century or more after Hume to bring to light the distinction he did not see and by which the problem of induction is solved.

STUDY QUESTIONS

1. What "disastrous consequences" does Empiricist say would follow if we were to accept Hume's skeptical conclusions regarding induction? Do you think he is right? If so, does this constitute a *reductio ad absurdum* of inductive skepticism, as Empiricist says it does?

2. What is the Principle of Uniformity? Is Empiricist right in saying that this principle constitutes "the ultimate major premise of all inductive reasoning"? Is it true that we would have a logical warrant for making inductive inferences if we could somehow establish the truth of this principle?

3. What exactly is the distinction that Empiricist makes between "informal" induction and "scientific" induction? What use does he make of this distinction in his subsequent argument?

4. How does Empiricist attempt to answer the objection that if the Principle of Uniformity is established by the relatively insecure method of "informal" induction, then all the reasoning based upon this principle must be equally insecure? Are you convinced by his answer? Can you present a better one?

10

RATIONALISM AND THE PROBLEM OF INDUCTION

It is a continuous source of interest to observe the various ways in which empiricists twist and squirm in their vain attempts to find an acceptable alternative to the inductive skepticism of Hume. Hume's question has been, as Empiricist has hinted, a distinct embarrassment to empiricists—so much so that I suspect that more converts to rationalism may have been won on this single point than on any other point to which rationalists commonly appeal in support of their position.

The empiricist is in a serious predicament. On the one hand, he is aware that inductive skepticism does lead to disastrous and, indeed, unacceptable consequences with respect to the status of a good deal of our knowledge of the world. On the other hand, he is committed to the proposition that empiricism is true—and Hume appears to have shown that on empiricist premises his skeptical conclusions cannot be avoided. But on empiricist grounds, Hume still has the final word. Two long centuries of effort have not produced a single convincing defense of inductive reasoning that does not violate the central tenet of empiricism. On the problem of induction, the only viable alternatives are skepticism and rationalism.

Critique of Constructive Empiricism

It should be apparent to anyone who is not blinded by empiricist dogmatism that the argument set forth in the preceding chapter does not succeed in its attempt to show that induction is a valid logical procedure. It is inadequate, as a matter of fact, in several different ways.

First, it fails to grasp the true purport, the really radical character, of Hume's argument. Hume did not say, as Empiricist implies in the latter part of his essay, that it was only the reasoning of scientists that was placed in jeopardy by his critical questioning of the validity of induction. All inductive reasoning, he argued, proceeds on the assumption that nature is uniform, that the future will be like the past. This means, therefore, that anyone who would answer Hume must do one of two things: either show that Hume was mistaken in his claim that all inductive reasoning presupposes the Principle of the Uniformity of Nature, or show that the principle is not itself a product of inductive reasoning. Since Empiricist has done neither of these, it is apparent that he has not really understood the radical character of Hume's question.

Second, it is also clear that Empiricist's argument turns on a distinction that is more apparent than real. Inductive reasoning, like anything else, can be done either carelessly or carefully, and there is no harm in calling attention to this difference by calling the one "informal" and the other "rigorous" or "scientific" induction. But as soon as we recognize that this is all the distinction amounts to, it becomes apparent that we cannot make the use of it that Empiricist has attempted to make. Even "informal" induction, according to Hume's analysis, presupposes the Principle of Uniformity. Unless Empiricist can exhibit the logical structure of "informal" induction in a way that escapes Hume's criticism, it will not be of any help to him as a foundation for "scientific" induction.

It is fair to say, therefore, that in the last analysis Empiricist's argument is circular. The very principle that he hopes to establish by means of "informal" induction—the Principle of the Uniformity of Nature—must be presupposed before the first such inductive generalization can be made.

Empiricist seems to have realized that his argument leaves something to be desired, and near the end of his essay he tries to patch it up as best he can. He does this by (a) a vague reference to the subsequent "purification" of the principle of uniformity once it has given birth to "scientific" induction, and (b) gratuitously assuming the general principle that "the wider the generalization, the more certain it is."

I do not rightly know how to distinguish between a "purified" and an "unpurified" principle, but I think I know what Empiricist has in mind. The Principle of the Uniformity of Nature, according to his account, still carries the taint of its unscientific past: it is not, in its natural state, a suitable principle for "scientific" use. It needs, therefore, to be "purified"—or, to put the point more prosaically, to be reëstablished by scientific induction. But this, quite obviously, cannot be done, since on Empiricist's own account "scientific" induction presupposes the unbaptized principle. It is no wonder that the reference to "purification" was rather vague!

Nor is Empiricist's case rendered any more convincing by the introduction of Mill's suggestion that the broader the generalization is, the more certain it is. This does not even appear to be true: it rather seems to be the case that the more cautious we are about generalizations— the closer we stay to what we actually observe—the more confident we may be about the correctness of those generalizations. But let us assume, for the moment, that Mill is right in this. How does he claim to know that it is true? Is it a priori? Obviously, no empiricist can allow this. Is it the product of inductive reasoning? If so, the validity of induction must already be assumed, and no principle that is established thereby can be called in to enhance its validity.

The Logical Premise of Inductive Reasoning

There are, I have suggested, only two possible ways to counter Hume's attack on inductive reasoning. One is to show that the Principle of the Uniformity of Nature is not itself the product of inductive reasoning. The other is to show that Hume was mistaken in his belief that all inductive reasoning presupposes the Principle of the Uniformity of Nature.

Some rationalists have attempted the first of these two alternatives as a way of reëstablishing the validity of inductive reasoning, but, in my opinion, not successfully. It seems evident, in the first place, that we do not know a priori that the Principle of the Uniformity of Nature in its "strong," or deterministic, form (P_1, see p. 75) is true. I myself have grave doubts about the truth of the principle when it is stated in this way; hence, I cannot justly be said to "know" it either a priori or a posteriori. A defense of inductive reasoning that depends on an appeal to a priori knowledge at this point seems, therefore, to be weak. On the other hand, we do know that the principle in its weaker form (P_2 or P_3) is true, but it is quite obvious that the principle in this form is itself an inductive generalization—that is, known a posteriori. Our knowledge of the principle in this form, therefore, presupposes the validity of inductive reasoning, and the ground of that validity must be sought in some other place.

A clue to the correct solution of this problem may be found in the way that we are able to proceed from premises to a conclusion in deductive reasoning. Our ability to do so depends on certain rules of inference that we know a priori (see Chapter 7). May it not be, then, that in inductive reasoning it is some logical principle that enables us to make our inferences? Let us reëxamine the logical structure of an inductive argument to see whether this is not, in fact, the case.

We may take as our example the well-worn one about the crows. We start, in this case, with what we shall call the observational premise —that N crows have been observed, and all of them have been black. From this we feel justified in inferring the probable but not certain conclusion that all crows are black. The argument appears to be this:

| Observational premise: | N crows have been observed, and all of them have been black. |
| | ... |

| Inductive conclusion: | It is more or less probable that all crows are black. |

If we are on the right track, we ought to look for some logical principle—some rule of inductive inference—that will enable us to draw the general conclusion. The principle should (a) provide a warrant for our drawing the inference and (b) account for the fact that the inference is only probable, never absolutely certain.

The principle for which we are seeking might be stated: "The more often two things have been observed to be conjoined in nature, the more probable it is that they are always so conjoined." Putting this principle—which I shall call the logical premise—in the place of the elliptical dots in our argument, we get the following:

| Observational premise: | N crows have been observed, and all of them have been black. |
| Logical premise: | The more often two things have been observed to be conjoined in nature, the more probable it is that they are always so conjoined. |

| Inductive conclusion: | It is more or less probable that all crows are black |

There are three observations that I should like to make regarding this principle. First, it should be noted that when this premise is supplied, it is no longer a mystery how we are able to draw our inductive conclusion. The reasoning that is involved is, in fact, deductive: the conclusion is validly inferred from the premises, as in any sound deductive argument.

Second, the principle does account for the fact that inductive generalizations are made with varying degrees of certainty. The conclusion —that it is more or less probable that all crows are black—follows rigorously from the premises and is known with the same certainty that the premises are known. The proposition that all crows are black is itself only more or less probable (as is the case with any empirical generalization), and this probability is explicitly stated in the conclusion.

Third, the argument, thus stated, exhibits the fact that the probability of the empirical generalization that appears in the conclusion varies directly with the quantity of evidence upon which it is based. If I have seen one crow, my generalization has a low degree of probability. If I have seen a hundred, the probability increases. And if I have seen thousands and have checked the reports of others who have seen thousands more, the probability becomes very high. The principle as stated does, therefore, correspond to our intuitive conviction that the greater the quantity of evidence upon which a generalization is based, the greater the probability that it is true without exception.

Our Knowledge of the Logical Premise of Inductive Arguments

I spoke just now about "our intuitive conviction" with regard to the quantity of evidence upon which a generalization is based. It seems clear to me that we do, in fact, have such a conviction—indeed, that we know that this is the case. What we have called the logical premise of all inductive reasoning, however, is nothing more nor less than a statement in slightly different terms of this very truth. To say that something is known intuitively is to say that it is known a priori. In identifying this logical premise, therefore, we may plausibly claim to have discovered the a priori ground of the validity of inductive reasoning.

Hume's chief error, if this analysis is correct, consists in his assertion that inductive reasoning always involves an appeal to the Principle of the Uniformity of Nature. This principle, he correctly observed, is itself a product of inductive reasoning. He, accordingly, drew the conclusion that all inductive reasoning is circular—is, in fact, no reasoning at all. Empiricist accepted Hume's analysis of the structure of inductive reasoning and attempted unsuccessfully to show that the Principle of the Uniformity of Nature could be established without appealing in the process to that very principle. It is only when this initial assumption as to the structure of inductive reasoning is rejected that the correct solution to the problem becomes apparent.

I do not suppose, however, that the solution I have proposed will be of any comfort to empiricists, because it carries with it the rather surprising conclusion that there is an a priori element even in most a posteriori knowledge—in all that goes beyond the particular data of direct observation. This includes, obviously, all the general findings of the natural sciences as well as the everyday truths that we all take for granted. To an empiricist, however, this conclusion is not only surprising, it is totally unacceptable; for to accept it is to concede that empiricism is a misguided epistemological theory.

It seems fair to say in conclusion, therefore, that properly understood the *reductio ad absurdum* argument that Empiricist directed against inductive skepticism is an equally effective demonstration of the absurdity of empiricism itself. The real merit of Hume's argument is to have shown precisely that skepticism with respect to inductive reasoning is an inevitable consequence of empiricism. It follows, therefore, that anyone who wishes to maintain the empiricist position must be prepared to accept the consequences of inductive skepticism. If those consequences are indeed absurd—as Empiricist and I both believe they are—then empiricism itself is an absurd and untenable position. When this is clearly understood, the correctness of the solution proposed here may become even more apparent.

STUDY QUESTIONS

1. Rationalist suggests that anyone who would answer Hume on the problem of induction "must do one of two things." What are they? Are these the only ways of answering Hume? Is it true that Empiricist has done neither?
2. Is Rationalist right in saying that the difference between "informal" and "scientific" induction is nothing more than the difference between careless and careful reasoning? Is the logical structure the same in both instances? If so, does this seriously damage Empiricist's argument?
3. What "clue" to the solution of the problem of induction does Rationalist claim to find in "the way by which we are able to proceed from premises to a conclusion in deductive reasoning"? Does this strike you as a promising way to approach this problem?
4. Which of the "two things" that Rationalist says one must do to answer Hume does Rationalist himself attempt to do? Does he succeed? How would you expect Hume to reply to Rationalist's argument?

11

THE PROPOSAL
OF PRAGMATISM

Whenever the discussion of a philosophical question reaches a complete impasse, as the discussion of the problem of induction appears
to have done, it is a good idea to ask whether there is not something
wrong with the question itself—whether, for example, some incorrect
assumption is not being made, or some impossible requirement is
being set up for any answer that is to be regarded as acceptable.
Should this prove to be the case with regard to some particular dispute, it is not surprising that all the parties to the dispute should end
up by proving nothing at all, and that their attacks and counterattacks
should serve no other purpose than to convince saner people that the
disputants simply do not understand the business that they are attempting to prosecute with such ostentatious vigor.

That the three-way discussion of the problem of induction has,
indeed, reached an impasse cannot be seriously doubted by any impar-
tial observer. The absurdity of inductive skepticism and the inadequacy of what is quaintly called "constructive empiricism" have
already been sufficiently demonstrated. If Rationalist appears for the
moment to have the upper hand in the argument, it is only because,
for the time being, he has had the opportunity to speak last. It is an
easy matter to show, however, that his position is as untenable as the
other two, and by way of clearing our minds for a fresh and more
promising way of looking at this old problem, we shall begin by pointing out what is wrong with the rationalist position.

Critique of Rationalism

We may begin by observing that the principle that "the more often two
things have been observed to be conjoined in nature, the more proba-

ble it is that they are always so conjoined" is hardly a promising candidate for an a priori truth, even according to the criteria that rationalists themselves commonly employ in identifying such truths. Most rationalists are in the habit of following Immanuel Kant on this point, and the two criteria of a priori knowledge to which they customarily point are what Kant called the "necessity" and the "universality" of such truths. Kant said:

> If we have a proposition which in being thought is thought as necessary, it is an a priori judgment, and [if] a judgment is thought with strict universality, that is, in such manner that no exception is allowed as possible, it is not derived from experience, but is valid absolutely a priori.[1]

It may be argued with some plausibility that Rationalist's "rule of inductive inference" has the requisite universality, though we could question whether it really does exhibit the "strict" universality of which Kant spoke. It does not seem that an exception to this principle is inconceivable in the way that an exception to an arithmetical truth is inconceivable; but I shall not press this point. What is clear is that this principle does not exhibit the necessity that is alleged to be the hallmark of truths known a priori. There is nothing self-evidently true about this principle, as there is, for example, about the axioms of geometry. If we are convinced that the principle is sound, the reason, surely, is because we have found that it *works.* And this has certain implications for our whole understanding of the problem, which we shall have to develop shortly. For the present, however, we may be content to have shown that even on Rationalist's own terms it cannot be plausibly maintained that what has been offered as the principle of all inductive reasoning is known a priori.

In addition, I do not think that Rationalist has succeeded in disengaging inductive reasoning from the assumption that nature is uniform. The logical principle is, after all, only as secure as our belief that nature does not behave in a way that is wholly capricious—as secure, in short, as the Principle of the Uniformity of Nature. Hume's objection is equally as devastating in its effect on Rationalist's position as Rationalist has perceived it to be on constructive empiricism: "If there be any suspicion that the course of nature may change, and that the past may be no rule for the future, all experience becomes useless and can give rise to no inference or conclusion."[2] To doubt the Principle of the Uniformity of Nature is, at the same time, to doubt the validity of the proposed rule of inductive inference. Thus, Rationalist's solution to the problem is no better than that of Constructive Empiricist, whom he so roundly criticizes.

---

[1]Immanuel Kant, *Critique of Pure Reason,* Intro., II, trans. Norman Kemp Smith (New York: St. Martin's Press, 1965), pp. 43–44.
[2]David Hume, in Charles W. Hendel (ed.), *An Inquiry Concerning Human Understanding* (New York: Liberal Arts Press, 1955), p. 51.

We are left, therefore, with three positions—inductive skepticism, constructive empiricism, and rationalism—all of which are seen to be untenable. Yet these are the only positions that it is possible to take with respect to the question that has been stated. Something, evidently, has gone wrong. There is something artificial, something incorrect, about the assumptions upon which the whole argument thus far has been proceeding. Let us try to locate the error and raise the discussion to a new and more fruitful level.

Truth

There is one assumption that all three previous writers on this question share in common: that a statement is true if and only if what it asserts to be the case really is the case. They have all assumed the correspondence theory of truth. Proceeding on this assumption, they have asked: How can we possibly know that reality corresponds to the assertions that we make when we utter an empirical generalization? We know, indeed, that reality corresponds to the simple observational statements with which we begin. But how can we know that it corresponds to the statement with which we conclude—a statement that leaps far beyond what we have observed and purports to describe phenomena that we have not observed and perhaps never shall observe?

To ask this question is, I submit, to ask a question that cannot be answered. That is why none of the illustrious philosophers who have tried to do so have been able to answer it. To show why this is an unanswerable question is our task in the remainder of this essay.

William James provided the key with which we may hope to unlock this old puzzle when he said:

> There can *be* no difference anywhere that doesn't *make* a difference elsewhere—no difference in abstract truth that doesn't express itself in a difference in concrete fact and in conduct consequent upon that fact, imposed on somebody, sometime, and somewhere ... Ideas ... become true just in so far as they help us to get into satisfactory relation with other parts of our experience, to summarize them and get about among them by conceptual short-cuts instead of following the interminable succession of particular phenomena.[3]

Let us examine these ideas and see how they can help us in coming to a satisfactory view with respect to the problem of induction.

"There can be no difference that doesn't make a difference." This means that the meaning of any idea consists precisely in the consequences that it is supposed to have for either our own experience or that of someone else. The meaning of the idea that there are tigers in

---

[3]William James, *Pragmatism* (New York and London: Longmans, Green, 1959), pp. 49–50, 58; see also pp. 197–234. (Italics added.)

India, for example, consists simply in—to quote James again—the "procession of mental associates and motor consequences that follow on the thought, and that would lead harmoniously, if followed out, into some ideal or real context, or even into the immediate presence, of the tigers."[4] The notion that there could be two different ideas that have identical practical consequences is simply meaningless.

Another way to put this is to say that ideas are "plans for action." We never desire to know just for the sake of knowing. We desire to know in order that we shall be able to get about in the world of our experience, in order that we shall be able to pursue our purposes in the world (no matter what those purposes might be). It is only in this way that we are able to choose, from among the infinite things that we might conceivably attempt to understand, those things that we do, in fact, seek to understand; it is *our interests, our purposes,* that determine the selection.

To say, then, that an idea is true is not to say that it is an exact "copy" of reality. Rather, it is to say that it works, that it enables us to move about in the world of our experience. "True ideas are those that we can assimilate, validate, corroborate and verify. False ideas are those that we can not."[5] This is the only sense of truth and falsehood that has any relation to the purposes for which we wish to distinguish the two—the only meaning, therefore, that this distinction can possibly have for us.

Truth, therefore, is always truth for someone. The things that were true for medieval man—the ideas that were adequate to enable him to get around in the world of his experience—are not necessarily true for us. Experience, as James so aptly put it, has ways of "boiling over," thus compelling each generation to modify what was received from the previous generation as the truth—to make its own truth, so to speak. But the idea of a purely objective truth, a truth that has no practical consequences for human experience, is an empty and meaningless concept. The reasons that lead us to call an idea true are precisely the reasons that make it true.

The idea of an "absolute truth," therefore, can be nothing other than the idea of a truth that would be adequate to all possible experience, a truth that no experience could ever require us to modify or reject. Such truth may be the ideal goal toward which all of our attempts to know the truth are aiming, but it is not the quality of those provisional and temporary truths that constitute the truth-for-us. The truth-for-us is simply the truth that works, the truth that enables us to get about in the "booming, buzzing confusion" that is the world of our experience. It is, as James said, "the expedient in the way of our thinking."

---

[4]William James, *The Meaning of Truth* (New York and London: Longmans, Green, 1910), pp. 44–45.
[5]William James, *Pragmatism,* p. 201.

The Problem of Induction Revisited

Let us now return to the problem of induction and see how the ideas we have just been considering can aid us in reaching the correct solution of that problem.

Suppose someone speaks to us as follows: "In all of my experience thus far, I have observed nothing but black crows. It seems to be true, therefore, that all crows are black. But how can I be sure that this is true absolutely? How can I be sure that the future will be like the past, that all 'future' crows will be black just as all 'past' crows have been? How can I infer from the observed to the unobserved?"

If we have understood the ideas set forth in the preceding pages, we shall have no difficulty in responding to such a query. We shall have to say, obviously, that our puzzled friend cannot be sure that the generalization that summarizes his or her past experience will hold in the future. But until experience itself contradicts the belief that all crows are black, the questioner would, nonetheless, be well advised to regard the generalization as true. And what we would mean by this is, quite simply, that so long as no facts arise to require an alteration of the generalization, it will serve to enable us to get around within a certain segment of our experience (to tie together, for example, what we see in the forest, what we read in books, and what we hear in the conversation of others). If something occurs within our field of experience that gives the lie to this belief, then and only then will it cease to be true. Then, too, we will be compelled to seek a new generalization that is sufficient to encompass this new experience as well as the old.

All parties to the dispute about the validity of inductive inferences have been obsessed with the idea of "absolute truth." It is this idea of truth that they have in mind when they ask: How can we know that the generalizations that are the products of our inductive inferences are true? They have sought, accordingly, to find a logical method that would somehow guarantee their truth. Hume, at least, saw that this was not possible and drew the skeptical consequences with which we are all familiar. Those who came after him continued the search for a method, with the inconclusive results that have made this problem the scandal of philosophy.

It is interesting to note that both rationalists and empiricists who have addressed themselves to this problem have attempted to validate induction by exhibiting it as a concealed form of deductive reasoning. The assumption has been, apparently, that deductive reasoning somehow "guarantees" the truth of its conclusions and that if induction could be shown to be deduction, then somehow the "absolute truth" of its conclusions could be conclusively established.

The truth of the matter is, however, that the mere form of one's reasoning can never guarantee the truth of one's conclusion. The conclusion of a valid deductive argument must, of course, be true if the premises are true, since the conclusion does nothing more than to assert explicitly what has already been asserted implicitly in the premises. But the form of the argument tells nothing at all about the truth of the premises. To determine that, you must go to experience; to go to experience is, in the last analysis, to invoke the pragmatic criterion of truth.

The way of wisdom in this matter, therefore, is to refuse to answer Hume's question on its own terms. The question, Is induction a valid logical procedure? presupposes that it is the validity or lack of validity of the procedure that must decide whether or not we are warranted in believing that our empirical generalizations are true, and that the truth of our generalizations consists in their being exact "copies" of reality. Both of these assumptions, we have argued, are mistaken. The truth of our generalizations consists in the fact that they work (in the sense already described), and our warrant for believing them is also simply the fact that they work. To see this is not, obviously, to answer Hume's question. It is, on the contrary, to see that no answer is required.

The root of the difficulty is the failure to recognize that intelligence is simply a tool that man has acquired through the evolutionary process, the precise function of which is to enable man to cope with a highly complex environment. The function of reflective thought is to transform a situation in which we experience obscurity, doubt, conflict, or disturbance of some sort into one that is clear, coherent, settled, and harmonious. Insofar as we do not encounter obscurity, doubt, conflict, and the like in our experience, our habitual patterns of behavior serve us adequately, and intelligence does not come into play. The business of intelligence, then, is to find suitable behavior patterns when experience confronts us with a situation containing some novel elements. The "problems" that intellect is equipped to solve are, therefore, profoundly practical problems.

The problem of induction is not a practical problem. Hume himself admits this when he says, "As an agent, I am quite satisfied on the point."[6] It is a purely theoretical problem that arises only if we try to press intelligence into a task for which it was never intended, namely, the disinterested pursuit of abstract truths having no practical bearing on the conduct of life. To recognize this, and to draw the appropriate consequences from this recognition, is, at last, to find an answer to Hume—not, indeed, the answer he sought, but the only answer to which his question is entitled. For the best answer to this question is the one that satisfies us in such a way that we are no longer inclined to bother ourselves about it.

STUDY QUESTIONS

1. What criticisms does Pragmatist direct against Rationalist's attempted solution of the problem of induction? Can you think of any

---

[6]Hume, *op. cit.,* p. 52.

way that Rationalist might defend himself against these criticisms?

2. Are you inclined to agree with Pragmatist that the discussion of the problem, thus far, has reached an impasse, and that the reason for this may be that all the parties to the dispute have been making some incorrect assumption? Are you equally persuaded that the assumption in question is the one Pragmatist says it is? Explain.

3. What is the theory of truth that Pragmatist offers as an alternative to the "correspondence" theory? Does this strike you as a correct description of what we ordinarily mean by "truth"? Or, is Pragmatist not suggesting that this is what we *do* ordinarily mean, but rather what we *ought* to mean?

4. How, according to Pragmatist, does the pragmatist theory of truth aid in the solution of the problem of induction? How do you think a Humean skeptic might respond to Pragmatist's proposal?

12

A FOOTNOTE TO HUME

Although I find myself in general agreement with the sentiments expressed in the opening paragraphs of the last chapter, I am not at all convinced that Pragmatist has succeeded in identifying whatever it is that makes the problem of induction, as he says, "artificial." Pragmatist writes with the enthusiasm and the disdain of one who has just taken in hand a new and, to him, exciting principle, by means of which he proposes to lay low all sorts of problems that have troubled able minds for centuries. However, the precise connection between the pragmatist theory of truth—even if we accept that theory—and the problem of induction is, to say the least, somewhat difficult to discern. Moreover, it has not yet been proved that the theory itself is one that it would be wise or prudent for us to accept.

Rather than attempting to assess the strengths and weaknesses of Pragmatist's argument, however, I propose that we return to the original problem as stated by Hume. Hume, as I shall hope to show, was not right in everything that he said about this problem, but his analysis is still more perceptive than any of the subsequent attempts that have been made to find a satisfactory answer to him. If we find that we are able to answer Hume without adopting the questionable theory of truth that is advocated in the previous chapter, I think we may safely ignore what is proposed there.

I spoke just now about finding an "answer" to Hume. Strictly speaking, however, I do not intend to propose an answer to Hume. Instead, I will show that his question ought not to trouble us in the way that it has troubled so many. I shall, as a matter of fact, agree with a great deal that Hume has said. My comments, therefore, should not be construed as an attempt to refute Hume. They are, rather, only a footnote to Hume's own penetrating remarks on induction that appear in Section IV of *An Inquiry Concerning Human Understanding.*

Where Hume Was Right

Hume argued, it will be recalled, that there is no possible way of showing that induction is a valid logical procedure. Induction depends, said Hume, on the assumption that nature is uniform, and that what has been observed to be the case in the past is, therefore, a safe guide as to what may be expected to occur in the future. This assumption, as Hume correctly perceived, can in no way be established. It is evidently not known a priori, nor can it be established inductively (since we could not reason inductively without assuming the very principle that is to be proved). We must conclude, therefore, said Hume, that induction is not a valid logical procedure and that our propensity to draw inductive inferences is nothing but a habit that is itself a product of the repeated observation of "constant conjunction."

It seems to me that after two full centuries of more or less vigorous discussion of this problem, Hume remains triumphant on each of the following points:

1. *Inductive reasoning does presuppose the Principle of the Uniformity of Nature.* Constructive empiricism, as we saw, does not even attempt to deny this; what it attempts to do, with notorious lack of success, is to establish the principle by a kind of "preinductive inference" in order that induction proper can get under way. Rationalist's attempt at a defense of induction does, indeed, pretend to deny the necessity of this assumption. But it has already been sufficiently shown that the "logical principle" that Rationalist attempts to put in its place derives whatever plausibility it has from this very assumption. On this point, therefore, Hume must be judged to have been correct.

2. *The Principle of the Uniformity of Nature cannot itself be established by inductive reasoning.* Hume wrote:

   We have said that all arguments concerning existence are founded on the relation of cause and effect, that our knowledge of that relation is derived entirely from experience, and that all our experimental conclusions proceed upon the supposition that the future will be conformable to the past. To endeavor, therefore, the proof of this last supposition by probable arguments, or arguments regarding existence, must be evidently going in a circle and taking that for granted which is the very point in question.[1]

   Constructive Empiricist's essay, with its obvious circularity, is the best possible demonstration that on this point also Hume was right.

---

[1]David Hume, in Charles W. Hendel (ed.), *An Inquiry Concerning Human Understanding* (New York: Liberal Arts Press, 1955), pp. 49–50.

3. *The Principle of the Uniformity of Nature is not known a priori.*
This is a point that is not susceptible to direct proof, since the
statement that something is or is not known a priori can never be
either proved or disproved. It is significant, however, that even
many rationalists are far from convinced that this principle is
known a priori, and they have directed their efforts toward finding
some other principle upon which to ground the validity of induction. If anyone is disposed to hold, therefore, that the Principle of
the Uniformity of Nature is known a priori, I can think of no
argument that might change his mind. But the majority of philosophers who have struggled with this question, rationalists and empiricists alike, are united in their judgment that in so saying he
would be simply mistaken. On this point, too, the decision must be
in favor of Hume.

The conclusion appears inescapable, therefore, that induction is
based on a principle that is known neither a priori nor a posteriori;
consequently, it is not known at all. Induction must, therefore, be
judged to be incurably irrational. This was Hume's conclusion, and
since it follows from the three propositions that we have just considered, we must also agree with Hume on this. *Induction is not a valid
logical procedure.*

Where Hume Was Wrong

It seems to me, however, that there are two points on which Hume was
clearly mistaken. It is the failure of most of Hume's critics to see these
mistakes that makes his attack on induction appear to have such devastating consequences.

First, Hume was mistaken in his view that our propensity to believe
that nature operates according to certain invariable laws is nothing
but a habit that, like other habits, is a product of repetition. In this
case, it is repetition of the repeated observation of what Hume called
"constant conjunction." "From causes which appear similar," he
wrote, "we expect similar effects."[2] Induction has no logical foundation, but it has a psychological foundation in the phenomenon that we
call "habit."

The reduction of the process of induction to habit is not consistent
with what we know about the way in which habits become established. What typically occurs when a habit is getting established is
that things that at first have to be done consciously and deliberately
come, at length, to be done effortlessly and, as we say, almost automatically. In learning to drive, for example—or to type, or to ski, or to speak
a foreign language—we begin by applying certain rules, certain
"laws" if you will. But when the operations in question have become

---

[2]*Ibid.,* p. 50.

a matter of habit, we are scarcely aware of applying rules: we simply do what we have learned to do. Nothing comparable to this seems to occur in the case of induction. We do not, at first, "induct" deliberately and with effort, and then perform with less and less conscious effort as we become better at doing it. It seems highly unlikely, therefore, that our propensity to draw inductive inferences is, as Hume said, a habit established by repetition.

Even if Hume's account of our inductive propensity as a habit established by repetition were psychologically sound, it is inadequate in yet another respect. There is no such thing as "repetition" pure and simple: repetition must be repetition *for someone.* There must be someone who interprets some event as a repetition of some earlier event. This means, however, that there must be some point of view, some system of expectations or interests, that leads us to note certain similarities between what is happening now and what happened at some earlier time. It is our point of view—the interests and the expectations that we bring to an event—that determines what is to count as a repetition of some earlier event or events. It is evident, therefore, that these expectations are *prior to,* and not *products of,* repetition. Hume's attempt to explain our expectation that the future will resemble the past as a product of repetition must, therefore, be regarded as a failure.

This brings us to Hume's second error: his uncritical and mistaken assumption that it is by induction that we arrive at interesting, general conclusions regarding the laws that govern empirical phenomena. Hume assumed that the everyday general truths that we all take for granted in ordering our lives, as well as the more subtle generalizations that we claim to establish in the natural sciences, are one and all "inductive inferences." Having shown that induction is not logically valid, he concluded that we have no rational basis for believing these generalizations to be true. It is because these truths appear threatened, and because we cannot tolerate the thought that so much of our supposed knowledge should turn out to be no knowledge at all, that we are so upset at the thought that induction is not a valid logical procedure. It is the rationality of our belief in these truths, not the logical credentials of induction itself, that we feel obliged to defend. If, therefore, we can succeed in showing that our knowledge of general empirical truths is indeed obtained by a noninductive procedure, we should have no difficulty in accepting with equanimity Hume's negative conclusion regarding the rationality of induction.

How General Empirical Truths Are Known

It is my contention that the correct account of the origin and status of our knowledge of empirical truths is as follows:

1. Our aim, in seeking empirical knowledge, is to achieve a true description of the world. The ideal goal of all science is to achieve

a description that is so accurate and so complete that everything that occurs can be understood as an instance of some general law or laws. (It will be noted that in saying this I am disagreeing with the so-called "pragmatist" or "instrumentalist" theory of truth set forth in the preceding chapter.)

2. We can never be sure that the description of the world that at any time we suppose to be true, really is true, though we can sometimes be reasonably sure that in some respects it is false.

3. The method by which we replace inadequate descriptions of the world with more adequate ones is not the method of induction but the method of *conjecture and refutation.* All our knowledge of general empirical truths is at best hypothetical. To say that some empirical generalization is true is only to say that despite our best efforts to do so we have thus far been able to discover no counterexamples.

To hold a certain hypothesis about the world, to believe that certain phenomena are governed by such-and-such laws, is to have a certain set of expectations about what will happen under such-and-such conditions. In science we express this by saying that on the basis of this or that law we can "make predictions," and our predictions are descriptions before the fact of what we expect to occur whenever a given set of conditions is fulfilled. Contrary to what is sometimes said, it is not the case that an empirical hypothesis is only as secure as the evidence on which it is based. Rather, a hypothesis is secure in direct proportion to the amount of effort that has been expended in the attempt to disprove it. Any number of hypotheses may be invented to account for almost any set of empirical facts. It is not the hypothesis that is supported by the greatest number of favorable examples, but the one that survives our best efforts to find counterexamples, that wins the right to be admitted to the fund of human knowledge.

Our knowledge of empirical truths, therefore, is nothing but the set of beliefs about the world that we have adopted in order to account for our expectations with respect to the world. There is nothing infallible, nothing final, nothing definitive, about such knowledge. A hypothesis that seems adequate for a time may, at length, have to be revised, as phenomena are discovered that do not conform to the expectations (predictions) we were led to have (make) on the basis of our supposition that the hypothesis is true. Then, we must seek to devise a new hypothesis, one that will account for the new phenomena as well as the old, and the search for counterexamples to the new hypothesis must begin anew.

Advances in our knowledge of general empirical truths, accordingly, always come about by way of revising our earlier hypotheses, of replacing less adequate hypotheses with more adequate ones. Every hypothesis that we propose will, of course, have been preceded by observations—the observations it was invented to explain. But those observations, in turn, must have been made within the context of an earlier hypothesis or set of hypotheses: it was precisely because the earlier hypothesis did not explain the observations in question that the new hypothesis had to be devised.

Where, then, does the whole process begin? The answer must be that it begins with the inborn expectations with which we enter the world. A newborn child expects the world to serve its needs—to feed it when it is hungry, warm it when it is cold, and so on. The child's initial hypothesis, we might say, is that the world is always just as the child wants it to be. This is not a very adequate hypothesis, but it (or something like it) must be the starting point for every human being. And from that point to the affirmation of the most subtle and sophisticated theory in nuclear physics, the process must lead through countless revisions and refinements of hypotheses successively advanced and discarded. Every instance of learning is a modification of what was previously known.

Among the expectations with which each of us enters the world is, apparently, the expectation that we will find some uniformity among the diverse phenomena that occur in the world of our experience. The experience of finding regularity does not create the habit of expecting it, as Hume incorrectly affirmed. On the contrary, the expectation that we will find regularity gives rise to the practice of looking for it, of demanding it, of searching for it, even when it is not obviously present. This is a most fortunate practice, for without it scientific inquiry could never flourish—but that is another matter.

It is time to conclude. Hume argued, as we have seen, that induction is not a valid logical procedure. In this, according to our view, he was right. Hume also believed, however, that in demonstrating the invalidity of inductive reasoning he was demonstrating the irrationality of our supposed knowledge of general empirical truths. In this, if our account is correct, Hume was mistaken. The true import of Hume's analysis of induction does not consist in the questions it raises about the status of empirical generalizations. Rather, it consists in the convincing demonstration that induction cannot, in fact, be the method by which scientific inquiry is carried on. It is one of the ironies of intellectual history that so much effort should have been devoted to the futile effort to find a suitable defense for induction instead of being directed toward a more searching analysis of the true nature of scientific inquiry.

STUDY QUESTIONS

1. The author of this chapter mentions three specific points on which, in his judgment, Hume was right. Do you agree? What is the view of each of the previous writers with respect to each of these points?

2. What objections does the author of this chapter raise with respect to Hume's account of induction as a "habit"? Are his objections

sound? (Consider, for example, poor study habits. Do they get established in the way described? How about driving habits? eating habits? shaving habits?)

3. What, exactly, does the author of this chapter propose as an alternative to induction? Is he right in saying that this method, rather than induction, is the method by which advances are made in our knowledge of general empirical truths? Does this account really avoid the difficulties raised by Hume?

4. Would you classify the author of this chapter as a rationalist or an empiricist? On what basis?

5. With which of the views set forth in this chapter are you inclined to agree? With which do you disagree? About which, if any, are you still in doubt?

6. If you had now to take some position with respect to the problem of induction, what would that position be? What seem to you to be the strongest reasons in favor of this position? What do you regard as the most serious objections that might be raised against it?

CORRELATED READINGS[1]

---

1. Aristotle. "Induction." *Analytica Posterioria,* Section 19.
2. Hume, David. "Induction Is Not Reasoning." *An Enquiry Concerning Human Understanding,* Section IV, Part II. Inductive Skepticism.
3. Russell, Bertrand. "On Induction." *The Problems of Philosophy.* New York: Oxford University Press, 1959, Chap. VI. A rationalist account.
4. Hospers, John. "The Justification of Probability Statements." *An Introduction to Philosophical Analysis.* New York: Prentice-Hall, 1953, pp. 171–177. An empiricist account of induction.
5. Popper, Karl. "The Myth of Induction." *The Logic of Scientific Discovery.* New York: Basic Books, 1959, pp. 27–33. An alternative to rationalism, empiricism, and skepticism.

FOR FURTHER READING

Black, Max. *Problems of Analysis.* Ithaca, N.Y.: Cornell University Press, 1954, Chaps. 10–12.

Feigl, Herbert. "The Logical Character of the Principle of Induction," in H. Feigl and W. Sellars (eds.). *Readings in Philosophical Analysis.* New York: Appleton-Century-Crofts, 1949.

James, William. *Pragmatism and Other Essays.* Cleveland, Ohio: World Publishing Co., 1965. See Lecture VI, "Pragmatism's Conception of Truth."

Mill, John Stuart. *A System of Logic.* Toronto: University of Toronto Press, 1966. See especially Book III, Chaps. 1–5.

Nagel, Ernest. *Logic Without Metaphysics.* New York: Free Press, 1956. See Part II, Chap. 7, "The Ground of Induction."

Popper, Karl. *Conjectures and Refutations.* New York: Basic Books, 1963. See especially pages 33–59.

Russell, Bertrand. *Human Knowledge.* New York: Simon and Schuster, 1962 (paperbound). See Part VI, "Postulates of Scientific Inference."

Salmon, W. C. "Russell on Scientific Inference," in G. Nakhnikian (ed.). *Bertrand Russell's Philosophy.* London: Duckworth, 1974.

Strawson, P. F. *Introduction to Logical Theory.* New York: Wiley, 1952, Chap. 9.

Wright, Georg Henrik von. *Treatise on Induction and Probability.* Paterson, N.J.: Littlefield, Adams, 1960 (paperbound).

---

[1] *Concise Readings in Philosophy,* Part III.

PART IV

REALISTS AND PHENOMENALISTS

13

COMMON-SENSE REALISM AND ITS CRITICS

The problem to which we now turn our attention is closely related to the epistemological problems that we have been concerned with in the preceding two sections. It is the problem of the ontological status of the physical world. Now "ontological status" is a phrase that is not used in ordinary conversation; rather, it is a part of the technical vocabulary of philosophers. Let us begin our discussion of the problem, then, by trying to make clear what philosophers are talking about when they use this rather forbidding-sounding combination of words.

To talk about the ontological status of something is to talk about the kind of being that it has. To say that the ontological status of X is this or that is to say something about X's mode of existence: it is to state in precisely what sense it is true to say that there are X's. Let us look at a few examples.

First, we will consider dreams. It makes sense to say that there are such things as dreams. The word "dream" does not denote a nonentity. It denotes something real, some real occurrence. But what sort of occurrence? What are dreams? What is their ontological status? Someone might reply that a dream is an experience that a person has in his astral body while his physical body is asleep. Most of us would probably say that a dream is a series of occurrences that takes place in our imagination while we are asleep. To reply in either of these ways is to say something about the kind of reality that a dream has. The disagreement that is apparent in these two answers is a disagreement about the ontological status of dreams, a disagreement about what sort of thing the item in question is.

Consider the case of angels. What are angels, really? Someone might say that angels are rational, sexless, winged creatures existing in heaven and serving God in a variety of ways. Someone else might say that angels are mythical beings imagined to exist in a mythical heaven, no more real than the elves and fairies of children's tales. Once again, the disagreement is over the ontological status of angels. To affirm either position is to hold a particular view regarding the kind of being or mode of existence of whatever it is that is denoted by the term "angels."

Let us consider a third example. Someone remarks, "I was at the theater last night and saw Othello kill Desdemona. What a bloody sight!" A bystander exclaims (not in jest), "How terrible! Did they catch the murderer? Is he in jail now? Will you have to be a witness at his trial?" The bystander, in this example, has mistaken the ontological status of the event in question. He has interpreted a murder in a play as if it were an actual murder. He has treated Othello and Desdemona as if they were living, breathing people instead of fictitious characters in a dramatic production.

Three observations may be made at this point. The first is that what we are prepared to regard as live options with respect to questions of ontological status depends in part on our world view, on the picture of reality we have. The astral-body theory of dreams is a live option only for someone whose world view includes a belief in astral bodies that are able to leave their physical counterparts on occasion, have adventures with other wandering astral bodies, and so on. The same is true of the theory that angels are real inhabitants in a real heaven. Some disputes about ontological status, therefore, resolve themselves into disputes about the credibility or incredibility of this or that world view.

The second observation is that within any given world view there can be genuine disagreement as to the ontological status of this or that particular class of phenomena. Indeed, for the most part it is only insofar as people share a relatively common world view that they can fruitfully discuss questions of ontological status. When this is not the case, there is a high likelihood that some parties to the dispute will be proposing answers that are not considered by the others to be live options.

The third observation is that the number of ontological categories available within the context of any given world view is fairly large and not capable of exhaustive enumeration. There are, to take some fairly noncontroversial examples, bodies and properties of bodies; minds and their ideas; living creatures and their behavior; and so on. To "place" something ontologically is to assign it to its proper place in a world view, to interpret it as belonging to such-and-such a kind of being. To ask about the ontological status of something is to ask what its proper "place" is.

Ontological Dependence

Some things could not exist without other things, upon which they may, accordingly, be said to be "dependent" for their existence. Dreams, for example, could not exist without dreamers. It is ridiculous to talk of dreams as if they went about on their own looking for someone to "have" them.

To say that something A is dependent on something else B for its existence is to affirm a relation of ontological dependence: it is to say that A is ontologically dependent on B. Thoughts are ontologically dependent on thinkers, dreams on dreamers, actions on actors, and so on. If the ontological status of B is assumed to be known, the question of the ontological status of A may be satisfactorily answered by pointing out its ontological dependence on B. If the ontological status of B is itself in question, then the ontological status of everything held to be ontologically dependent on it is also in question.

The Physical World

The question considered in this section concerns the ontological status of a large class of objects that we designate by the collective phrase "the physical world." It includes everything that we perceive by means of our five senses.

There is no serious disagreement, either among philosophers or among nonphilosophers, about what we perceive the physical world to be. It appears to consist of a vast number of individual objects— trees, stones, birds, animals, human beings—that exhibit a wide variety of colors, shapes, sounds, smells, temperatures, tastes, textures, and so on. Were anyone to deny that this is how the physical world appears, we would be inclined to think that either that person was not being honest with us or else was lacking some of the normal faculties of sense perception.

But is the physical world as we perceive it an exact copy of the physical world as it really is, or is the reality "out there" different in some ways from our perception of it? To ask such a question is not to ask about the ontological status of the physical world; it is only to call in question the trustworthiness of our perceptions. Nevertheless, it is only a short step from this question to the ontological one: *Is the physical world to any degree dependent on a perceiver for its existence?* Does this varicolored, varishaped, varisounding reality that we perceive exist even when someone is not perceiving it, or is it in some sense constituted by and therefore dependent on perception?

Four Alternatives

The common-sense answer to this question, and certainly the view held by most people prior to any sophisticated reflection on it, goes something like this: there is a real physical world that causes us to have the perceptions that we have, and our perceptions are more or less exact copies of the qualities that are really present in those objects. An object that appears to be brown really is brown; one that is perceived to be hard or cold or smooth really is hard or cold or smooth; and so on. In short, the physical world exists and is in no way dependent on our perception for its existence. If all perceivers were annihilated, the varicolored, varishaped, varisounding world that these perceivers had formerly perceived would still be there, though there would not, of course, be anyone around to perceive that it was there.

The view that we have just stated is often called "naïve realism" by philosophers who address themselves to this problem. The name is somewhat unfortunate, however, since the term "naïve" seems to suggest that the position is obviously not worthy of serious consideration. In the discussion that follows, therefore, we shall refer to this position as *common-sense,* or *direct, realism* and to someone who holds it as a *common-sense,* or *direct, realist.*

A second position that may be taken with respect to this question is the view known as subjective idealism, or phenomenalism. The former name is rather closely associated with George Berkeley, an early eighteenth-century Irish philosopher, and is not in general use at the present time. Nevertheless, although it now goes by the name of phenomenalism, and the grounds upon which it is commonly held are somewhat different from those upon which Berkeley first maintained it, the position is essentially Berkeley's.

In the scale of possible answers concerning the ontological status of the physical world, phenomenalism stands at the opposite extreme from common-sense realism. It explicitly rejects the "copy" theory of perception and asserts that the physical world is, accordingly, completely dependent on the perceptions of a perceiver for its existence. Berkeley's classical formula for this view was *esse est percipi,* "to be (a physical object) is to be perceived." Strange as this position may seem initially, it can be supported by a number of powerful arguments, and it is held by many philosophers at the present time.

In addition to common-sense realism and phenomenalism there is only one other approach to this question. It is that the physical world is partly dependent on a perceiver for its existence and partly independent of a perceiver. What is perceived is in some ways like and in some ways unlike what is really "out there." There is both similarity and dissimilarity between the world as we perceive it and the world as it really is. This view is called critical realism.

Within this view, however, there are significant differences, depending upon whether the emphasis is on the similarity between our perceptions and the real world (thus being fairly close to the realist end of the scale) or on the dissimiliarity between the two (thus coming closer to the phenomenalist view). We shall, in the discussion that follows, make a semantic distinction to mark these two forms of critical realism, calling the more mild form *critical realism* and the more radical form *hypercritical realism.* The difference between them, it must be remembered, is one of degree only.

In philosophical writings on this problem, the term *sense datum* (plural, *sense data*) occurs rather frequently. Sense data are what we immediately perceive whenever we are ordinarily said to be perceiving something, without regard to whether there is anything "out there" corresponding to our perception. Thus, a person who is hallucinating, for example, and who "sees" a pink elephant is said to have the same kind of sense data as people who are not hallucinating and who see a real pink elephant.

Employing this term, we can distinguish the four positions defined above in the following way. Common-sense realism is the view that the sense data that people have when their senses are not impaired are accurate copies of the physical world, and that, accordingly, the physical world is not constituted by sense data in any way whatsoever. Phenomenalism is the view that what we call the physical world is simply the inferred totality of our actual and possible sense data (except when we are hallucinating, for example) and does not exist apart from these sense data. Critical realism (in any form) is the view that the sense data that we directly have when we are perceiving the physical world are in some respects similar to the characteristics objectively present in the physical world and in other respects dissimilar. Hypercritical realism, which is simply a variant of this view, claims that the dissimilarity between the two is significantly greater than most critical realists recognize.

There is a special form of phenomenalism—some philosophers would say it is a logical implication of phenomenalism—known as *solipsism.* This view is difficult to state with precision, but a fair approximation is the following: *I* alone exist in the primary or fundamental sense of "exist," and everything else that exists does so only in the secondary sense of being my perception or thought. Just as my dreams do not exist unless I am dreaming them, so nothing exists unless I am having the perceptions or thoughts that constitute the existence of something. This view, though difficult to refute, is universally considered highly implausible. To the best of my knowledge, it has not been seriously advocated by any major thinker in the whole history of Western philosophy. Solipsism stands, however, as the fantastic limit to which skepticism regarding the inferences made from the data of sense experience can be carried, and it does come up occasionally in discussions of the problem of the ontological status of the physical world.

It is possible to discuss many of the matters in this section in terms of a slightly different question: can our senses be trusted to give us accurate information about the world? Actually, many philosophers prefer this question, partly because discussions of ontological status have been more or less out of style in recent years. However, the classical examinations of perception—those of John Locke, George

Berkeley, David Hume, Immanuel Kant, and others—were quite openly directed toward a determination of the ontological status of the physical world. Moreover, it seems evident that any view we might adopt with respect to the veracity of our perceptions would have important implications for our view of the ontological status of the physical world. For these reasons, we shall focus our discussion on the ontological question.

Chapters 14–16 may be viewed as three successive critiques of common-sense realism, each one progressively rejecting more of what common-sense realism affirms concerning the ontological status of the physical world. The discussion moves from a mild form of critical realism to hypercritical realism and then to phenomenalism. Finally, a defender of direct realism is given an opportunity to show what, if anything, can be salvaged of the common-sense view.

STUDY QUESTIONS

1. What ontological status would you be inclined to assign to each of the following: a hunch, a plan, redness, temperature, weight, Huckleberry Finn, Abraham Lincoln, a headache?
2. What, precisely, is the main question posed for consideration in this chapter? Restate it in at least three different ways (without changing the point of the question).
3. In brief summary, what answers do the four alternatives defined in this chapter offer to this question? As you understand the problem, do these four alternatives exhaust the logical possibilities?
4. Do you find anything odd about the following statement? "The arguments in favor of solipsism are so convincing that I find myself compelled to adopt the position; I am surprised that more people do not come to the same conclusion."

14

CRITICAL REALISM

It is obvious that most people trust their sense perceptions and, accordingly, believe that the world is really very much as they perceive it to be. Most people would grant, I suppose, that they can err in *judgment:* for example, they might see a stone in the distance and mistakenly judge it to be a dog. But they would not, for this reason, mistrust their senses. They would realize that they had judged too hastily and, perhaps, would resolve to be more careful in the future. Once they had identified the object in question as a stone, however, they would not doubt that the stone really is hard, rough, heavy, porous, and gray, as it appears to be. And if one were to ask them how they *know* that the stone really has these characteristics, they would reply with some indignation, "Because I have seen it with my own eyes, and felt it with my own hands!"

No matter how accustomed we may be to thinking of the world in this way, however, the view that the world really is as we perceive it to be—that it really has all the characteristics we perceive it to have —is one that cannot survive critical reflection. Let us see why this is so.

Critique of Common-sense Realism

That common-sense realism is not a defensible position is evident, in the first place, from the fact that we sometimes have illusory perceptions. A straight stick immersed in water, for example, looks as though it is bent. There is no point of view we could adopt that would make it look any other way. It is only because such a stick does not feel bent, and because it looks straight when removed from the water, that we have learned not to rely on our visual sense data in this instance. Or consider a mirage that taunts a traveler in the desert. He sees it just as surely as we can see real water and real trees; it is only because the mirage recedes or disappears as he "approaches" it—only because he can never reach it, drink its water, be cooled by the shade of its trees —that he calls it an illusion. The phantom pains of persons who have suffered the loss of a limb may also be mentioned as a case in point.

There is, of course, no reason to conclude that because our senses deceive us at times, they deceive us all the time. Indeed, it is only on the assumption that they do not deceive us all the time that we can identify our perceptions of the bent stick, the mirage, and the phantom pains as illusory. But in view of these examples of illusory perception, we cannot reasonably maintain that the physical world exactly corresponds to our perception of it. The most that can be maintained is that the world is like some, perhaps the majority, of our perceptions.

The same conclusion is reinforced by a second consideration, namely, that certain changes in a perceiver produce changes in his perceptions of the physical world. Suppose, for example, that a quantity of water is kept at a constant temperature. On one occasion, I come from a hot bath, immerse my hand in the water, and pronounce it cold. On another occasion, I come from having handled ice, immerse my hand in the water, and pronounce it warm. The water is not really cold in the first instance and warm in the second, but is the same temperature. It is my perception that varies, not the water itself.

As another example, consider what happens when we wear colored glasses—pink, brown, green, or what have you. The world, as we all know, then appears more pink, more brown, more green, than otherwise. How can we be sure that the colored glasses do not enable us to see more clearly what the world is really like? Similarly, persons under the influence of certain drugs perceive the world differently than they do when not under their influence. Which set of perceptions provides an "accurate copy" of the real world?

A particularly interesting phenomenon to consider with regard to this question is color blindness. Two observers, A and B, look at patches of color. A perceives some patches to be red and others to be green; B perceives them to be all the same color. B, accordingly, is said to be color blind. But note that it is only because, like A, most people are able to make the distinction between "red" and "green" that those unable to do so are said to be color blind. Were the statistics reversed, persons who perceive a distinction would perhaps be regarded by the majority as subject to a strange illusion. Whose perception is to be regarded as an accurate copy of the real world? We cannot say, "Those who are normal," since normalcy is here defined in terms of the perceptions of the majority. It does not make sense to decide a question of this sort by means of a referendum.

We could, of course, save some vestiges of the common-sense view by making a number of arbitrary decisions. For example, we could say that what tells us about the world as it is really is the majority of the perceptions of people who have normal perception—people who suffer no impairment of sensory responses, who are not color blind, who are not wearing colored glasses, who have been for some time in a room whose temperature is exactly 68° Fahrenheit, and so on. However, since such decisions are purely arbitrary, each new difficulty that appeared would require a new condition to be introduced. To realize this is to realize that something other than common-sense realism must be adopted.

The Case for Critical Realism

The principle that should guide us in determining what is real about what we perceive is the one enunciated by Locke: qualities that are utterly inseparable from a physical object, such that a particle of matter however small could not be conceived to exist without it, are real qualities of that object; everything else that we perceive, though it indeed may appear to us to be a real quality in the object, is in truth nothing but a modification of our faculty of perception.[1] We shall, following Locke, call these *primary qualities* and *secondary qualities,* respectively. We shall say, accordingly, that primary qualities reside in the object and, with respect to these qualities, the object is as we perceive it to be. Secondary qualities, however, are not in the object at all but are only modifications of our faculty of perception caused by the object through its primary qualities. Let us see what account of the physical world can be given on the basis of this distinction.

Every object that we perceive appears to have the following qualities: color, shape, size, temperature, solidity, texture, and either rest or motion. Some objects also have some odor, some taste, and some sound. These are the qualities that our various senses perceive to be present or absent in the objects that come before us.

Which of these qualities really are present in the object? Applying Locke's principle, we see that if we take any object and divide it up into as many tiny parts as we please, each part will still have some shape, some size, some temperature, some degree of solidity, and some texture, and it will be either in motion or at rest. These, therefore, are the primary qualities of an object.

The qualities that remain to be accounted for are the secondary qualities of an object—its color, odor, taste, sound, and apparent degree of warmth or coldness. These, it is clear, depend on the sense apparatus of the perceiver and consist of nothing more than a modification of that apparatus by the object. Were the senses associated with

---

[1]See John Locke, *An Essay Concerning Human Understanding,* II, xxiii (New York: Dover, 1959), pp. 390–423.

our eyes, our ears, and our nose capable of being affected differently, things would appear to have different colors, different sounds, different odors than they now appear to have. Were our body temperature higher or lower than it is, things would not be perceived to be warm or cold in the proportions that they now are.

The qualities that are objectively present in an object—shape, size, temperature, texture, solidity, and either rest or motion—cause, via the mechanism of our sense apparatus, (a) impressions that are like the qualities themselves, which we call impressions of primary qualities, and (b) impressions unlike the qualities, which we call impressions of secondary qualities.

There is one further point that must be made to complete our account. It is impossible to conceive of an object as being made up simply of its several qualities randomly thrown together. An object has a certain unity for which our account thus far has made no provision. Formerly, it was possible to posit a "substance" or a "substratum" that underlay and supported the object's qualities—an admittedly vague concept that Locke himself disparaged as merely "the supposed but unknown support of those qualities we find existing, which we imagine cannot subsist . . . without something to support them."[2] With the more sophisticated knowledge of matter that we have now, however, it is impossible to account for the unity of objects in this way. We say, therefore, that this unity is simply the natural consequence of the laws of nature acting upon the particular particles of matter in question. In the case of inanimate objects, the relevant laws are physical and chemical laws, and the resultant unity is merely structural. In the case of living things, this account must be supplemented by citing certain relevant biological laws, and the resultant unity (so long as the organism is alive) is organic as well as structural.

To come to a decision about the physical world's ontological status, we may safely ignore the more recondite facts about matter that have been reported by modern science. Whatever science may conclude concerning the nature of the physical world at the atomic and subatomic level, at the macroscopic level this world exhibits real qualities of shape, size, temperature, texture, solidity, and either rest or motion. These are real, and although they undoubtedly are dependent on atomic and subatomic processes for their reality, they are in no way dependent on us as human perceivers.

But critical realism does hold that color, sound, taste, smell, apparent degree of warmness and coldness—the secondary qualities of objects—are, indeed, dependent on a perceiver. In fact, they are nothing but modifications that occur within the perceiver. If there were no perceivers capable of being modified in this way, there would be no color, sound, taste, odor, warmness or coldness in the world (whereas

---

[2] *Ibid.*, p. 391.

primary qualities would continue to exist even in the total absence of perceivers).

The chief reason for adopting critical realism is that it enables us to solve the puzzles about perception that originally caused us to question the common-sense view. It enables us to explain the fact that alterations in a perceiver result in certain changes in that person's perception—to see, for instance, that what is perceived to be cold at one time may, without changing, be perceived to be warm at another time (or even simultaneously, if one of the perceiver's hands is warm and the other is cold). Similarly, the puzzles that arise in connection with our perception of color are easily solved: things appear to be colored differently to persons who are color blind, under the influence of certain drugs, or wearing colored glasses, because such conditions alter the visual sense apparatus and because color is nothing but a modification of this apparatus.

There are other puzzles in connection with perception that can also be solved in the context of this view. For example, some people are able to hear high-pitched signals that are completely inaudible to others. From the point of view of common-sense theory, this fact immediately poses a question: Is a signal that is inaudible to all but a few people a sound or is it not? For critical realists, this phenomenon causes no difficulty. Sound is nothing but a modification of the hearing apparatus of a perceiver, and any such modification is a sound. It is simply the case that some people are capable of being affected by air vibrations of a higher frequency than others; hence, the difference. Individual differences with respect to taste and smell can be accounted for in the same manner.

Some Remarks About Perception

It is evident that we must reject the common-sense view regarding the ontological status of the physical world, along with the "copy" theory of perception. The real world is not exactly as it appears to be; if our sense impressions are a "copy" of the real world, they are very poor copies indeed. What, then, shall we say of the status of our sense impressions? How are sense data related to the objects in the real world that are their causes?

The answer implied in the position I am advocating is that the sense data represent the real objects before our minds. We directly perceive the sense data, and we make certain inferences about the objects that they represent. What we see, hear, taste, touch, and smell, we really do see, hear, taste, touch, and smell. But what we infer about the objects that are represented to us by these various kinds of sense data may be in error. Common-sense realism is thus seen to consist in the view that for every sense datum that appears in our perceptual field there is something just like it in the physical world. And this view, as we have seen, is one that is not consistent with the facts.

We must take care, however, not to reject more of the common-sense view than the facts require us to, and this, so far as I can see, is no more than we already have rejected. There are, I am aware, certain considerations that seem to favor the phenomenalist view on this matter, and these obviously are worthy of being considered on their own merits. That view, however, involves certain difficulties that I do not think can be resolved without returning to something like the view proposed here. It seems to me that every argument that tends to support the phenomenalist position is equally persuasive, if it is persuasive at all, as an argument in support of solipsism—a view so patently absurd that the arguments in its support must be regarded as highly suspect. That we must depart as far from the common-sense theory as I have proposed seems obvious; but it seems equally obvious that to depart any further would be neither wise nor prudent.

STUDY QUESTIONS

1. What considerations does Critical Realist bring forward to support the view that common-sense realism is not a defensible position? Can you think of any way to defend common-sense realism against this critique?
2. What is the criterion by which Critical Realist proposes to distinguish between primary and secondary qualities? Does he apply it consistently in drawing up his two lists? In your opinion, is the criterion itself a valid one?
3. What, according to Critical Realist's account, are the primary and secondary qualities, respectively, of each of the following: a red brick? a book? a bowling ball? a siren? a mirage?
4. What reasons does Critical Realist give for adopting his theory regarding the status of the physical world? Do you find his reasons convincing? Can you think of any way that his case might be strengthened?

15

HYPERCRITICAL REALISM

I think my readers should be advised that "hypercritical realism" is a term they are not apt to find in any philosophical writings prior to the early 1960s. It was originally coined by Herbert Feigl, obviously in jest. However, it is remarkably suggestive of what I hold concerning the relation of our percepts (what we perceive) to the physical world, and I would not object if it were to come into general use as a descriptive title for the position that I represent.

Anyone who is at all familiar with the advances that have been made in the science of physics during the past few decades will recognize immediately, I think, that we cannot stay as close to common-sense realism as Critical Realist has urged us to do. This rough-and-ready description of the world in terms of primary and secondary qualities may have deserved some credence a century or two ago, but certainly not today. We have learned a good deal since the time of Locke. It is now a matter of common knowledge that the particles of which material objects are composed are not little nuggets of matter, each retaining the "primary qualities" of which Critical Realist speaks—shape, size, motion, and all the rest. We know, or at least we think we know, that everything in the physical world is a compound made up of basic elements. Every element is reducible to molecules; every molecule to atoms; every atom to protons, neutrons, electrons, and numerous other, smaller particles. To try to understand the relation of our percepts to a world thus conceived in terms of Critical Realist's theory is like trying to do fine etching with a pickax: the tool is simply too unrefined for the task.

There is no need to plunge into the complexities of modern physics, however, in order to see that so minimal a departure from the common-sense theory as Critical Realist has proposed will not do. A number of far less recondite facts are as evidently fatal to his theory as the facts he does mention are to the common-sense theory. Let us consider in some detail the damaging facts that Critical Realist has overlooked.

Some Paradoxes of Perception

Critical Realist has pointed out a number of rather unusual perceptual phenomena—the refraction of light as it passes through a transparent liquid (the example of the bent stick), mirages, phantom pains, and the like—and has rested the case for his view on the claim that he is able to account for them. However, a number of paradoxes arise in connection with some far less unusual perceptual phenomena that cannot be easily accounted for in the context of his theory.

The first such group of paradoxes has to do with what I shall call the "perspectification" that accompanies all visual perception. Consider, first, the quality that we call shape. The shape that an object appears to have depends entirely on the point of view from which it is viewed. A sheet of typing paper, for example, appears to be a rectangle if you view it from a point directly above its center; each of its four corners, accordingly, appears to be a right angle, or very nearly so. Turn it at a slight angle, however, step away from it a few feet, and two of the corners will appear to be acute angles and two obtuse. The same phenomenon occurs in all cases of visual perception: the apparent shape varies depending on the point of view of the observer, and it is constantly changing as the observer moves in relation to the object being viewed (or vice versa). A lake that looks round when viewed from the air (directly above its center) looks like a wide oval when viewed from the top of a nearby mountain and like a very long and thin oval when viewed from any point along its shore. A penny looks round from one point of view, oval from another, and rectangular from yet another, and so on.

Which of the many shapes that every object appears to have is supposed to be really present in the object? Why should the topside view of a printed page, or the air view of a lake, or the front-and-center view of a penny be granted a privileged status? Such selectiveness is obviously arbitrary. To say that something is round, for example, is only to say that it will appear to be round if it is looked at from such and such a point of view. No reason can be given, however, for saying that this point of view rather than some other is the one from which the "real" shape of the object can be seen. In the case of three-dimensional objects, there is, in fact, no point of view from which an object appears to have the shape that it is usually said to "really" have.

Consequently, if we wish to maintain Critical Realist's position, we must be prepared to do one of two things. Either we must say that an object has many shapes, and that the one seen depends on the point of view from which the object is observed; or, quite arbitrarily, that this or that point of view puts us in a position to see the object's "real" shape. If we are not willing to accept one or the other of these alternatives—and I for one am not—then we must give up the view that objects have a "real" shape that corresponds to some shape we perceive.

The same perplexities arise in connection with size. From a long distance, a tractor-trailer may seem to be the size of a child's toy. As it moves closer, it appears to grow larger and larger. So it is with all visual perception: the size that an object appears to have depends on how close you are to it. I have yet to meet a person to whom the moon, when viewed from earth with the naked eye, does not appear to be about the size of a basketball. Through a telescope, of course, or from a spaceship near its surface, it looks much larger.

Which of the apparent sizes of an object is to be considered its "real" size? Is it the close-up view? How close? We are faced, evidently, with alternatives comparable to those that we had to contend with in connection with shape. Either we must hold that an object really has many sizes, and that the one perceived depends on how far away the observer is from the object; or we must claim to know that there is some precise distance from which the "real" size can be perceived. Or, we must give up the view that objects have a "real" size to which some perception of ours exactly corresponds.

What, then, can be retained of Critical Realist's account? Is temperature a real quality in an object? Perhaps. But we do not perceive temperature; we merely infer it from what we see on a thermometer. What we perceive is only impressions of warmness and coldness, and these even Critical Realist admits to be modifications in the perceiver. Can texture be retained as a real quality in objects? Here, too, difficulties arise. What feels smooth to the touch looks rough when viewed under a microscope, which reveals a terrain of hills and valleys in a surface that previously seemed perfectly even. Which is it "really," rough or smooth? Or is it both? We are back in our old dilemma.

It is scarcely necessary to discuss the paradoxes that arise if we try to regard rest and motion as real qualities objectively present in objects. Since motion is relative, it is obvious that whether a thing is to be regarded as being in motion or at rest depends entirely on what is assumed to be at rest in making the judgment. If the earth is assumed to be at rest, then a boulder lying on a terrestrial mountainside is also at rest; if the sun is assumed to be at rest, then the earth and everything on it, including the boulder, are in motion. To an observer on earth, the earth appears to be at rest, and the sun, the moon, and the stars appear to revolve around it. To an observer on the moon, or on Mars, the surface on which he or she stood would appear to be at rest and everything else would appear to be in motion in relation to the observer. Since whether a thing is perceived to be in motion or at rest depends on the point of view of the observer, our alternatives are (a) to say that every object in the universe really has many motions, (b) to say that only one of these is its "real" motion and give some reason for so saying, or (c) to concede that rest and motion are not real qualities of objects at all but merely "appearances" perceived by an observer.

There remains of Critical Realist's list of primary qualities only solidity, and by this time I suspect we are prepared to concede that it, too, is unlikely to stand up under close scrutiny. It seems evident, in the first place, that "solidity" can only mean the resistance of one object to another, and that this resistance must vary depending on the size and strength of the invading object. To a fly a piece of balsa wood must appear quite solid; to a human being it does not. To a small child, a piece of stiff paper appears quite solid; to an adult, it appears soft and malleable. What is the case "really"? Any answer that we might give would be completely arbitrary.

In point of fact, we know that nothing in the whole world is "really" solid. The desk upon which I am writing appears to be solid, to have such and such a color and texture, and to stand absolutely motionless here in the center of my study. In reality, it has none of these qualities. They are all relative to the particular senses with which I happen to be equipped and the particular point of view from which I happen to observe the desk. What really is "out there" is quite different, radically different, from what I perceive to be out there. What, then, are we justified in believing about the real qualities of physical objects?

Appearance and Reality

In order to solve these paradoxes, we must make a clear distinction between the world of our percepts and the world as it really is, between appearance and reality. The world appears to us to consist of a multiplicity of objects of various sizes, shapes, colors, textures, temperatures, and so on. On the basis of these appearances, common sense constructs a theory of a real three-dimensional space in which all these objects are believed to exist and to possess the various characteristics that they appear to have. When subjected to close scrutiny, however, this whole common-sense theory collapses.

What is really "out there"—the physical world as it really is—is being discovered with greater and greater accuracy by the natural sciences, especially physics. This is hardly the place to summarize even the main outlines of what we now know about the constitution of the universe, but a brief sketch may indicate how we ought to think about an object if we want to conform in some degree to what physics tells us is the case.

Consider the above-mentioned desk, for example. According to modern physics, it is not, as it appears to be, a solid block of "matter" that occupies some particular position or series of positions in a fixed three-dimensional space. It consists, rather, of several series of events occurring in a four-dimensional manifold that physicists call space-time, these several series being interrelated in a vast variety of ways.

What I refer to as "my desk" is, in short, something that happens; it is, in fact, a vast conglomeration of happenings that occur in the particular region of space-time that it occupies. None of the particles involved in the events constituting my desk—the protons, neutrons, electrons, and so forth—is solid, or colored, or warm, or cold, or anything else that we perceive when we perceive the desk. The language that is appropriate to the desk as I perceive it is totally inappropriate for a description of the atomic events of which it is really composed.

It is logically possible, of course, that the atomic events comprising my desk should be occurring without my being aware of them, just as radio waves are constantly passing through the region of space-time that I occupy without my being aware of them. It happens to be the case, however, that as a result of the atomic events that constitute my desk, and as a result of certain other atomic events that are related in various ways to the atomic events that constitute my desk, radiations are emitted that, when I am properly situated, cause a series of occurrences in my brain that I call "perceiving the desk."

Consider, for example, the perception of solidity. I perform the activity that I call "pressing my hand against the desk" and say that the desk is "hard," or "solid." In reality, however, no particle that is involved in the events of which my hand is composed comes in contact with the particles involved in the events of which the desk is composed. What really happens is that an electrical force is created by the nearness of the former to the latter, and this force, through a complicated process involving my nerves and my brain, causes the event that I call perceiving the "hardness" or "solidity" of the desk.

Or consider color. My desk looks brown; according to the common-sense view, it really is brown. Physics, however, tells us otherwise. What is really happening when I am "perceiving brown" is that electromagnetic waves of various frequencies are being emitted from the sun and, after a journey requiring roughly eight minutes, are streaming through my window and striking my desk. Some of these waves enter the desk, causing certain changes in it that we describe as an increase in its temperature. Others are scattered by the particles that constitute the surface of the desk, and some of these (by way of my eyes, optic nerve, and brain) create the event in me that I call "perceiving brown." And so on for all sensible qualities.

Thus, hypercritical realism holds that the physical world is dependent on a perceiver for the existence of all of what we may call its common-sense qualities: color, sound, taste, odor, shape, size, solidity, and all the rest. It is only because of the constitution of our faculty of sensation—the particular modifications of which that faculty happens to be capable—that the world appears to us to have these qualities. If we, or beings having a faculty of sensation like ours, were to be annihilated, all such qualities would accordingly disappear. What would not disappear, however, are the atomic and subatomic events that constitute the physical world and cause us to have the particular perceptions we do have. To that extent, the physical world has a real existence of its own and is in no way dependent on a perceiver for its existence.

Perception

I find myself, therefore, in agreement with old-fashioned critical realism on two important points: (a) there is something "out there" that constitutes the real world, and (b) it is what is "out there" that causes us to have the perceptions we have. Perceptions do represent realities in the external world, but they do not represent them as they really are. To infer that the physical world is just like, or somewhat like, the world as it appears to us is to ignore most of what science has taught us and to become involved in endless paradoxes. The way to resolve these paradoxes is to make the distinction we have made between appearance and reality, and to allow that the perceptions that represent physical realities to us are in no way like the realities they represent.

In conclusion, I should like to state that I am well aware that it is not easy for any of us to relinquish the idea that the physical world really is as we perceive it to be. Looking now at the desk that I have recently been so busy dissolving into atomic and subatomic events, I am as powerfully tempted as the most unconvinced common-sense realist to think that it really has the solidity, the color, the smoothness, that I perceive it to have. It is only when I attend carefully to the arguments, only when I consider the difficulties involved in maintaining the common-sense view, that I know it cannot be so. As a theory, common-sense realism, or anything close to it, simply will not do. But as a way of looking at the world, as an attitude that governs our everyday commerce with the world, it is very much with us. None of us is able to divest ourselves of it. For the world that we must take account of in most of our affairs is the world of appearance, not the world of reality.

STUDY QUESTIONS

1. What paradoxes does Hypercritical Realist mention that, according to him, cannot be explained in the context of a mild form of critical realism? Can you think of any way that Critical Realist might be able to defend his position against this attack?

2. What is Hypercritical Realist's general answer to the question posed in this section? What, if anything, makes his position a form of "realism"?

3. What, according to this theory, is the ontological status of color? of sound? of temperature? of electrons? of atoms? of molecules?

4. What criterion does Hypercritical Realist use in distinguishing between "appearance" and "reality"? Is it, in your opinion, a sounder criterion than that employed by Critical Realist?

16

PHENOMENALISM

Phenomenalism is the view that the existence of a physical object is dependent upon its being perceived; that is, a physical object is a construct made up of the percepts that are the immediate objects of perception. It follows directly from this that the physical world is completely dependent on some perceiver(s) for its existence and that, if all perceivers were to be annihilated, the physical world would, accordingly, cease to exist.

The task of explaining and defending this view is rendered easier than it might otherwise be, because much of what I ordinarily would have to say in order to build my case has already been said by the two writers who have preceded me in this discussion. The latter has, indeed, left us at the very borders of phenomenalism, and I propose to show that precisely the considerations that have brought the argument to this point require us to take a further step that leads to the phenomenalist position.

The Inconsistency of Hypercritical Realism

Hypercritical Realist has argued, quite rightly, that we cannot validly infer from the fact that the world appears to us as a multiplicity of objects of various colors, shapes, sizes, textures, and so forth, that it really is so. If we try to say this, a host of puzzles arise that we cannot solve without departing rather far from the common-sense view. He also suggests that we know, nonetheless, that there is something "out there" that causes us to have these sensations, and that what this something is can be learned by studying physics. He then proceeds to give us a short course in atomic physics and supposes, thereby, that he has persuaded us that so much at least can be retained of the realist view.

But surely it is fair to ask how we know that the atomic events that we do not see are objectively real, when we evidently do not know that the physical phenomena that we do see are objectively real. How have the physicists come by this esoteric knowledge of what is supposed to lie behind the appearances?

We know the answer, of course. They have inferred it from certain observed phenomena. Common-sense realism is the consequence of an unsophisticated inference from some more or less obvious facts of observation; hypercritical realism is the consequence of a sophis- ticated inference from some less obvious facts of observation. But if the inference is not justified in the first instance, neither is it justified in the second. There is no more reason to say that the latest theory of the physicists is an accurate description of something real "behind the appearances" than that the description of a common-sense realist is accurate. The two differ considerably in their respective degrees of sophistication, but so far as validity is concerned, they are on the same ground. Realism is equally naïve, whether it is maintained in a com- mon-sense or in a scientific version.

It is useful to note that Hypercritical Realist's mistake of regarding scientific theories as descriptive is not always made by scientists themselves. What Andreas Osiander said in his preface to Nicolaus Copernicus's treatise *On the Revolutions of the Heavenly Bodies* may be said of all scientific theories: there is no need for these hypotheses to be true, or even to be at all like the truth; one thing is sufficient— that they should yield a calculus that agrees with the observations. Scientific hypotheses are, in short, nothing more than instruments useful for purposes of calculation. Their function is not to tell us what the world is really like but to aid us in controlling the world as it appears to us.

It seems clear, therefore, that the very arguments that have been used in the preceding chapters to establish some form of critical real- ism actually tend to support the phenomenalist view instead. We have no basis for inferring a universe of signaling stations beyond or be- hind the perceptual signals that we constantly receive. The only world of which we have or can have any knowledge is the world of our perception. This is precisely what we mean by the phrase "the physi- cal world"; hence, it is clear that the physical world is altogether dependent on perceivers for its existence.

A Common-sense Argument for Phenomenalism

Let us return again to the example of the desk. If I want to teach a child the meaning of the word "desk," I have to show one to him and let him see it and touch it, and I have to say the word "desk" so that he will associate that word with the sense data he is receiving. After he has learned this word, what can he possibly understand it to mean but the impressions of hardness, brownness, flatness, and so on, that he has been taught to associate with it? Surely all of us learned the names of such familiar objects as desks, chairs, tables, stones, trees, and so on, in just this way.

What does it mean, then, to say that a thing *exists*? It can mean only that if you go to a place where, say, a desk is said to exist, you will, if the statement is true, have percepts of the sort that you have learned to associate with the word "desk"; if the statement is false, you will not. A statement affirming the existence of something is always a statement about percepts.

Do things exist, then, when nobody is perceiving them? Yes, they do. But to say that something exists when nobody is perceiving it is still to say something about percepts, namely, that if someone were to go to the place where a particular thing is said to exist, he would have particular kinds of percepts. Every statement to the effect that something exists is a statement about actual or possible percepts. Any meaning that we try to ascribe to the word "existence" in addition to this is simply unintelligible.

Consequently, if a person says that something exists behind percepts that is the cause of our having them, that person is saying something that has no meaning. It makes sense to say that there are real actors in a real studio that cause us to have the particular percepts we have when we look at television, because we know what it is like to have the percepts that constitute the set of events we call "actors in a studio." Here, we can "go behind the scenes," so to speak, without forsaking the realm of percepts. But to talk about a reality behind the appearances, a nonperceptual something that causes us to have percepts, is to talk nonsense. The appearance *is* the reality. If there is anything beyond the world as it appears to us (whatever that might mean), we must remain forever in ignorance of what it is.

The physical world, therefore, exists only in our percepts. If there were no perceivers, there would be no percepts and, hence, no physical world. Berkeley was right: to be a physical object is to be perceived.

Objections and Replies

I do not think that the phenomenalist view of the ontological status of the physical world is really very vulnerable to attack. The various forms of critical realism that have been proposed are, I am convinced, nothing more than temporary stopping places for "backsliding realists." Philosophers who have failed to complete the route to phenomenalism have done so more by default than by acute philosophical argument. There are, however, some common-sense objections that are sometimes raised against the phenomenalist view. To demonstrate just how strong the case for phenomenalism really is, I should like to state these objections and show how easily they can be met.

It is sometimes objected, for example, that it is silly to say things like "I had some Wheatieslike percepts for breakfast this morning," or "Help! Someone has stolen my carlike percepts." But according to the phenomenalist view, this ought to be a perfectly proper way of speaking. However, the phenomenalist theory does not imply that it is proper to talk in this way. Indeed, it is never proper to mix ordinary language and technical theory in this way. It would be equally absurd to say, "I had a bowl of Wheatieslike protons, neutrons, and electrons for breakfast," or "Someone stole my carlike atoms." The objection is quite beside the point.

A second objection is that phenomenalism provides no basis for distinguishing between valid and illusory percepts. If to be is to be perceived, then mirages and other things that even common sense regards as illusions must be as real as anything else, for these illusory phenomena are obviously perceived. Because we can distinguish between illusory and nonillusory perceptions, it is sometimes concluded that phenomenalism must be in error.

To answer this objection it is necessary only to point out that the difference between illusory and nonillusory perceptions is a difference among perceptions. The reason that we call some perceptions illusory is that they lead us to have certain expectations that are not subsequently fulfilled. We regard a mirage as illusory, for example, precisely because it leads us to expect certain other perceptions—those constituting what we call "drinking water" and "resting in the shade of a tree"—that are not forthcoming. To say that a thing is real is not to posit an unperceived metaphysical reality "behind" our percepts of the thing; it is to say that the expectations created in us by our percepts of the thing can be fulfilled. Try as we will, I do not think we shall find any further reason for making the distinction between illusory and nonillusory percepts. If the water-and-shade percepts that we anticipate when we see a mirage were forthcoming, we would not call it a mirage; it would then be identical with what we call an oasis.

It is sometimes argued that according to the phenomenalist account, physical objects—trees, stones, freight trains, skyscrapers, and other such apparently solid and substantial things—are constantly popping in and out of existence. When someone is perceiving them, they exist; when nobody is perceiving them, they cease to exist. And this, it is said, is absurd. Even Berkeley, it may be pointed out, found this idea so preposterous that he advanced the idea that things exist continually in the omniscient perception of God—a view that is wittily parodied in this often quoted limerick:

There was a young man who said, "God
Must think it exceedingly odd
   If he finds that this tree
   Continues to be
When there's no one about in the Quad."

Dear Sir:
    Your astonishment's odd:
I am always about in the Quad.
    And that's why the tree
    Will continue to be,
Since observed by
                    Yours faithfully,
                        God.[1]

My form of phenomenalism, however, can easily account for the continued existence of objects during those times when they are not being perceived—and I do not have to invoke a "perpetual perceiver" in order to accomplish this. According to my view, to say that something continues to exist even when it is not being perceived is simply to say that *if* someone were to fulfill such and such conditions, he would have such and such perceptions. Physical objects, as John Stuart Mill once said, are permanent possibilities of sensation. A physical object consists of percepts, actual and possible; the intervals of time during which the object is not being perceived are filled in by the continuing "possibilities of sensation" that remain.

Even after hearing this explanation, however, we may be inclined to ask how it is that common sense comes to take it for granted that objects when they are not perceived continue to exist in exactly the same way that they do when they are perceived. Where does the common-sense idea of an objectively real, ontologically independent physical world come from? The answer, I think, is that certain features of our perceptual experience lead us to posit such a world. The most important of these features are (a) the resemblance between the various percepts that we call percepts of the "same thing," (b) the occurrence of these similar groups of percepts in the context of a relatively stable perceptual environment, (c) the fact that we can, within certain limits, predict what kinds of percepts we shall have under such and such conditions, and (d) the fact that the perceptions we have can be varied in a more or less systematic way depending on our own movements. The idea of an independently existing world of physical objects, which appear to us in the vast variety of ways evident in our actual perceptions, is an ingenious hypothesis that common sense has erected to account for these features of our perceptual experience; but it is, as we have seen, a hypothesis that does not stand up under close scrutiny.

How are we to account for the consistency and the order that obtain among our percepts if there is no independent physical world that is the cause of them all? Phenomenalism cannot satisfactorily answer

---

[1]Ronald Knox, as quoted by Bertrand Russell in *A History of Western Philosophy* (New York: Simon and Schuster, 1945), p. 648.

this question, but neither can the realist theory. The realist theory only pushes the problem one step back. It accounts for order among our percepts by positing an ordered world and either takes the order of the world for granted or leaves it unexplained. Phenomenalists say that the order that evidently obtains among our percepts *is* the order in the world, because the only world of which we have any knowledge is the world of our percepts. If there is some explanation of why there is order in the world, then that is why there is order among our percepts; if there is no explanation, then there is none for the order among percepts either. The discussion about order, in any case, in no way favors the realist view.

Therefore, it is not to the point to argue that the phenomenalist view is refuted by the fact that people in the same general vicinity possess more or less the same kinds of sense data. Of course they do; if they did not, they would not be able to speak and act as if they lived in a common world. That our percepts are more or less alike, and that they are systematically related in a wide variety of ways, are simply ultimate facts that have to be taken for granted. To try to explain them by positing an ordered world "behind" the percepts is like trying to explain the sleep-producing effect of some drugs by saying they have a "soporific power." Not only is such a statement an inadequate explanation; it is not even a meaningful combination of words.

The final objection with which I should like to deal is that if phenomenalism were true, we could never know that other minds exist. If to say that something exists is to say that we are having, or could have, such and such percepts, then other minds do not exist since no actual or possible percepts can warrant our saying that they do. By this argument, it is concluded that phenomenalism must lead to skepticism regarding the existence of any mind other than one's own, and in the end, to solipsism.

This question has always been a difficult one for empiricists, and I shall not pretend to give a definitive answer to it. I may say, however, that neither I nor any other phenomenalist known to me is a solipsist; therefore, it is evident that being a phenomenalist does not entail accepting the solipsist position. But it is not easy to say how we know of the existence of other minds.

Much of the difficulty results from the obscurity of the very notion of a "mind." In some senses that have been given to that word, I do not think we know of the existence of any mind, including our own. What we really want to know when we ask if other minds exist is whether other conscious and sentient beings exist. It seems to me that the phenomenalist can answer as follows: (a) our own existence as conscious and sentient beings is immediately evident to us (our existence consists, as Berkeley said, in perceiving, not in being perceived); (b) we perceive beings that look, talk, and act much the way we do; and (c) by analogy, we infer that they, too, are conscious and sentient beings. Common sense, in my opinion, can do no better.

Phenomenalism and Empiricism

In conclusion, I want to state briefly what I consider to be the relation of phenomenalism to the epistemological questions discussed in the preceding sections of this book. In my opinion, anyone who intends to be absolutely consistent in his or her adherence to empiricism must adopt the phenomenalist view with respect to the ontological status of the physical world. If we are serious about the view that all we know is what comes to us in experience, then it is clear that all we know is our percepts. To posit an unseen world "behind" the world of our percepts is to claim that by means of experience we can go beyond experience, and this is just what an absolutely consistent empiricism will not permit us to do. The point, briefly put, is this: phenomenalism is the ontology of empiricism. Let phenomenalism be overthrown and rationalism will have won the day.

STUDY QUESTIONS

1. What argument does Phenomenalist use to enforce the conclusion that hypercritical realism is no more tenable than common-sense realism? Is this argument sound? Can you think of any way to defend Hypercritical Realist's view against this argument?
2. How does Phenomenalist attempt to establish his position? Is this a sound argument in your opinion?
3. Summarize the "common-sense objections" to his position that Phenomenalist mentions, and his reply to each. Are you satisfied with his replies? Can you think of any other difficulties with this theory that Phenomenalist may have neglected to mention?
4. Phenomenalist says: "Neither I nor any other phenomenalist known to me is a solipsist; therefore it is evident that being a phenomenalist does not entail accepting the solipsist position." Is this a good argument?

17

RETURN TO REALISM

A wise old professor of mine once said, "There are times in the study of philosophy when you must listen very carefully to that still, small voice that whispers insistently in your ear, 'Poppycock!'" Surely this is one of those times. From the simple common-sense view that we live in a world that exists whether or not it is perceived—a world whose features we are able to discern to some extent at least by means of our five senses—we have been led step by step to the preposterous views (a) that the physical world "exists only in our percepts," (b) that "to be is to be perceived," and (c) that the idea of an independently existing world is nothing but a mistaken hypothesis for which there is no evidence at all. Now this conclusion is utterly absurd, and I propose to begin by pointing out some of the most glaring absurdities inherent in the phenomenalist position.

Critique of Phenomenalism

First, let us take another look at the "common-sense objections" that Phenomenalist attempts to refute. He states five such supposed objections to his position and offers answers to each. The first two of these —the semantic absurdities to which phenomenalism allegedly leads, and the problem of distinguishing valid and illusory percepts—are not valid objections to phenomenalism, in my opinion, so I shall say no more about them. The other three arguments, however, are quite decisive, and I want to show how inadequate Phenomenalist's replies are.

To begin with, it is absurd to say, as Phenomenalist does, that physical objects are forever hopping back and forth between the status of "possible percepts" and "actual percepts," depending on whether or not someone is perceiving them. Phenomenalist dismisses Berkeley's view that the world is saved from an intermittent existence because it is perceived at all times by God, and takes obvious delight in reciting Ronald Knox's famous mocking limerick about the tree that, thanks to God's perpetual observation, "Continues to be/When there's no one about in the Quad." But Phenomenalist's view lends itself to well-deserved ridicule no less than does Berkeley's, as may be seen from the following bit of verse which I modestly admit is from my own pen:

"I wish," said a possible tree
"That someone would come *stare* at me;
    For to be very factual,
    I'd like to be actual:
I am tired of mere possibility."

REPLY

"Be patient," replied an old stone,
"You trees really ought not to moan;
    Why, for billions of years
    There were no eyes or ears:
We survived on possibility alone."

Let me state my point very plainly. When I say that a physical object exists even when I am not perceiving it, I do not mean that it exists because God is perceiving it, nor do I mean merely that if someone were to fulfill such and such conditions, he would have percepts of a certain kind. I mean, quite simply, that it *exists*. Now, it is true that if something exists, it will be perceived by a person who gets himself or herself into a position to perceive it. The existence of the object is a factual precondition of its being perceived, but the statement that it exists is not logically identical with the statement that it is being perceived.

Note that in order to sustain his view, Phenomenalist must hold that prior to the evolution of sentient life, nothing at all existed except, of course, potentially. The generally accepted view that the universe existed—really existed—for billions of years prior to the emergence of life becomes unintelligible on this view. Yet in studying the rock samples recently brought back from the moon, we obviously are not trying to determine what kinds of "percepts" an observer might have had four and a half billion years ago if he had been on the moon: we are trying to determine what really happened there (and elsewhere in the solar system) during those eons of time prior to the emergence of life.

Phenomenalist argues, further, that the realist theory is no more capable of explaining order in the world than is the phenomenalist theory; hence, he says, the fact that phenomenalism has no explanation for "the consistency and order that obtain among our percepts" ought not to count against it. I think, on the contrary, that the consistency and order of what we perceive does count, decisively, against Phenomenalist's view. There are two facts that have to be explained. First, each individual perceives the world as being relatively ordered: objects appear to be more or less permanent, change usually occurs in an orderly and intelligible way, and so on. Second, people in the same general vicinity perceive the same world—to use Phenomenalist's language, they perceive similar sense data. Now, it is totally unconvincing to say that the order and consistency that are thus perceived are ultimate facts to be taken for granted. These facts are easily explained within the context of a realist ontology; they become inexplicable only from the phenomenalist position.

Consider a simple analogy. Most of us occasionally have the experience of standing in a television showroom and observing a number of sets that all display what we call "the same picture" and emit what we call "the same sounds." Suppose that someone who knows nothing at all about television were introduced into this situation. What hypothesis would such an observer be justified in forming to explain these identical pictures? He or she could, of course, hypothesize that for no reason at all the sets just happen to be displaying the same pictures, but that would hardly be a satisfactory explanation, no matter how primitive the observer might be. Surely, the observer would be inclined to say, there must be some *common source* of these pictures. And in so saying the observer would, of course, be right. Just so with respect to the present point, except that in the present case it is the consistency of the perceptions of hundreds of millions of people that has to be explained. Phenomenalism has no explanation for this, whereas realism does. I consider this a decisive argument against phenomenalism.

The last objection that Phenomenalist attempts to refute is that a completely consistent phenomenalist ought to be a solipsist, since no actual or possible percepts warrant our saying that another mind exists. What is Phenomenalist's reply to this objection? That "neither I nor any other phenomenalist known to me is a solipsist; therefore it is evident that being a phenomenalist does not entail accepting the solipsist position." Now I submit that the fact that Phenomenalist and his friends are not solipsists in no way demonstrates that solipsism does not follow logically from their position. It proves only that they do not have the courage to draw this particular logical inference. It is not by logical argument, but by mere fiat, that Phenomenalist rejects the solipsist dilemma. Phenomenalism implies solipsism: this is the ultimate *reductio ad absurdum* of phenomenalism. Phenomenalist acknowledges the absurdity of solipsism and attempts to escape the *reductio* by pleading that his position does not really commit him to solipsism. But the question crucial to phenomenalism remains unanswered: If on the basis of our percepts we are not justified in affirming the existence of a real world that is the cause of those percepts, how on the basis of those same percepts can we be justified in affirming the existence of minds other than our own? Until Phenomenalist answers this question, we must hold that he is saved from solipsism not by rational argument but by a small residuum of common sense.

Further absurdities, which Phenomenalist does not mention, follow if we adopt his position. If phenomenalism is true then it follows, for example, that some merely *possible* things are the causes of some *actual* things. The collisions that are believed to have created the craters on the moon were (so far as we know) observed by no one. The supposed collisions, on the phenomenalist theory, are nothing but some possible percepts that were not actualized. Their existence is purely hypothetical and nonactual. But the craters on the moon are actual (at least part of the time), since they are frequently observed by astronomers, astronauts, and people who visit observatories. Now according to the phenomenalist theory, the statement that "the craters on the moon were caused by the impact of meteors that strayed into the moon's gravitational field" means, roughly, "the actual crater percepts that you get when you look at the moon through a sufficiently powerful telescope are the result of some possible collision percepts, the conditions for which existed some billions of years ago when, unfortunately, there were no perceivers to actualize them." This statement, to say the least, is more than a little difficult to swallow. I am not convinced that it makes sense to say that one set of actual percepts (rain percepts) causes another set of actual percepts (wet-pavement percepts); but I am completely convinced that it makes no sense at all to say that some actual percepts are caused by some merely hypothetical possible percepts. Phenomenalism reduces the notion of causality to utter nonsense.

One final objection. Phenomenalism implies that if there were no perceivers, nothing would actually exist, since all that exists is minds and their perceptions. The annihilation of all sentient life is, however, logically conceivable and is, in fact, a ghastly empirical possibility that we have been forced to think about since the advent of the atomic age. But surely it is absurd to say that the annihilation of all sentient life would terminate the actual existence of the whole physical universe. I think it makes more sense to say that in the event of such a tragedy the sun, the moon, the stars, and the planets would continue to exhibit the motions they now exhibit; that on this sad old planet we call Earth the winds would still blow, the snow and the rain would still fall, and, perhaps in time, grass would grow and flowers would bloom once more; only no one would be here to observe these occurrences. Still, phenomenalism would insist that such statements make no sense, or that they make a kind of sense (the possible-percepts story) that is about as close as you can come to no sense at all. Thus, we may add one more item to the long list of absurdities that follow from the phenomenalist position.

Realism Reconsidered

Where, then, has Phenomenalist gone wrong? If phenomenalism is really as vulnerable as the preceding argument has shown it to be, how can so many able philosophers be persuaded of its truth? Most important of all, what view are we warranted in holding about the ontological status of the physical world?

I suggest that the initial error that has sent so many philosophers down the slippery slope to phenomenalism is the innocent-looking claim that the immediate objects of perception are sense data. I shall argue, on the contrary, that the immediate objects of perception are sights, sounds, tastes, smells, tactual qualities. I shall, in short, defend the view known as direct realism. In order to do this, I must refute the argument from illusion, which is the principal basis for the erroneous claim that the immediate objects of perception are sense data.

What, exactly, is an illusory perception? It is nothing more than a combination of the mistaken belief that something exists and the mistaken belief that one is immediately perceiving it. A mirage, for example, is the mistaken belief that at a certain place in the desert there is an oasis, combined with the mistaken belief that one is immediately perceiving the oasis mistakenly believed to exist. Were these two beliefs not mistaken, one would not be the victim of a mirage but would instead be having the experience called "seeing an oasis."

What, then, is a person perceiving when "seeing a mirage"? The answer is that he or she is perceiving nothing at all. Normal perception is the true belief that an object exists together with the true belief that we are immediately perceiving it. Illusory perception is the false belief of these same propositions. The immediate object of normal perception is the object that we believe we are perceiving—sounds, color patches, shapes, and so on. Since in the case of illusory perception there is no real object, it follows that nothing is being perceived. Illusory perception is not the perception of sense data to which nothing corresponds in reality, but the holding of certain *beliefs* that happen to be false. Sense data are mere phantoms, introduced to provide an object for perception in those cases in which someone is said to "see" something that does not really exist. My analysis of illusory perception shows that no such object is required; thus, we can simply dispense with the whole concept of sense data.

The immediate objects of perception, when perception is actually occurring, are the colors, shapes, sounds, tastes, odors, and so forth that we perceive by means of our senses. The term "immediate" here means simply that these are the phenomena that appear directly in our perceptual field: they present themselves to us, and under appropriate conditions we perceive them. In a derivative sense, however, we may say that what we perceive are not colors, shapes, sounds, tastes, odors, but trees, stones, automobiles, steaks, perfumes. That is, we may add to the immediate perception the *judgment* that the sound we just heard was from an approaching automobile, or that the object we see in the distance is a tree—and in so doing, we may be mistaken. It seems perfectly proper to say, however, "I hear an automobile," "I see a tree," or "I smell perfume." In such cases, we are expressing what I should call *mediate* or *indirect* perception. The immediate objects of perception are colors, shapes, sounds, tastes, odors, and the mediate objects of perception are the objects that have those colors, shapes, sounds, tastes, odors.

Is the physical world, then, in any degree dependent on a perceiver for its existence? No. The physical world is altogether independent of the perceptions of any perceiver. It existed for billions of years before the emergence of sentient life and may well exist for billions of years after all such life has vanished from the scene. In the meantime, however, our unaided senses reveal to us some of the shapes, colors, sounds, and so forth, that are really there; by the use of various instruments that magnify the powers of our senses—microscopes, telescopes, amplifiers, and what not—we are able to perceive features of the world that are not discernible to the unaided eye or ear. The account of the physicist does not conflict with but supplements the account of common sense. To say that the observations of physicists are valid whereas those of ordinary people are not (hypercritical realism) is purely arbitrary.

I would observe, in conclusion, that there is no need to develop a constructive argument in support of direct realism. Common-sense realism is the position from which everyone sets out in this controversy: people become critical realists or phenomenalists (or even solipsists) only because they are persuaded by some argument or other that they must abandon their "naïve" or "common-sense" views. In order to reëstablish the realist position, we have only to refute the arguments that led to its abandonment in the first place. Direct realism is merely common-sense realism that has become sure of itself through having defended itself against its critics. Hence, the arguments of direct realists are typically directed not toward the positive fortification of their position but rather toward the refutation of the arguments commonly leveled against it.

STUDY QUESTIONS

1. "The existence of the object is a factual precondition of its being perceived, but the statement that it exists is not logically identical with the statement that it is being perceived." Explain.
2. Does the fact that "people in the same general vicinity perceive the same world" count against the phenomenalist position? Defend your answer.
3. "Phenomenalist is saved from solipsism not by rational argument but by a small residuum of common sense." Do you agree? Explain.
4. What, according to Direct Realist, is an illusory perception? Do you agree with this analysis?
5. "Sense data are mere phantoms introduced in order to provide an object for perception in those cases in which someone is said to 'see' something that does not really exist." Does this seem plausible to you?
6. "There is no need to develop a constructive argument in support of direct realism." Attack or defend this statement.
7. Has Direct Realist answered all the objections to common-sense realism raised by the previous writers? List the objections, and show how they have or have not been refuted.

CORRELATED READINGS[1]

1. Locke, John. "The World As We Perceive It and As It Really Is." *An Essay Concerning Human Understanding* (1690), Vol. I, Book II, Chap. VIII, Sections 7–24; Vol. II, Book IV, Chap. XI, Sections 1–9. Critical realism.

2. Berkeley, George. "To Be Is to Be Perceived." *Of The Principles of Human Knowledge,* Vol. I, Sections I–XX. An early formulation of subjective idealism.

3. Mill, John Stuart. "Matter as a Permanent Possibility Of Sensation." *An Examination of Sir William Hamilton's Philosophy.* 5th ed. London: Longman's, Green, Reader and Dyer, 1878, Chap. XI. A further refinement of Berkeley's view.

4. Barnes, Winston H. F. "The Myth of Sense Data." *Proceedings of the Aristotelian Society,* Vol. XLV (1944–1945), pp. 89–117. A defense of direct realism.

FOR FURTHER READING

Adams, E. M. "The Nature of the Sense-Datum Theory," *Mind,* 67 (1958), 216–226.

Alexander, Peter. "Curley on Locke and Boyle," *Philosophical Review,* 83 (1974), 229–237.

Armstrong, D. M. *Perception and the Physical World.* New York: Humanities Press, 1961.

Austin, J. L. *Sense and Sensibilia.* London: Oxford University Press, 1962 (paperbound).

Ayer, A. J. *The Foundations of Empirical Knowledge.* New York: St. Martin's Press, 1958 (paperbound), Chaps. 1, 2, 5.

————. *The Problem of Knowledge.* New York: St. Martin's Press, 1956, Chap. 3.

Bergmann, Gustav. *Logic and Reality.* Madison: University of Wisconsin Press, 1964, Chap. 14.

Chisholm, R. M. "The Problem of Empiricism," *The Journal of Philosophy,* 45 (1948), 512–517.

Cornman, J. W. *Perception, Common Sense and Science.* New Haven, Conn.: Yale University Press, 1975. An important recent defense of direct realism.

Curley, E. M. "Locke, Boyle and the Distinction Between Primary and Secondary Qualities," *Philosophical Review,* 81 (1972), 438–464.

Dewey, John. *Essays in Experimental Logic.* New York: Dover, 1960 (paperbound), pp. 1–74, 250–302.

Dretske, Fred I. *Seeing and Knowing.* Chicago: University of Chicago Press, 1969.

[1]*Concise Readings in Philosophy,* Part IV.

Eddington, A. S. *The Nature of the Physical World.* Ann Arbor: University of Michigan Press, 1958 (paperbound).

Ewing, A. C. *The Fundamental Questions of Philosophy.* New York: Macmillan, 1951, Chap. 4.

Garnett, A. C. *The Perceptual Process.* London: Allen & Unwin, 1965. Short, highly readable, critical realist view.

Gibson, James J. *The Senses Considered as Perceptual Systems.* London: Allen & Unwin, 1968.

Hinton, J. M. *Experiences: An Inquiry into Some Ambiguities.* New York: Oxford University Press, 1973.

Jackson, F. *Perception: A Representative Theory.* New York: Cambridge University Press, 1977. A critical realist account.

Joske, W. D. *Material Objects.* New York: Macmillan, 1967.

Lewis, C. I. *An Analysis of Knowledge and Valuation.* LaSalle, Ill.: Open Court Publishing Co., 1947 (paperbound), Chap. 7.

Locke, D. *Perception and Our Knowldege of the External World.* London: Allen & Unwin, 1967.

Mandelbaum, M. *Philosophy, Science, and Sense Perception.* Baltimore, Md.: Johns Hopkins Press, 1964. Defends critical realism.

Mundle, C. W. K. *Perception: Facts and Theories.* New York: Oxford University Press, 1971 (paperbound).

Pitcher, George. *A Theory of Perception.* Princeton, N.J.: Princeton University Press, 1971.

Price, H. H. "The Argument from Illusion," in H. D. Lewis (ed.). *Contemporary British Philosophy,* Third Series. New York: Macmillan, 1956, pp. 391–400.

——————. *Perception.* 2nd ed. New York: Dover, 1950.

Rogers, G. A. J. "The Veil of Perception," *Mind,* 84 (1975), 210–224. Attempts to combine a causal theory of perception with a form of direct realism.

Russell, Bertrand. *Human Knowledge.* New York: Simon and Schuster, 1962 (paperbound). See Part III, "Science and Perception."

——————. *The Problems of Philosophy.* New York: Oxford University Press, 1959 (paperbound), Chaps. 1–4.

Warnock, G. J. *Berkeley.* Baltimore, Md.: Penguin Books, 1969 (paperbound).

PART V

THE EXISTENCE OF GOD

18

ON PROVING THE EXISTENCE OF GOD

There are a number of questions about God that philosophers have asked at various times in the history of Western philosophy. Many of these have been concerned with the *nature* of God: Is God rightly described as a "person"? Is God absolutely eternal and immutable, or does He in some sense change? If God does not change, how is it possible for Him to experience love, or solicitude, or compassion? These, and dozens of other questions of this kind, figure prominently in the writings of such Christian philosophers as St. Augustine, St. Anselm, St. Thomas Aquinas, and Duns Scotus. To modern ears, such questions often sound exceedingly strange, even insignificant; but to the philosophers of the Middle Ages they were questions of great importance. Indeed, one measure of the distance that modern thought has traveled from that of the Middle Ages is the infrequency with which such questions are discussed today.

There is another question, however, that has been of interest to at least some philosophers in every age. That is the question, Does God exist? Some philosophers—St. Augustine, for example—thought the existence of God so self-evident that it did not even require proof (though he does offer one such proof in his treatise *On the Free Will*). Others, like St. Albert the Great, St. Thomas Aquinas, and René Descartes, thought the existence of God required proof, but they considered the task of producing such a proof a relatively simple matter. Aquinas, for example, offers no less than five "proofs" in the space of just two or three pages. Most philosophers today are at least in agreement that the proof of the existence of God, if it is possible at all, is no easy matter; and it is probably true to say that the majority of them regard it as impossible.

The Meaning of the Term "God"

Before we can intelligently discuss the various arguments that have been offered as proofs of the existence of God, it is necessary that we consider carefully a prior question, namely, What is the meaning of the term "God"? Let us see why this is such an important question, in connection with the arguments concerning the existence of God.

Suppose that someone proposed for discussion the question, Do *snergs* exist? Now, it would be obviously futile to begin to construct arguments for or against the existence of snergs until some agreement had been reached as to what was meant by the term "snergs." Indeed, confusion would most surely occur, for those who affirm the existence of snergs might have one thing in mind, and those who deny their existence might have another. As a result, their disagreement would be merely verbal rather than real. Unless there is agreement on this key point, and thus agreement on what is the point of the question, the question itself cannot be intelligently discussed.

Even philosophers, unfortunately, have not always understood clearly the crucial importance of this prior question. As a consequence a good deal of confusion has been created in the discussion of God's existence. Some philosophers have supposed, for example, that the question, Does God exist? is equivalent to, Does there exist, some place beyond the reach of even our most powerful telescopes, a very wise and powerful being who once upon a time brought the world into existence, who occasionally even now interferes in its orderly operations, and who will some day reward the righteous and punish the wicked? They have supposed, that is to say, that it is God *as conceived by popular, unsophisticated Christian piety,* whose existence is in question; and they have relatively little difficulty in showing that none of the arguments that have been offered in proof of the existence of God succeeds in proving the existence of such a being. But, then, no philosopher who has seriously proposed an argument for the existence of God has ever intended to prove the existence of a being so conceived.

What, then, have those philosophers who have attempted to prove the existence of God meant by the term "God"? It is very difficult to answer this question with the precision that might be desired. Those philosophers who have entered most seriously and profoundly into the discussion of this question—philosophers such as St. Anselm, St. Thomas Aquinas, Descartes, and Immanuel Kant (who are far from agreeing on the soundness of the various arguments for the existence of God)—appear to have meant by the term "God" at least the following:

1. A reality that transcends space and time
2. The ground of being and value
3. A reality worthy of human worship

Substituting this definition for the term "God," our question becomes, "Is there a reality that transcends space and time, is the ground of being and value, and is worthy of human worship?" To answer this question in the affirmative is to affirm that God exists. To answer it negatively is to deny that God exists. To affirm or deny the existence of any other sort of being is to miss the point of the question, Does God exist?

However, certain terms in this formulation of the question are unclear, notably "reality" and "ground." Let us try to clarify them.

Perhaps the best way to get at the meaning of "reality," as used in this context, is to note the reasons for using this term instead of "being." To speak of God as "a being" would not do justice to what many philosophers who have attempted to prove the existence of God have meant by the term "God." Why? Because our notion of "a being" is one of a spatiotemporal something that exists alongside other spatiotemporal somethings. To speak of "a being" is to speak of something that exists in some places but not in others, at some times but not at others. Philosophers who have believed that God exists, and that His existence could be proved, have not intended to assert the existence of a being occupying some particular region of space-time. Rather, they have meant to assert the existence of a reality that is not subject to the categories of space and time, a reality, in other words, that transcends space and time. Hence, we must speak of God not as a being but as a reality.

To say that God is to be conceived as a reality that transcends space and time is to say that God is not to be conceived simply as a natural object, as one of the many objects that we might encounter within the realm of nature. No telescope will ever be constructed, no space journey ever undertaken, that will reveal God's habitation—not because the distance is too great, but because the question of God's existence does not concern distance at all. If we cannot attach some meaning to the phrase "a reality that transcends space and time" (and many philosophers today insist that they cannot), then we simply cannot enter into the discussion of the question, Does God exist?

The same reasoning obtains in the use of the term "ground" rather than "cause." "Cause" is (in contemporary usage) too closely tied up with the notions of space and time. A cause is a spatiotemporal something that stands in a certain relation to something else that we call its effect. But the notion of God, we have said, is the notion of a reality that transcends space and time; hence, we must not speak of God in a way that suggests "a spatiotemporal something." We want, however, to affirm something like the relation of cause and effect between God and being and value. How shall we do this? Philosophical usage has given us the term "ground," which means roughly (in philosophical usage) "nonspatiotemporal cause." Let us say, then, that God is the ground of being and value.

What, finally, does it mean to say that the idea of God is the idea of a reality "worthy of human worship"? This is in many ways the most puzzling of the three statements. Yet something like this must be said to take account of the fact that the term "God" is, in the first instance, a *religious* term—so much so that we would not be too far from the truth if we were simply to define "God" as "the object of the act of worship." The supposition is, however, that the object of worship is somehow worthy of human devotion, which in our philosophical tradition, at least, has meant that God is conceived to be holy, just, good, merciful, and so on. Many philosophers (Aquinas, once again, is an excellent example) have attempted to construct proofs of a number of such attributes of God, but it seems clear that the very notion of God includes in embryonic form the idea that He possess in an eminent degree those virtues that we normally admire in one another. It is this notion that we are including in the idea of God when we say that God is to be conceived as "a reality that is worthy of man's worship."

The question whether God exists—whether there exists a reality that transcends space and time, is the ground of being and value, and is worthy of human worship—is not a trivial question. I think most people would agree with the sentiments of the philosopher who said (though he himself rejected all the arguments for the existence of God):

> If we found that any of the traditional arguments for the existence of God were sound, we should get out of our one hour this ... afternoon something of inestimable value, such as one never got out of any hour's work in our lives before. For we should have got out of one hour's work the answer to that question about which, above all, we want to know the answer.[1]

Many philosophers who believe that none of the traditional arguments for the existence of God is sound believe, nonetheless, that the question of the existence of God is an exceedingly important question. In fact, some of those who hold that God does not exist (for example, Friedrich Nietzsche and Jean Paul Sartre) have recognized that such a conclusion must profoundly alter one's understanding of oneself, one's fellows, and one's world. It is probably safe to say that anyone who does not regard the question of the existence of God as a serious and important question has not really understood the point of the question.

A Related Question

To the question, Does God exist? there are just three possible answers: yes (theism), no (atheism), I don't know (agnosticism). Philosophers,

---

[1] J. J. C. Smart, "The Existence of God," a public lecture given at the University of Adelaide in 1951, published in Antony Flew and Alasdair MacIntyre (eds.), *New Essays in Philosophical Theology* (London: SCM Press; and New York: Macmillan, 1955), pp. 28–46; see p. 28.

however, are not interested just in people's opinions on this matter; they are interested primarily in the reasons that might be given in support of an opinion. Therefore, let us for the moment approach the question of the existence of God by asking whether there are any rational grounds for believing in the existence of God, whether there are any good reasons for believing that the proposition "God exists" is true. Such a question may be answered in a number of ways.

First, we could assert that there are some rational grounds for believing in the existence of God—in which case we ought to be prepared to say what those grounds are. In practice, this means that an argument for the existence of God is put forward and an attempt is made to show that the argument succeeds. (Chapters 19–21 attempt to do this in terms of three of the traditional arguments for the existence of God.) It should be noted at this point that what is to be allowed to count as "rational grounds" in this connection depends very much on one's epistemological persuasion. If one is an empiricist, for example, one cannot agree with the proponent of the cosmological argument when he makes an appeal to "rational insight" (Chapter 20). If, on the other hand, someone is persuaded by the cosmological argument, then he or she must be prepared to draw the epistemological consequences. Here, as with every philosophical problem, intricate and important interrelationships with other philosophical issues are evident.

A second way of answering this question is to say that none of the arguments offered in support of the existence of God is sound and, therefore, one must draw the conclusion that God does not exist. Since philosophical naturalism cannot allow the existence of God (as defined above), it is incumbent upon a naturalist to take this second position. A critique of the arguments from this perspective is offered in Chapter 22.

Not all those who deny the soundness of the traditional arguments for the existence of God are philosophical naturalists, however. Some theologians, for example, deny that the existence of God can be established by rational argument; yet they obviously do not draw the conclusion that God does not exist. The view that there are no sound arguments by which the existence of God can be proved, but that God nonetheless exists and His existence is certified in certain presumably nonargumentative ways represents a third response to the question posed in this section. Chapter 23 attempts to build the case for such a view.

A Preliminary Look at the Arguments

Since the question of the existence of God is one in which many people have been extremely interested, it is not surprising that a rather large number of arguments have been constructed in an attempt to prove that the proposition "God exists" is true. No less than five types of arguments have been put forward. Let us survey them briefly before proceeding to a more detailed consideration of three such arguments.

First, it is possible to argue that the existence of God can be correctly inferred from the idea of God. Such an argument is termed an *ontological* argument for the existence of God. This type of argument, the most famous example of which was formulated by St. Anselm of Canterbury (1033–1109), is considered in some detail in Chapter 19.

Second, it is possible to argue that the existence of the world presupposes, implies, or points to, the existence of God. This type of argument is called a *cosmological* argument for the existence of God. Among the best-known arguments of this type are those of Avicenna (980–1037) and St. Thomas Aquinas (1225–1274).

A third type of argument attempts to reason from the assertion that there is order in the world to the conclusion that God exists. An argument of this type, advocated by such men as William Paley (1743–1805) and F. R. Tennant (1866–1957), is called a *teleological* argument.

The *moral* argument for the existence of God attempts to reason from certain features of moral experience to the conclusion that God exists. Immanuel Kant (1724–1804) defended a version of this argument, as did the British philosophers W. R. Sorley (1855–1935) and A. E. Taylor (1869–1945).

A fifth type of argument is the *argument from religious experience,* which begins with certain features of religious experience and attempts to reason from these to the conclusion that God exists. It is rarely encountered in serious philosophical discussion, but it is attacked from time to time—apparently on the supposition that there are people who endorse some version of it.

Few areas of philosophical inquiry evidence the poverty of language more plainly than does discussion of the arguments for the existence of God. The "five ways" of Aquinas, for example, are stated in the language of Aristotelian metaphysics and are quite unintelligible apart from an understanding of that metaphysical system. Since Aristotelian metaphysics is not part of the conceptual vocabulary of most people today, an intelligent appraisal of Aquinas' arguments is simply impossible for them. It will be evident in the essays that follow that the advocates of the various arguments for the existence of God are groping for a terminology that is both adequate to express their ideas and intelligible to modern ears.

STUDY QUESTIONS

1. Why is it necessary to come to some agreement about the meaning of the term "God" before engaging in a discussion of arguments purporting to prove the existence of God?
2. Does the definition of God proposed here agree with what you have ordinarily understood the term to mean? If not, how would the definition have to be altered to do so?
3. What are the reasons given for using the terms "reality" and "ground," rather than "being" and "cause," in the definition of

God? Do these strike you as being sound reasons? What difference would it make in the discussion if the terms "being" and "cause" were substituted for "reality" and "ground"?

4. What is an ontological argument for the existence of God? a cosmological argument? a teleological argument? a moral argument? an argument from religious experience?
5. What is your present opinion regarding the central question posed in this chapter? Where have you gotten that opinion?

19

THE ONTOLOGICAL ARGUMENT

The history of the controversies concerning the problem of the existence of God during the past sixteen hundred years provides an interesting commentary on the development of Western thought during this period of time. Initially, in the work of St. Augustine especially, the existence of God is simply taken for granted. It is regarded as a matter so self-evident that a proof of God's existence would be utterly superflous. At the present stage of this development (I do not say the last), the *non*existence of God is so commonly taken for granted that any attempt to prove the existence of God is viewed by many of our contemporaries as anachronistic and futile. The intervening chapters in this history, marked by the explicit formulation of the ontological argument (St. Anselm), the rejection of the ontological argument in favor of the cosmological argument (Aquinas), and the rejection of both of these in favor of the teleological argument (deism), indicate the course by which our culture generally has moved from an implicit belief in the existence of God to an implicit disbelief. An advocate of any argument for the existence of God today has little reason to be hopeful of winning many adherents.

Moreover, the task is rendered even more difficult by the widespread ignorance regarding what is actually to be proved. A reasonably well-educated person should know that philosophers who believe it is possible to demonstrate that God exists emphatically do *not* believe in the existence of "the Old Man in the Sky" of primitive supernaturalism. Even St. Augustine, who might have been excused for holding what we would regard as "primitive" ideas, knew better. If our only alternatives were naturalism and supernaturalism, it is clear that the honest choice would have to be naturalism. Supernaturalism, with its demons and its angels, its throne in the heavens, and its Old Man in the Sky, belongs to the childhood of our culture. These things may survive indefinitely in the symbolism of religious communities and as the picture language of simple religious faith, but they have no place in serious discussion of the existence of God. It would be better if the question were not discussed at all than to have it reduced to such childish and superficial terms.

There is, happily, an alternative. It is to enter earnestly and passionately into a consideration of what it means to affirm that God exists, to try to grasp this great affirmation so profoundly and so intimately as to understand how some of the intellectual giants of our culture could have regarded it as unthinkable that anyone *who knew what he or she was doing* could refuse to affirm it. Let this question be our point of departure: How could intelligent and learned thinkers such as St. Augustine and St. Anselm have been persuaded, as almost nobody is today, that the existence of God is self-evident? What did they see, or think, or feel, or understand, that most people today apparently do not? Perhaps by considering this question we may begin to understand what a twentieth-century version of the ontological argument would be, and why, even today, it deserves our attention and respect.

St. Anselm

St. Anselm of Canterbury (1033–1109) was one of the few truly original thinkers who appeared during the long interval between St. Augustine (354–430) and St. Thomas Aquinas (1225–1275). Like St. Augustine, whom he sought to emulate, St. Anselm conceived his role to be that of an apologist for Christian orthodoxy. All his writings reflect his theological and apologetic concerns; indeed, he did not make a hard and fast distinction between theology and philosophy. However, in two of his writings, the *Monologium* and the *Proslogium,* he advanced a number of arguments for the existence of God. These are worthy of study in themselves, quite apart from the apologetic context out of which they arose.

The ontological argument was the product of St. Anselm's quest for

> a single argument which would require no other for its proof than itself
> alone; and alone would suffice to demonstrate that God truly exists, and
> that there is a supreme good requiring nothing else, which all other
> things require for their existence and well-being.[1]

The arguments that he had previously offered (in the *Monologium*) were, St. Anselm realized, extremely complex and, therefore, uncon-

---

[1]St. Anselm, *Proslogium and Other Writings,* trans. S. N. Deane (LaSalle Publishing Co., Ill.: Open Court, 1962), p. 1.

vincing to many readers. The argument he sought and believed he now had found was to be so simple and so cogent that no one could fail to understand it and be convinced by it.

Unfortunately, the argument as developed by St. Anselm is far from simple, at least to modern ears. The crucial passage reads as follows:

> Even the fool is convinced that something exists in the understanding, at least, than which nothing greater can be conceived. For, when he hears of this, he understands it. And whatever is understood, exists in the understanding. And assuredly that, than which nothing greater can be conceived, cannot exist in the understanding alone. For, suppose it exists in the understanding alone: then it can be conceived to exist in reality; which is greater. Therefore, if that, than which nothing greater can be conceived, exists in the understanding alone, the very being, than which nothing greater can be conceived, is one, than which a greater can be conceived. But obviously this is impossible. Hence, there is no doubt that there exists a being, than which nothing greater can be conceived, and it exists both in the understanding and in reality ... There is, then, so truly a being than which nothing greater can be conceived to exist, that it cannot even be conceived not to exist.[2]

Analysis of the Argument

This is a far more forceful argument than most of St. Anselm's critics have realized. In order to appreciate its cogency, however, it is first necessary to understand it, and this is not easy. Perhaps the following restatement will help.

Proposition 1.   By the term "God" is meant a being than which none greater can be conceived.

Proposition 2.   Whether we affirm or deny the existence of God, a being than which none greater can be conceived exists in the understanding.

Proposition 3.   It is possible to conceive of a being than which none greater can be conceived existing not only in the understanding but in reality as well; and this is greater.

Proposition 4.   If, therefore, a being than which none greater can be conceived exists *only* in the understanding, it is not a being than which none greater can be conceived.

Proposition 5.   Therefore, a being than which none greater can be conceived exists also in reality.

I do not think that anyone would deny that if Propositions 1–4 are allowed to stand, Proposition 5 (the conclusion) would follow from them. Let us consider what may be said in defense of Propositions 1–4.

---

[2]*Ibid.,* pp. 8–9.

Proposition 1 simply asserts a minimal definition of the term "God." St. Anselm is saying, in effect, that people who believe in the existence of God believe in the existence of a being than which none greater can be conceived, that the only way to deny the existence of God is to deny the existence of a being than which none greater can be conceived. Thus far, it seems to me, St. Anselm's opponents have no reason to object. At most, they could only quibble over terms, since it is this definition that determines the substance of what St. Anselm means when he affirms that God exists.

Proposition 2 points out the obvious fact that anyone who affirms or denies the existence of God must, first, understand the meaning of the term "God." If people say the words "God does not exist" but mean something other than "a being than which none greater can be conceived does not exist," they are only denying the existence of something else to which they incorrectly give the name "God." In order to really affirm or deny the existence of *God*—in order, that is, to be a party to this debate at all—we must understand what the term "God" means. And since, as St. Anselm says, "whatever is understood, exists in the understanding," Proposition 2 must be affirmed.

This brings us to Proposition 3, which is surely the crux of St. Anselm's famous argument. It states that it is possible for us to distinguish in thought between (a) a being that exists only in our concept and (b) a being that exists in our concept and in reality, and that a being of the latter sort is greater than one of the former. Let us consider this matter carefully in terms of two important questions: Can we make the distinction St. Anselm says we can make? Is it self-evidently true that a being existing in concept and in reality is on that ground alone greater than a being existing only in concept?

Concerning the first question, it seems evident that in at least some cases we have no difficulty making the distinction that St. Anselm asks us to make. We can distinguish without difficulty, for example, between an imaginary dog and a real dog, the proof being that we have certain expectations in connection with the one that we do not have with the other. I am thinking at this moment, for example, of a particular Dalmatian. I expect to see him occasionally as I drive by the yard where he usually is kept, I expect to observe him playing with the neighborhood children, and so on. But I can also form the concept of a dog identical with him in every respect save one: this dog exists only in my concept, not in reality. This dog, I know, will never be lying in the yard as I drive by, will never play with the neighborhood children, will never chase my car—unless, of course, I provide some *imaginary* children and cars for him to frolic with. Thus, if Kant's often quoted statement that existence is not a predicate means, as it is usually supposed to mean, that it is not possible for us to make this distinction between real and merely conceptual existents, then I think we must conclude that on this point Kant was simply mistaken. We can and do make the distinction that St. Anselm is asking us to make.

Is it self-evidently true, then, that a being existing in reality is on that ground alone greater (more perfect) than an otherwise identical being existing only in concept? Here, it seems to me, we must choose among three alternatives: either (a) whatever order of excellence may be attributed to a thing in concept, some additional excellence accrues to that thing if, in addition, it is conceived to exist in reality; or (b) whatever order of excellence may be attributed to a thing in concept, that excellence is totally unaffected if, in addition, it is conceived to exist in reality; or (c) whatever order of excellence may be attributed to a thing in concept, that excellence is diminished if, in addition, it is conceived to exist in reality. I know of no way to *prove* that the first of these alternatives is to be preferred. For myself, however, I have no doubt that St. Anselm's assumption on this point is correct, and I think that the burden of proof must lie with those who would adopt either of the other two alternatives.

I urge my readers to ponder carefully what St. Anselm is saying at this point, for if they can understand and accept Proposition 3, they should have no difficulty in agreeing with the remainder of the argument. Can we distinguish between a being that exists only in concept and a being that exists both in concept and in reality? The answer certainly is that we can. Then, it makes sense to say that existence in concept and in reality is better than existence in concept alone. Peace in the world is certainly better than a mere concept of peace. That God should exist in reality is certainly better than that we should merely have a concept of Him. We can and do distinguish between mere conceptual existence and real existence, and we do regard the latter as superior. It *is* possible to conceive of a being than which none greater can be conceived existing not only in the understanding but in reality as well; and this *is* greater.

It follows (Proposition 4) that if a being than which none greater can be conceived exists in the understanding only, that being is not a being than which none greater can be conceived. As has already been shown (Proposition 3), a being existing in concept and in reality is superior to an otherwise identical being existing in concept only. If, therefore, you say that this being exists in concept only, you are contradicting yourself; for you are saying that a being than which none greater can be conceived is not in fact a being than which none greater can be conceived. Such a statement is contradictory in the same way that the statement "Some round figures are not round" is contradictory: it asserts something in the subject that is denied in the predicate.

Thus *you cannot deny the existence in reality of a being than which none greater can be conceived without contradicting yourself.* Since by the term "God" we mean a being than which none greater can be conceived, it follows that the statement "God exists" is necessarily true. God, as St. Anselm says, "cannot even be conceived not to exist."

Some who reject this argument reason that if it were a sound argument, it should be possible to prove in the same way the existence of many things—for example, an island than which a more beautiful one could not be conceived. The reasoning is not parallel, however, so the conclusion does not follow. There is no logical necessity in the existence of an island than which a more beautiful one could not be conceived, for the concept of existence is not implicit in the concept of maximum beauty. The reasoning applies only in the unique case of a being than which a greater cannot be conceived, for existence *is* implicit in the concept of such a being (Proposition 3). In this one case, and only in this one case, real existence follows necessarily from the mere concept of such a being.

We began with the question, Are there any rational grounds for believing in the existence of God, and if so, what are those grounds? I have argued that the very concept of God as a being than which none greater can be conceived makes it logically necessary that God exists, that is, that our belief in the existence of God rests on the very secure rational ground of logical necessity. It follows, then, that to deny the existence of God is not only to make an error of fact, it is also to be involved in a self-contradiction, to make a logical error. Thus, we ask with St. Anselm:

> Why, then, has the fool said in his heart, there is no God (Psalms 14:1), since it is so evident, to a rational mind, that [God] dost exist in the highest degree of all? Why except that he is dull and a fool?[3]

STUDY QUESTIONS

1. Does the restatement offered here accurately reproduce St. Anselm's argument? If not, how should it be revised in order to do so?
2. We are advised in this chapter that we ought to accept the first two premises of St. Anselm's argument without question. Do you agree? Defend your answer.
3. "It is possible for us to distinguish in thought between (a) a being that exists only in our concept, and (b) a being that exists in our concept and in reality." Do you agree or disagree? Defend your position.
4. "A being that exists in our concept *and* in reality is superior to an otherwise identical being existing in concept only." Do you agree or disagree? Defend your position.
5. In your opinion, is the ontological argument a sound argument? If not, where do you think it goes wrong?

---

[3] *Ibid.,* p. 19.

20

THE COSMOLOGICAL ARGUMENT

Anyone seriously involved with the problem of the existence of God—or, more specifically, the problem of assessing the cogency of the several arguments for the existence of God that have been put forward—is painfully aware that the present-day advocate of any such argument faces a number of difficult obstacles. Chief among these are the following: (a) the apparently inescapable vagueness of the concept "God," (b) the antimetaphysical bias of much modern thought, and, as a corollary, (c) the absence of a vocabulary acceptable to the modern mind that is suitable for the construction of a proof of the existence of God. I am not sanguine about the prospects for overcoming these obstacles in what follows, but I do think the existence of God is capable of strict demonstration. Therefore, I shall try to state my proof in a form that I trust will be intelligible as well as persuasive to a modern reader.

It is not surprising that the concept of God is less precise than most of the concepts that we customarily employ. Most of our concepts are of objects that exist in space and time—objects concerning which it is appropriate to ask questions like, Where is it? How big is it? What color is it? and so on. If the concept of God were to be given that kind of precision, we would no longer be talking about God at all; for whatever we do mean by "God," it is clear that we do not mean "one object (or being) among others in the world of space and time."

The question concerning the existence of God is, therefore, unique. It would be silly to try to prove the existence of a spatiotemporal object. The existence of any such object is a purely contingent fact: to convince anyone of its existence you must produce not an argument but *the object itself.* Only if it presents itself in some way to at least one of our senses are we willing to say that it "exists." And rightly so.

But we cannot know of God's existence in the same way that we know of the existence of spatiotemporal objects. If we are to know of the existence of God, therefore, it must, in this one, unique case, be by way of argument or demonstration. The question we must ask is this: Is there any feature of the world of space and time that points to a reality that transcends space and time, is the ground of the being and value of this world, and is worthy of man's worship? To answer this question in the affirmative is to construct (or at least to affirm that it is possible to construct) a cosmological argument for the existence of God.

St. Thomas Aquinas

"The existence of God," said Aquinas, "can be proved in five ways."[1] Thereupon, in a scant three pages, the great Angelic Doctor gave to the world five of the most famous arguments for the existence of God that have ever been formulated.

None of the "five ways" is original with Aquinas (nor, of course, did he claim that they were), and they are not equally persuasive. The first three, in particular, are very similar, and differ markedly from both the fourth and the fifth arguments. There are reasons for regarding the third way as the fundamental, or centrally important, one. The complete text of this argument reads as follows:

> *The third way is taken from possibility and necessity, and runs thus. We find in nature things that could either exist or not exist, since they are found to be generated, and then to corrupt; and, consequently, they can exist, and then not exist. It is impossible for these always to exist, for that which can one day cease to exist must at some time have not existed. Therefore, if everything could cease to exist, then at one time there could have been nothing in existence. If this were true, even now there would be nothing in existence, because that which does not exist only begins to exist by something already existing. Therefore, if at one time nothing was in existence, it would have been impossible for anything to have begun to exist; and thus even now nothing would be in existence—which is absurd. Therefore, not all beings are merely possible, but there must exist something the existence of which is necessary.* Every necessary thing either has its necessity caused by another, or not. It is impossible to go on to infinity in necessary things which have their necessity caused by another, as has been already proved in regard to efficient causes. Therefore we cannot but postulate the existence of some being having of itself its own necessity, and not receiving it from another, but rather causing in others their necessity. *This all men speak of as God.*[2]

---

[1]St. Thomas Aquinas, *Summa Theologica*, I, ques. 2, art. 3, trans. by Fathers of the English Dominican Province (New York, Cincinnati, and Chicago: Benziger Brothers, 1910), p. 24.

[2]*Ibid.,* p. 26. (Italics, which are mine, are explained below.)

Although I hold this to be a sound argument, I do think it is more complicated than it needs to be because of Aquinas' inclusion of a multiplicity of "necessary things which have their necessity caused by another." This may have served some polemical purpose at the time that Aquinas was writing, but to a modern reader it appears as excess baggage that only clutters up the argument. Nothing essential to the argument is lost, I think, if we simply omit this reference to a series of hypothetical "necessary beings" (everything not in italics above) and conclude directly from the existence of "beings [that] are merely possible" to the existence of "something the existence of which is necessary ... [that] all men speak of as God."

Ontological Contingency

Both defenders and critics of this argument sometimes assert that the starting point of the argument is a fairly obvious feature of the world, namely, that something exists. I think this assertion indicates a serious misunderstanding of the argument. The starting point of the argument is not that something exists (that *is* obvious) but that some *contingent beings* exist, and this is not nearly so obvious. It is precisely at this point that we determine whether or not we are going to go along with Aquinas's argument. Either we share his insight into *the contingency of finite beings,* or we remain unconvinced by his argument.

What does it mean to say that something is ontologically contingent? It means that the thing in question can be conceived to not exist, that it does not have the cause of its existence within itself. In every moment that it exists, its existence is in question, in jeopardy. It is perpetually threatened by nonbeing, by nothingness, and there is nothing within it to protect it against this threat.

By way of analogy (not example), consider for a moment a beam of light proceeding from a flashlight. One could imagine a naïve person —a child, perhaps, who knows nothing about the physics of light— supposing that the beam of light is self-subsistent in the same way that most people regard trees and stones and other physical objects as being self-subsistent. (Whether they really are so is a question to which we shall return in a moment.) But we, of course, know that a beam of light does not have the same degree of ontological independence as a tree or a stone—or a flashlight. The beam of light, in each moment that it exists, proceeds from and is dependent on the flashlight. In each moment that it exists its existence is in question, in jeopardy: it can be turned off, extinguished, made *not to be* in an instant.

To say that the tree, the stone, the flashlight are ontologically contingent is to say that, as in the case of the beam of light, the cause of their existence does not lie within themselves. Just as a child would be mistaken in thinking that a beam of light is self-subsistent, so we would be mistaken if we believed any physical object to be totally self-subsistent. For every physical object—everything that we can see, smell, taste, touch, or feel, *including ourselves*—is ontologically contingent. We too can be turned off, extinguished, made not to be.

Two Common Criticisms

It will be convenient to deal here with two criticisms that are frequently made of this argument. The words "necessary" and "contingent," it is sometimes said, are words that apply not to *things* but to *propositions.* To speak of God as a "necessary being," or "something the existence of which is necessary," must mean (if it means anything at all) "The proposition 'God exists' is a necessary proposition." But this is precisely the claim of the ontological argument. Therefore, according to this argument, the cosmological argument reduces ultimately to the ontological argument, and if the ontological argument is not sound, then neither, obviously, is the cosmological.

It is easy to show, however, that this is a superficial criticism. It starts with purely arbitrary definitions of the terms "necessary" and "contingent" and then attempts to employ these definitions to make Aquinas—or anyone else who advocates this form of the cosmological argument—say something he clearly did not say and did not mean to say. Granted that in logic the terms "necessary" and "contingent" apply only to propositions, not to terms or to arguments. In logic a necessary proposition is one the negation of which involves a self-contradiction, whereas a contingent proposition is one the negation of which does not involve a self-contradiction. Does this exclude the possibility that outside the realm of logic—in metaphysics, for example—these same terms may have a somewhat different meaning? Of course not.

The cosmological argument, in whatever form, always moves from the *ontological contingency* of finite being to the *ontological necessity* of the ground of being. Aquinas does not, in the argument quoted above, use the term "contingent"; he speaks instead about "things that are possible to be or not to be." But that, as we have just noted, is precisely what "ontological contingency" means.

A second common—and, in my view, mistaken—objection to Aquinas's argument concerns his claim that "it is impossible to go on to infinity," which is essential to his argument. Some critics have asked, Why can you not go on to infinity? Mathematicians regularly employ the notion of an infinite series. Why should we regard it as self-evident that a series of "contingent beings" or "causes" cannot proceed to infinity?

This objection, like the first, rests on a misunderstanding of the cosmological argument. Aquinas's point is not that a particular being —a man, let us say—is dependent on his parents for his existence, and they on their parents, and they on theirs, and so on, all the way back to God. The cosmological argument has nothing to do with the relation between parents and children. It has to do with the *present* ontological contingency of some being and its *present* dependence for its existence on some noncontingent ground. The possibility of an infinite mathematical series is, therefore, totally irrelevant to the argument.

That the cosmological argument has nothing to do with this story of one generation's succeeding another may also be seen in the fact that if the argument is construed in this way, it can, at best, prove that *at some time in the past* there was a remote ancestor of this presently existing contingent being. It is not the purpose of the cosmological argument to prove the present existence of somebody's great-great-great-great ... grandfather. Therefore, it should be evident that to construe the argument in this way is to *mis*construe it, indeed, to render it altogether ludicrous.

I have dwelt briefly on these two objections to the cosmological argument for two reasons: first, because they are frequently accepted as sound, and, second, because they reveal some of the most common misunderstandings of the cosmological argument. Discussion of them affords an opportunity to point out and attempt to remove these misunderstandings. I may be wrong in my view that the cosmological argument is a convincing proof of the existence of God, but I am surely not wrong in insisting that any opinion of this argument should be based on a serious effort to understand the argument as it is understood and intended by those who support it.

A Restatement

So that the truly persuasive character of the cosmological argument may be exhibited as clearly as possible, I should like to offer a restatement of the argument in what I take to be its simplest possible form. I propose to state it in terms of two premises and a conclusion and to indicate the grounds on which each of the premises rests. I hope that at least a few of my readers may then find it possible to join me in affirming the conclusion.

Reduced to its simplest possible form, the cosmological argument may be stated as follows:

Some contingent beings exist.
Contingent beings require a noncontingent ground of being in order to exist.

A noncontingent ground of being exists.

The crucial step in this argument, as I have already indicated, is the first premise. The question that must be asked, then, is *On what basis* is it affirmed that "some contingent beings exist"? The answer that must be given will, I fear, be disappointing to many. I am obliged to reply that the ontological contingency of finite beings cannot be demonstrated on the basis of some other more evident truths: it must be grasped directly. I know only too well that the notion of "rational insight" is distinctly out of favor at present; but if we do not have such direct insight into the ontological contingency of finite things, we cannot know it at all.

Even though this truth cannot be demonstrated, it may be possible to suggest a few things that will help to "elicit the insight." Aquinas does this, for example, when he calls attention to the fact that things in nature are subject to "generation and corruption"—they come into being and pass away. "My days," says the Psalmist, "are like a shadow that declineth, and I am withered like grass."[3] The coming into being and the passing away of individuals is, of course, an observable fact, one that often gives rise to the feeling of the transitoriness of all things, of the tenuous and precarious character of finite existence. From this awareness, it is but a step to the rational insight into the ontological contingency of finite being upon which the cosmological argument rests.

Or we may take a slightly different approach. At the present moment you are, of course, existing—a fact that, like most people, you probably take for granted. Concerning the future (tomorrow, for example), you ask not, Will I be? but, What will I be doing? Yet in all seriousness, how can you simply take your own existence for granted? Is not existence a gift received anew moment by moment? It is certainly conceivable that at any second, we could simply cease to exist, that individually or collectively we and our world could be annihilated —in short, that the gift of existence could be withdrawn, and in our place would be . . . nothing. To ponder our own existence in this way is to feel the uncertainty, the precariousness, the gratuitousness of all finite existence, including our own. To conceptualize this feeling is to grasp the ontological contingency of finite being, the rational insight with which the cosmological argument begins.

The second premise of the argument—that contingent beings require (presuppose) a noncontingent ground of being in order to exist —is analytically true. To say that something is "contingent" is to say that it is "ontologically dependent"; it is to affirm a relation and, therefore, implicitly to posit that to which the relation refers. If we understand what we have said when we have affirmed the contingency of finite being, there is no difficulty in affirming this second premise. Its function is simply to spell out what is implied in the initial insight into the contingency of finite being, and this in such a way as to make it evident that this insight does indeed imply the existence of God.

---

[3]Psalms, 102:11.

The Object of Worship

Although in my discussion thus far I have had in mind chiefly those critics of the cosmological argument who think it tries to prove too much (that God exists), I know there are other critics who object that the argument proves too little. A deeply religious person may respond to the cosmological argument with profound indignation because the "ground of being" who appears at the conclusion of the argument—this "God of the philosophers," as Blaise Pascal said—bears little or no resemblance to the loving Heavenly Father of living religious faith. "Away with these abstractions!" is the cry of such well-meaning people. What is to be said in answer to such an objection?

The only answer I shall attempt to give is that it is not the business of the philosopher to attempt to prove everything about God that is of importance for religious faith. Faith simply presupposes the reality of God and by means of a rich symbolism seeks to worship Him in a way that is worthy of Him. Faith lives in symbolism and imagery, not primarily in concepts; this is why all conceptions of God—even those formulated by theologians—seem, from the point of view of faith, woefully inadequate.

But philosophers *qua* philosophers are not entitled to such a presupposition. For philosophy, the question whether God exists is a legitimate and, indeed, inescapable question. As I have indicated, I believe that we are entitled to answer this question in the affirmative. I believe, further, that the conception of God that emerges at the conclusion of the cosmological argument is capable of considerable enrichment, when the argument is applied to a wide variety of contingent existents (as Aquinas does, for example, in the first three of his five ways). But the God whose existence is thus established, though surely worthy of humankind's worship, can never acquire by philosophical argument the rich (but profoundly anthropomorphic) connotations that religious faith ascribes to Him in poetry, prayer, and song. In comparison with the God of living faith, the God of the cosmological argument must appear highly abstract, austere, and remote. Philosophical argument is limited to concepts, which it must strive to make as precise as it possibly can. It cannot deal in imagery. It cannot disclose to us the richer reality that is the object of religious faith. But it can and does disclose to us the reality of God as the ground of the being of finite things. We must not expect of it more than this.

STUDY QUESTIONS

1. What is meant by the statement that the question concerning the existence of God is "a unique question"? Is it? What assumptions is one making if one holds that it is? If one holds that it is not?
2. Restate St. Thomas Aquinas's "third way" premise by premise, just as St. Anselm's argument was restated in the previous chapter.

3. What does it mean to say of something that it is ontologically contingent?
4. The author of this chapter offers the account of the "beam of light" as an analogy, not an example. What is the difference? What is the analogy supposed to illustrate?
5. What are the "two common criticisms" of the cosmological argument that our author attempts to refute? Do you find the refutation convincing?
6. What is the difference between attempting to "prove a proposition" and attempting to "elicit an insight"? Why does the author of this chapter resort to the latter?
7. Who would be apt to criticize the cosmological argument on the ground that it proves too much? on the ground that it proves too little? What is your own opinion of the argument?

21

THE TELEOLOGICAL ARGUMENT

Like the two writers who are to succeed me in this discussion, I am not at all persuaded by either the ontological or the cosmological argument for the existence of God. I have never been impressed with them in their "classical" formulations—those of St. Anselm and Aquinas, respectively—and I am equally unimpressed after reading the explanations offered by the preceding two writers. Both these arguments are vulnerable to a really devastating and, I think, decisive critique, which I assume will be forthcoming in the chapters that follow. I shall be content, therefore, to simply state my rejection of these arguments, leaving the detailed criticism to others, and shall proceed directly to the formulation and defense of a third argument that, in my estimation is far more persuasive.

The argument of which I speak is commonly called the teleological argument (from the Greek word *tēlos,* meaning "end" or "goal"). Aquinas's fifth way is a version of this argument, but the "classical" statement of the argument is in William Paley's *Evidences of the Existence and Attributes of the Deity.*[1] It is an argument that deserves to be studied with great care.

The Sense of Wonder

We shall be better prepared to both understand and appreciate the teleological argument if we first consider briefly the kind of human experience out of which the argument has come to be formulated.

---

[1]William Paley, *Natural Theology,* ed. Frederick Ferrè (Indianapolis: Bobbs-Merrill, 1963).

All but the most pedestrian of human beings must, at times, be impressed by the vastness, the grandeur, the beauty, and the order of the universe. There is a feeling of awe and wonder when we stand upon the shore of a stormy sea, gaze upward on a starry night, or survey the rugged beauty of a range of mountains. Here is power, restless and profound; here is vastness, staggering in magnitude; yet, here is order, beautiful to behold.

Scientists in whom the sense of poetry is still alive tell us of a similar experience when they have penetrated some of the less obvious wonders of nature. To understand the structure of the atom is to marvel at its ordered complexity. To survey the course of evolution is to view a magnificent process unfolding through millenniums of time. To grasp the genetic code is to possess a key that may unlock yet further mysteries of nature. Here are phenomena capable of inspiring awe of which our ancient predecessors could not even dream. How much there is, in the world as we perceive it, to inspire that sense of awe of which we have been speaking.

It seems very natural, when some feature or other of the universe impresses us in this way, to say that it could not be by chance that the universe is the way it is. A beautiful poem, a great symphony, a particularly inspiring work of architecture, a remarkable engineering achievement—these are impressive and rightly cause us to give honor to their creators. But more wonderful still is the poetry, the harmony, the power, the beauty, the structure of the universe itself. Surely it, too, has an Author, an Architect, a magnificent Craftsman, whose wisdom and power are commensurate with the mighty work that He has wrought. Every person living, at some time in his or her life, must have entertained sentiments such as these.

The teleological argument is simply an attempt to extract and to render conceptually precise the argument that is implicit in the natural reflections inspired by this experience of wonder.

The Argument

Paley's formulation of the argument in *Evidences of the Existence and Attributes of the Diety* does not, unfortunately, lend itself to a brief summary statement. It is, as he says, cumulative; his whole book is the argument. However, I shall try to indicate the general course Paley takes.

He begins by noting that whenever we observe of something that "its several parts are framed and put together for a purpose" (a watch, for example) we conclude, without hesitation, that it has been devised for this purpose by some intelligent designer. Nothing that we may subsequently learn about the watch (that it sometimes fails to work perfectly, that it is capable of reproducing itself, or anything else) can dissuade us from this belief. Paley states:

> There cannot be design without a designer, contrivance, without a contriver; order, without anything capable of arranging; subserviency and

relation to a purpose, without that which could intend a purpose; means suitable to an end, and executing their office in accomplishing that end, without the end ever having been contemplated, or the means accommodated to it. Arrangement, disposition of parts, subserviency of means to an end, relation of instruments to a use, imply the presence of intelligence and mind.[2]

So much for the first part of Paley's argument. The second part attempts to show that the universe abounds with phenomena that, like the watch, exhibit teleological order:

Every indication of contrivance, every manifestation of design, which existed in the watch, exists in the works of nature; with the difference, on the side of nature, of being greater and more, and that in a degree which exceeds all computation ... The contrivances of nature surpass the contrivances of art, in the complexity, subtlety, and curiosity of the mechanism; and still more, if possible, do they go beyond them in number and variety: yet, in a multitude of cases, are not less evidently mechanical, not less evidently contrivances, not less evidently accommodated to their end, or suited to their office, than are the most perfect productions of human ingenuity.[3]

Paley's favorite example of design in nature is the eye, whose delicate and intricate mechanism he discusses in great detail. But countless other examples are to be found.

The conclusion, Paley suggests, must therefore be drawn: design in nature points to the existence of an intelligent Designer of nature, just as design in a watch or other machine points to the existence of its designer.

Were there no example in the world of contrivance except that of the eye, it would be alone sufficient to support the conclusion which we draw from it, as to the necessity of an intelligent Creator. It could never be got rid of because it could not be accounted for by any other supposition, which did not contradict all the principles we possess of knowledge.[4]

I think that this argument is sound and convincing. I propose to reduce it to its barest essentials and to add a few comments by way of elucidating its fundamental structure.

Elucidation and Defense of the Argument

The teleological argument contains two premises. One, straightforwardly factual, is that nature exhibits a number of instances of means ordered to ends. The other, a general principle, is that the ordering of means to ends presupposes the existence of a designer whose intelli-

---

[2] *Ibid.,* p. 10.
[3] *Ibid.,* p. 13.
[4] *Ibid.,* p. 44.

gence and power are sufficient to do the ordering. The whole argument, therefore, is as follows:

Nature exhibits a number of instances of means ordered to ends.
The ordering of means to ends presupposes the existence of a
   designer whose intelligence and power are sufficient to do the
   ordering.

The ordering of means to ends in nature presupposes the existence of a designer whose intelligence and power are commensurate with the magnitude of the product wrought.

It is important to note, in attempting to assess this argument, that it does not say, nor does it presuppose, that the whole universe is cooperating to achieve some single ultimate purpose. This may or may not be the case: the argument is neutral with respect to this question. Unfortunately, some critics of the teleological argument have failed to grasp this point.

It should also be observed that the argument does not say, nor presuppose, that the several "ends" toward which the various means are ordered are necessarily good, or are what human beings would always approve of, or tend to serve our needs. For example, the various endowments that make the tiger a dangerous animal serve the end of the *tiger's own* self-preservation—sometimes, at the expense of human beings. This is an "end" in the sense in which that term is used in this argument, human preferences in the matter notwithstanding. Numerous other examples could be given.

The factual premise in this argument seems to me beyond dispute. The evidence is all around us, and it is overwhelming. Animals have eyes in order to see, ears in order to hear, teeth in order to chew their food, digestive organs in order to utilize their food, lungs in order to breathe, and so on. In the plant world, too, we observe the adaptation of means to ends: root systems in order to draw nourishment from the soil, leaves in order to derive the benefits of the sunlight, and so on. Look where we will, the evidence is the same. Every species of living thing known to us, every plant, every insect, every fish, every mammal, is endowed with those characteristics necessary to its existence and way of life.

We know, of course, as Paley did not, that this remarkable state of affairs has come about through a long process of evolution in which the forms of life now found in nature have developed from other forms no longer extant. But this alters the argument not at all. Consider this process at any point you will, the kind of evidence we are now considering abounds there. No matter how far we press our inquiry into the remote past, we find not chaos but order: means subservient to ends, processes conducive to the emergence of life, circumstances conducive to the proliferation of life, powers adapted to the preservation of life. So much for the factual premise.

The second premise—that the ordering of means to ends presupposes the existence of some intelligent designer to "do the ordering" —is an inductive generalization well substantiated by experience. It is beyond dispute that in every such instance of which we have any reasonably certain knowledge, the principle holds true. We know of no watches without watchmakers, ships without shipbuilders, or planes without planebuilders. We would never allow, if we were to be shown one of these objects, that without the intelligent direction of any mind whatsoever the object in question just "happened to happen." Where we find *means ordered to ends,* "chance" is as good as no answer at all; for in every such instance of which we do have knowledge, we find mind—intelligence—behind it. Every day we observe countless examples of this principle; we have never observed, or been offered, a counterexample. The principle would seem to be as secure, therefore, as it is possible for an inductive generalization to be.

If the argument is to be attacked, then, it must be on the ground that the order that we find in nature is not sufficiently similar to the order that we find in human contrivances to justify applying the principle. David Hume saw this clearly and, in his *Dialogues Concerning Natural Religion* (published posthumously in 1779), he exercised, as he says, "all [his] sceptical and metaphysical subtilty" in an attempt to weaken the analogy. But after doing his best, or rather his worst, to find some alternative to intelligent design as a principle of explanation, even Hume was forced to conclude (in the words of Philo, his chief spokesman in the *Dialogues*):

> In many views of the universe and of its parts, particularly the latter, the beauty and fitness of final causes strike us with such irresistible force that all objections appear (what I believe they really are) mere cavils and sophisms; nor can we then imagine how it was ever possible for us to repose any weight on them.[5]

The order that we find in nature calls for some explanation. The analogy between it and the order found in contrivances known to be the product of intelligent purpose is infinitely stronger than any other analogy so far suggested. Against this objection, therefore, the teleological argument stands secure.

The Wider Teleological Argument

We have, of course, learned a great deal about the world since the days of Paley and Hume. I can well imagine a reader acknowledging that such an argument had some persuasive power prior to the work of Charles Darwin, but pointing out that the adaptation of means to ends as we find it in nature is adequately explained by the principle of natural selection. According to this opinion, there is no need for expla-

---

[5]David Hume, *Dialogues Concerning Natural Religion,* ed. Norman Kemp Smith, 2nd ed. (New York: Social Sciences, 1948), p. 202.

nation through "divine intelligence." Since this objection appears serious to many people, it deserves to be treated with respect, though it is by no means fatal to the teleological argument. Its true import is that it forces us to broaden the scope of the field within which we may discern the workings of the divine intelligence.

Consider the following remarkable facts about the world as we know it:

1. The world is intelligible in a very high degree. The world, somehow or other, is capable of being understood by means of the logical and mathematical categories of the human mind.
2. The evolutionary process, which posits "chance" mutations whose survival depends on their suitability to enhance the organism in its struggle for life, has operated *as if* it were intended to produce variety, beauty, mind, and intelligence.
3. The inorganic world, which according to current theory existed for hundreds of millions of years before life emerged on our planet, is remarkably well adapted—physically, chemically, thermally, and so on—to the maintenance of life.
4. Nature has developed in such a way that there are numerous phenomena that elicit in human beings a sense of beauty.
5. The conditions of human life have developed in such a way that man is able to postulate, pursue, and, to a high degree, achieve moral ideals.

How are we to account for these remarkable facts? What hypothesis will do justice to the truly astonishing fact that out of a mass of inorganic matter there has emerged, through a process that might have worked in countless other directions, not only life (which is remarkable enough in itself) but a being possessing intelligence, morality, and a sense of beauty? Say, if you will, that it is all a matter of chance, that the laws of nature had to produce *some* kind of world, and that this just happend to be the one that developed. I for one do not believe it. If this world evolved by a "throw of the dice" then I cannot escape the conclusion that the dice were loaded. There is, as Sir Arthur Eddington once remarked, a "cheater" some place in the vicinity. The hypothesis that the world is the way it is because God so arranged it is, I think, strongly supported by facts such as those enumerated above. Evolution, far from destroying the teleological argument, provides new evidence of adaptation of means to ends and thus supports the God-hypothesis that it is the purpose of the teleological argument to establish.

The Limits of Philosophical Argument

The teleological argument by itself does not and cannot be expected to give us a rich, "full-blown theology," such as would satisfy a religious community. For that is needed the images evoked and provided by religious literature, the sentiments that are nourished in various rites of worship, and the vocabulary and ideas that have life and meaning only in the context and the tradition of this or that worshiping community. Any philosophical attempt to "fill out" the concept of God in these essentially religious ways would be rightly resisted both by philosophers and by nonphilosophical adherents of religion.

The God whose existence is proved by the teleological argument is not the Brahman of Hindu faith, the Yahweh of Jewish faith, or the Heavenly Father of Christian faith. The God of the teleological argument, strictly speaking, is simply an unknown Mind and Power, by virtue of whose workings we find order in the world about us. About this austere notion cluster the sentiments of awe and wonder at the marvels of nature—the natural precursors, perhaps, of that "sense of the holy" that is so distinctive of religious communities. Perhaps, too, the awareness of the beauty of nature and of the greatness of the privilege of being alive leads to some intimation of the goodness of God, so that He is conceived not only as Mind and Power but also as Goodness.

Philosophical reflection on the awesome spectacle of order in nature cannot take us beyond the bare knowledge of God's existence and the faint intimation of some few of His attributes. But it can take us that far. We may or may not then turn to religion to further enrich our conception. That is another matter altogether. Philosophy is not theology, and philosophical understanding is not religious faith. But the understanding that philosophy can give us, limited though it is, may serve as a foundation for faith.

STUDY QUESTIONS

1. What relevance, if any, does the discussion of "the sense of wonder" have for the subsequent discussion of the teleological argument?

2. Look up St. Thomas Aquinas's fifth way (*Summa Theologica*, Part I, Question 2, Article 3), and compare it with the argument given in this chapter. What similarities do you find between the two arguments? What differences?

3. How does one go about identifying an instance in nature of "means ordered to ends"? What right have we to say, for example, that the "end" served by the ferocity of the tiger is the self-preservation of the tiger rather than the death of its prey? Is some criterion at work here that has not been made explicit?

4. Is the analogy between "order in nature" and "order in human contrivances" sufficiently close to support the second premise of the teleological argument? How important is this alleged analogy to the argument?

5. "Evolution, far from destroying the teleological argument, provides new evidence of adaptation of means to ends and thus supports the God-hypothesis that it is the purpose of the teleological argument to establish." What is your opinion?

22

THE NONEXISTENCE OF GOD: A NATURALISTIC REJOINDER

It is a fundamental tenet of philosophical naturalism that the whole of reality consists of objects and events occurring in space and time, and that the system of spatiotemporal events that we call the world is self-dependent and self-operating. It is an obvious negative corollary of this view that there is nothing real that transcends this world—no gods, no values, no anything. To say that something exists is to say that it is, or is reducible to, some spatiotemporal events that we can perceive, or that we could perceive under such and such circumstances, or that (at a minumum) are causally related to events of this kind. It makes sense to say that grasshoppers exist, because we can see them. It makes sense to say that mountains exist on Venus, because we know what mountains are and what it would be like to see them through a telescope. It makes sense to say that electrons exist, because the event that we call the existence of an electron is causally related to other events that we perceive. It does not make sense, in any of these ways, to say that God exists.

But no sooner do we naturalists point out that the statement "God exists" is, at best, exceedingly odd (and at worst meaningless), than theists turn this very observation against us. "Quite so," they say, "but the reason is that the existence of God is a unique instance. Grasshoppers, mountains, and electrons exist only *contingently*, but God's existence—the only one of its kind—is *necessary*. That is why the statement 'God exists' strikes us as being so odd." On this whole question of the existence of God, I would like to make just one assertion and then be done with it: the statement "God exists" has no clear meaning. It is as senseless to deny it as it is to affirm it. But in view of the rejoinder ("This is a unique case"), we have no choice but to go over the worn-out old arguments to show why they do not establish the proposition "God exists" in any meaningful acceptation of those terms. What follows, then, is a *disproof of the proofs* for the existence of God.

The Ontological Argument

There is one strong prima facie reason for doubting the soundness of the ontological argument: practically everybody who has studied it carefully has, in the end, rejected it. St. Anselm, of course, who invented the argument, believed it to be sound; so also did René Descartes and Gottfried Wilhelm von Leibnitz. But Gaunilon in the eleventh century, Aquinas in the thirteenth, Hume and Kant in the eighteenth, and nearly every major philosopher since then have rejected it. If we can determine the soundness of an argument on the basis of the consensus of those who are most competent to judge, the ontological argument must be adjudged a failure.

The critics of the ontological argument have rejected it principally for three reasons, all of which I find convincing. First, if the reasoning contained in the ontological argument were sound, it should be applicable in other instances as well—namely, to the superlative instance of any positive quality. It should be possible to prove (by a parallel argument) the existence of an island than which none more beautiful can be conceived (that was Gaunilon's example), a mountain than which none taller can be conceived, and so on. But this is clearly absurd. It seems evident, therefore, that something is wrong with the argument.

We begin to understand just what is wrong with it when we consider, in the second place, that it really is not the case that when anyone either affirms or denies the existence of God, a being than which none greater can be conceived "exists in the understanding." Let it be granted that we can utter the *words* "a being than which none greater can be conceived"; I contend that we have no *concept* of a being so described.

The third reason for rejecting the argument is the most decisive. Existence, as Kant said, is not a predicate. To assert that something is red, for example, is to make an assertion that requires us to alter our concept of that thing; "red," therefore, is a predicate. But the assertion that something exists in no way modifies our concept of that thing. The ontological argument hinges on an alleged contrast (Proposition 3 of the summary) between (a) a being existing only in the understanding and (b) an otherwise identical being existing both in the understanding and in reality. But this is a contrast, a distinction in thought, that it is not possible for us to make. Our concept of a real Dalmatian differs in no way from our concept of an imaginary one. The difference between the two consists not in anything found in the concepts themselves but rather in the different ways in which they are related to our (actual or possible) perceptions. Hence, even if it were possible to form a concept of a being than which none greater can be conceived (and I have questioned this), it still would not be possible to conclude to the existence of God. The crucial distinction upon which the whole argument turns is one that it is impossible to make.

The Cosmological Argument

There are many forms of the cosmological argument, and it would be a tedious job to review and criticize each in detail. Chapter 20 presents the argument in a form that many contemporary supporters regard as persuasive, and I shall restrict my remarks to this version. Anyone who understands what is wrong with the argument in this form will have no difficulty in detecting the weaknesses in any other form of the argument.

The cosmological argument as stated suffers from three serious defects. To begin with, the first premise ("Some contingent beings exist") is either unintelligible, or it is a truism. If it is unintelligible, it is not deserving of serious consideration. If it is a truism, nothing of importance follows.

I am at this moment looking at an ashtray. It, presumably, is one of the "contingent beings" that this premise says exists. Very well. What does it mean to say that this ashtray is "contingent"? I can think of three possibilities. It may mean that (a) there was a time when this ashtray did not exist and now it does—it has "come into being" and will, presumably, some day cease to exist. Or it may mean that (b) the nonexistence of this ashtray is conceivable. Or it may mean that (c) there are certain things without which the ashtray would cease to exist. If *a*, nothing of importance follows. You may, if you wish, argue to the existence at some time in the past of an ashtray-maker, but this is quite obviously beside the point. If *b*, again nothing of importance follows. We can conceive of the nonexistence of anything simply by thinking of it as occupying space and then imagining that space to be empty. If *c* is meant, the situation is a little more complicated, but the result is the same. It is apparent, for example, that the continued existence of this ashtray depends on the continued validity of certain laws of physics—the cohesion of its parts, its tolerance of the temperature levels to which it is subjected, and so on. But this does not take us any distance at all toward establishing the proposition "God exists."

If the proposition "Some contingent beings exist" does not mean one of these three things, I can only insist that I find it unintelligible. If there is something else that I am supposed to "see directly," I can only confess that I do not see it. Until the defenders of the cosmological argument tell us plainly and explicitly what they mean by the statement, I think we are justified in suspecting that they do not see it either. Either they mean one or more of the three things suggested above, or they mean nothing at all.

Let us, however, be as charitable as we can. Let us suppose that the supporters of this argument do mean something when they assert that "Some contingent beings exist." What might they mean? Option *c* would seem to be their most promising choice. They might insist that something of significance does follow from it because we cannot be satisfied with an infinite regress. If something Z (the ashtray, for example) is dependent on something else Y for its continued existence, they might say, then we can ask the same question about Y. Is it contingent or not? Eventually we must come to a *non*contingent cause, and this is what we mean by God.

But there is something very wrong with this argument from ashtrays to physics to God. We know that by means of physical laws we can reason only to other physical laws or to some spatiotemporal event or events. Physical laws are passports that enable us to move from one range of phenomena to another *in the natural world*. They do not give us an exit visa to pass outside spatiotemporal reality. Moreover, what is wrong with a series of contingent causes, even an infinite series of contingent causes? In this case, every member of the series is contingent in the sense defined above, and there is no first member. Is this any harder to conceive of than an infinite mathematical series, or infinite space?

Finally, the conclusion of the argument is so ambiguous that it seems quite impossible to either affirm it or deny it. How could anyone decide for or against the statement "A noncontingent ground of being exists"? What concrete difference would it make in your experience or mine whether this statement (if it is a statement) is true or false? None whatsoever. It is a meaningless combination of ponderous words, designed to intimidate rather than to elucidate. But one thing is clear: whatever these words are supposed to mean, the premises that precede them do not establish the existence of God. We may not like it, but it happens to be the case that this world and its laws are the only reality there is. Any attempt to reason from this or that feature of the world to some reality not of the world is sheer fantasy.

The Teleological Argument

Although it is popularly regarded as one of the most persuasive of the traditional arguments for the existence of God, the teleological argument is by far the weakest. Since the defects of the argument have only to be pointed out to be seen, I shall restrict myself to a summary statement of them.

The assertion "Nature exhibits a number of instances of means ordered to ends" is subtly ambiguous. What nature exhibits is a high degree of *lawlike regularity*. If this is all that is meant by "means ordered to ends," all well and good; but it seems that more than this is intended. The language suggests "purposiveness," or "ordering," and thus subtly suggests in an allegedly factual premise that we ought to look for a "purposer," or "orderer." We seem to have here a case of syllogistic smuggling.

Furthermore, the alleged analogy between the lawlike regularity that we find in nature (to substitute for the offending terms) and that which we find in human contrivances is notably weak. We do indeed posit a human intelligence whenever we encounter an implement that (a) serves some conceivable purpose and (b) is evidently not altogether a product of nature. But neither of these characteristics applies to the regularities that we find in nature, not even to those offered by the author of Chapter 21 as examples of the sort of thing he has in mind. On what basis, then, are we supposed to see an analogy?

It is quite beside the point to argue that "the analogy between (order in nature) and the order found in contrivances known to be the product of intelligent purpose is infinitely stronger than any other analogy so far suggested." This may well be. I am no more impressed than was Hume, for example, by the suggestion that the universe could be likened to a giant plant or to a spiderweb rather than to a machine. But why should it be likened to anything at all? A human contrivance, after all, utilizes in some way or other certain laws of nature that human beings, by careful inquiry or by good luck, have discovered. May not these laws be themselves the ultimate facts to which appeal can be made, and may not the universe itself be the model of regularity in relation to which every other instance of regularity is only a pale analogy?

Moreover, even if the argument were sound, the being whose existence it establishes would be nothing more than a finitely wise, finitely powerful architect. The inventor of a machine does not create the materials with which he works; he only shapes them. Hence, the "orderer," whose existence is supposedly established by this argument, is merely a craftsman, not a creator. The argument, if it is sound, requires only that this cosmic "orderer" be very wise and very powerful. It does not establish the existence of an *infinitely* wise and powerful being. Moreover, the argument requires nothing at all in the way of goodness. Since there is evil in the world that this God is supposed to have designed, it may be assumed that He is something less than perfectly good; at best He must be considered amoral, at worst malevolent. This is hardly a description of God in any religiously meaningful sense of the term.

Finally, even if the argument did establish the existence of this strange being, it would establish only his past existence, not his present one. The existence of a watch implies only the existence of a watchmaker *at the time the watch was made;* it does not in any way assure me of his *present* existence. Similarly, if the existence of an ordered universe implied anything at all (which I doubt), it would be that once upon a time, long, long ago, there was a worldmaker. He may since have died or changed his occupation.

The teleological argument is not a good one. It derives its prestige entirely, I suspect, from the fact that it unites the "natural wonder" of which we heard in the last chapter with the apparently kindred feeling of "reverence" in a way that is satisfying to religious people. It may even be that the feeling of reverence arose originally out of this feeling of natural wonder. Be that as it may, it is perfectly evident that the belief in the existence of God did not come about because of the cogency of the teleological argument.

A Final Word

None of the arguments for the existence of God is able to withstand careful scrutiny. Why, then, do so many people believe that God exists? The answer can only be that this belief is irrational—an illusion (Sigmund Freud), a personification of society (Émile Durkheim), or something else. The persistence of this belief, in spite of the demonstrable fallaciousness of the arguments used to support it, suggests that it must fulfill some deep emotional need of many people. Therefore, it may be thought cruel to show, as I have done, how weak those arguments are. However, since people who believe in God obviously did not arrive at this belief by means of rational argument, it is unlikely that the removal of the arguments will by itself destroy that belief. People who need this particular illusion will probably keep it, with or without intellectual props. Moreover, we have addressed ourselves to this problem only in the interest of knowing the truth. Are there or are there not rational grounds for believing in the existence of God? As a convinced naturalist, I hold that there are not. I think that this is the truth. If the truth is painful, it is still the truth. Things are the way they are; the best we can do is to try to see them that way, not the way we might like them to be.

STUDY QUESTIONS

1. What objections does Naturalist bring against the ontological argument? In your opinion are they all sound objections? (Compare Naturalist's third objection with the defense of Proposition 3 in Chapter 19.)
2. What are Naturalist's objections to the cosmological argument? Do they apply with equal force to Aquinas' third way and to the shorter formulation offered in Chapter 20?
3. What are Naturalist's objections to the teleological argument? Do they apply with equal force to Paley's argument and to Aquinas' fifth way? Do you think Naturalist is right in calling this "by far the weakest" of the arguments for the existence of God?
4. Select whichever of the traditional arguments you consider to be the strongest and attempt to defend it against Naturalist's criticisms.

23

THE FAILURE OF THE ARGUMENTS: A SYMPATHETIC APPRAISAL

In the debate about the existence of God, there would seem to be only two plausible positions: either (a) there is some sound argument for the existence of God, and everybody ought to believe that God exists; or (b) there is no sound argument for the existence of God, and everyone ought to hold that the existence of God is improbable, or at best, highly problematic. The absence of an argument proving that something exists does not, of course, prove that the thing in question does not exist. It must be admitted, however, that the burden of proof rests with those who make the affirmative claim. (For example, I cannot prove that there are no little, two-headed green animals living on the planet Venus; there may well be, but sanity seems to require that I assume that there are none unless, or until, some evidence is produced to indicate that there are.)

I find myself in disagreement with both positions, and I fear, therefore, that my own position must, at first, seem somewhat strange. I hold, with the author of the last chapter, that there is no sound argument for the existence of God; but I also hold with the authors of the previous three chapters, that God exists and that His existence can be known by us. This position represents, I think, the only possible way in which the impasse between theists and naturalists concerning the problem of the existence of God can be overcome.

Arguments and Rational Grounds

One way of stating the position that I should like to defend is this: there are no sound *arguments* for the existence of God, but there are, nonetheless, valid *rational grounds* for believing in His existence. Naturalists are right in rejecting the arguments for the existence of God but wrong in denying His reality; theists are right in affirming the reality of God but wrong in insisting that His reality is capable of proof.

Strictly speaking, it is not possible to *prove* the reality of anything. Reality manifests itself to us, or it does not. Only in the former case is it possible for us to know it. One cannot even prove the reality of the physical world, as the futile discussions between realists and phenomenalists over this very question show. Solipsism is the only consistent alternative to a direct cognition of the reality of that which manifests itself to us as real.

Few philosophers who have addressed themselves to the realist-phenomenalist controversy have realized, I suspect, that their reflections concerning that problem are intimately related to the question of our knowledge of the reality of God. But they are. The root question, in both cases, is, How do we cognize *reality*? How do we get beyond perception and feeling to an awareness of the reality of that which seems to lie behind them? The solution to both the realist-phenomenalist controversy and the problem of the reality of God depends on the answer to these questions.

The chief obstacle to satisfactorily resolving these and a number of other related problems is the very limited (and limiting) concept of *reason* that prevails in our culture at the present time. In the great classical tradition of Western philosophy—and I include all the major figures from the Golden Age of Greek philosophy down to and including the German Idealists of the nineteenth century—reason was conceived as the structure of the conscious self by virtue of which man is able to both grasp and shape reality. It is one and the same reason, according to this view, that seeks to know the true, to love the good, and to appreciate the beautiful. Human beings, it is evident, relate to their world in a variety of ways, each qualitatively different from the others: they know (cognition), they feel (emotion), they appreciate (taste), they strive (conation), they act (practice). Reason, in the classical view, is the ground and locus of all these; it expresses the unity of the self even as it acknowledges the multiplicity of its relations to the world.

In our culture, however, this concept of reason has been lost. Reason is regarded by most people today simply as the human capacity for *reasoning*. Its function is conceived to be purely cognitive, and all the other functions formerly assigned to reason are, therefore, judged to be "irrational." Feelings, it is alleged, may be appropriate or inappropriate, but they cannot be rational; acts may be discreet or indiscreet, but they cannot be right or wrong (consistent with or contrary to right reason). Even in its cognitive function, the scope of reason has been radically narrowed. To espouse a moral or aesthetic value is no longer regarded as an instance of cognition, but simply as the expression of a private taste. The whole business of reason, according to this view, is to attain scientific knowledge, and what is not scientific knowledge is not considered knowledge at all. It is, in other words, irrational.

If any culture were absolutely consistent in maintaining this view, the consequences would be truly appalling. The outstanding characteristics of such a culture would be an impressive degree of technical competence, that is, an ability to do an enormous variety of things exceedingly well, and a complete lack of conviction as to whether any of these things are really worth doing. People in such a culture would be (as F. Scott Fitzgerald once described himself) like a little boy alone in a big house, who, now that he was free to do anything, suddenly discovered that there was nothing he wanted to do. All of human life, on such a view, would be made up of technical knowledge and totally irrational feelings and inclinations. Such technical knowledge could not even include a knowledge of the reality of the world toward which it is supposedly directed.

Fortunately, no culture, not even ours, has been absolutely consistent in maintaining this view; but ours has gone far in this direction. We are more than a little embarrassed about espousing values that cannot be defended "scientifically." We are reluctant to engage in public discussion of issues that do not admit of clear-cut factual answers—issues such as the responsible use of atomic power or the obligations of industrialized nations toward underdeveloped countries.

No argument for the existence of God can be successful, for argument does not belong to the level of reason where the reality of God is manifest. Argument belongs to the level of "technical" or "scientific" reason; it can take us no further. On this point, naturalism is right. But then, without making some gratuitous assumptions, no argument for the existence of anything else can succeed either. If we are to know of the reality of anything, reality must disclose itself to us; there is no other way.

Our knowledge of the reality of God might be described as "nontechnical," "nondiscursive," "nonargumentative," or even "nonscientific"—but not as "nonrational." Too much of what is of value in human life belongs to the deeper levels of reason to allow scientific reason alone to determine what is rational and what is not. That scientific reason is and must be supreme in its own sphere is an important truth that was established only after a long and bitter struggle (witness the experience of Galileo). That the sphere of scientific reason is limited is also an important truth, however, one our culture is dangerously close to forgetting. The penalty for ignoring the former was the temporary retardation of the progress of modern science, and that was most unfortunate. But the penalty for forgetting the latter would be an overwhelming sense of the futility of life, and that, if it occurred, would be disastrous. Man can abide discomfort; but robbed of meaning, he is reduced to nothing.

The Self-Disclosure of God

Material reality manifests itself to us in sense experience. The reality of the tree that I see through my office window is disclosed in the very process by which I see it. I do not first have sense data and then infer that there is something "real" corresponding to them. Investigation, experimentation, and reasoning may tell me much about *what* it is, but they cannot tell me *that* it is. Either its reality is immediately evident to me or I must remain ignorant of it. Scientific reason cannot persuade me of the reality of the tree; indeed, it is only as this reality is given that scientific reason can begin its work.

Human reality manifests itself in *interpersonal communication,* notably in conversation. Scientific reason cannot demonstrate the existence of other minds: this is the inescapable conclusion of the endless discussions of this topic carried on ever since Hume. In love, in friendship, even in our relations with the countless people whose lives barely touch ours, the reality of other rational selves is manifest to us. Here we are more aware, perhaps, of the limitations of scientific reason than in the case of material objects, for we know full well that the richness of a human personality defies exhaustive description. We know, but we sometimes forget.

God manifests Himself to us in the event called *revelation.* I do not mean by this anything odd or unusual—nothing in the way of an "ecstatic vision" or anything of that sort. I mean simply that our longing that life shall have some significance, our desire that the future shall have some hope, and our anxiety over the transitoriness and insecurity of everything that we perceive are somehow overcome. I do not think that any human being is without this experience. There is a need, a longing, an anxiety, a concern, an emptiness in human life. Somehow, from deep within ourselves, these are overcome, the void is filled, and we find courage. This "finding of courage," or "being grasped by meanings," or "being sustained in the conviction of the significance of life" is what I mean by revelation. The source or ground of this experience is what we are talking about when we use the term "God."

Please note that I am not setting forth here another argument for the existence of God. I reject all such arguments, including the argument from religious experience. What I am saying is that at a level of our selves far deeper than that at which reasoning and argumentation occur, God discloses Himself to us. We are, all of us, implicitly aware of the reality of God. We may choose to call this reality by some other name—that is a very trivial matter. Or we may turn away from this deeper dimension of our selves and try to live without meaning and without courage—and that is not a trivial matter.

I have no serious quarrel with the definition of God suggested in the introductory chapter and basically adhered to by the other writers. The reality that is disclosed to us in the way I have described does, indeed, reveal itself as the ground of being and value. There can be little doubt that if and when we are moved to an act of worship, it is this reality that is the intended object of our devotion. But precisely because we are dealing with a reality that is apprehended by reason in its depth rather than by scientific reason, this concept is bound to be obscure. Theology is an attempt, among other things, to make the concept "God" more precise; but the best theologians know that you cannot give this concept scientific precision without robbing it of its deepest meaning. "The heart has its reasons, which reason does not know."[1] The "reasons of the heart" are not blind, irrational emotions. They are a function of reason itself in a dimension vastly more profound than that with which we engage in scientific "reasoning."

This matter of the inevitable obscurity of the concept "God" deserves to be emphasized more than it has been thus far. H. D. Lewis is right when he says:

> the skeptic and agnostic do not so much find themselves unconvinced that in fact there is a God as fail to see what is meant by "God"; and we cannot first tell them what we mean and then proceed to show that God is also real. If they can be induced to see what we mean when we speak of God they will at one and the same time be convinced of His existence . . . [2]

The chief difficulty in acknowledging the reality of God, however, is not the inescapable ambiguity of the concept; rather, it is the fact that in popular religion the concept *has* been made precise, but in an absurdly childish way. Often, people who do not believe in the existence of a Bearded Father somewhere off in space mistakenly think that this constitutes disbelief in the existence of God. But the God who is the ground of being and value, whose reality is manifest to every person in the deepest reaches of the self, bears little or no resemblance to this Celestial Despot of popular fantasy. To deny the reality of the latter is to topple an idol and so to be on the side of God. To seriously deny the reality of the former is impossible.

Another Look at the Arguments

If, now, we look at the traditional arguments from the perspective developed briefly in this chapter, it is not difficult to see why the debate concerning them has been so inconclusive. The critics of the arguments have, quite rightly, found fault with their argumentative form; the supporters of the arguments have defended their implicit meaning. For reasons already given, the arguments cannot succeed *as arguments;* on this point the critics are right. But the arguments do express, albeit inadequately, the awareness of the reality of God that is embedded deep in the consciousness of every human being.

The ontological argument attempts to put this fundamental awareness of the reality of God into a form acceptable to scientific reason.

[1]Blaise Pascal, "Fragment 277," *Pensées* (New York: Everyman's Library, 1932), p. 78.
[2]H. D. Lewis, *Our Experience of God* (London: Allen & Unwin; New York: Macmillan, 1959), p. 44.

It affirms, accordingly, that *the proposition "God exists" is self-evident.* This, as the critics of the ontological argument have pointed out, is not the case; hence, the argument is no good as an argument. But the self-disclosure of God to reason in its depth is not the same thing as the alleged self-evidence of the proposition "God exists." As an argument, the ontological argument is a failure; but the insight that it intends to express in this very inadequte way is both true and important.

The cosmological argument seeks to express this same insight in a slightly different way. The truth of the cosmological argument is that we are aware, in the depth of our selves, of the reality of the ground of our being and of all being. But the cosmological argument distorts this fundamental insight by attempting to exhibit it to scientific reason as a bit of propositional knowledge that can be gotten by correct syllogistic reason. This, as the critics of the cosmological argument have correctly pointed out, cannot be done; the cosmological argument is no good as an argument. However. the insight that it is attempting to express, and that no argument can adequately express, is both true and important.

This insight is most weakly reflected in the teleological argument, which, at least in the form made popular by Paley and other writers in the eighteenth century, almost inevitably conjures up the image of an Ultimate Artisan going about the business of making a world. This conception expresses little, if anything, of what is meant by the concept "God." Often, when we look upward on a starry night, there is, indeed, a sense of mystery, which is probably best understood as a momentary heightening of our awareness of the reality of the ground of all being. But very little of this sense of mystery carries over into the teleological argument itself. People who find the teleological argument impressive are not usually convinced by the argument as such. They respond to it because it directs their consideration to certain features of the universe that tend to enhance the awareness of God that all human beings have. If the argument does this for some people, to that extent it is of value; but its value is that of poetry, not logic.

Former Harvard President Nathan M. Pusey once said, "It would seem to me that the finest fruit of serious learning should be the ability to speak the word God without reserve or embarrassment, certainly without adolescent resentment; rather with some sense of communion, with reverence and with joy."[3] To do this, we must rid ourselves of concepts and images that make God into a thing among things, whose existence is accordingly open to question. Even our secular age knows, though it does not acknowledge, that there is a depth of reason and of reality. Without this awareness there would be no sense of worth, of destiny, or of hope. When we learn that it is at this level of

---

[3]Nathan M. Pusey, *The Age of the Scholar* (Cambridge, Mass.: Harvard Universtiy Press, 1963), p. 145.

our being that the reality of God is manifest, perhaps we shall learn once again "to speak the word God without reserve or embarrassment ... ; rather with some sense of communion, with reverence and with joy."

STUDY QUESTIONS

1. How does the author of this chapter propose to overcome "the impasse between theists and naturalists concerning the problem of the existence of God"?
2. What exactly is the distinction drawn in this chapter between *arguments* and *rational grounds*?
3. What do you make of the discussion of the various dimensions of reason? Is it true that there is a tendency today to limit reason to what is here called "scientific reason"? Are you persuaded by the suggestion that there are dimensions of reason other than the "scientific"?
4. Is it correct to say that existence is not capable of demonstration —that either we must recognize it directly or else be ignorant of it? Is this true, for example, of our knowledge of the existence of physical objects? of other minds?
5. What does the author of this chapter mean by "revelation"? Is this, in fact, another argument for the existence of God?
6. Is there, as this writer affirms, an analogy between this problem and the realist-phenomenalist controversy?

CORRELATED READINGS[1]

1. Anselm of Canterbury. "The Ontological Argument." *Proslogion,* in *Anselm,* trans. Sidney Norton Deane. Chicago: Open Court Publishing Co., 1903, Chap. II–IV. The original formulation of this famous argument.
2. Gaunilon of Marmoutier. "In Behalf of the Fool." S. N. Deane, *op. cit.* pp. 145–53. A critique of the ontological argument by a contemporary of St. Anselm.
3. Anselm of Canterbury. "Reply to Gaunilon." S. N. Deane, *op. cit.,* pp. 153–70. An elaboration and defense of the original argument.
4. Aquinas, St. Thomas. "The Five Ways." *Summa Theologica,* Part I, Ques. II, Art. 3. Five proofs of the existence of God.
5. Hume, David. "The Teleological Argument." *Dialogues Concerning Natural Religion,* Part II. A devastating critique of the teleological argument.
6. Pascal, Blaise. "It Is Reasonable to Wager That God Exists." *Pensées,* Fragment 233. A mathematician's substitute for a proof of the existence of God.
7. Freud, Sigmund. "Theism Is an Illusion." *The Future of an Illusion,* tran. James Strachey. New York: Norton, 1975, Chap. VI. Freud's explanation of why belief in God persists, notwithstanding the absence of a convincing proof.

FOR FURTHER READING

Alston, William P. "The Ontological Argument Revisited," *The Philosophical Review,* 69 (1960), 454–474.

Bowker, John. *The Sense of God: Sociological, Anthropological, and Psychological Approaches to the Origin of the Sense of God.* Oxford: Clarendon Press, 1973.

Brown, Patterson. "St. Thomas' Doctrine of Necessary Being," *The Philosophical Review,* 73 (1964), 76–90.

Devine, P. E. "Does St. Anselm Beg the Question?" *Philosophy,* 50 (1975), 271–81. Argues that St. Anselm does not beg the question.

Ducasse, C. J. *A Philosophical Scrutiny of Religion.* New York: Ronald Press, 1953.

Ebersole, Frank B. "Whether Existence is a Predicate," *The Journal of Philosophy,* 60 (1963), 509–524.

Ewing, A. C. *The Fundamental Questions of Philosophy.* New York: Macmillan, 1951, Chap. 11.

Ewing, A. C. *Value and Reality, The Philosophical Case for Theism.* London: Allen and Unwin, 1973. Argues for the possibility of an intuitive knowledge of the existence of God.

---

[1]*Concise Readings in Philosophy,* Part V.

Flew, Antony. *God and Philosophy.* London: Hutchinson, 1966. Detailed critique of arguments for theism.

Harris, E. E. *Revelation Through Reason.* London: Allen & Unwin, 1959.

Harrison, C. "Totalities and the Logic of First Cause Arguments," *Philosophy and Phenomenological Research,* 35 (1974–75), 1–19.

Hartshorne, Charles. *Anselm's Discovery: Re-examination of the Ontological Proof of God's Existence.* LaSalle, Ill.: Open Court Publishing Co., 1966.

—————. *The Logic of Perfection and Other Essays in Neoclassical Metaphysics.* LaSalle, Ill.: Open Court Publishing Co., 1962.

—————, and W. L. Reese. *Philosophers Speak of God.* Chicago: University of Chicago Press, 1963 (paperbound).

Hawkins, D. J. B. *The Essentials of Theism.* London: Sheed and Ward, 1949.

Hick, John. "God as Necessary Being," *The Journal of Philosophy,* 57 (1960), 725–734.

Hurlbutt, Robert H. *Hume, Newton and the Design Argument.* Lincoln: University of Nebraska Press, 1966.

Jack, Henry. "A Recent Attempt to Prove God's Existence," *Philosophy and Phenomenological Research,* 25 (1965), 575–579.

Kant, Immanuel. *Critique of Pure Reason,* trans. by Norman Kemp Smith. New York: St. Martin's Press, 1965 (paperbound). See section entitled, "The Ideal of Pure Reason."

Kenny, Anthony. *The Five Ways: St. Thomas Aquinas' Proofs of God's Existence.* London: Routledge and Kegan Paul, 1969. Detailed analysis by a competent and sympathetic critic.

Leslie, J. "Efforts to Explain All Existence," *Mind,* 87 (1978), 181–94. An inconclusive examination of some alternative ways of "explaining all existence."

—————. "God and Scientific Verifiability," *Philosophy,* 53 (1978), 71–9. A defense of the teleological argument against several common criticisms of that argument.

Lewis, H. D. *Our Experience of God.* London: Allen & Unwin; New York: Macmillan, 1959.

McIntyre, John. *St. Anselm and His Critics.* Edinburgh, Scot.: Oliver and Boyd, 1954.

Malcolm, Norman. "Anselm's Ontological Arguments," *The Philosophical Review,* 69 (1960), 41–62.

Martin, C. B. *Religious Belief.* Ithaca, N.Y.: Cornell University Press, 1959.

Mascall, E. L. *Existence and Analogy.* London: Longmans, Green, 1949.

Mavrodes, George I. (ed.). *The Rationality of Belief in God.* Englewood Cliffs, N.J.: Prentice-Hall, 1970.

Mill, John Stuart. *Three Essays on Religion.* New York: Henry Holt, 1874.

Paley, William. *Evidences of the Existence and Attributes of the Deity.* Many editions. Originally published in 1802.

Plantinga, A. *God and Other Minds.* Ithaca, N.Y.: Cornell University Press, 1967. A study of the rational justification of belief in God.

Plantinga, A. (ed.). *The Ontological Argument from St. Anselm to Contemporary Philosophers.* Garden City, N.Y.: Doubleday, 1965 (paperbound).

Reichenbach, B. R. *The Cosmological Argument: A Reassessment.* Springfield, Ill.: Charles C. Thomas, 1972. Sympathetic to this type of argument.

Rowe, W. L. *The Cosmological Argument.* Princeton, N.J.: Princeton University Press, 1975. A detailed analysis of the argument and a defense of the argument against some common criticisms.

Shepherd, J. J. *Experience, Inference, and God.* London: Macmillan, 1975. Defends a type of cosmological argument.

Shrader, K. S. "A Critique of Freud's Philosophy of Religion," *Philosophy Today,* 19 (1975), 213–227. An analysis of what the author calls the "Linus-Blanket Theory" of religious belief.

Smart, Ninian. *Philosophers and Religious Truth.* New York: Macmillan, 1970 (paperbound).

————. *Reasons and Faiths.* New York: Humanities Press, 1958.

Smith, J. E. *The Analogy of Experience.* New York: Harper & Row, 1973. A point of view somewhat similar to the last chapter in this unit.

Taylor, R. *With Heart and Mind.* New York: St. Martin's Press, 1973. Again, somewhat similar to the last chapter in this unit.

Tillich, Paul. *Systematic Theology,* vol. 1. Chicago: University of Chicago Press, 1951, pp. 204–235.

Torrance, Thomas F. *God and Rationality.* New York: Oxford University Press, 1971.

PART VI

THE PROBLEM OF EVIL

24

GOD AND EVIL

Shortly before his death, Robert F. Kennedy published a book, bearing the title *To Seek a Better World,* in which he discussed various programs that he believed should be adopted in order to cure some of the major ills of society. Ironically, Senator Kennedy himself fell victim to the violence that has been one of the characteristic ills of recent years, and the search for a better world was left to others.

Can you and I not imagine a better world than the one we know? Surely we can. We can imagine a world, for example, in which there would be no illness, no suffering, no starvation, no violence, no death. In such a world, parents would not have to stand helplessly by as the bodies of their children waste away under the onslaught of some dread disease, nor would children be left homeless and orphaned, innocent victims of the ravages of war. There would be no earthquakes, no hurricanes, no floods in such a world, for nature would be congenial to human life. And the Kennedy brothers and Martin Luther King, Jr., would not have been cut down in the prime of life by the bullets of assassins. Every time we support a "cause," every time we seek constructive change—whether we seek a cure for cancer, try to find a solution to poverty, work for improved government, long for peace—we are affirming our belief in the possibility of a better world.

No doubt, if a group of us were to discuss this matter thoroughly we would disagree, in some respects, about what would constitute an "ideal" world. You might insist, for example, that everyone in the world should subscribe to the principles of a certain political party, or the creed of a certain church—and I might very well contend with you on this. Or you might be willing to allow certain lifestyles that someone else feels should not be tolerated in an "ideal" world. We are, after all, amateurs in the art of world-making, and some disagreement is to be expected. Certainly, however, we can agree that the things we have enumerated above—illness, suffering, starvation, violence, death— would not exist in an "ideal" world, and that one who works to eradicate these things from human life—one who visits the sick, or feeds the hungry, or comforts the suffering, or works for peace, or restores life to those who are dying—is doing a good work. In this respect, surely, we would be in agreement about what would constitute a perfect world.

In whatever degree the world is less than perfect, to that degree the world is "evil." Evil is that which takes the place of a good that can be conceived to exist, but that cannot come into being unless the evil is destroyed. Evil is to good as illness is to health, hunger to satiety, death to life. Let all evil be destroyed, and this would be a perfect world.

Evil as a Problem

The problem of evil arises for any world view that affirms that the universe is constituted in such a way that we might reasonably expect that it would contain no evil. If the universe is the result of the mind- less working of purely natural forces, as naturalism affirms, then it is not surprising that the world is the way it is. If, however, the universe as we know it is the creation of a God who is all-knowing, all-powerful, and all-good, then it *is* surprising that there is evil in the world; for one would expect that such a God, if He is going to create a world at all, would create a *good* one. Indeed, one would expect Him to create a perfect world, a world containing no evil of any kind.

The dilemma facing the theist may be stated as follows. According to traditional theism, all of the following statements are true:

1. God is perfectly good.
2. God's power is unlimited (that is, He is omnipotent).
3. God is all-knowing (omniscient).
4. God is the sole creator of everything that exists.
5. There is evil in the world.

Note that if any one of these statements is held to be false, the problem disappears. If, for example, one denies that God is perfectly good, then the occurrence of evil can be understood as a consequence of God's willing it to exist. If one denies that God's power is unlimited, then God can be absolved of responsibility for evil on the ground that He did His best. If God's omniscience is denied, He can be excused on grounds of ignorance. If He is only a *co*creator of the world, then perhaps evil can be attributed to the other creator(s) (though this apparently entails a denial of God's goodness, omniscience, or omnipotence as well). And finally, if one denies that there really is evil in the world, there is nothing left to be explained.

David Hume once put the theist's dilemma like this: "Is God willing to prevent evil, but not able? then is he impotent. Is he able but not willing? then is he malevolent. Is he both able and willing? whence then is evil?"[1] Can the apparent fact of evil in the world be reconciled with belief in a creator who is perfect in goodness, knowledge, and power? That is the problem with which we shall be concerned in the present section.

The technical name for an essay or treatise that attempts to achieve such a reconciliation is *theodicy.* A number of theodicies have been written by such writers as St. Augustine, Leibnitz, and F. R. Tennant. Chapter 25, "The Exoneration of God," summarizes the principal arguments usually put forward by theodocists. The following chapter, "A Skeptical Rejoinder," subjects these arguments to a critical analysis and concludes that they are unsuccessful.

Solutions Not Open to Theists

Before turning to a consideration of the principal attempts by theists to reconcile the apparent contradiction between their theological beliefs and the apparent fact of evil, it may be useful to review two philosophically interesting "solutions" to this problem that are not available to the theist.

The first of these is the solution offered by Plato. In his great creation myth *Timaeus,*[2] Plato depicts the originator of the material world as a divine Craftsman who makes the ordered universe out of preëxisting matter according to a plan, or "blueprint," of a perfect world. The Craftsman, says Plato, is perfectly good. His desire in making the world is to create an absolutely perfect world, one in which there will be no evil of any kind. If He could succeed in making the material world according to this plan, it would, in fact, be a perfect world. Why, then, is there evil in the world? Because, says Plato, the matter with which the Craftsman has to work contains a certain resistance to order which He cannot wholly overcome. God did the best He could, says Plato—no evil that exists is to be ascribed to Him—but His best was simply not sufficient to mold a recalcitrant matter into an altogether perfect world. Thus, there is evil in the world.

Such an explanation of evil is, of course, not acceptable to a theist for at least two reasons. First, it denies the omnipotence of God, for according to traditional theism, God can do anything that does not

[1]David Hume, *Dialogues Concerning Natural Religion,* ed. Henry D. Aiken (New York: Hafner, 1957), p. 66.
[2]See B. Jowett (ed.), *The Dialogues of Plato* (New York: Random House, 1937), Vol. II, pp. 13–14.

imply a contradiction. Second, it assumes that matter is itself eternal (or at any rate, not a product of God's creative activity), and thus denies that God is "Creator of heaven and earth, and of all things visible and invisible" (Nicene Creed).[3] Indeed, from the point of view of traditional theism, this account is objectionable in yet another way, for the plan according to which Plato's Craftsman is said to have formed the world is also independent of the Craftsman; it is a preëxisting plan that the Craftsman, like a builder who is not his own architect, must follow as best he can.

Another philosophically interesting explanation of evil is that offered by an ancient Persian religion called Zoroastrianism (also known as Zarathustrianism), according to which the world as we know it is the joint creation of a good deity (Ahura Mazda) and an evil deity (Angra Mainyu). All that is good in the world is due to the former, all that is evil, to the latter. Every human life is a battleground for the struggle between these two deities, which is to say, the struggle between good and evil. In the end, according to Zoroastrianism, the evil deity will be conquered, and evil will be destroyed forever; but in the meantime, life and history must be lived out in a world where good and evil are intermingled in countless ways.

Although to some people this account could be made quite acceptable by the simple expedient of substituting the more familiar names Jehovah and Satan for Ahura Mazda and Angra Mainyu, it requires but little reflection to see that it cannot be reconciled with traditional theism, for roughly the same reason that Plato's account is unacceptable to theism. If God is conceived as the Creator of everything that exists, then it is no more acceptable to affirm the existence "from the beginning" of an evil deity (whatever be his name) than it is to affirm the eternal existence of a recalcitrant matter. Moreover, if God is, indeed, infinite in power, there does not seem to be any reason for Him to delay until some unknown (but presumably remote) future date the final overthrow of evil.

In the final analysis, then, Platonism and Zoroastrianism both explain the existence of evil by affirming an ultimate ethical dualism. God is thereby relieved of responsibility for evil in the world—and of the possibility of being proclaimed omnipotent and Creator of everything that is.

Whatever may be said in favor of ethical dualism as an explanation of the existence of evil, therefore, it is evident that such an explanation is not acceptable to theism. Hume's taunt remains: Is God both able and willing to prevent evil? Whence then is evil? Let us see how a theist might attempt to take up this challenge, and how a critic might respond to such an attempt.

---

[3]The Nicene Creed is one of three ancient creeds of the Christian church (the other two being the Apostles Creed and the Athanasian Creed). It dates from the Council of Constantinople, held in A.D. 381.

STUDY QUESTIONS

1. What is the meaning of the term "evil"? What characteristic(s) must something have in order to be properly described as evil?
2. What, exactly, is the *problem* of evil? For whom does this problem arise? For whom does it not arise?
3. What is Plato's solution to the problem of evil? Why is it not acceptable to a theist?
4. What is the Zoroastrian solution to the problem? Why is it not acceptable to a theist?
5. What is a "theodicy"?

25

THE EXONERATION OF GOD

That there is evil in the world obviously constitutes a serious problem for theism, for it does, indeed, appear to be a contradiction to say that our imperfect world is the creation of a God who is perfect in knowledge and power and goodness. The contradiction might be stated thus:

> If God is perfect in knowledge, power, and goodness, then any work that He performs or has performed will be altogether good.
> This universe is a work that God has performed, but it is not altogether good.
> Nonetheless, God is perfect in knowledge, power, and goodness.

How shall we resolve the contradiction? Shall we deny the first premise? That does not seem very promising, for one would then be in the position of asserting that God directly and knowingly causes evil. Shall we deny the second premise? It appears that we cannot do that either, for it merely affirms that the universe is God's creation, and that there is evil in it. How then can we avoid drawing the conclusion that God must be lacking in knowledge, power, or goodness?

Apparent Evil and Real Evil

The first observation that I wish to make is that *some things that we call evil are merely things that are not to our liking.* In some respects we are all like the little child who cries bitterly because its mother will not allow it to have everything it wants. We desire something and count it an evil that other people possess it and we do not. Or we desire to do something—to play tennis, let us say—and we count it an evil that the weather does not cooperate. Much of our muttering about evil is nothing more than the tantrum behavior of God's spoiled children.

Some philosophers have gone so far as to say that *everything* that we call evil is, rightly considered, simply that which is contrary to our wishes. "The perfection of things," said Spinoza, "is to be reckoned only from their own nature and power; things are not more or less perfect, according as they delight or offend human senses, or according as they are serviceable or repugnant to mankind."[1] One suspects, however, that the victims of Auschwitz or Hiroshima or My Lai might find this view a bit difficult to swallow.

We who would "justify the ways of God to man," as John Milton put it, must be careful that in our great concern to exonerate God we do not become insensitive to the reality of pain and suffering in the world. There is evil in the world, and our clear duty as human beings is to help bear the burden of those who suffer evil, and to do all in our power to eliminate it. Yet, we should recognize that some things perceived as evil are not really so, but are simply the consequence of our desiring more in the way of pleasure or possessions than it is reasonable for us to expect.

Evil as an Instrumental Good

Second, I would observe that *some things that are indeed evil in and of themselves are, nonetheless, productive of a good that could not have been produced in any other way.* We clearly recognize this principle in the case of surgery: the pain experienced by the patient, considered simply as an instance of suffering on the part of a sentient creature, is certainly evil; but it is an evil that is willingly endured because it is a means to a good end, that is, healing and health.

What I am suggesting, then, is that evil may play a role in the total economy of the universe analogous to the role of pain in the process of surgery. The patience that comes through enduring hardship over a long period of time, the joy that accompanies the achievement of a long-sought goal—these would not be possible in the absence of all difficulty and want. It is not unthinkable that God in His infinite wisdom should have allowed some evil in the world so that He might use it for man's moral training and, thus, for his ultimate good.

Evil as a Logical Corollary of Good

Third, I would point out that *some things that are indeed evil are logical corollaries of certain goods.* Consider, for example, the virtues

---

[1]Benedict Spinoza, *Ethics,* Appendix to Part I, in *The Rationalists* (Garden City: Doubleday, undated), p. 215.

of compassion, sympathy, and generosity. A world having these qualities is clearly better than one devoid of them. Yet, these virtues would be nonexistent in a world in which there was no pain, no suffering, no want of any kind.

The point, of course, must not be overdrawn. There is obviously much suffering, much want, much sorrow, that does not call forth any such corollary sentiment or act of love. Moreover, it is extremely difficult to say what measure of, say, compassion would morally compensate for a given quantity of want or pain. All I wish to suggest is that there are some undoubted goods that could not exist without the correlative evils. It is quite possible that a world lacking those goods *and* evils would, in fact, be poorer than the world as it is.

Evil as a Consequence of Human Actions

A more profound understanding of the occurrence of evil in the world begins, however, when we recognize that *much of the evil in the world is a result of human actions, and could have been prevented by God only at the price of making us all automata.* Consider for a moment how much of what we normally regard as evil in the world is accounted for by (a) individual human acts of cruelty, (b) war, and (c) manmade social structures and customs that enable the strong to oppress the weak. If we, who are so quick to point an accusing finger at God, could only eliminate from this world the evil that *we ourselves* do, the evil that would remain to be explained would be but a fraction of that which we now observe.

It is, of course, true that God could have prevented all the evil attributable to human beings had He simply made them incapable of doing evil. Such creatures, however, would hardly be worthy of being called human, for they would be like the lower animals in that they would do everything by necessity rather than by free choice. And the universe, which would then be rid of all the evil that is now caused by human beings, would lack those remarkable beings who are certainly the crowning glory of God's creation by virtue of the fact that they can *freely choose* to do the good.

Consider a simple analogy. As a parent, I desire that my son should be spared as much pain and sorrow as possible when he goes out into the world. Now, it would be theoretically possible for me (though admittedly grotesque) to protect him from whatever dangers may await him out in the world by literally *imprisoning* him in my home, and perhaps "brainwashing" him from childhood to believe that life within the confines of one small house is quite enough for him. But though my son would in this way be spared some things that might indeed be painful and unpleasant, no one in his right mind would approve of my treating him in this way. Why? Because it is the universal judgment of humankind that to be deprived of one's freedom— even the freedom to be hurt—is an incomparable loss, and that freedom with its concomitant dangers is preferable to the kind of safety that can be purchased only at the price of giving up one's freedom. I demonstrate my love for my son, not by absolutely preventing him from being harmed, but by giving him his freedom in the hope that he will use it in ways that prove to be for his good.

If it is granted that the creation of beings capable of doing either good or evil is consistent with belief in a God who is perfect in knowledge, power, and goodness, then it is possible to extend the same reasoning to account for *all* evil in the world, not just that directly attributable to man. For according to a very ancient teaching, the whole creation as we know it is "fallen" from its original perfect state, and all the evil that we observe is a result of its fallenness. The precise nature of this fall from an original perfection is admittedly a mystery, and I shall not pretend to be able to trace every example of evil in the world to a specific aspect of the rebellion against the Creator that is the essence of the idea of the fall. To one who is sincerely seeking a solution to the agonizing problem of evil, however, the doctrine of the fall is a highly plausible and strangely comforting doctrine. Indeed, it is, in the last analysis, the only possible explanation of why there is evil in a creation that was once pronounced "very good" by its Creator.

The Best of All Possible Worlds

The proposition that we must finally defend if we would convincingly exonerate God of blame for the evil in the world is the proposition that this is the best of all possible worlds. God could have willed not to create any world at all, in which case He alone—He who is infinitely good—would exist. Or, He could have created any one of an infinite number of possible worlds which He did not in fact create. Undoubtedly among those possible worlds that God chose not to create are some that would have been free of everything that we call evil. Why, then, did God choose to create this world, knowing (as He must have known) that it would contain much evil? The only possible answer is that of all the worlds He might have created, the one He did create—this one —contains more total good than any other world that He could have created. "The best plan," as Leibnitz said, "is not always that which seeks to avoid evil, since it may happen that *the evil be accompanied by a greater good.*"[2]

It is, of course, easy for us to sit back smugly and say (in the spirit of Voltaire), "How can this be the best of all possible worlds when it contains such horrors as Auschwitz and My Lai? Even I can imagine a better world than that!" The problem is that we *cannot* really imagine a better world than that *because we do not know all the ways that God would have had to alter the design of the world in order to ensure that such things did not occur.* We are all Monday-morning quarterbacks when it comes to the game of world-making.

Consider, for example, the assassination of President Kennedy. I do

---

[2]Gottfried W. Leibnitz, *The Philosophical Works of Leibnitz*, trans. George M. Duncan (New York: Tuttle, Morehouse and Taylor, 1890), p. 195.

not deny that this was an evil thing, for the violent death of a human being whenever it occurs is a tragedy that mars the perfection of the world. Undoubtedly, in my view, God in His Omniscience knew "from the beginning" that this tragedy was going to occur, and could, in fact, have created the world in such a way that it would not occur. But what would God have had to do in order to prevent it? It is impossible for us to say. Perhaps, as I suggested earlier, He would have had to deprive all men of their freedom in order to prevent a Lee Harvey Oswald from exercising his freedom with such tragic consequences. Or perhaps, like a celestial Superman who always manages to deflect the bullet before it reaches its intended target, He would have had to personally intervene whenever misused human freedom was about to produce some evil result—with the further consequence, perhaps, that people would never learn to use their freedom responsibly, since God would always be seeing to it that no matter what they did, things turned out right.

Now, to say that we would prefer a world without freedom or a world with a "Divine Intervener" to the world as it actually is would be simply naïve, not because we positively know that such a world would be inferior to the world as it is, but precisely because we do *not* have a sufficient knowledge of what such a world would be like to say that it would be preferable to this one. It certainly appears that such a world would be inferior to the actual world at least in this, that it would lack some of the undoubted goods that this world clearly does contain; but that is not the point I am chiefly trying to make. The main point is that the concept of an alternative world is so complex that we can never know whether the difference that we glibly say we would prefer, *together with all the other differences that this would entail in the infinitely complex system of the world,* would yield a world that would, in fact, be preferable to the world as it is.

The Contradiction Revisited

Returning now to the apparent contradiction with which we began, it is evident that the thrust of our argument is to challenge the assertion that "if God is perfect in knowledge, power, and goodness, then any work that He performs or has performed will be altogether good." We have argued, rather, that any work that God performs will be productive of a greater *total* good than any alternative work that He might have performed. In order to show God blameworthy for the evil in the world, therefore, a critic would have to describe in complete detail an alternative world, a possible world, containing more total good than we find in the world as it actually is. It seems to me that this is, in principle, impossible, both because of the limitations of our knowledge of the world and because we cannot predict how much good will yet emerge in the infinite future that is revealed to us but one moment at a time; from which it follows that no one can ever be in a position to criticize God for making the world the way He did.

STUDY QUESTIONS

1. "Everything that we call evil is, rightly considered, simply that which is contrary to our wishes." Attack or defend this statement.

2. Is God "exonerated" to the extent that some evil can be shown to be a necessary condition of the existence of some good? Defend your answer.

3. Is it true that a world in which there are human beings who exhibit the virtues of compassion, sympathy, and generosity is better than one in which no such qualities would be present? What relevance does your answer have for the controversy concerning the problem of evil?

4. "The creation of beings capable of doing either good or evil is consistent with belief in a God who is perfect in knowledge, power, and goodness." Attack or defend this statement.

5. Theodicist argues that, contrary to what might appear to be the case, we cannot, in fact, imagine a better world than the one that actually exists. Summarize his argument in support of this proposition.

26

A SKEPTICAL REJOINDER

As I read Theodicist's "exoneration" I was reminded of a famous passage in David Hume's *Dialogues Concerning Natural Religion* in which Philo (a principal spokesman in the *Dialogues*) likens the world to a house or palace so ill-planned that "there [is] not one apartment convenient or agreeable." Now, it simply would not do in such a case, says Philo, for the architect to point out that if this or that feature of the structure were altered, even greater ills would result. Philo continues:

> What [the architect] says may be strictly true: the alteration of one particular, while the other parts of the building remain, may only augment the inconveniences. But still you would assert in general that, if the architect had had skill and good intentions, he might have formed such a plan of the whole, and might have adjusted the parts in such a manner as would have remedied all or most of these inconveniences.[1]

Philo expresses precisely my own sentiments as I prepare to respond to the arguments of the preceding chapter. I concede that the problem is more complex than it might initially appear to be. Before one considers the matter carefully, one is, indeed, inclined to say that it is self-evident that the occurrence of evil in the world is inconsistent with belief in a God who is perfect in knowledge, power, and goodness. Theodicist's arguments at least succeed in destroying this illusion of self-evidence. But do they really succeed in "exonerating" God of blame for the evil that is in the world? I think they do not. Let me explain why.

---

[1]David Hume, *Dialogues Concerning Natural Religion,* ed. Henry D. Aiken (New York: Hafner, 1957), p. 72.

Moral Evil and Natural Evil

Philosophers who are concerned with the problem of evil often make a distinction—an important one for our purposes—between *moral* evil and *natural* evil. Any evil that occurs as a result of deliberate human doing is termed moral evil. Any evil that occurs as a result of the ordinary working of natural laws is termed natural evil. An act of murder would be a typical example of the former, animal suffering (other than that inflicted by human beings) an example of the latter. There is nothing difficult about this distinction, and everyone can easily supply additional examples of both types from his or her own knowledge and experience.

There are, to be sure, instances of evil that appear to be "mixed" evils, that is, both natural and moral in certain respects. Suppose, for example, that a building contractor (perhaps with the collusion of the fire-safety inspector) constructs a building that he knows does not meet certain standards of fire safety, and suppose further that the building is struck by lightning with an ensuing fire that results in serious injury and loss of life. Are the suffering and death in this case instances of natural or of moral evil? The answer appears to be that they are both. The building contractor is culpable because he knowingly subjected the inhabitants of the building to a hazard that he could have and should have prevented, though he did not explicitly will that the building should catch on fire or that his negligence should lead to suffering and death. The occurrence of lightning, however, is a natural phenomenon that sometimes causes suffering and death even in the absence of any negligence such as we have just described, and the fact that human negligence was a contributing factor in this particular case does not prevent this from being an instance of natural evil as well. Again, it would not be difficult to invent, or perhaps recall, numerous additional examples of evils that appear to be the joint product of human negligence or evil-doing and natural occurrences.

For our present purposes, however, we need not be concerned about these instances of mixed (natural and moral) evils. There are plenty of examples of *un*mixed evils of both kinds to support the distinction, and once we have the distinction clearly in mind, we may begin to see what is wrong with Theodicist's account.

God and Moral Evil

Consider first Theodicist's account as it applies to moral evil, which is the kind that he appears to have principally in mind. All such evil, he says, may be understood as a consequence of man's misuse of his God-given freedom. But is not God, then, blameworthy for having made man capable of misusing his freedom in this way? No, says Theodicist, for a world in which there are creatures who have the freedom to choose good *or* evil is intrinsically better than one in which there are no such free creatures, even though the latter world would be free of all moral evil. Indeed, if we are to take Theodicist's second argument seriously, he seems to be suggesting that the occurrence of moral evil is only an episode in the moral training of the human race —that evil is really good in the way that surgery is, because it leads to a good result that could be gotten in no other way.

But I must ask, Is not Theodicist forgetting that the God whose innocence he is trying to establish is supposed to be omnipotent? How, then, can he say that the good things that God is allegedly trying to accomplish by subjecting the world to the "surgery" of evil "could not have been produced in any other way"? If God is omnipotent, then He can do anything that does not imply a contradiction. Why, then, could God not have created human beings *already morally trained,* thus avoiding the horrors of assault and murder and oppression and war and the whole long litany of woes that result from our terrible inhumanity to each other? Where is the contradiction in that? If a surgeon were capable of producing health without subjecting the patient to the pain of surgery, we would not think well of the surgeon if he or she put the patient through the operation anyway. How, then, is God, if He is omnipotent, not blameworthy for subjecting His creatures to the consequences of human cruelty when presumably He could have achieved His end without such terrible means?

Theodicist says that we can never "be in a position to criticize God for making the world the way He did" because we do not know all the ways that God would have had to alter the design of the world in order to ensure that evil did not occur. Note, however, that Theodicist's "moral training" argument posits a world at some future time that *is* better than this world at the present time by virtue of the "moral training" that is supposed to occur between now and then. I admit the ignorance with which Theodicist charges all of us. I confess that I do not know how to alter the system of the world to make it better—less evil—than it is. But God apparently does, for He is using evil (says Theodicist) "for man's moral training and thus for his ultimate good." But why, if He is omnipotent, does He not produce this good result immediately, without all that suffering in between? Why must an omnipotent God act like an irresponsible surgeon?

God and Natural Evil

If Theodicist's arguments fall short of exonerating God with respect to the occurrence of moral evil, they are even less adequate as an attempt to explain the occurrence of natural evil in the world.

Consider, for example, animal suffering. If we pay attention to the terror and the suffering that helpless animals are forced to endure, the history of the evolution of species is one of the most depressing stories imaginable. Think of it! Millions upon millions of sentient creatures were cast forth into a world in which the prevailing law was simply "The fit shall survive for a short time, the unfit shall perish immediately." Countless millions of creatures were able to survive for but a moment in such a hostile world before becoming the prey of other animals whose own survival depended upon using them for food. And if one of them happened to survive, he in turn sought out other animals that were *his* natural prey, and terrorized and killed them even as he would eventually be terrorized and killed by his natural enemies. The present state of affairs in the animal world is just the same: the strong prey upon the weak, species is at war with species, terror and suffering and violent death are the rule rather than the exception.

How do Theodicist's arguments speak to this dimension of the problem? They hardly touch it, so far as I can see. Animal suffering certainly is not something that can be dismissed as a mere "apparent evil" (argument 1). It can hardly be said to make any contribution to man's moral training (argument 2). It is difficult to see what goods might be "corollaries" of such suffering (argument 3). Theodicist must be arguing, then, that animal suffering is somehow a characteristic of a world that is "fallen" from its original state of perfection, and that such suffering is somehow consistent with the idea that this world is nonetheless the best of all *possible* worlds.

I do not want to caricature Theodicist's view of the matter, but, in all honesty, I do not see how it can reasonably be argued that the "law of the jungle," with all the animal suffering that it entails, is a consequence of the "fallenness" of the world, or how that would absolve God of responsibility even if it were the case. It is a basic fact of every ecosystem that *life feeds upon life.* It is only in the poet's imagination that the lion and the lamb live at peace with one another: in the real world, the lion who will not eat an innocent lamb dies of starvation, and the less peace-loving sort live on to propagate the species. In a world capable of sustaining only a finite number (albeit a very large number) of living beings, every living thing is potentially at war with every other living thing. A world "before the fall" in which all of God's creatures lived together in a presumed perfect harmony is a mere figment of pious imagination.

Moreover, even if such a state of affairs could be imagined, there is nothing in Theodicist's account to explain why God is not responsible for the animal suffering that is said to be a feature of the "fallenness" of this world. What has the lamb done to deserve a cruel death in the clutches of a hungry lion? Nothing. What has the lion done to deserve the spear of the man whose lamb he has just killed? Nothing. If the "fall" occurred as a result of human rebellion against God, then it is unjust that animals should suffer the consequences of that fall. And is not He who is reputed to have set the rules for this whole sorry game then guilty of a terrible injustice? Is it not implausible—really implausible—to argue that this world in which most animals (though innocent of any wrongdoing) live a pitifully short life characterized by terror, suffering, and violent death is *the best of all possible worlds?*

Nor is animal suffering by any means the only kind of natural evil that cries out for a better explanation than Theodicist has given us.

Who is reponsible for the famine that is ravaging the inhabitants of central Africa at this very hour? How shall we explain the suffering and death that result from such natural occurrences as hurricanes and earthquakes in a world that is supposed to be the handiwork of a God who is perfect in knowledge, power, and goodness? What account can be given of the occurrence of disease in the best of all possible worlds? We search in vain through all the theodicies that have been written for an answer that will stand the test of careful scrutiny, but always we come away as empty-handed as we began. Evil simply *does not make sense* in a world whose creator is all that God is said to be.

A Choice

We must conclude, therefore, that the fact that there is evil in the world cannot be reconciled with belief in a God who is perfect in knowledge, power, and goodness. If we believe in the existence of God —and in the absence of such a belief we ought to have no interest in this problem—we must reëxamine our concept of God to see if we cannot bring it into conformity with the facts. Can we accept the idea of a God whose knowledge, though great, is limited? Then God may be excused for the evil that is in the world on grounds of ignorance. Can we live with the idea of a God whose power, though great, is less than infinite? Then God may be excused for the evil that is in the world on the ground that He did the best He could—and we may dare to hope that in the very long run evil will be overcome. These, it would appear, are our only alternatives, for it would hardly be exculpatory to suggest that there is evil in the world because God's goodness is limited. He who would believe in God in a world such as ours must, therefore, choose between a God who is limited in knowledge and one who is limited in power. Or else he must live with the recognition that deep within his world view there is a contradiction between his knowledge of the world and his beliefs about God, a contradiction that is and will forever remain unresolved.

STUDY QUESTIONS

1. How does Skeptic propose to distinguish between "moral evil" and "natural evil"? Is this a valid distinction? What relevance, if any, does it have for the discussion of the problem of evil?
2. Skeptic asks, "Why must an omnipotent God act like an irresponsible surgeon?" Translate this rhetorical question into an argument against Theodicist's position.
3. Does Theodicist's argument provide a way to account for animal suffering? disease? natural disasters? Are these unexplainable evils, as Skeptic implies?
4. "He who would believe in God in a world such as ours must . . . choose between a God who is limited in knowledge and one who is limited in power." Is this correct? If not, what are the remaining alternatives?

CORRELATED READINGS[1]

1. Augustine of Hippo. St. "God and Evil." *Confessions,* Book VII, Chaps. V, XII–XVI. St. Augustine relates the story of his own struggle to solve the problem of evil.

2. Spinoza, Benedict. "Good and Evil." *Short Treatise on God, Man, and His Well-being,* First Part, Chap. X; and *Ethics,* Part I, Appendix. An account similar to that of St. Augustine.

3. Leibniz, Gottfried Wilhelm. "God Created the Best of All Possible Worlds," "Abridgment to the Theodicy," *The Philosophical Works of Leibniz.* New Haven, Conn.: Tuttle, Morehouse, and Taylor, 1908, pp. 284–285. Leibniz' own summary of the argument of the *Theodicy.*

4. Hume, David. "The Unsolved Problem of Evil." *Dialogues Concerning Natural Religion,* Part X. A thorough discussion of the problem that leaves little doubt that Hume considers it insoluble.

5. Dostoievsky, Fyodor. "The Suffering of Children." *The Brothers Karamazov,* trans. C. Barnett. New York: Grosset & Dunlap, 1900, pp. 266–269. A great novelist struggles with the problem of evil as exemplified in the cruel suffering and death of an innocent child.

6. Tennant, Frederick R. "A Theist's Account of Evil." *Philosophical Theology,* Vol. II. Cambridge, Eng.: Cambridge University Press, 1930, Chap, VII. An attempt at a theodicy by a twentieth-century theist.

FOR FURTHER READING

Adams, Robert Merrihew, "Must God Create the Best?" *The Philosophical Review,* 81 (1972), 317–332.

Ahorn, M. B. *The Problem of Evil.* New York: Schocken Books, 1971. Argues that the problem of evil leaves the existence of God an undecided issue.

Augustine, St. *On Free Will.* Several editions.

————. *The Nature of the Good.* Several editions.

Bayle, Pierre. *Bayle's Historical and Critical Dictionary—Selections,* ed. by Richard Popkin. Indianapolis, Ind.: Bobbs-Merrill, 1965 (paperbound). Contains Bayle's objection to theism based on the problem of evil. Leibnitz seeks to answer Bayle in his theodicy.

Farrer, Austin. *Love Almighty and Ills Unlimited.* Garden City, N.Y.: Doubleday, 1961.

Ferre, Nels. *Evil and the Christian Faith.* New York: Harper & Row, 1947. A defense of theism.

Hick, John. *Evil and the God of Love.* New York: Harper & Row, 1966. From a theistic standpoint.

Lewis, C. S. *The Problem of Pain.* New York: Macmillan, 1962. A readable defense of theism.

---

[1]*Concise Readings in Philosophy,* Part VI.

Madden, E. H., and P. H. Hare. *Evil and the Concept of God.* Springfield, Ill.: Charles C. Thomas, 1968. Critical of theism.

Martin, M. "Is Evil Evidence Against the Existence of God?" *Mind,* LXXXVII (1978), 429–432. Argues, *contra* Pargetter (see below) that it is.

McCloskey, H. J. *God and Evil.* The Hague: Martinus Hijhoff, 1974. Argues that the attempts of theists to reconcile the fact of evil with belief in God are not successful.

————. "God and Evil," *The Philosophical Quarterly,* 10 (1960), 97–114. Argues against the theist's appeal to natural law as a solution to the problem of evil.

Mill, John Stuart. *Three Essays on Religion.* New York: Henry Holt, 1874.

Pargetter, R. "Evil as Evidence Against the Existence of God," *Mind,* LXXXV (1976), 242–245. Argues that the claim that the existence of evil is strong evidence against the existence of God has not been established.

Pike, Nelson (ed.). *God and Evil.* Englewood Cliffs, N.J.: Prentice-Hall, 1964 (paperbound). Contains Pike's reply to Hume.

Plantinga, A. *God, Freedom and Evil.* Grand Rapids, Mich.: Eerdmans, 1978. Argues that the fact of evil does not contradict belief in the existence of God.

————, Adams, R. M., and Rowe, W. L. "God and Possible Worlds," *The Journal of Philosophy,* LXX (1973), 539–555. A discussion of Leibniz' thesis that this is the best of all possible worlds.

Reichenbach, B. "Natural Evils and Natural Laws: A Theodicy for Natural Evils," *International Philosophical Quarterly,* 16 (1976), 179–196. A critique of McCloskey (see above).

Sutherland, S. R. *Atheism and the Rejection of God: Contemporary Philosophy and "The Brothers Karamazov."* Oxford: Blackwell, 1977.

PART VII

MIND AND BODY

27

THE MIND-BODY PROBLEM

Man, it has been said, is a mystery to himself. We know that we are a part of nature, and yet we feel that we stand outside nature as does no other species. We know that we share a common evolutionary heritage with everything on this planet that is alive. Yet we believe that human reality—*Homo sapiens*—is not merely another link in the evolutionary chain but a radically different and higher form of being that cannot be adequately comprehended in the categories appropriate to even the highest forms of nonhuman animal life. Socrates's ancient dictum "Know thyself" identifies a task that human beings apparently can neither avoid nor complete.

This is not, of course, to deny that the *scientific* study of man has achieved impressive results in modern times. We understand a great deal today about the workings of the human organism—about the mechanical and chemical and electrical processes involved in the various systems necessary to human life—that was not understood as recently as two or three decades ago. This new understanding has enabled medical science to achieve astonishing results in the prevention and cure of disease, in the implantation of "borrowed" organs (heart and kidney transplants, for example), and even in the creation of artificial organs. There is certainly every reason to believe that further medical research will continue to enlarge indefinitely our knowledge of the human organism, and will enable us to prolong and restore useful life where at present we are unable to do so.

One of the most puzzling questions that human beings have ever posed about themselves, however, is one that falls outside the scope of biological and medical science. That is the question regarding the relation of *mind* and *body.*

Mental Events and Physical Events

We are all acquainted with a class of events that it seems natural and proper to describe as "mental" events. We know what it is like, for example, to have pleasurable and unpleasurable sensations: a cool shower after a hard day of work provides an example of the former, a dentist's drilling too close to a nerve, an example of the latter. We know, moreover, what it is like to experience *emotions:* love, hate, affection, concern, jealousy, and so on. Certain kinds of activities also appear to be mental, or at least partly mental, such as perceiving, remembering, imagining, deliberating, and inferring. Finally, volition—willing or deciding to do something in preference to something else—is a mental occurrence.

Events of the kinds just mentioned appear to be different in a number of ways from "physical" events. The most obvious apparent difference is that mental events, unlike physical events, are not publicly observable. If I am in pain, for example, nobody but me feels the pain. Other people may, of course, infer that I am in pain from the way I act (I may grimace, cry out, or perhaps clutch the part of my body that has been injured), but they cannot feel the pain that I feel. Indeed, I can fool other people into inferring that I am in pain by going through the motions of someone who is in pain; but I cannot fool myself on this score. Either I feel pain or I do not. It makes no sense to say, "I thought I felt a pain, but I was mistaken." (At this point we need not raise the question of how we are aware of such mental events. The question is worth consideration, but it will come up only incidentally in the discussion that follows. We may observe, however, that the name that some philosophers use for this process by which we appear to be directly aware of our own mental states is *introspection.* We know our own mental states by introspection and the mental states of others, if at all, by inference.)

A second feature of mental events that distinguishes them from physical events is that they cannot properly be said to be locatable in space. With respect to a physical event, it is always meaningful to ask, Where, exactly, did it occur? But with respect to a mental event, such a question (unless it is construed to mean, Where were you when you felt, or decided, thus and so?) has no precise meaning. A volition, an emotion, or a recollection is not the sort of thing that can occur, say, on the sidewalk in front of the White House, about six feet in front of the main gate, whereas an explosion, a collision, a demonstration, or anything else that we would classify as a physical event is.

The differences, most people would say, result from the fact that the subjects of physical events are *bodies,* whereas the subjects of mental events are *minds.* Bodies occupy space and are locatable in space; hence, the events in which they participate are also locatable in space. Minds, however, do not occupy space (they are neither round, nor square, not any other shape, nor do they come in various sizes) and are not, properly speaking, locatable in space; consequently, the events of which they are the subjects are not locatable in space.

What, precisely, is this notion of "mind" (or "consciousness") that is so deeply embedded in the common-sense view of man? It is difficult to say precisely. It involves, certainly, the idea of something that is the subject of what we call mental events—feeling, willing, desiring, thinking, and so forth—and it involves the denial that it can be described in terms of shape or size or other qualities applicable only to bodies. It is evidently closely associated with the brain, but because the brain is locatable in space (and for other reasons) mind is not usually considered identical with brain. It probably does no injustice to the common-sense view to say that each mind is thought to "inhabit" a particular body. In any case, it is clear that each mind is believed to be intimately related in some way or other to some particular body.

We do sometimes use spatial language in talking about certain mental phenomena. We say things like "I can't seem to get this idea *into my head,*" and "Intentions are hard to detect because they occur *in a person's mind* where no one else can see them"; but when we speak in this way, we clearly are using spatial language metaphorically. We could, without altering the meaning of these statements, say instead, "I can't seem to comprehend this idea" and "Intentions are hard to detect because they are mental events and thus not publicly observable." It seems doubtful, in any case, that the common-sense view of the nature of mind would allow that spatial categories are properly applicable to it.

There is something else about body and mind that is a part of the common-sense view, however, and that is that a given mind and the body with which it is associated mutually influence one another. The mental event that we call "seeing a flash of lightning," for example, seems to be related causally to a series of physical events involving an event in the sky, light waves, the optic nerves, and so on. The mental event that I call "feeling a pain" seems to be causally related to (a consequence of) certain physical events occurring in my body: the flame touching my finger, the bee stinging my ear, the dentist drilling my tooth, and so on. To be sure, I cannot always infer a physical event from the mental event of feeling a pain. Some pains are "psychosomatic"; they do not appear to be caused by the organic disturbances that normally cause such pains. In many cases, however, the mental event that we call "feeling a pain" does seem to be caused by a physical event that we might call "receiving an injury"; and this supposition—that some mental events are caused by some physical events—seems clearly to be a part of the common-sense view.

It is also commonly supposed that some causal series run in the opposite direction—that some mental events cause, or at least partly cause, some physical events. At the present moment, for example, I am engaged in writing, which obviously consists of a series of physical (publicly observable) events. But at least part of the cause of my writing now is the fact that some time ago I decided to spend this particular day in this way. Part of the cause of my writing these particular words, this particular sentence, is my desiring (a mental activity) to clarify the point that I am currently trying to make and my thinking (another mental activity) that the activity in which I am currently engaged—writing—offers a suitable example of a series of physical events apparently caused in part by certain antecedent mental events. Our thoughts, our wishes, our decisions—mental events—seem to make a difference in the content and form of our speaking and acting, which are physical events.

These common-sense beliefs about body and mind may be stated in two simple propositions: (1) body and mind are two distinct entities, neither of which can be adequately explained as simply a special form of the other; (2) body and mind are capable, nonetheless, of causally acting on each other. The first proposition states the central thesis of what is called *mind-body dualism*. The second, which presupposes the first, states the central thesis of the view called *interactionism*. Interactionism, then, is simply the technical name for the "plain man's" view regarding the relation of body and mind.

Some Questions Regarding the Common-sense View

To most people, the facts that we have just recounted seem commonplace enough, and for them the mind-body problem never arises. Many philosophers, however, find some features of the common-sense view extremely puzzling chiefly because of (a) the alleged unclarity of our notion of "mind," (b) certain difficulties in the way of knowing that such an entity exists, (c) the difficulty of understanding how there can be causal relations between physical and nonphysical entities, and, more recently, (d) the belief of some philosophers that the interactionist account presupposes metaphysical views that they find unacceptable. The effect of these problems is to raise doubts about the correctness of the common-sense (interactionist) account and subsequently to stimulate a search for a more adequate alternative.

The mind-body problem may be considered in terms of two related questions arising out of the common-sense view: Are body and mind two distinct entities, neither of which can be explained as a form or function of the other? and, How are the apparent two-way causal relations between them to be understood? The first part of the problem calls in question the dualism implicit in the common-sense view. The latter part asks for some explanation of the fact that body and mind appear to be involved in mutual causal relations.

Historically, it was the latter part of this problem that first caught the attention of philosophers; the dualism implicit in the common-sense view was simply taken for granted. During the seventeenth and eighteenth centuries, the question that philosophers debated was, How are we to understand the apparent mutual causation between body and mind? A number of interesting and sometimes far-fetched answers were forthcoming.

René Descartes (1596–1650), whose reflections on the problem really launched the modern discussion, advocated the interactionist view. Body and mind, said Descartes, are radically distinct entities, two different kinds of substances, neither of which is reducible to the other; body is "extended, unthinking substance" and mind is "thinking, unextended substance." Nonetheless, Descartes thought it evident that body and mind interact, and even conjectured that the precise point where this interaction occurs is in the pineal gland—for which, it may be said in his defense, no one had previously found any worthwhile function.

Descartes's successors by and large accepted his dualistic account of man, but some of them found his pineal-gland theory rather unconvincing. A number of alternatives to interactionism were therefore proposed. Gottfried Wilhelm von Leibnitz (1646–1716), for example, advocated a theory known as *parallelism.* Body and mind do not interact, said Leibnitz, but they appear to do so because God has created the world in such a way that there is a perfect "preëstablished harmony" between any given series of mental events and a corresponding series of physical events. Mental events are always caused by prior mental events, and physical events by prior physical events, but thanks to God's thoughtful provision for a perfect harmony between the two kinds of events, the appearance of interaction results. Nicholas de Malebranche (1638–1715), a contemporary of Leibnitz, advocated a special form of parallelism known as occasionalism, which might be described as harmony on the installment plan: God, said Malebranche, did not establish perfect harmony between physical and mental events "in the beginning," but as the occasion arises (presumably rather frequently), He does what needs to be done to keep the two series parallel. The result is the same, except that Malebranche's theory provided for the possibility of a certain kind of freedom for mind that Leibnitz's theory did not. Benedict de Spinoza (1632–1677) advocated what has been called a double aspect theory, the details of which we shall not pause to recount. Suffice it to say that none of these proposals has commended itself to more than a few. It seems safe to conclude that anyone who wishes to maintain the dualism that is inherent in the common-sense view must be prepared to maintain interactionism (mutual causation) as well. In the discussion that follows, in any case, we shall ignore all except the interactionist version of the dualist account.

The Alternatives

Are body and mind two distinct entities, neither of which can be understood as a form or function of the other? There appear to be only three possible answers to this question.

First, it is possible to deny that they are radically distinct and to argue that mind is a determination of matter—that mind is, so to speak, a purely physical phenomenon that is governed by, and explicable according to, the same laws as any other physical phenomenon. Mind, in this view, is not ontologically unique: it is not a "spiritual substance," a nonphysical reality, that acts apart from and independent of the laws of nature. It is a part of nature, a product of nature, and wholly subject to its laws. The collective name for views that attempt to account for the relationship between mind and body in this way is *identity materialism.*

Second, it is possible to take a position just opposite to that of identity materialism—to reject the dualism implicit in the common-sense view, and to argue that body is explicable in terms of mind rather than the reverse. It would be tempting, for the sake of terminological consistency, to call this view "identity mentalism," or something of that sort, but common usage dictates otherwise. We shall, accordingly, refer to this view as *panpsychism.*[1]

Third, it is possible to hold that the common-sense view in this matter is the correct one—that is, to maintain the interactionist position, which we have already described. One must then attempt to show that the interactionist position, with whatever problems it may involve, is nonetheless more believable than either of the other two alternatives.

All three positions have one task in common, however, and that is to give some account of the apparent casual relations between mind and body. Whether we adopt the identity materialist, the panpsychist, or the interactionist position, the problem with which the philosophers of the sixteenth and seventeenth centuries wrestled so unsuccessfully remains a genuine problem that demands some kind of answer.

A Word About Metaphysics

To make any headway with this problem, we are going to have to venture into the rather forbidding area of metaphysics. None of the views we shall be considering really stands by itself: each is integral to a particular metaphysical position and can scarcely be made intelligible apart from the more inclusive view. Identity materialism, for example, is not just one view among many with respect to the mind-body problem. It is the view of humankind, and especially of mind, that is implicit in *monistic materialism,* that is, that the whole of reality consists of matter and its determinations. The panpsychist view of mind and body, on the other hand, is implicit in the broader metaphysical view of *panpsychism.* And interactionism, or at any

---

[1] Strictly speaking, panpsychism is a general metaphysical theory, whereas identity materialism is a theory about the relation between mind and body. There is no parallel term for the panpsychist theory of mind and body, however, so we shall have to use the single term "panpsychism" for both the metaphysical theory and for the theory of mind and body that it entails.

rate the mind-body dualism that it presupposes, is the view of humankind that is implicit in *ontological dualism,* that is, that matter and mind are ontologically distinct and that reality includes both. It is possible to carry on the discussion for a greater or shorter period of time without explicitly bringing in these wider metaphysical views, but they are always hovering in the background when the problem of mind and body is being discussed.

It has been said that the mind-body problem has given rise to more "isms" than any other problem in the history of philosophy, and this is probably true. The mind-body problem is a complex one. We have attempted in this introductory chapter to narrow it down somewhat in order that we may concentrate on just three theories—identity materialism, panpsychism, and interactionism. Any theory on the nature of body and mind, it would seem, must be reducible to one of these three types, and a comprehension of them will facilitate an understanding of related matters with little difficulty.

STUDY QUESTIONS

1. Give some examples of what are here called "mental events" and "physical events." Do you in practice have any difficulty in distinguishing the two? By what criteria do you make the distinction?
2. Summarize what you understand to be the common-sense view regarding body and mind. Is this also your view? What "puzzles," if any, seem implicit in this view?
3. What exactly is identity materialism? panpsychism? interactionism? Do these three exhaust the logically possible alternatives with respect to the mind-body problem? Explain.
4. Is anything of importance at stake in the discussion of this problem? Do you see any possible implications for psychology? for sociology? for ethics? for religion? Be specific.

28

IDENTITY MATERIALISM

There are four main reasons why people generally have adopted—or perhaps have unconsciously presupposed—the dualist view regarding mind and body. First, the apparent irreducibility of mental events and physical events seems to imply that they occur, respectively, in minds and bodies. Thinking, feeling, desiring, wishing, willing, and the like, appear to be different in kind from moving, being moved, accelerating, decomposing, and so on. The most plausible explanation of this difference, it is asserted, is that mind is the subject of the one set of events and body the subject of the other. Hence, it is concluded, mind and body must be regarded as two distinct entities.

Second, the fact of personal continuity seems to favor the dualist account. Not one single particle of the matter of which my body is now composed was in my body twenty years ago, yet it seems that there is some sense in which I am the same "person" that I was twenty years ago. The only acceptable explanation of this fact, it is held, is that there is something that remains unaltered by these physical changes, namely, my "mind" or "soul." So on this ground, too, it appears that mind or soul must be something different from body.

Third, certain facts alleged to be discoverable by introspection—for example, our awareness of acting "deliberately" or "purposively"—are sometimes said to demonstrate that conscious activity cannot be adequately described as a physical process. In the act of "weighing alternatives," for example, it seems that I am directly aware of the fact that I am not simply observing a process that is going on, say, in my brain: I am actively doing something, and this something that I am doing, it is held, is irreducibly "mental." The point of this argument is that we are directly aware of the uniquely "mental" character of such activities in the act of performing them; hence, they are not reducible to some other kind of process different from what we allegedly know them to be.

For many people, the same conclusion is strongly reinforced by a fourth and very different sort of consideration. In Western culture, a widespread belief in, and hope for, life after death prevails. This evidently presupposes a soul capable of existing apart from the body, for it is evident that after the event that we call death, the body decomposes and is eventually reduced to its basic elements. If, then, we are to give any meaning to the phrase "personal immortality," something must be presupposed in the constitution of man that is not subject to the process of decomposition; and this something is called soul, mind, or consciousness. The emotional fervor with which the dualist account is sometimes maintained is, in my opinion, largely a result of this consideration.

These, then, are what I take to be the chief grounds upon which the dualist theory of body and mind has been erected. Some of these reasons are very persuasive, since they exhibit the dualist theory as an explanation of certain undeniable facts—facts that must be accounted for in some way or other by any theory that may be proposed. Nonetheless, a number of other considerations provide strong grounds for doubting the correctness of this account, and I propose now to indicate in some detail what they are.

Reasons for Doubting the Correctness of the Dualist View

The dualist theory is suspect, in the first place, because it is impossible to form a clear concept of an entity called a mind, soul, or consciousness. We have, here, a case parallel to that of the now thoroughly discredited idea of a "material substratum," which John Locke whimsically defined as "something I know not what that supports qualities."[1] Mind, apparently, is a something we know not what that thinks, feels, decides, and so on. It is the name for our ignorance of the true nature of mental events. To infer mind as the cause of mental events is equivalent to inferring wind gods as the cause of the blowing of the wind: the inference, in both cases, is vacuous.

In addition, whatever it is that is supposed to be meant by "mind" or "soul," there seem to be insuperable difficulties in the way of our knowing that any such entity exists. That some organisms are capable of perception and feeling seems evident: more or less definite criteria can be established to determine when such an event is or is not occurring. But there appear to be no criteria on the basis of which we could

---

[1]John Locke, *An Essay Concerning Human Understanding,* II, xxiii (New York: Dover, 1959).

say in any given instance, "There is a mind." There is nothing that we can see, hear, taste, touch, or smell—no observational evidence, in other words—that is in any way relevant to confirming or disconfirming the statement "A mind exists." To the purely conceptual difficulty of trying to understand just what it is that is being affirmed to exist when mind is being affirmed to exist, we must, therefore, add the epistemological difficulty that there seems to be no conceivable way by which the existence of these elusive entities could ever be known.

Even if it were possible to give conceptual clarity to the notion of mind, and even if some evidence could be adduced to render the existence of mind probable, it would still be quite impossible to conceive how mind could be involved in causal relations with body. Let me illustrate. Given a minimal knowledge of the laws of physiology, I can understand without too much difficulty how the movement of an arm, say, can be caused by the contraction of certain muscles, how the contraction of those muscles can be caused by certain nerve impulses, and how the nerve impulses can be caused by certain neural events —events occurring, that is, in the brain. All these, it will be noted, are physical processes that are theoretically observable by anyone who approaches them with the proper instruments and the requisite knowledge. But how are we to understand these neural events as being "caused" by an allegedly nonphysical event called a "volition"? Is volition a sort of causation—perhaps an instance of pushing or pulling, or the passage of an electrical current, or what? No answer given to this question would be intelligible; that is what I mean when I say that it is impossible to conceive how body and mind can be involved in causal relations. The same difficulty arises, of course, whether it is mind that is alleged to act causally upon body (as in volition) or body upon mind (as in sensation).

Moreover, what we know about the structure of the nervous system makes it extremely unlikely that the process of deliberation, for example, and the purposive behavior that commonly follows it are different in kind from processes universally taken to be nonmental. Indeed, it seems likely that the only difference between purposive activity and the reflex action of higher animals is degree of complexity. It is only because of the lapse of time between the stimulus and the response that we regard purposive behavior as something different in kind from reflex action.

Another serious objection to the interactionist view is that if it were true, it would violate the principle of the conservation of energy, for which there is a vast amount of supporting evidence, including experimental evidence with regard to human activity. Briefly, the principle of the conservation of energy may be stated thus: in all physical processes, the total amount of energy in the universe remains constant; its form may be altered, but never its quantity. Moreover, every instance of causation known to us involves the transference of energy from the cause to the effect. If, then, it is said that some events in the body have effects in the mind, there must be some transfer of energy from the body to the mind. Since mind is allegedly unperceived, this energy should supposedly "disappear" for a time: the measurable energy in the body should decrease. And if the mind causes effects in the body, the amount of energy in the body should then increase. This does not appear to be the case. Thus, either body-mind interaction does not occur, or body-mind interaction is a remarkable exception to the principle of the conservation of energy.

Finally, it seems implausible to me that there should be one large class of events—those associated with "mind" or "consciousness"—that cannot be understood in terms of the same principles that explain all other phenomena. Scientific research is steadily revealing to us a world that is best understood as an immense mechanism whose parts are interrelated and interdependent. That this system is incredibly complex is obvious. Indeed, some subsystems (that is, identifiable parts of the total system) are so complex that it takes many years of painstaking research to understand their workings (the genetic code, for example). Nonetheless, area after area of inquiry is yielding its secrets to the patient efforts of scientific researchers. It is simply unbelievable that "mental" phenomena should be the lone exception to a world that otherwise can be understood in terms of the laws of physics.

I think it must be conceded that the objections to which I have called attention constitute substantial grounds for doubting the correctness of the dualist theory and thus justify the search for a more adequate alternative. Such an alternative is to be found, in my opinion, in the materialist view of mind.

A Materialist Theory of Mind

One difficulty of a purely semantic nature stands in the way of the general acceptance of a materialist view of mind: the term "materialism" frequently has strong negative connotations, due chiefly to its association with some rather crude theories advocated about a century ago. Let me make it clear, then, that I do not propose to account for mind in terms of tiny nuggets of matter that act and react upon one another according to Newton's Laws of Motion. Nothing except a few fairly simple macroscopic phenomena can be accounted for in this way. Nor is it my intention, in this account of mind, to "dehumanize" humanity in any way. Human beings are clearly noble and fortunate creatures, and their capacity for intelligent behavior remains their most noble endowment, however it is to be understood.

Suppose that we try to understand human beings without positing a nonmaterial "mind" or "consciousness." How, then, must they be conceived? Clearly, they must be seen as complex psychophysical organisms capable of correspondingly complex behaviors. Some of these behaviors may sometimes be described (and appropriately so) in mentalistic terms, but there will be no activities of this organism that are purely "mental" activities, none that could only be understood as activities of a "mind" or "consciousness."

What I am asserting is that the universe as I understand it contains *no minds:* it contains organisms that behave in ways that have led some philosophers, and most nonphilosophers, to draw the erroneous conclusion that there are some entities called "minds." There is no such thing as a mind activity that might be called "thinking"—but there is a kind of human behavior that can rightly be described as "thoughtful." Similarly, there are no mind activities that can properly be called willing, remembering, wishing, and so on—but human beings do sometimes behave purposively, reflectively, or with desire. Mentalistic terms, in short, denote some of the ways in which human beings behave; they do not denote the activities of an unperceived nonspatial entity that is somehow "within" those human beings. The dualist account of body and mind has been aptly called "the dogma of the ghost in the machine."[2] Identity materialism is sometimes thought to consist simply in exorcising the ghost, leaving only the machine. I am arguing, on the contrary, that human beings are neither ghosts nor machines: they are complex psychophysical organisms capable of a peculiarly complex type of behavior that we sometimes describe in mentalistic terms.

"But surely," it will be objected, "people do not only behave thoughtfully; they also *think.* They not only act purposively; they *will,* they *decide.* Thinking, willing, choosing, sensing, deciding—surely these are activities in which human beings engage, not merely adverbial dimensions of other kinds of behavior. How can identity materialism account for such activities?"

It is evident that a complete answer to this objection would require an extensive analysis of each of the types of events commonly called "mental." Limitations of space make this impossible, and we must, accordingly, be selective. Let us take, then, the alleged mental process that we call "thinking." If we can show that thinking is capable of being understood without recourse to a substantival theory of mind, we may justly claim to have defended our view in what must be regarded as a crucial test case; for thinking is without doubt the activity *par excellence* of which minds are supposed to be the subjects.

A typical example of what we call "thinking" would be a student's attempting to solve a problem—for example, trying to find the square root of 196. What does the student do? If the student does not know the procedure for finding square roots, he or she will have to tackle the logically prior problem of finding out how to do them. If the student does know the procedure, he or she will simply apply it, presumably with the help of pencil and paper. And if the student is bright and has

---

[2]Gilbert Ryle, *The Concept of Mind* (New York: Barnes & Noble, 1949), p. 15 and elsewhere.

had a lot of practice solving problems of this sort, he or she may even be able to dispense with pencil and paper and do it, as we say, "in his (or her) head."

But what is going on "in one's head" when one is attempting to solve this or any other problem? The answer seems to be that certain processes are occurring in one's brain. One may, as an aid to these processes, put some numbers down on paper, but this is not essential to the process itself. (It is not even essential to such a process that the person engaged in it be directly aware of what he or she is doing. Mathematicians frequently are able to give the answer to a problem without consciously going through the steps by which the answer is deduced. The same conclusion can be drawn from the fact that we sometimes wake up knowing the answer to a problem that we tried unsuccessfully to solve the night before. The relevant "thinking" occurred, apparently, during sleep.) What is essential is only that the answer one comes up with should, in fact, be the square root of 196— that one should end up by "knowing" what the square root of 196 is.

A number of further considerations may be adduced in support of the view that thinking is nothing more or other than a physical process occurring in the brain. For one thing, we are able to do it better at some times than at others. When we are fatigued, for example, we do not do it nearly so well as when we are rested. Also, our ability to think can be enhanced or decreased by administering certain drugs. Drugs and fatigue do have certain effects on the body, including the brain; hence, it seems likely that the process itself is a process occurring in the brain.

It may be objected that *awareness* of thinking is not itself a process going on in the brain. Perhaps. But this awareness, as we have already noted, does not always accompany the process that we call "thinking," though sometimes, admittedly, it does. Moreover, to explain this awareness we should have to analyze introspection; and this, too, is a physiological process, as are all the phenomena we call "mental events."

Replies to Objections

The most serious objections that could be raised against the materialist view of mental occurrences are precisely those considerations that led to the adoption of the dualist theory in the first place. Let us review them once again.

The apparent irreducibility of "mental events" and "physical events" amounts, in my opinion, to little more than the irreducibility of the *language* of personal experience to the *language* of objective occurrences. We recognize that the sentence "I am seeing a blue object" is not translatable into a sentence of the form "Such and such processes are occurring in my brain," and we conclude from this that the two sentences are not about the same thing. That we have these two kinds of language to describe mental events is undeniable, but no conclusion about the status of such events follows from this fact.

The notion of personal continuity is something of a puzzle. That it is not to be accounted for by positing a nonphysical soul or self that persists throughout all bodily changes is evident, however, when we consider the fact that institutions and other complex entities are also said to exhibit continuity. Take, for example, a university that has been in existence for a century or more. None of the original faculty, students, administration, or regents are now associated with the university. It is very possible that none of the original books are any longer to be found in the library, and that no building now on the campus was there in the beginning. Yet, in *some* sense it is said to be the "same" university, for over relatively short spans of time a number of the elements that constitute the university—physical plant, faculty, student body—remain relatively unchanged. Perhaps continuity in the case of persons ought to be understood in much the same way. My continuity with the self of yesterday consists in the fact not that some one element remains constant throughout, but that change occurs in the context of a relatively stable structure.

No conclusion about the status of mind can be drawn, it seems to me, from the fact that we are, allegedly, directly aware on occasion of acting "deliberately" or "purposively." We are apparently in a position to know our own mental states in a way that others are not (although it is to be noted that fairly precise criteria can be established for judging someone's behavior to be "deliberate" and/or "purposive"), but it can scarcely be argued that it, therefore, follows that a mental state consists in some determination of a nonphysical entity that we call our "mind." It is just as plausible to hold that this awareness is simply one of the by-products of the occurrence of such and such a neural process.

On the question of life after death, certainly the hope for such a thing does not constitute a valid reason for holding that the conditions for it do, in fact, obtain. In the materialist view of mind, when death occurs, mind perishes no less than body; it is as meaningless to talk of the continuation of mind after the deterioration of the brain as it is to talk of the continuation of running after the deterioration of one's legs. "Mind" is the collective, and misleading, name for those dimensions of human behavior that we call "intelligent." When the human organism dies, it ceases to behave at all; thus, intelligent behavior also ceases. When running stops, "swiftly" cannot continue by itself; when behavior ceases, "mind" no longer has any meaning.

The old puzzle about how mind and body could interact, or how the appearance of interaction was to be accounted for, is evidently a consequence of the mistake of separating body and mind in the first place and regarding the latter as a substantial entity that has then to be rerelated to body in some odd way. Mind is minding; it is adjectivally, adverbially, related to the body and its behavior. But body is explicable

in terms of the laws governing matter, particularly matter as organized in complex living organisms. Hence, mind, too, is explicable in
terms of those self-same laws.

STUDY QUESTIONS

1. What are suggested in this chapter as the main reasons why people
   generally have tended to favor the interactionist view of body and
   mind? Can you think of any additional reasons for this? How would
   you rank these reasons, from "strongest" to "weakest"?
2. Summarize Materialist's reasons for doubting the correctness of
   the dualist view. Which list of reasons—this list or the one written
   in answer to the previous question—strikes you as being the most
   convincing?
3. What exactly is the view of mind that Materialist is proposing?
   What arguments does Materialist use to support this view?
4. What are Materialist's answers to what are asserted to be the chief
   arguments in favor of the interactionist view? Which do you personally find more convincing, the arguments in support of the
   interactionist view or Materialist's replies to them?

29

PANPSYCHISM

If we are to arrive at an acceptable view on the question of mind and body, it is important to distinguish carefully between (a) the considerations against the dualist account and (b) those supporting a materialist theory. It is sometimes assumed that if the dualist theory can be shown to be inadequate, the materialist account of mind will readily be seen to be correct. This idea, I am convinced, is erroneous. I hope to show that the correct view is, instead, that body, or "matter," is to be understood mentalistically.

I should like to begin by reinforcing an observation made, almost incidentally, in the introductory chapter of this section. Although the problem of the relation between body and mind appears to be straightforwardly about how we are to understand human beings, at root it is a metaphysical problem. To argue that mind is nothing but a particular determination of matter is simply not plausible. No one, I think, who confined his or her attention to the known facts about the relevant physical and psychological phenomena would ever be tempted to subscribe to such an account. The philosophers who, nonetheless, do take this approach do so, I think, out of a prior conviction that *all* phenomena are ultimately to be understood in terms of matter and its laws. They are, in other words, committed from the start to the metaphysics of monistic materialism. The existence of mental phenomena, therefore, constitutes an embarrassing problem for them, and they are, accordingly, compelled to try to "reduce" mind to matter on pain of having their metaphysical theory discredited. This is true whether the metaphysics that inspires the attempt is overt, as in the case of the nineteenth-century materialists, or covert, as it is with many philosophers at the present time.

The materialist account of mind is so utterly unconvincing that my preference would be simply to ignore it and to proceed directly to an exposition of what I consider to be a much more plausible alternative. However, many people today apparently do find monistic materialism very attractive, so I must take time to point out some of the most serious inadequacies of Materialist's account. And since identity materialism is needed to maintain the metaphysics of monistic materialism, my critique of the materialist theory of mind may also be construed as a *reductio ad absurdum* of that metaphysical theory.

Critique of the Materialist Theory of Mind

The materialist theory of mind is inadequate in at least four respects. First, this theory does not provide a believable account of what is happening when we are thinking, feeling, perceiving, remembering, desiring, willing, and the like. Let us consider "thinking," since this is the example that Materialist has briefly discussed. It seems evident that (a) whether or not a neural process of some unique sort is occurring whenever a person is thinking of some particular thing, this certainly has never been shown to be the case; and (b) even if thinking of a determinate sort is always accompanied by some corresponding neural process, it does not follow that thinking simply *consists in* this neural process. The question of what neural processes are correlated with what mental states is, surely, an empirical question, and the investigation of this matter has not yet proceeded to the point where anyone can claim a one-to-one correspondence between the two. Even if this were to be established, however, it is extremely implausible to hold that thinking is the *same thing* as the neural process that accompanies it. A well-designed and properly programmed computer, for example, is capable of solving certain kinds of problems far more quickly than even the brightest of mathematicians; yet we would not (except metaphorically) describe the process by which it does so as "thinking." What is the difference? The difference is that to say that something is an instance of thinking is to posit a mind, a consciousness, as the subject of the thinking. Nothing other than metaphysical prejudice could ever induce someone to give a different answer.

Materialist has, in a way, attempted to answer this objection. According to Materialist, the apparent irreducibility of mental events and physical events amounts to little more than the irreducibility of the *language* of personal experience to the *language* of objective occurrences. But this way out of the difficulty is not open to the materialist. If the materialist account of mind is correct, then a sentence like "I am seeing a blue object" ought to be logically equivalent to the sentence "Such and such processes are occurring in my brain." The statement "Rutabagas do not taste good," for example, can be translated "So-and-so does not like rutabagas," since these statements are *about* the same thing—the likes and dislikes of some particular person or persons. Alternative descriptions of the same state of affairs are always interchangeable. If, then, it is conceded that in the present case the two descriptions are not interchangeable, then they obviously are not describing the same state of affairs: mental states are not *equivalent to* neural processes.

Materialist's account of personal continuity is also quite obviously inconsistent with what we know about this phenomenon from the one case each of us actually experiences—our *own* continuity. My knowledge that I stand in a relation of continuity with that certain person born on such and such a date at such and such a place rests, surely, on the fact that I have recollections of experiences that are so related that I necessarily see them as members of a single series. I know that I am the "same person" who last evening watched a baseball game, last year took a trip to Chicago, some years ago attended a certain university, and before that lived in a certain city, because I *remember* having the experiences that constitute these several events. It may well be that the "stuff" of which my body is composed has been completely changed during this long span of time; but certain patterns, a certain more or less constant organization of this "stuff," and certain serially related memories have endured. It is to these that I have reference when I say that throughout this time I have been the "same person."

It seems grossly misleading, therefore, to explain personal continuity on the analogy of the continuity of a nonorganic complex like a university. The analogy, if there is one, must surely be applied in the other direction. An institution has, admittedly, a kind of fictional unity that bears some analogy to the unity of a person (as does a nation, a club, a political party, and the like); and the recorded history of an institution might be compared in some ways to the remembered experience of a human being. We can even personify a university and sing "her" praises in song and verse, but we know well enough that the "person" we thus posit does not really exist except in a metaphorical sense. It is not nearly so evident that Materialist is aware of the fact that one is using a metaphor, and a misleading one at that, when one attempts to "thingify" our experience of personal continuity.

One final objection. The materialist theory of mind implies that people never act in terms of conscious purposes freely chosen but only as a result of external causes. In our own experience, at least, we know that this is not true. Despite Materialist's disavowal of the older mechanism, materialism inescapably involves a mechanistic view of human behavior; and mechanism, old or new, is a bitter pill to swallow. We surely believe ourselves to act freely and purposively a good deal of the time. Indeed, I should say that we know ourselves to do so. Unless we are to regard this knowledge as no knowledge, as illusory, we must reject the materialist account of mind. If we do adopt that account, we must be prepared to accept its mechanistic consequences.

Another Alternative

So far we have agreed with Materialist that the dualist account of body and mind—the view that body and mind are two distinct entities involved in mutual causal relations—is untenable, and we have rejected the materialist alternative of attempting to account for mind as a peculiar determination, or set of determinations, of matter. There now appears to be only one possibility remaining, and that is to regard *mind* as fundamental and body as explicable in terms of mind. What case can be made for this alternative? Since we have acknowledged that any resolution of this problem presupposes some metaphysical theory, let us begin by noting some of the more important features of such theories.

Metaphysics consists in the attempt to elaborate a system of concepts in terms of which every phenomenon that we encounter can be interpreted and understood. The requirements that a metaphysical system must meet are that (a) some phenomena shall be explicable in terms of it, (b) no phenomena shall be inexplicable in terms of it, (c) it shall be internally consistent, and (d) it shall not have implications that are absurd or contrary to fact. The method by which such systems are elaborated consists in (a) generalizing some concepts that are known to have application in some limited sphere and (b) attempting to apply the concepts thus developed to all phenomena—attempting, in other words, to give them a universal application. Monistic materialism, for example, is a metaphysical system whose central concepts were originally adapted from the science of mechanics. My criticism of it is that it does not provide a plausible explanation of mental, or psychological, phenomena.

Suppose, then, that we relinquish the idea that everything that occurs is explicable in terms of tiny units of lifeless matter that act and react upon one another according to certain laws. Let us see if we can give a better account of things by saying instead that the ultimate constituents of which the universe is composed are to be conceived on the analogy of *mind*. Everything is to be conceived as being composed of a greater or lesser number of "droplets of experience," or "atoms of consciousness," each of which is in some degree aware of the environment that constitutes its world, and each of which, accordingly, takes account of its environment in a way that is appropriate to its particular level of awareness. Following Alfred North Whitehead (1861–1947), we shall call such a center of experience an "actual occasion."[1]

Since the idea of an actual occasion is derived from our direct

---

[1]See Alfred North Whitehead, *Process and Reality* (New York: Harper & Row, 1960), p. 113.

awareness of our own selfhood, it is natural that we should develop the idea in terms of other concepts derived from the same source. We know, for example, that our own lives are describable as careers in which we are constantly obliged to make choices. Our past and the constitution of the rest of the world severely limit the possibilities open to us, but there are some possibilities for each of us, a variety of alternatives from which we must choose. Let us say, then, that the life of every actual occasion is a career in which it must choose, from among the possibilities available to it, what it is to become. Its possibilities, like ours, are determined by (a) its past, (b) the constitution of the rest of the world that it has to take into account, and (c) its own level of awareness. Every actual occasion, then, will experience something—something appropriate to its own level of awareness—analogous to what in human beings is called perception, feeling, remembering, willing, and so on.

According to this account, what is a "material object," for example, a stone? Let us call it a "society of actual occasions," an aggregate of actual occasions united together in a quasi-unity analogous to that of a society of persons. No doubt, the level of awareness of the actual occasions that compose a stone is of a very low order—lower, for example, than that of the lowest organism—and the alternatives open to them are so severely limited that so far as we can see they do little more than perpetuate themselves virtually unchanged from moment to moment. So unvarying are their choices, in fact, that we can observe statistical uniformities in the behavior of the society—can formulate, in other words, certain laws descriptive of the behavior of the aggregate. We can do the same thing, it is to be noted, with respect to a colony of ants or bees.

Our way of taking account of such aggregates is through what we call "perception"—in the case of our perceiving a stone, by means of sight and touch. Its way of taking account of us is to resist our efforts to penetrate it, to allow itself to be moved on occasion, and so on.

The level of awareness of actual occasions appears to vary greatly, and the options available to an actual occasion seem to widen as the level increases. In inorganic substances, the level appears to be at its lowest: we cannot even begin to imagine what it would be like to be a grain of sand or a particle of calcium. With the simplest organisms, the level is higher: the very simplest plants are able to exercise a degree of freedom that is unknown to any particle of inorganic matter. The level increases when we come to insects, still more when we come to the higher animals, and reaches the fullest realization of which we have any knowledge in man. So great is it in the case of the higher animals such as dogs, horses, monkeys, and the like, that we can almost imagine what it would be like to be such a creature; in any case, we cannot seriously doubt that they have a consciousness in many ways similar to our own.

A Panpsychist Account

How, then, ought we to conceive of a human being? As a society of actual occasions of varying levels of awareness. Some one of these dominates and gives unity to the society; this we call the "mind" or "soul." In the experience that we call perception—feeling a pain, for example—the pain is experienced by the finger, say, as a pressure or a piercing, by the nerves as an electrical current, by the brain as certain brain waves that occur in it, and by the mind as the feeling of pain. The experience that we call willing is experienced by the mind as deliberation and decision, by the brain as a directive to enact such and such an alternative, by the nerves as electrical impulses of a certain kind, and by the appropriate muscles as a directive to contract in such and such a way. The society, when it is healthy, is a cooperative society, each member doing its part to ensure the welfare of the whole under the guidance of its dominant member. When a hostile "foreigner" enters (as in the case of an infection), or when some members of the society become uncooperative (as in the case of cancer), the whole society suffers; and if it cannot repel the invaders, or get rid of the uncooperative members, the whole society may be destroyed.

Limitations of space have permitted only the briefest sketch of the metaphysical scheme in terms of which, I believe, the relation of body and mind can be correctly understood. Much more detail and countless additional examples of its explanatory power would have to be provided before I could hope to persuade many of my readers that what I am suggesting is, at least, in the direction of the truth. For now, I must be content to let the plausibility of my proposal rest on its ability to solve the familiar puzzles of the relation between body and mind. These, it will be recalled, are (a) the alleged impossibility of forming a clear concept of "mind," (b) the alleged difficulty of knowing that any such entity exists, (c) the difficulty of trying to understand how unthinking body and unextended mind can interact, (d) the problem of how we are to conceive of personal continuity in the case of conscious organisms, and (e) the problem of how certain mental events are related to the so-called physical events with which they are associated.

My answer to each of these puzzles is as follows. First, there is no difficulty whatsoever in forming a perfectly clear concept of mind unless we demand that the concept be formed in spatial terms. The question, What kind of body is a mind? is not a proper question and deserves no answer. I cannot form an "image" of a mind because a mind is not the sort of thing that occupies space, and only things that occupy space can be "imaged." But I know as clearly as I know anything what a mind is: a conscious center of feelings, perceptions thoughts, and volitions.

There is also no difficulty in knowing that mind exists. In the very act of thinking, feeling, doubting, and so forth, I know that I exist. In the intelligent behavior of other organisms, especially in the intelligible communication that I have with other minds, I know that other minds also exist.

There are no unthinking bodies; hence, there is no "gap" between body and mind that has to be bridged by some half-mind-half-body "connecting link." There are only minds of varying levels of awareness; and every mind is able to take account of those that constitute its world in ways appropriate to its level of awareness. (Minds at a relatively low level of awareness, for example, take account of one another by means of what we call "mechanical causation.")

Personal continuity in the case of any organism—whether or not it is "conscious" in the strict, unextended, sense of that word—consists in the persistence of its structural unity and its unique relation to its past history, which past history it must take into account in choosing the next stage in its career. Something analogous to memory, therefore, must characterize the experience of every actual occasion.

There are no such things as purely physical events properly so-called. Everything that occurs is an event in the career of some actual occasion or society of actual occasions. It is only when we abstract from this and view it, so to speak, "from the outside" that we get the derivative notion of a "physical event." A given event may be perceived as a feeling of pain by the actual occasion (mind) that is dominant in the society constituting a human brain; the same event may be perceived by a neurosurgeon as the occurrence of certain neural processes. It all depends on how one actual occasion takes account of the experiences of other actual occasions, which in turn depends in large part on the particular ways in which that actual occasion happens to be related to them.

STUDY QUESTIONS

1. What inadequacies does Panpsychist claim to find in the materialist theory of mind? Are these serious objections to the materialist theory? How might Materialist attempt to answer them?
2. What precisely is panpsychism? How well, in your opinion, does it measure up to the "requirements that a metaphysical system must meet" as itemized by Panpsychist?
3. What theory of man does Panpsychist propose? How is this theory supposed to provide a solution to the mind-body problem?
4. What do you consider to be the strongest arguments in favor of the panpsychist theory of body and mind? What seem to be the strongest arguments against it?
5. Write a critique of panpsychism from the point of view of a materialist, answering the objections raised by Panpsychist against the materialist theory and raising appropriate objections to the panpsychist theory.

30

DUALISM RECONSIDERED

Let me begin this defense of dualism by saying that on two points I am in very close agreement with Panpsychist. First, I think he is quite right when he says that there is no special difficulty in forming a clear concept of "mind"—except for those who are really looking for an *image* rather than a *concept*. No nonspatial entity can be "imaged," since "image-ing" is modeled after visual perception, and visual perception is always spatially determined. Any attempt to form an "image" of mind or soul—such as Plato's famous word picture (in the dialogue *Phaedrus*) of the two horses and the charioteer—clearly must be metaphorical in character, and, hence, a pale reflection of reality itself. I find nothing obscure, however, in the concept of mind as a conscious center of feeling, perception, thought, and volition.

Second, I agree with Panpsychist that there is no special difficulty in knowing that mind exists. Descartes was essentially right, I think, in saying that our own existence as a thinking being (*res cogitans*) is the most indubitable fact we can know. Even if we doubt that anything else exists, we must exist in order to do the doubting. As for the existence of other minds, we obviously have to infer from the outward behavior of the other person that he or she is in a mental state such as we know ourselves to be in when we behave in such and such a way (tears when we are sad, grimaces when we are in pain, laughter when we are happy, and the like). But our inferences in such cases are as warranted, surely, as any inference can be.

I am not at all persuaded, however, by Panpsychist's suggestion that the problem of how mind and body can interact, or appear to interact, is to be solved by simply disallowing that there is any such thing as body, any more than I am by Materialist's mechanistic explanation. Communication between minds by means of intelligible discourse, and communication between bodies by means of mechanical causation, are both processes that I can understand well enough not to feel puzzled about them. Now, whatever it is that goes on between mind and body—in perception and in volition—does not seem to be reducible to either of these. We must look further for our explanation of body-mind intercausality.

Is it, indeed, even meaningful to say that the ultimate constituents of which a stone, for example, is composed are minds with a very low level of awareness? It makes sense, I think, to talk about animals and insects having something like a human consciousness, because something like the behavior that we know to be associated with consciousness in human beings is to be observed in the behavior of animals. We have, in this case, three points of reference in relation to which we can fill in the fourth: human consciousness is to certain kinds of human behavior as x is to somewhat similar animal behavior. But in the case of stones, and in the case of individual parts of the human body, we lack the "similar behavior" that would permit us to work the equation. What, then, does it mean to posit "low-level consciousness" in such things? I am afraid we must conclude that it means nothing at all.

With respect to the nature of personal continuity, I am not sure that I understand what Panpsychist is suggesting; consequently, I am not sure whether I agree or disagree with his view. It seems clear to me, in any case, that our awareness of our own personal continuity is tied up with our awareness of having a mind that is one and the same mind from the beginning to the end of our life. In the strict sense of the word, therefore, I do not think that we should attribute personal continuity to any beings except those who have minds like ours. In an analogous sense, however, we can attribute continuity to animals on the ground that they possess a consciousness somewhat similar to our own, and we can attribute organic continuity to any organism so long as it maintains its organic structure and unity. Aggregates of inorganic matter —stones, for example—can be said to have continuity only in the sense that they have a relatively stable structure. But this is a loose application of the notion of continuity: a piece of a stone is also a stone, and it has as much structure as the larger one from which it came.

Finally, it appears wholly gratuitous to say, as Panpsychist does, that there are no such things as physical events "properly so-called." In one sense of this statement, it is obviously false: there *are* lightning flashes, thunderclaps, planetary motions, and things of that sort. These are surely more properly described as "physical events" than as anything else we might be inclined to call them. But this, obviously, is not what Panpsychist means to deny. What he is contending, rather, is that we should not think of such events as the consequences of the actions and reactions of bits of lifeless, unconscious matter operating according to certain invariable laws. What is really the case, he wants to say, is that everything that exists—including electrons, protons, and so on—is composed of tiny "droplets of consciousness," and everything that occurs, including what we call "physical events," is, properly understood, an experience in the career of some such droplet or droplets. This whole account seems to me, for reasons already given, altogether gratuitous, fantastic, and meaningless; it is, as someone has said, so incredible that no one but a very learned man could ever have thought of it.

The attempt to reduce body to mind must be regarded as a failure, just as the attempt to reduce mind to body has been shown to be a failure. Since, then, there appears to be no viable alternative to the dualist view of body and mind, let us look once again at the difficulties allegedly involved in the dualist view to see if they cannot be removed without doing violence to our sense of what is credible. Certainly, the prima facie evidence must be conceded to be on the side of dualism. It is only the apparent difficulties of this view that have led to the fruitless search for a monistic alternative. Let us see whether on this matter common sense cannot, for once, be vindicated.

The Alleged Difficulties of the Dualist View

The difficulties alleged to be inherent in the dualist view of body and mind have been nicely summarized by Materialist as follows: (a) the conceptual difficulty of trying to understand what the term "mind" is supposed to denote; (b) the epistemological difficulty of knowing anything about such an entity, if there is one; (c) the alleged impossibility of conceiving how body and mind could interact; (d) the alleged impossibility of distinguishing between purposive behavior and "reflex action" behavior in view of the fact that the same nervous system is apparently involved in both; and (e) the suggestion that interaction, if it occurred, would violate the principle of the conservation of energy. Let us consider each of these difficulties in turn.

To what I have already said regarding the first two points, I should like to add that it is materialist dogmatism alone that creates the first-mentioned difficulty, and empiricist dogmatism alone that creates the second. Otherwise, enough has already been said on the first point; anyone who is able to distinguish between a concept and an image should have no difficulty forming a precise concept of mind. On the second point, I can only say, *"Of course* we cannot see, feel, taste, touch, or smell minds: they are not the sort of thing that can be perceived in that way." But we have already discussed this point sufficiently in our earlier remarks.

Let us leave the interactionist puzzle for a moment and consider the two quasi-scientific arguments. With respect to what I shall call the "nervous system argument," there surely must be *some* difference between deliberate actions and reflex actions that leads us to make the distinction in the first place. What is it, then, that leads us to call some instances of behavior—blinking, sneezing, flinching, and so on—reflex actions? The answer, surely, is that these actions occur without deliberation or decision on our part: there is a stimulus (a thrown object, a tickle in the nose, a loud noise) and the response follows immediately—"automatically," as we say. We do not have to decide to do something in such cases; we just do it. Reflex actions are, as it were, natural habits of the human organism. With deliberate actions, the situation is different: we must decide both what we shall do and when we shall do it; and the process of deliberation may be as brief or protracted as we choose to make it.

It is not at all plausible to argue that the difference between these two kinds of behavior is due only to the relatively greater complexity of the neural processes involved in deliberate behavior, for even if these processes are more complex than those involved in reflex action (whatever "complexity" means in this context), it does not follow that this is the only difference. Certainly, the same nervous system must be employed in the two cases: it is the only nervous system we have! But our own experience tells us that there is, nonetheless, a qualitative difference between the two. The most plausible explanation of this difference is that in the one case mind is active and in the other case it is not; in the one case mind is agent and in the other it is only a spectator. The "nervous system argument," therefore, has no force whatsoever as an objection to the dualist view. Indeed, reflection upon the evident difference between reflex behavior and purposive behavior tends to strengthen the dualist view.

Nor, I think, is the "conservation of energy" argument any more convincing. There are, actually, two different forms of this argument. One would have it that the dualist theory implies that in man the principle of the conservation of energy is violated, and that because we know this principle to be universally valid, the dualist theory is therefore false. The other asserts that the dualist theory implies that in man the principle of the conservation of energy is violated, and that because we have experimental evidence to show that this is not the case, the dualist theory must be false. The argument, in either form, is usually put forward with a great show of scientific learning, leaving the impression that either the dualist or the late Professor Albert Einstein must be mistaken—and there is little doubt, in such a contest, who will be the winner.

Whether or not the principle of the conservation of energy is universally valid is a question for physicists to decide, and neither Materialist nor I have any basis for an opinion. Be that as it may, however, the argument cannot succeed unless it can also be shown that the interaction of body and mind, if it does occur, involves the transfer of energy from one to the other. This has never been demonstrated: it has only been presupposed. It may well be that every instance of purely physical causation involves such a transfer of energy; this, again, is a question for the physicist, not the philosopher, to decide. But it is surely begging the issue simply to presuppose that body-mind interaction, if it occurs, must be an instance of physical causation and must, therefore, conform to the laws governing such events.

Both the "nervous system argument" and the "conservation of energy" argument are thinly veiled attempts to bring not scientific facts but scientific *prestige* to bear against the interactionist view. Neither argument arises because of any puzzles inherent in the dualist view: they are arguments invented for the purpose of discrediting the dualist view, after that view has already been rejected on other grounds. These grounds, as I think Panpsychist has amply shown, are metaphysical ones: the dualist view of body and mind is distinctly uncongenial to the metaphysics of materialism. We are left, then, with only one difficulty in the way of adopting the dualist view of body and mind, that of understanding how body and mind can interact. What is it about this phenomenon that strikes us as being so odd?

Why Interaction Is Puzzling

Perhaps the reason that mind-body interaction appears so puzzling is that mind and body seem to be so dissimiliar to one another. How can a nonspatial and nonphysical entity, like a mind, be involved in mutual causal relations with an unthinking physical entity, like a body? But a moment's reflection makes it evident that this question does not locate precisely the source of our bewilderment, for there are innumerable examples of causation between dissimilar entities that pose no such puzzlement. We believe without difficulty that there is a causal relation between a mosquito bite and malaria, between the throwing of a switch and the blowing of a siren, between the pressure on an accelerator and the increasing speed of an automobile; yet, the two terms in each of these examples are highly dissimilar. We must look further for the source of our bewilderment.

Perhaps the reason that we are mystified about apparent instances of mind-body interaction in a way that we are not mystified by instances of intraphysical causality is that in cases of the latter kind we conceive of the cause and the effect (however dissimilar they may be) as being parts of a *single system,* governed by the *same laws.* We assume that there is some coherent set of laws—chemical, physical, biological—in terms of which the several series of events from the mosquito bite to the malaria, the throwing of the switch to the blowing of the siren, and the pressing of the accelerator to the increase in speed of the automobile are all explicable. If we are mystified at this level, it is because we do not know which laws are relevant to the phenomena in question. (Compare: How do mosquitoes cause malaria? How do burns cause feelings of pain?) In the case of mind-body interaction, it seems that we have to deal with two "systems," and the laws governing the interaction of body and mind do not seem to be assimilable to either.

Let me illustrate. We can explain a burn, up to a certain point. We can, with the help of the relevant physical laws, relate the occurrence of the flame to the increase of temperature on the surface of the skin; this increase in temperature to the occurrence of tiny electrical impulses in certain nerves; and the occurrence of these impulses to the occurrence of a certain pattern of brain waves. But then we reach a gap in our explanation: we have no laws—none that are coherent with, or a part of, the system of laws we have been using thus far—that will enable us to relate the occurrence of the brain waves to the *feeling of pain* in the consciousness of the injured person.

Once we posit the feeling of pain in that consciousness, however, we have no difficulty understanding subsequent mental events. The injured man "deliberates" between going to the doctor and treating himself; he "remembers" that his wife warned him to be careful about lighting camp stoves; he "decides" to treat the burn himself; and so on. Once we get to mind, we can "lock in" on the other system, and everything is all right. But then there is volition and the ensuing behavior (brain waves, nerves, muscles, and the like), and, once again, we encounter the gap.

Our puzzlement about the interaction of body and mind is, therefore, an expression of our desire to reduce all phenomena to some single unitary system, with one set of laws applicable to all events. But the only possible ways of fulfilling this desire would be to explain mental phenomena in terms of physical laws (identity materialism), or physical phenomena in terms of mental laws (panpsychism), and neither of these explanations is adequate to the facts. We are left, therefore, with an ultimate and irreducible dualism, a dualism that may leave us puzzled and dissatisfied, but which we must nonetheless accept.

Although we cannot understand mind-body interaction, either in terms of the laws governing physical phenomena or in terms of the laws governing mental phenomena—cannot construe it, that is, either as a physical phenomenon or as a mental phenomenon—we have the best possible evidence that such interaction does occur, namely, our own experience. Physical events do cause mental events: we know this from countless instances of what we call perception. Mental events do cause physical events: we know this from countless instances of willed, deliberate behavior. These are the facts, and they cannot be denied, however puzzled we may be about the *modus operandi* of that unique mode of causality that occurs in the mutual relations of body and mind.

To realize why we find it difficult to comprehend mind-body interaction, however, is in some degree to rid ourselves of the puzzle. We then understand why this particular sort of causality seems so odd, and we are free to look at it without being tempted to deny the obvious in order to assimilate it to some other mode of explanation; we are no longer "bothered" by its oddness. It is only in this sense that an informed dualism constitutes a "solution" to the mind-body problem. The odyssey that begins with common sense, and that seeks a solution to its puzzles in either materialistic or mentalistic monism, reaches its culmination in a view that might be best described as common sense made sure of itself. To accept such a view is to accept the puzzle of how mind and body interact in preference to the even more bewildering puzzles that result if the reality of either is denied.

STUDY QUESTIONS

1. On what points does Dualist agree with Panpsychist? What objections does Dualist raise against Panpyschist's position? Could Materialist, without abandoning his own position, join Dualist in urging these same objections?

2. Write a defense of panpsychism against the objections raised by Dualist. Which of Dualist's arguments do you find most difficult to refute?

3. What is the "nervous system" argument against dualism, and how does Dualist attempt to answer it? Who do you think has the stronger case on this particular point?

4. What is the "conservation of energy" argument against dualism? What is Dualist's answer to this argument?

5. What, according to Dualist, makes apparent mind-body interaction so puzzling? Do you think Dualist is right about this? Are you satisfied with Dualist's final answer to the puzzle?

CORRELATED READINGS[1]

1. Descartes, René. "Thinking Things and Extended Things." *Meditations on the First Philosophy,* Meditations II and VI; and *A Discourse on Method,* Part V. The classic statement of mind-body dualism.
2. Minsky, Marvin L. "I Think, Therefore I Am." *Psychology Today,* 2, 11 (1969), 30–32. An intriguing comparison of human beings and advanced computers.
3. Hintz, Howard. "Whitehead's Concept Of Organism And The Mind-Body Problem," *Dimensions of Mind,* ed. Sidney Hook. New York: New York University Press, 1959, pp. 100–109. A lucid statement of the panpsychist view of mind and body.
4. Feigl, Herbert. "The Identity Theory," ed. Sidney Hook, *op. cit.,* pp. 24–34. An exceptionally compact statement of the identity theory.

FOR FURTHER READING

Armstrong, D. M. *A Materialist Theory of the Mind.* London: Routledge and Kegan Paul, 1967.

Aune, Bruce. "Feelings, Moods, and Introspection," *Mind,* 72 (1963), 187–207.

————. "The Problem of Other Minds," *The Philosophical Review,* 70 (1961), 320–339.

Borowski, E. J. "Identity and Personal Identity," *Mind,* 85 (1976), 481–502.

Borst, C. V. *The Mind-Brain Identity Theory.* London: Macmillan, 1970 (paperbound). A collection of papers pro and con.

Broad, C. D. *The Mind and Its Place in Nature.* Paterson, N.J.: Littlefield, Adams, 1960 (paperbound), Chaps. 3, 14.

Campbell, Keith. *Body and Mind.* Garden City, N.Y.: Doubleday, 1970 (paperbound). Contains a good bibliography.

Cornman, James W. *Materialism and Sensations.* New Haven, Conn.: Yale University Press, 1971. Defends an adverbial theory.

Dewey, John. *Experience and Nature.* LaSalle, Ill.: Open Court Publishing Co., 1958 (paperbound).

Dilman, I. *Matter and Mind.* London: Macmillan, 1975.

Ducasse, C. J. *Nature, Mind and Death.* LaSalle, Ill.: Open Court Publishing Co., 1951.

Evans, C. O. *The Subject of Consciousness.* London: Allen & Unwin, 1970.

Ewing, A. C. *The Fundamental Questions of Philosophy.* New York: Macmillan, 1951, Chap. 6.

Feigl, Herbert. *The "Mental" and the "Physical."* London: Oxford University Press, 1968 (paperbound).

————. "The Mind-Body Problem in the Development of Logical

Empiricism," in M. Brodbeck and H. Feigl (eds.). *Readings in the Philosophy of Science.* New York: Appleton-Century-Crofts, 1953, pp. 612–626.

Grossman, Reinhardt. *The Structure of Mind.* Madison: University of Wisconsin Press, 1965. Detailed critique of arguments for phenomenalism from a realist perspective.

Hume, David. *A Treatise of Human Nature.* Many editions. See Book I, Section VI.

Joske, W. D. "Behaviorism as a Scientific Theory," *Philosophy and Phenomenological Research,* 22 (1961), 61–68.

Krikorian, Y. "A Naturalistic View of Mind," in Y. Krikorian (ed.). *Naturalism and the Human Spirit.* New York: Columbia University Press, 1944, pp. 242–269.

————. "The Publicity of Mind," *Philosophy and Phenomenological Research,* 22 (1962), 317–325.

Lachs, John. "Epiphenomenalism and the Notion of Cause," *The Journal of Philosophy,* 60 (1963), 141–146.

Laird, John. *Our Minds and Their Bodies.* London: Oxford University Press, 1925.

Laslett, Peter (ed.). *The Physical Basis of Mind.* Oxford: Basil Blackwell, 1951.

Lewis, H. D. *The Elusive Mind.* London: Allen & Unwin, 1970. Defends mind-body dualism against its major contemporary critics.

Locke, Don. *Myself and Others: A Study in Our Knowledge of Minds.* London: Oxford University Press, 1968. Current and lucid.

Malcom, Norman. "Knowledge of Other Minds," *The Journal of Philosophy,* 55 (1958), 969–978.

Mucciolo, L. F. "The Identity Theory and Criteria for the Mental," *Philosophy and Phenomenological Research,* 35 (1974–1975), 167–180. Examines the logic of the identity theory.

Nelson, R. J. "Mechanism, Functionalism, and the Identity Theory," *The Journal of Philosophy,* 73 (1976), 365–385.

O'Connor, John (ed.). *Modern Materialism: Readings on Mind-Body Identity.* New York: Harcourt, Brace & World, 1969. Useful bibliography.

Polten, E. P. *Critique of the Psycho-physical Identity Theory.* The Hague: Mouton, 1973. Attacks identity materialism as represented by Herbert Feigl.

Popper, K. R. "Some Remarks on Panpsychism and Epiphenomenalism," *Dialectica,* 31 (1977), 177–186. A critique of the two theories named in the title.

Rosenthal, D. M. (ed.). *Materialism and the Mind-Body Problem.* Englewood Cliffs, N.J.: Prentice-Hall, 1971.

Russell, Bertrand. *The Analysis of Mind.* New York: Humanities Press, 1958.

Ryle, Gilbert. *The Concept of Mind.* New York: Barnes & Noble, 1965 (paperbound).

Shaffer, Jerome. "Could Mental States Be Brain Processes?" *The Journal of Philosophy,* 58 (1961), 813–822.

Skinner, B. F. *Science and Human Behavior.* New York: Macmillan, 1953. See "The Self," pp. 283–294.

Smart, J. J. C. *Philosophy and Scientific Realism.* New York: Humanities Press, 1963. See Chap. V. "Consciousness." Defends identity materialism.

Smythies, J. R. (ed.). *Brain and Mind*. London: Routledge and Kegan Paul, 1965. A valuable collection of essays by various writers.

Spicker, Stuart F. (ed.). *The Philosophy of the Body*. New York: Quadrangle Books, 1970 (paperbound). Classical and contemporary selections.

Stevenson, L. "Mind, Brain and Mental Illness," *Philosophy*, 52 (1977), 27–43. Explores the psychiatric implications of materialist theories of mind.

Strawson, P. F. *Individuals*. Garden City, N.Y.: Doubleday, 1959, pp. 87–116.

Teichman, J. *The Mind and the Soul*. New York: Humanities Press, 1974. A short, well-written introduction to the mind-body problem.

Vesey, G. N. A. *The Embodied Mind*. London: Allen & Unwin, 1965. A Cartesian view in modern dress.

Wiggins, D. *Identity and Spatio-Temporal Continuity*. Oxford: Basil Blackwell, 1967.

Wilkerson, T. E. *Minds, Brains and People*. London: Oxford University Press, 1974. See especially Chap. 7. Critique of identity materialism.

Wisdom, John. *Other Minds*. New York: Philosophical Library, 1952.

————. *Philosophy and Psychoanalysis*. New York: Philosophical Library, 1953.

————. *Problems of Mind and Matter*. New York: Cambridge University Press, 1963 (paperbound).

Woodhouse, M. "A New Epiphenomenalism?" *Australasian Journal of Philosophy*, 52 (1974), pp. 163–169. A critique of Keith Campbell's theory (see above).

PART VIII

FREEDOM AND DETERMINISM

31

THE PROBLEM OF FREEDOM
AND DETERMINISM

We now turn to one of the most frequently discussed, and most vexing, problems in philosophy: the problem of freedom and determinism. This issue is closely related to the mind-body problem that we have just been considering, as will become apparent as we go along. If you have made up your mind about the mind-body problem, chances are that you will have little difficulty in deciding where your preferences lie with respect to the present issue as well. If you had trouble deciding where the truth lies with respect to the former problem, perhaps a careful consideration of the issues involved in the freedom-determinism controversy will help you make up your mind on the mind-body problem too.

Like many philosophical problems, the freedom-determinism problem arises because of an apparent conflict between beliefs based on two different groups of facts. On the one hand, certain facts of moral experience convince most of us that we are accountable for our actions. For example, we praise and blame one another on the basis of observed behavior, and we accept praise and blame from others (and occasionally from ourselves) for our own acts. We say things like, "I ought not to have done that," "What he did was shameful," and so on. In other words, we believe ourselves to be morally responsible, and we treat others as if they were too. It would naturally seem to follow that if we are morally responsible, then we must be free: moral responsibility seems to presuppose moral freedom. This is one side of the picture.

But there are other facts that seem to support the view called universal determinism, the theory that every event in the universe is an inevitable consequence of antecedent causes. It seems self-evident to many people, for example, that "every event has a cause." Every scientific inquiry seems to presuppose that the phenomena under investigation are governed by some laws, and that these laws are capable of being discovered and stated with mathematical precision. We all act, as a matter of course, as if the universe is orderly: we expect pure water always to freeze at 32° Fahrenheit at sea-level barometric pressure; we expect the laws of aerodynamics to remain constant when we take a plane trip; and so on. Moreover, an immense and steadily growing quantity of scientific evidence appears to bear out the hypothesis that this is an orderly universe, that every event has a cause, that everything that occurs is an inevitable consequence of antecedent causes. Thus, we are also readily persuaded that the determinist hypothesis is correct.

However, if we try to affirm both these views, we encounter a serious problem. How can we be free in the way required to render us morally responsible if every event in the universe (including our decisions and our actions) is an inevitable consequence of antecedent causes? Does this not imply that we are not the real agents of our acts, and that our belief that we are morally responsible is mistaken? Or, if we are, indeed, free in the sense required to render us morally responsible, how can every event be an inevitable consequence of antecedent causes? Do moral responsibility and the freedom it requires contradict the mass of evidence supporting our belief in the orderliness and regularity of the universe?

It is apparent that a correct understanding of "moral freedom" is imperative. So far, we have spoken of moral freedom simply as that freedom (whatever its nature) that is a condition of moral responsibility. But what is the nature of this freedom? Is such freedom consistent with universal determinism or is it not? If not, which is the case?

Three Alternatives

The question about freedom and determinism can be answered in three different ways. One answer is (a) the freedom that is a condition of moral responsibility is not compatible with universal determinism, and (b) universal determinism is the case; therefore, (c) we are not free in the sense required to render us morally responsible. This position is commonly called *hard determinism.* It has been maintained by a large number of eminent thinkers and is more plausible than it appears when stated in summary form as it is here.

A second answer is (a) the freedom that is a condition of moral responsibility is not compatible with universal determinism, and (b) we have this freedom; therefore, (c) universal determinism is not the case. This position is commonly called *libertarianism.* It also can claim a large number of eminent defenders, and is probably the view of most people prior to systematic reflection on the problem.

The third possibility is (a) the freedom that is a condition of moral responsibility is compatible with universal determinism, and thus (b) we may be morally responsible even if determinism is the case. This view is commonly called *soft determinism* or *compatibilism.* It has been supported by such well-known philosophers as David Hume and John Stuart Mill, and it is probably the dominant view among British and American philosophers at the present time.

It should be noted that a soft determinist is no less a determinist than a hard determinist: both hold that every event in the universe is an inevitable consequence of antecedent causes. The difference between them is only in the consequences that they draw from this view. A hard determinist, who believes that the freedom that is a condition of moral responsibility is not compatible with universal determinism, draws the "hard" conclusion that human beings are not morally responsible. A soft determinist, who sees no incompatibility between universal determinism and moral freedom, draws the "soft" conclusion that human beings may be morally responsible even though universal determinism is the case. This is a point that people who are only casually acquainted with the freedom-determinism problem often fail to understand.

Terminology

Before considering the grounds upon which any one of these positions is maintained, it is advisable to clarify some of the terminology that frequently enters into discussions of this problem.

Let us consider first the terms "determinism" and "indeterminism." *Determinism* (or universal determinism, as it is called above) is a theory about the universe—the theory that every event in the universe is an inevitable consequence of antecedent causes. According to this theory, the state of the universe at any given moment determines *in every detail* what it will be like at any future moment. An omniscient observer, if one existed, could, according to this theory, predict with perfect accuracy each and every detail of the future—precisely when each organism would come into being, every detail of its life, the exact moment of its death, and so on. That we cannot, in fact, make such predictions now, say determinists, is due only to our ignorance of the relevant laws. If we did know the relevant laws—as we do in the case of the motions of the planets—such prediction would be theoretically possible.

Indeterminism is simply the denial of determinism. Like determinism, therefore, it is a theory about the universe. It asserts that the universe is so constituted that some events occur that are not the inevitable, and therefore theoretically predictable, consequences of antecedent causes; rather, they are uncaused, spontaneous, original. This does not mean, of course, that the universe as conceived by the indeterminist is utterly chaotic. An indeterminist readily admits that there are vast areas of the universe in which events are not only theoretically predictable but actually predictable. The indeterminist's position is simply that however wide the domain of causal law may be, it is not universal. Some events are not subject to it; they are not inevitable, and our hypothetical omniscient observer could not have predicted them despite his exhaustive knowledge of the universe.

We may also observe, at this point, that since determinism either is or is not true, and since indeterminism is identical with the view that determinism is not true, it is evident that either determinism or indeterminism must be the case. A great deal of confusion in the literature relating to this problem might have been avoided if this simple point had been clear to everyone who has written on it.

Two other theories that must be clearly understood are behaviorism and the free-will theory. Unlike determinism and indeterminism, these theories are about man rather than the universe.

Behaviorism may be defined as the view that human beings are so constituted that the whole of their behavior—their every wish, thought, decision, and act—is the inevitable consequence of antecedent causes. Behaviorism, then, is determinism as it applies to us. We, according to this view, are not, in any degree, the original cause of our own actions; our decisions and our choices are merely links in a complex chain of causes whose ultimate origin lies outside of ourselves.

The *free-will theory,* stated negatively, is simply the denial of behaviorism (just as indeterminism is simply the denial of determinism). Positively stated, the free-will theory may be defined as the view that we are so constituted that we are in some degree the original cause of our own actions—that it is impossible in principle to predict every detail of a person's behavior, since some of the causes of his or her future behavior are not now present. Similarly, it is impossible in principle to reduce a given act to a set of antecedent conditions lying outside the agent. However strong the influence of antecedent conditions may be, they are not, according to this view, sufficient to produce the act.

We shall have occasion in a later chapter to note in some detail the difficulties surrounding this notion of free will. For the present, however, the reader should concentrate on what the theory denies rather than what it affirms. We may justly expect that Libertarian, who is committed to affirming the free-will theory, will give a positive account of this theory in the course of stating and supporting this position.

Assuming the definitions that have just been given, the logical relations that obtain among these four theories may be summarized as follows:

1. If determinism is true, then
   a. indeterminism is false

    b. the free-will theory is false

    c. behaviorism is true

2. If determinism is false, then
    a. indeterminism is true
    b. the truth or falsity of behaviorism is unknown
    c. the truth or falsity of the free-will theory is unknown

3. If indeterminism is true, then
    a. determinism is false
    b. the truth or falsity of behaviorism is unknown
    c. the truth or falsity of the free-will theory is unknown

4. If indeterminism is false, then
    a. determinism is true
    b. behaviorism is true
    c. the free-will theory is false

5. If behaviorism is true, then
    a. the free-will theory is false
    b. the truth or falsity of determinism is unknown
    c. the truth or falsity of indeterminism is unknown

6. If behaviorism is false, then
    a. the free-will theory is true
    b. indeterminism is true
    c. determinism is false

7. If the free-will theory is true, then
    a. behaviorism is false
    b. indeterminism is true
    c. determinism is false

8. If the free-will theory is false, then
    a. behaviorism is true
    b. the truth or falsity of determinism is unknown
    c. the truth or falsity of indeterminism is unknown

Two other somewhat technical terms occasionally encountered in discussions of this problem are fatalism and predestination. We shall not use them in the debate that follows, but it seems advisable to clarify them briefly in order to avoid future confusion.

Fatalism may be defined as the view that (a) determinism is true, therefore, (b) whatever is going to happen is going to happen, no matter what anyone does. Fatalism implies what might be called a what-the-hell attitude toward life, since it would make no sense to try to bring about some result when its occurrence depends solely on whether or not the desired result is "fated" (determined) to occur. For the same reason, obviously, it would make no sense to take any steps to prevent some event from occurring. A fatalist would say, "I'll go when my time comes—and until then, no matter what I do, I'm safe; when that time comes, nothing can save me." Fatalism, then, is not so much a theory as an attitude toward life. Insofar as it is a theory, however, it is clearly mistaken in asserting that on the premise that determinism is true it follows that whatever will be will be *no matter what you or I or anyone else may do.* What determinism implies is that what you or I or someone else may do can be very influential (as intermediate causes) in determining events, but that our behavior, whatever it may be, is itself determined by antecedent causes. Much more could be said on this topic, but perhaps these few remarks are sufficient to show that fatalism is not a particularly useful concept in attempting to understand the freedom-determinism problem.

An equally unhelpful concept for our purposes is *predestination.* This is a theological concept, and in Christian theology it has a very precise meaning. It is the view that God determines absolutely, without regard to any quality or condition, who shall be saved and who shall be damned; it has to do only with this alleged decision, nothing else. Its only relevance to the freedom-determinism controversy is that it denies that we are free to decide what our eternal destiny will be. Since we have no need for this concept in the following discussion, there is no need to say any more about it.

It is crucially important for the discussion that follows, however, that the four concepts discussed earlier—determinism, indeterminism, behaviorism, and the free-will theory—be clearly and thoroughly understood. They will bear occasional review as we proceed with the debate.

STUDY QUESTIONS

1. State in two or three different ways what you understand to be the freedom-determinism problem.
2. How might this problem arise for each of the following: a physicist? a psychologist? a sociologist? a theologian? a juror?
3. Is it true that this problem is capable of being answered in just three ways? If so, explain why; if not, describe the additional alternatives.
4. Define carefully each of the following: hard determinism, soft determinism, universal determinism, indeterminism, libertarianism, behaviorism, free-will theory.
5. X says, "I do not believe in either determinism or indeterminism: I believe in self-determinism." Criticize this statement.

32

THE CASE FOR HARD DETERMINISM

I intend to show that of the three possible ways of answering the question posed in the preceding chapter, hard determinism is the most plausible. I shall begin by pointing out exactly what, as a hard determinist, I am obliged to defend. I shall then show why a careful consideration of this issue requires that one adopt the hard determinist position.

Hard determinism is the view that (a) the freedom that is a condition of moral responsibility is not compatible with universal determinism, and (b) universal determinism is the case; therefore, (c) we are not free in the sense required to render us morally responsible. I hold a certain view of what would have to be the case if one were to be morally responsible; I hold that this condition of moral responsibility is not compatible with universal determinism; and I hold that universal determinism is true. I conclude, therefore, that we are not, in fact, morally responsible. This conclusion—the assertion that human beings are not morally responsible—cannot be avoided if my two premises are true.

What Constitutes Moral Freedom?

It is first advisable to distinguish two different meanings that are often conveyed by the single word "freedom." One is "the opportunity to do what you want to do." In this sense, we have the freedom to do whatever we are not hindered from doing by external constraints or natural limitations. Thus, I am "free" at this moment to write or not to write, to remain sitting at my desk or to get up and leave it, to open my office door or to keep it closed. I am not "free" to help myself to all the money in the vault of the nearest bank (because of external constraints) or to jump thirty feet into the air (because of natural limitations). Let us call this kind of freedom the "circumstantial freedom of self-realization."[1]

It is apparent that freedom in this sense varies greatly, depending on abilities and circumstances. The strong are "free" to do some things that the weak are not; the rich are "free" to do some things that the poor are not; the average citizen is "free" to do some things that the prison inmate is not; and so on. Circumstantial freedom of self-realization, the opportunity to do what we want to do, is a matter of degree.

In another sense, freedom is seen as a power of the self to enact any one of a number of genuinely open alternatives. This is what libertarians ascribe to us when they credit us with having a "free will." The essential idea here is that of being an *original cause* of some action. We shall call this kind of freedom the "natural freedom of self-determination."

Suppose, for example, that a passerby observes a house on fire, hears a child's cry for help, and at risk to his or her own life and safety rushes in and rescues the child. This is an example of what many people would call purposive behavior, and, in calling it this, a part of what they mean is that the passerby's decision to respond to the child's cry for help was an *original cause* of this subsequent behavior. According to the free-will theory, the passerby had, as we said above, the power to enact any of several alternatives: he or she could have called for help, or rushed to the nearest telephone to call the fire department, or fled in cowardly fear. Why, then, did the passerby attempt the rescue? According to the free-will theory, because he or she *chose* to; and this choosing—this decision—was not itself the product of antecedent causes, but an original "uncaused cause."

I want to urge my readers to think carefully about the distinction that I have just made between these two conceptions of freedom, for the distinction is absolutely essential to a proper understanding of this whole problem. The first conceives of freedom as an *opportunity;* the second, as a *power.* To assert that people are free in the first sense is to assert something about their external circumstances; to assert that they are free in the second sense is to assert something about their internal makeup. Opportunity/power; external/internal; freedom A/ freedom B: these are the contrasts that we must hold firmly in mind as we try to decide what position to take with respect to this important problem.

I assume that everyone will allow that freedom in the first sense— the circumstantial freedom of self-realization—is a necessary condi-

---

[1]The terminology is borrowed from Mortimer J. Adler, et al., *The Idea of Freedom* (New York: Doubleday, 1958). This study constitutes the definitive analysis of the concept of freedom, and it is highly desirable that its terminological recommendations be adopted by all participants in the dispute over determinism and free will.

tion of moral responsibility. We do not hold people responsible for not doing something if we are satisfied that they wanted to do it but were simply unable to. This much is agreed to by everyone who is a party to the freedom-determinism dispute.

It is my view, however, that although the circumstantial freedom of self-realization is indeed a *necessary* condition of moral responsibility, it is not a *sufficient* condition. The libertarians are right in affirming that if people are to be regarded as morally responsible, it is also necessary to ascribe to them the natural freedom of self-determination—"free will," as they like to call it. They are wrong, however, in affirming that people have this kind of freedom.

The question of what constitutes moral freedom is a very difficult one, and we must be careful not to get lost in a forest of abstractions and arbitrary definitions. It would be easy, indeed, to arbitrarily define moral responsibility in such a way that the circumstantial freedom of self-realization would be a sufficient condition of its possibility. But we are not at liberty to define moral responsibility according to our fancy. What we really mean by moral responsibility is implicit in the ways in which we ascribe praise and blame and consider ourselves and others as deserving of reward or punishment.

In order to decide, therefore, whether or not the natural freedom of self-determination (free will) is a condition of moral responsibility, we have only to scrutinize the kinds of moral judgments we make. Then we may ask ourselves, Would we or would we not alter our judgment if we were persuaded that the agent of the act was not "free" in the sense of possessing the natural freedom of self-determination? I am confident that anyone who reflects carefully on a few hypothetical cases of this kind will find that we would alter our judgment, thereby demonstrating that our moral judgments do presuppose that people are free in the sense of possessing the natural freedom of self-determination.

Consider this hypothetical example. Two boys, Tom and George, are apprehended attempting the armed robbery of a supermarket. Subsequent questioning reveals that the holdup was first suggested by Tom, but that the detailed planning of the robbery was done cooperatively and that the two participated equally in the actual attempt. Therefore, both are guilty of committing a felony, and they are presumably deserving of equal punishment before the law.

If we were given no more information than this, our moral judgment on the matter would probably be nearly parallel to the legal judgment. Tom and George, we would say, are equally blameworthy for planning and attempting to execute this act. Indeed, if there is any difference at all in the blame attaching to the two boys, the greater blame must be Tom's since it was he who first suggested the idea. Nonetheless, we would say, both are highly blameworthy and deserve the punishment that they will now presumably receive at the hands of the law.

But suppose we then learn that Tom was raised in a family of habitual criminals, and that from earliest childhood he had been taught that armed robbery was a feat of heroism rather than a blame-worthy act. Suppose we also learn that George was the product of a very different kind of home: his father was governor, his mother a leader in civic affairs, and his elder brother a congressman. Would we now alter our previous moral evaluation? I am certain that we would, and in some readily predictable ways. We would say that George, having had the advantages of his upbringing, is more deserving of blame than Tom. We would say that Tom, owing to the untoward circumstances in which he was raised, is almost more to be pitied than to be blamed. Whatever the status of these two before the law, we would maintain that so far as their moral guilt is concerned, they are not deserving of equal blame.

But what is the principle according to which we alter our judgment of moral guilt? Why do we judge Tom less harshly than George? Clearly, it is because we partly attribute Tom's act to causes lying outside himself—to the environment in which he was raised—whereas we attribute George's act to his own perverse choice. In other words, *we do not hold a person responsible for any act insofar as we believe that act to be the consequence of causes lying outside that person.* Anyone who objectively considers a number of hypothetical cases of moral judgment will readily agree that this is an important principle on which our everyday moral judgments are formulated.

A person is morally responsible for his or her actions, then, only if, and insofar as, he or she is the original cause of those actions. Moral freedom—the freedom that is a condition of moral responsibility—includes the natural freedom of self-determination. Without this—without "free will," as the libertarians say—there is no moral responsibility.

The Case for Determinism

Unfortunately, it is impossible for human beings to have the natural freedom of self-determination, because this is a deterministic universe. To complete my case, I shall set forth a number of arguments that make it necessary to adopt the determinist hypothesis.

First, every instance of regularity in nature supports the hypothesis that all macroscopic phenonema are reducible to the regular operations of natural laws. The quantity of evidence now available from the many special sciences is so great as to make the contrary hypothesis exceedingly improbable.

The era of modern science began when people ceased asking for the *purposes* of natural phenomena and asked instead for their *causes.* To the question, What is the purpose of the revolution of the heavenly bodies? all sorts of fanciful answers are possible, and no answer can ever be demonstrated to be the right one. But to the question, What *uniformities* are exhibited in the motions of the heavenly bodies? or,

What are the *causes* of celestial phenomena? clear and mathematically precise answers can be given.

For a long time, it was assumed that "lawlike regularity" applied only to the realm of inanimate matter and that human behavior, at least, was exempt from the reign of such laws. Severe doubt was cast on this view by the work of Charles Darwin, however. A short time later, research was undertaken by Sigmund Freud and others on the supposition that human behavior, like any other phenomenon, is governed by laws that may be discovered by painstaking inquiry. This supposition has been progressively verified by Freud's successors. As B. F. Skinner says, "We cannot apply the methods of science to a subject matter that moves about capriciously."[2] Every advance in descriptive psychology, every discovery that is made with respect to the laws governing human behavior, adds to the rapidly growing evidence that human behavior, too, is thoroughly subject to the vast network of causes that govern all phenomena.

Should anyone be disposed to quarrel with what has just been said, let him or her reflect for a moment on what it would be like for a scientist to abandon the determinist hypothesis. Given the determinist hypothesis, a scientist can ask about any phenomenon chosen for investigation, What are its causes? What are the uniformities, the laws, exemplified in this phenomenon? Without the determinist hypothesis, a scientist could not ask such questions. Instead, the questions would have to be: Does this phenomenon have any causes—or is this, perhaps, one of those things that occur haphazardly, one of those things that do not have any regular causes? And this, I submit, would be absurd. It would cut the nerve of the whole scientific enterprise, which has made its advances on precisely the opposite supposition.

In a less rigorous but perhaps equally important way, we all make a similar supposition whenever we predict the behavior of other human beings. We know, for example, that if we want to avoid an argument, we had better stay off the subject of politics whenever Uncle George is around. We know this because, in a rough and ready way, we know some of the "laws," the "regularities," that govern Uncle George's behavior. Consider any person with whom you are reasonably well acquainted. Is it not true that you could, with a high degree of accuracy, predict how he or she would act in a wide variety of situations? To acknowledge this is to acknowledge that his or her behavior exhibits certain uniformities, uniformities that differ from the uniformities exhibited in the motions of planets, the interactions of chemicals, and the migration of birds only by virtue of being less well understood.

That human behavior is not exempt from causal laws also becomes evident when we reflect on the experience of "choosing among alter-

---

[2]B. F. Skinner, *Science and Human Behavior* (New York: Macmillan, 1953), p. 6.

natives." Here, if anywhere, we would expect the "natural freedom of self-determination," which libertarians defend, to be evident. But it is not. Consider: we never choose without a motive. Just as motives are determined by desires, so choice is determined by motive: we always choose that alternative for which we have the strongest motive. But what constitutes the strongest motive for any given individual depends on personal likes and dislikes, which are, in turn, the consequences of heredity and environment. Thus, the "chain of causes" leading to an act stretches back indefinitely; "decision" is not an original cause but merely one link in the chain.

Consider, once again, the passerby who courageously rescued the child from a burning building. Is it correct to say that the passerby's decision to attempt the rescue was an "uncaused cause" of his or her subsequent behavior? No. Being a particular kind of person—given a particular heredity and environment—it was inevitable, theoretically predictable, that he or she would decide to behave in a particular way. Another person, the product of a different heredity and environment, might have chosen differently, but this person—the passerby in our example—could not have chosen otherwise. He or she simply did that for which there was the strongest motive—as we all do. We are as integral a part of the all-embracing deterministic scheme of things as an atom, a molecule, a grain of sand. Our decisions, our actions, are only intermediate links in immensely long chains of events whose original cause or causes we shall never know.

I have dwelt at length on this matter of human behavior because it is, so to speak, the last outpost of indeterminism. If it is conceded that human behavior is as completely subject in principle to causal explanation as are other phenomena, then, so far as I can see, there will remain no further objection to adopting the determinist hypothesis. Thanks to the efforts of psychologists and sociologists, we have already come a long way toward adopting a behaviorist view. We now speak without hesitation of "the causes of crime," "the conditions that create antisocial attitudes," and the like. We still have, admittedly much to learn about the laws that govern human behavior. But it is not unreasonable to hope, with Skinner, that:

> eventually a science of the nervous system based upon direct observation rather than inference will describe the neural states and events which immediately precede instances of behavior. We shall know the precise neurological conditions which immediately precede, say, the response, "No, thank you." These events in turn will be found to be preceded by other neurological events, and these in turn by others. This series will lead us back to events outside the nervous system and, eventually, outside the organism.[3]

The foregoing considerations do not, of course, conclusively demonstrate the truth of the determinist hypothesis. However, they do sug-

---

[3] *Ibid.,* p. 28.

gest quite clearly that it is more reasonable to affirm the determinist hypothesis than it is to affirm its only alternative—indeterminism. And this is the conclusion that I have been attempting to establish.

I want to deal briefly with one objection that is frequently raised against the determinist position. It is sometimes stated that the principle of indeterminacy, which was first formulated by the German physicist W. K. Heisenberg and which is now an accepted part of modern physical theory, demonstrates that determinism is not the case and lends empirical support to the libertarian position. Now I will concede that it is possible that there is a real indeterminacy in the behavior of subatomic particles, as Heisenberg's theory affirms, although it seems to me most improbable that this is the case. The principle of indeterminacy is best understood, I think, as a limitation in *our knowledge* of subatomic events rather than a real hiatus in the network of mutually interacting events of which the universe is composed. Suppose, however, that I should turn out to be mistaken on this point. Suppose there is a real indeterminacy at the subatomic level. What are the consequences? I would, of course, be compelled to concede that in this one class of cases there does, indeed, seem to be some real indeterminacy in the universe, and that to that extent, determinism is incorrect. But this admission would in no way bolster the libertarian view that human decisions or actions are undetermined. To be sure, hard determinism is in considerable part an inference drawn from the belief that determinism is true, and to this extent hard determinists would (if Heisenberg's principle does, in fact, point to a real indeterminacy) have to modify their position. But the consequences for ethics are the same whether one is a determinist or merely a behaviorist, and the Heisenberg principle does nothing to undermine the behaviorist view. Thus the objection, while it is not exactly irrelevant to the issue we are discussing, suggests nothing that could be of any help to the defenders of moral responsibility.

Consequences for Ethics

The conclusions to which the foregoing considerations force me are, I confess, somewhat disturbing. Since moral responsibility presupposes the natural freedom of self-determination (free-will), since this freedom is not compatible with universal determinism, and since universal determinism appears to be the case, it seems evident that—contrary to what most people certainly believe—human beings are not morally responsible. And this inference, in turn, carries with it consequences such as the following:

1. No human act, however "noble" or "base," is ever worthy of either praise or blame. John F. Kennedy's heroism and dedication were as much a product of his heredity and environment as Lee Harvey Oswald's hatred and perversion were a product of his.
2. Punishment (or "retributive justice" as it is sometimes called) can-

not be defended on the ground that a person who acts in a certain way is "guilty" and therefore "deserving of punishment." It makes no sense to talk about a criminal "paying his debt to society." Like everybody else, the criminal has acted in the only way possible for him (given his heredity and environment) and therefore has incurred no such debt.

3. If we are to continue to praise and blame or reward and punish people on the basis of their behavior, it can only be on the ground that such things will tend to influence their behavior in certain desirable ways.

These are "hard" conclusions. I will even admit that personally I do not like them, and that I, in fact, continue to make judgments of praise and blame just as everyone else does. But as a philosopher I know that such judgments have no rational justification. Our beliefs about moral responsibility and what we now know about the structure of the universe (and about human beings in particular) are in hopeless and irremediable contradiction. As a philosopher, I have felt obliged to point out this contradiction, notwithstanding the unpalatable consequences for ethical theory.

STUDY QUESTIONS

1. What precisely is the difference between "the circumstantial freedom of self-realization" and "the natural freedom of self-determination"? In what sense, according to Hard Determinist, must people be free if they are to be morally responsible? Do you think he is right about this?

2. What is the point of Hard Determinist's insistence that in the discussion of this question one must constantly refer to the "facts concerning the actual ways in which we handle the categories of moral responsibility"? Does this seem to be at all important?

3. Does Hard Determinist's example bear out his claim that we do not hold a person responsible for an act insofar as we believe that act to be the consequence of causes lying outside that person? Suggest three or four additional examples that either confirm or disconfirm this principle.

4. What arguments does Hard Determinist offer in support of the truth of the determinist hypothesis? Does this evidence seem to be conclusive? Can you think of any additional arguments in support of this hypothesis that Hard Determinist has failed to mention?

5. Do the "disturbing consequences" that Hard Determinist itemizes at the end of his essay really follow from his view, as he says? Are there other similar consequences that Hard Determinist has neglected to mention?

33

THE CASE FOR SOFT DETERMINISM

It must certainly be acknowledged that Hard Determinist has made a strong case for determinism and the impossibility of the freedom without which, according to his view, people cannot be morally responsible. His arguments in support of the determinist hypothesis are particularly cogent, and I am delighted to accept everything he has to say on that score as a part of the case that I propose to build in defense of soft determinism or compatibilism.

Before I do this, however, I should like to note that I do not care for the name "soft determinism" that is commonly used to describe my position. There are two reasons for my dislike of this name. The first is that it was invented by William James, a noted libertarian, who coined it precisely for the purpose of disparagement. Just listen to James:

> Nowadays, we have a soft determinism which abhors harsh words, and, repudiating fatality, necessity, and even predetermination, says that its real name is freedom; for freedom is only necessity understood, and bondage to the highest is identical with true freedom.[1]

Now, if to avoid confusion I allow my position to be called "soft determinism," I insist that James' pejorative connotations be laid aside and that my position be considered simply on its merits. If I reject Hard Determinist's conclusions with respect to ethics, it is not because I am "soft," but because I think his conclusions are unwarranted.

---

[1]William James, "The Dilemma of Determinism," *The Will to Believe and Other Essays in Popular Philosophy and Human Immortality* (New York: Dover, 1956), p. 149.

The second reason for my displeasure with the name "soft determinism" is that it has led to a great deal of confusion concerning what
my position really is. I am no less firm in my adherence to determinism than is Hard Determinist. I, too, maintain that the universe is so
constituted that absolutely everything that occurs, including actions
by human beings, is an inevitable consequence of antecedent causes.
Both Hard Determinist and I are what may be called "strict determinists." The difference between us is not that he is more consistent in his
determinism than I, but that he draws certain consequences from his
determinism (with respect to ethics) that are, in my view, unjustified.
I propose now to show where Hard Determinist makes his mistake and
how it is possible to maintain a consistent determinism without drawing the dire conclusions that he insists must be drawn.

Moral Freedom

The crucial question that must be asked about the vexing problem of
moral freedom is, *In what sense* must one be "free" in order to be
morally responsible? Hard Determinist has argued that one must be
free in a contracausal sense, that is, must possess a natural freedom
of self-determination. My view, on the contrary, is that the circumstantial freedom of self-realization—the opportunity to do what you
please—is a necessary *and sufficient* condition of moral responsibility. I think that a careful consideration of the ways in which we actually ascribe praise and blame will demonstrate that this view is the
correct one.

Let us suppose that Hard Determinist were right in his contention
that people could be morally free only if this were not a deterministic
universe, that is, that they could be held morally responsible for an act
only if that act were not the inevitable consequence of antecedent
causes. We would then be in the position of saying that a person is
responsible for an act if and only if that act is uncaused. But to say that
something is uncaused is to say that it is a "chance" event, a mere
random occurrence. Apart from the difficulty of even conceiving of
such a thing, it is absurd to maintain that a person could be morally
responsible only if his or her actions, or some of his or her actions
(those for which he or she would be held responsible), occurred "by
chance." This is not what we have in mind when we say "So and so
is morally responsible for doing *r*."

What, then, do we have in mind? Simply, I submit, that the agent
had the opportunity—the circumstantial freedom—to do a number of
things, and that the agent took a particular action *because he or she
wanted to.* When appraising praiseworthiness or blameworthiness,
we do not ask whether the agent could have desired to do otherwise,
because that is not relevant to our judgment of the particular action.
What we do ask is whether the agent could have done otherwise had
he or she so desired.

Let us consider a hypothetical example. Johnny has been instructed always to come directly home from school, and his mother has learned (through repeated observation of Johnny's arrival time) that when he does, he normally arrives home no later than 3:15 P.M. A few times, however, Johnny has arrived home at a slightly later time, but on each of these occasions his mother has determined that he "could not have done otherwise": he had to stay after school, the extreme cold made it necessary for him to stop briefly at a store to warm himself, and so forth. But one spring day, Johnny arrives home at nearly 5 P.M., and Mother naturally asks, "Johnny, where have you been?" Johnny replies, "I've been playing in the puddles." "But Johnny," Mother objects, "don't you know that you are supposed to come directly home from school?" "Yes." "Well, why didn't you?" "Well, I just didn't want to. I wanted to play in the puddles." "Well, son, you will have to be punished for this." "But Mother," Johnny cries, "you can't punish me for that. I couldn't *want* to do anything else."

We obviously do not, and would not, consider Johnny's objection relevant. Why? Because in holding someone responsible for something, we do not ask why that person wants to do such and such but only whether doing such and such was a result of wanting to do it. So long as Johnny's late arrival was unavoidable—so long as his wanting to be home on time was thwarted by circumstances—Johnny was not held responsible for his late arrival. But when his late arrival was the consequence of his wanting to do something that caused him to be late, he was immediately held responsible *no matter what may have been the causes of his wanting to play rather than obey.*

Let us consider a second hypothetical case. The manager of a supermarket is apprehended in the act of removing the contents of the store safe at 2 A.M. and, of course, is suspected of attempted theft. Investigation discloses, however, that (a) a gunman is holding the manager's wife and children hostage and has threatened to harm them if the manager does not comply with orders; (b) a second gunman has forced the manager to drive to the supermarket and open the safe; and (c) the manager tried unsuccessfully to attract the attention of the police (at risk of his life) by exceeding the speed limit and running through a red light en route to the market.

Knowing these facts, we would not hold the manager responsible for the attempted theft, because we would then be satisfied that he was not doing what he wanted to do. And the reason that he was not doing what he wanted to do was that he did not have the circumstantial freedom, the opportunity, to do it.

Who was responsible, then, for the attempted robbery? Obviously, the gunmen, for *to be morally responsible is to be the person whose motives, whose desires, need to be changed if a given kind of behavior is to be encouraged or prevented.* We do not blame people for doing what, under the circumstances, was the only thing they could reasonably have been expected to do. We do blame them if a different desire on their part would have been sufficient to produce a more desirable kind of behavior.

Reasons for Confusion

The problem of freedom and determinism has been debated vociferously and inconclusively for many hundreds of years. Why is this if the solution is really as simple as I have suggested? Since the question may itself hinder acceptance of my position, I should like to deal briefly with it.

There are two reasons why the true solution to this much discussed problem has proved consistently elusive. The first, and in my judgment the most important, is that the nature of moral judgments has been misunderstood. To be morally responsible, as we said above, is to be the person whose motives need to be changed if a given kind of behavior is to be encouraged or prevented. Moreover, the function of moral judgments is precisely *to alter the motives of the person being judged and, thus, to influence his or her future behavior.* Praise and blame are simply mild forms of reward and punishment. The reason for employing either is always to discourage or prevent certain kinds of undesirable behavior (blame or punishment) or to encourage certain kinds of desirable behavior (praise or other rewards).

Let us now suppose that someone makes a moral judgment without understanding the true nature of moral responsibility. In all likelihood that person will construe such judgments on the analogy of statements of fact. Accordingly, he or she will interpret blameworthiness and praiseworthiness as "intrinsic qualities" of the persons or acts being judged. From this mistaken starting point it is only a short step to the view that some obscure power ("freedom") *within the agent* is a condition of moral responsibility.

The second reason involves a series of semantic confusions over the terms "law" and "freedom." Our understanding of the term "law" derives largely from its use in connection with statutes and ordinances —the kinds of things enacted by city councils, legislatures, and parliaments. It is the very nature of this type of law to prescribe behavior —indeed, by virtue of the threat of punishment, to coerce behavior. Implicit in every such law is the "or else" embodied in the system of fines or punishments that await the offender. If we disobey, we become subject to the prescribed punishment. Because we fear the punishment, we usually obey, whether or not the prescribed behavior is what we ourselves really want to do.

But in science, the term "law" is used to designate something very different, namely, an observed uniformity. Scientific law is merely a report about what has actually been observed to be the case in such and such a class of phenomena. Here, there is no coercion, no "or else." Pure water, at sea level, is not compelled or constrained to freeze whenever the temperature reaches 32° Fahrenheit. It just does. And the "law" that states this is simply a description of what, in fact, has been observed to occur.

Had this distinction between prescriptive and descriptive law been clearly recognized, it probably would never have occurred to anyone to insist that moral responsibility requires exemption from the laws of nature. Moral responsibility does, indeed, require exemption from coercion, but the laws of nature do not coerce. The opposite of causality is acausality, or indeterminism, whereas the opposite of compulsion is freedom. Hence, the failure to distinguish the two different kinds of law led to the absurd view that moral responsibility requires a contracausal, or indeterministic, freedom.

Moral Responsibility Requires Determinism

Thus far, I have argued only that moral freedom is consistent with the determinist hypothesis and that we do not need to conclude with Hard Determinist that people cannot be morally responsible in a deterministic world. It may appear that I am being purely defensive—that I am trying to "salvage" whatever I can of human moral responsibility in a deterministic universe. By way of countering this impression, which is implicit in James's unfortunate labeling of my position as "soft" determinism, I should like to conclude by taking the offensive in this argument. The thesis I propose to support is this: not only is moral responsibility consistent with the determinist hypothesis, but *moral responsibility would not be possible in anything other than a deterministic universe.*

That moral responsibility requires determinism is evident from my earlier argument concerning the absurdity of maintaining that a person can be responsible for only those of his acts that occur "by chance." For any event whatsoever, we can conceive of only two possibilities: either it has a cause or it does not have a cause. If it has a cause, then it is explicable within the context of the determinist hypothesis. If it does not have a cause, then it is a "chance event." To reject determinism, therefore, on the ground that it is incompatible with moral responsibility—or, alternatively, to reject moral responsibility on the ground that it is not possible in a deterministic universe —is to adopt the absurd position referred to above.

My thesis can also be supported in another way. Let us suppose that this were not a deterministic universe—that some things that occur were not the inevitable consequences of antecedent causes, and that a given set of circumstances would not, therefore, always produce a predictable effect. In such a universe, it would be impossible to hold a person responsible for *anything,* because he could never know what would be the result of any act he might perform. In such a universe, the glass of water that yesterday quenched the thirst of a dying man might today poison him, or turn him into a giraffe, or do any one of countless other thoroughly unpredictable things. It is only insofar as we can predict what the effects of a given course of action will be that we can act responsibly; hence, it follows that we can act responsibly only in a universe where certain predictable effects follow inevitably from certain causes. An indeterministic universe, in which the orderly sequence of events is interrupted by more or less frequent "chance events," would be a moral chaos. It is doubtful if life would even be possible in such a universe. Certainly, responsible behavior would not.

It seems, therefore, that the time has come to lay this old problem to rest. What is really of concern to Hard Determinist is the truth of the determinist hypothesis. It is this that he feels obliged to insist on, and in this he is right. What is really of concern to Libertarian is the truth of the conviction that human beings are morally responsible. This is what he feels obliged to insist on, and in this he is right. Where both Hard Determinist and Libertarian err—and this is the unargued assumption that has kept the debate alive for many years—is in assuming that moral responsibility requires contracausal freedom. Once the absurdity of this assumption is perceived, the problem is solved.

STUDY QUESTIONS

1. Where precisely does Soft Determinist agree with Hard Determinist, and where does he disagree with him? Is there any difference between them regarding the *method* by which each thinks this question must be decided?

2. Does it follow from Hard Determinist's position, as Soft Determinist says, that "a person is responsible for an act if and only if that act is uncaused"? How might Hard Determinist defend himself against this objection?

3. Do the hypothetical examples offered by Soft Determinist support his claim that the only relevant question in deciding moral responsibility is whether the person involved acted in a certain way because he or she wanted to? Could Hard Determinist explain these examples in a way consistent with his position?

4. What does Soft Determinist say is the meaning of "moral responsibility"? Do you think he is right? If not, what alternative would you suggest?

5. What considerations does Soft Determinist offer in support of the claim that moral responsibility actually *requires* determinism? Do you agree or disagree with this thesis? Why?

34

THE CASE FOR LIBERTARIANISM

Despite the formidable array of arguments that Hard Determinist and Soft Determinist have presented in support of their respective positions and against libertarianism, I am convinced that libertarianism can be shown to be true. I welcome the opportunity to demonstrate how the various objections raised against it can be rather easily overcome. Let me begin by indicating where I agree and disagree with each of my opponents.

Hard Determinist has argued that determinism is true, and that the freedom that is a condition of moral responsibility is not compatible with determinism. From these two premises, he has drawn the unhappy conclusion that human beings are not morally responsible. My position vis-a-vis Hard Determinist is clear: I reject his first premise, affirm his second, and, of course, do not accept his conclusion. I believe it can be established on independent grounds that human beings are morally responsible and that, therefore, determinism is not the case. I shall attempt to show in due time that the consequences of accepting this conclusion are not nearly so dire as some determinists would lead us to believe.

Soft Determinist offers a more elusive argument, so naturally it is more difficult to state precisely where we agree and disagree. Our prime disagreement, of course, centers on determinism: he holds that it is the case, I hold that it is not. We disagree, moreover, about the kind of freedom required to render a person morally responsible. He holds that the circumstantial freedom of self-realization is a sufficient condition of moral responsibility; I hold (in agreement with Hard Determinist) that people are not morally responsible unless they also possess the natural freedom of self-determination (free will).

It may seem as if Soft Determinist and I agree on one point, namely, that people are morally responsible. But anyone who is acquainted with both his position and mine will immediately recognize that our agreement is only verbal. When Soft Determinist says that A is morally responsible, he means that A is the person whose motives need to be changed if a certain kind of behavior is to be encouraged or avoided. When I say that A is morally responsible, I mean that A is fittingly, or deservingly, subject to praise or blame, reward or punishment.

Despite the fact that soft determinism is a widely held position, I am convinced that it is not a tenable one. Hard determinism, on the other hand, is a position worthy of respect, though I consider it mistaken nonetheless. At any rate, I believe that for any clear-thinking person the final choice must be between libertarianism and hard determinism, and I shall do my best to show that the strongest considerations are on my side.

Refutation of Soft Determinism

I have the greatest sympathy for the considerations that led Soft Determinist to adopt his position. The conclusions that Hard Determinist draws with respect to human moral responsibility are "hard," indeed, and it is not surprising that some determinists have sought a way to avoid them within the context of their deterministic beliefs.

Nonetheless, the mistake that Soft Determinist makes—the mistake that vitiates his whole position—is incredibly obvious. Starting from the assumption that determinism is true, Soft Determinist (a) arbitrarily redefines "moral freedom" in such a way as to render it compatible with determinism, and (b) arbitrarily redefines "moral responsibility" in such a way as to make "moral freedom" as he has defined it a sufficient condition thereof. He then proudly announces that he has "reconciled" determinism and moral responsibility, and that the traditional problem that has long divided libertarians and determinists has, at last, been solved. But all that has been accomplished by this little verbal sleight of hand is a blurring of the relevant concepts and a further confusion of the issue. That moral responsibility *as this concept is employed in our everyday judgments of praise and blame* is compatible with determinism is not shown to be true in the slightest by Soft Determinist's argument.

Consider an analogy. Suppose that we are interested in the question, Are all citizens of Flamenco absolutely loyal to their government, or do some of them occasionally commit acts of treason? Two straightforward answers are possible. Either (a) all citizens are absolutely loyal ("hard loyalism") or (b) treasonous acts are sometimes committed ("occasionarianism"). But it would be distinctly unhelpful to have someone say, "Look, I can define treason in such a way that occasional acts of what is now called treason do not contradict the view that all the people of Flamenco are absolutely loyal to their government." We do not want to know whether treason *as thus defined* can be made to square with "universal loyalism." What we want to know is whether treason in its ordinary unaltered meaning is compatible with "universal loyalism"; and it is evident that it is not.

Hard Determinist has already cautioned us to remember that we are not at liberty to define moral responsibility to suit our fancy. What we really mean by moral responsibility is implicit in the ways in which we ascribe praise and blame and deem ourselves and others deserving of reward and punishment. If one attends carefully to the actual employment of judgments of praise and blame, one will shortly discover, I am confident, that "being morally responsible" means more than simply "being capable of having behavior altered through an alteration of motives."

Consider for a moment some of the absurd implications of the view that moral responsibility means what Soft Determinist says it means. In the first place, it would follow that we ought to hold animals morally responsible no less than we do men, for there is every reason to suppose that reward and punishment will influence the behavior of dogs and horses just as much as they will influence the behavior of men. But, of course, although we do, indeed, reward and punish animals, we do not apply moral judgments to them.

Further, if moral responsibility means what Soft Determinist says it means, it would make no sense whatsoever to speak of a deceased person as "responsible" for something, since on this hypothesis there is no one whose motives could be influenced in such a way as to bring about a different sort of behavior. Yet, we do blame deceased persons for acts committed by them: Hitler and Stalin are examples.

And again, in judgments of praise and blame, we commonly "make allowances" for such things as a poor childhood environment. The boy who grew up in the slums, whose father was a petty thief, and so on, "did not have the chance" (as we say) that his more fortunate fellows had, so we judge him less harshly. On Soft Determinist's ground, we would have no reason to judge him less harshly, since we have no reason to suppose that his behavior is either more or less subject to influence than anyone else's behavior. Indeed, if Soft Determinist is right, we ought, if anything, to judge such a person more harshly, since there is reason to suppose that more counteracting influences are needed if his behavior is to be brought into tolerable conformity with society's norms.

Thus, at a number of crucial points, Soft Determinist's account of moral responsibility is at variance with our actual judgments of praise and blame. Since it is in reference to such judgments that we must decide this matter, Soft Determinist's inability to account for the cases just mentioned must be regarded as decisive against his position.

Soft Determinist has argued that moral freedom consists simply in having the circumstantial freedom of self-realization, and that this view is supported by the fact that in concrete cases we never inquire about anything else. "It is significant," he writes, "that the only question relevant to determining moral responsibility . . . is, Was the agent able to do what he wanted to do? That is, did he have the *circumstantial freedom* to actualize his own wishes?" But surely the reason for this is that we assume that every normal and healthy person has the natural freedom of self-determination—free will—at all times, and so we do not feel the need to inquire about it in each particular case. The reason that Johnny's mother (in Soft Determinist's example) does not accept his objection that he "couldn't *want* to do anything else" is not that his objection, if true, is not relevant, but rather that she does not believe him. If she were to become convinced that he had suddenly been afflicted with a puddle-playing syndrome that literally *compelled* him to want to play in puddles, her attitude would be very different.

We may safely conclude, therefore, that the recent attempts of some determinists to affirm the moral responsibility of human beings without relinquishing their belief in determinism do not succeed. If human beings are to be regarded as morally responsible, it is necessary, as Hard Determinist has argued, that they have both the circumstantial freedom of self-realization (the opportunity to do what they want to do) and the natural freedom of self-determination (free will). And since, as Hard Determinist has shown, the latter is not compatible with determinism, the choice must rest between Hard Determinist's position and my own.

Replies to Objections

Hard Determinist has admirably stated the arguments that he thinks effectively support the determinist hypothesis. Nevertheless, his arguments are not convincing. Let us review them once more.

First, he asserts that "every instance of regularity in nature supports the hypothesis that all macroscopic phenomena are reducible to the regular operations of natural laws" and that "the quantity of evidence now available from the many special sciences is so great as to make the contrary hypothesis exceedingly improbable." However, the determinist hypothesis is not a "superhypothesis," progressively being established by mounting evidence. Rather, it is a heuristic principle[1] that is presupposed in each particular scientific inquiry. It is important to scientific research that there be no preestablished limits to the scope of natural laws, since such limits would arbitrarily prevent inquiry beyond a certain point. But it is not important to the scientific enterprise to maintain, either as a dogma or as a hypothesis, that there are no such limits.

Suppose, for example, that my view that people are free in a contracausal sense were correct. This would not, so far as I can see, in any

---

[1]See Glossary, pp. 480–481.

way hinder the scientific study of humanity. My view does not deny that there are some laws governing human behavior: it only denies that human behavior is *completely* explicable in terms of such laws. Let the scientific study of humanity proceed as rapidly and as far as it can; let the independent variables affecting human behavior be discovered and stated with as great precision as possible; there will still remain the "freedom factor"; consequently, behavior will not become perfectly predictable and people will remain morally responsible. This factor may be more or less influential in determining a person's behavior than we now commonly suppose; outside influences may, as psychologists and sociologists are inclined to believe, play a much greater role in determining behavior than was once assumed. But unless and until laws have been discovered in terms of which *every detail* of human behavior is explicable, there is no reason whatsoever to deny the presence of this "freedom factor."Indeed, as we shall see presently, there is excellent reason to affirm it.

Hard Determinist's admission that the principle of indeterminacy might turn out to be a case of real indeterminacy in the universe illustrates my point exactly. Physicists have lived with this concept for many years now, and it has not appeared to hinder their research in the least. They have simply been forced to accept the fact that when they are dealing with subatomic particles, they have reached one of the limits of universal law, a realm where lawlike regularity apparently does not obtain. That the human will should constitute another such limit would not appear to raise any new problems. Certainly, I do not mean to suggest that the discovery of the principle of indeterminacy constitutes evidence in support of the freedom of the will: Hard Determinist is quite right in denying that this principle has any such direct relevance for the free-will problem. I do emphatically assert, however, that the fact that scientists have been able to accept with equanimity the principle of indeterminacy, astonishing as that principle was in the context of classical theory, completely destroys Hard Determinist's claim that the possibility of indeterminacy, such as would be required by a belief in free will, would "cut the nerve of the whole scientific enterprise."

Hard Determinist's second argument in support of determinism (actually it is in support of behaviorism) is that we can, in a rough-and-ready way, predict the behavior of people whom we know well. This, he contends, supports the hypothesis that their behavior is governed by certain "laws" or "uniformities," which we vaguely discern in making our prediction.

I grant that we can, within certain limits, make some informed guesses about how people that we know well will act in certain situations, but I fail to see how this in any way supports the behaviorist thesis. Such consistency of behavior as we actually observe in people of our acquaintance may be due to either (a) external causes such as a behaviorist believes completely dominate human behavior or (b) habits of character acquired through many years of training and experience—or both. Even if we grant that to some extent *a* is the case, we can still reasonably hold the libertarian view in the absence of evidence that *a* is the case totally. And to the extent that *b* is the case, we can plausibly hold that a person's character is in part a product of his or her past choices freely made, and that it may be further modified by future choices. Thus, it seems clear that such regularity as we do observe in the behavior of individuals in no way supports the hypothesis that *all* human behavior is the product of causes lying ultimately outside the agent.

Hard Determinist's third argument is that reflection on the experience of "choosing among alternatives" makes it evident that (a) we always do that for which we find the strongest motive, and (b) what constitutes the strongest motive for any individual depends on causes lying outside that individual. In one form or another, this is one of the oldest and most persuasive arguments used against the libertarian position. The refutation of it must, unfortunately, be somewhat complex.

The apparent force of this argument lies in the tacit adoption of a mechanical model to describe and explain human volition and action. According to this model, the self is conceived as a "thing" that is pulled, or pushed, in various directions by "motives" and is inevitably moved in the direction of the strongest pull, or push. But the model is not adequate. Selfhood cannot be conceived "from the outside"; it must be conceived from within, in terms of what it means to *be* a self. The reality of responsible selfhood cannot be adequately described in the paramechanical language of motives-determining-acts; it can be expressed only in the personal-life categories of decision and choice.

Space does not permit the detailed development of an alternative to the mechanical model employed by Hard Determinist. However, we may observe that it is the moral freedom of human beings, not the indeterminacy of some "faculty," that is here in question. As moral agents we know (a) that there are some situations in which we are "morally obliged" to act in a certain way—there is something that we "ought" to do—and (b) that often in such situations there is something that we "desire" to do that differs from what we "ought" to do. I am willing to allow that people are not free to choose what shall be their strongest desire in any given situation: that, it seems to me, is determined by their character in relation to all the other details of that situation. I would insist, however, that, in any given situation, people need not act in accordance with their strongest desire; they may, instead, act contrary to that desire because they believe it is their *duty* to do so. The person alone decides whether an action shall correspond to duty or to desire; hence, he or she alone is answerable for his or her behavior.

This is admittedly a gross oversimplification of the matter, since in actual experience the conflict between duty and desire is seldom so sharp and explicit as this account suggests. It is, nonetheless, truer to our actual experience as moral agents than the mechanistic model we are attempting to refute. Anyone wishing a fuller explanation of this matter can, and should, at some later time inquire further into the notion of the self. For the present, we have only to acknowledge that a self is not a "thing" and that its operations cannot be understood in terms of a mechanical model appropriate only to "things."

The Basis for Libertarianism

Even if my arguments succeed in removing the chief objections to libertarianism, the libertarian position is yet to be established. What is still required is some positive ground for its affirmation.

There is one, and only one, ground upon which libertarianism rests: that we know ourselves to be morally responsible, and that, therefore, we also know that whatever is necessary to render us morally responsible must be the case. There are, indeed, times when we have only one avenue of action open to us, and in such situations we accept neither praise nor blame for doing what, under the circumstances, was the only thing we could do. But more commonly we are faced with a variety of alternatives, some of which are, in varying degrees, attractive to us (instances of desire) and some of which may appear to make some moral claim on us (instances of duty). Here we must choose among the alternatives; and in the experience of choosing, of saying Yes to one of the alternatives and No to all the rest, we know directly that it is *our choice* that determines what shall be done. Our choice is not arbitrary: we can always give a reason for it ("I wanted to," "I felt it was my duty," and so forth). But neither is it predictable, because we alone decide whether and to what extent to follow duty or desire.

Since we are, and know ourselves to be, morally responsible, the universe must contain the possibility of moral responsibility. Therefore, it cannot be strictly deterministic, for in such a universe, moral freedom and responsibility could not exist. But neither, obviously, can it be a chaos, since in such a universe we could never accurately predict the result of any of our acts. (This last condition is the answer to Soft Determinist's claim that moral responsibility *requires* determinism. What moral responsibility does require is that the universe exhibit sufficient uniformity to enable us to know the probable consequences of this or that act.) The universe must, therefore, be sufficiently uniform in its operations to enable us to "count on" certain actions producing certain effects, and it must be sufficiently "loose" in its structure to permit human beings to make genuinely free and responsible decisions.

Fortunately, from my point of view, that is just how the universe appears to be. There certainly *is* a large area in which perfect uniformity appears to prevail. Thus I can, for example, depend on food to nourish, and I can feed the hungry confident that my action will not produce unintended results. Whether I actually do feed the hungry is up to me; consequently, I am fittingly held responsible for what I do or fail to do. Because there is a considerable degree of uniformity, science is possible; and I would not want to set any a priori limits to the extent of that uniformity. But because there is also a certain amount of "looseness" in the universe, moral freedom and responsible behavior have found a place as well; and I would be equally reluctant to set any a priori limits to the extent of man's moral responsibility. In a strictly deterministic universe, science would presumably be possible, but moral freedom and responsibility would not. In a chaotic universe, neither science nor morality would be possible. In the universe as it is, however, highly uniform but not strictly determined, there is ample room both for scientific knowledge and for moral freedom and responsibility. To abandon either would be to err in our understanding of human beings and their world.

STUDY QUESTIONS

1. Where exactly does Libertarian agree, and where does he disagree, with each of the two previous writers? Where on each of these points do your own sympathies lie at the present time?
2. How, according to Libertarian, has Soft Determinist accomplished the apparent reconciliation of determinism and moral freedom? Is this an accurate description of what Soft Determinist has done? If not, where does it go wrong?
3. Libertarian offers a *reductio ad absurdum* of Soft Determinist's account of moral responsibility. Summarize the argument. Does it succeed in your opinion?
4. What is a "heuristic principle"? How does the suggestion that the determinist hypothesis is a heuristic principle tend (if it does) to weaken Hard Determinist's case?
5. Summarize Libertarian's replies to Hard Determinist's arguments in support of determinism. Which of them, if any, do you find most convincing? Which least convincing?
6. What does Libertarian say is the "one, and only one, ground upon which libertarianism rests"? Do you find his argument at this point convincing? Why or why not?

CORRELATED READINGS[1]

1. Mill, John Stuart. "Necessity and Moral Freedom." *A System of Logic.* 5th ed. (1862), Vol. II, pp. 413–421. Soft determinism.
2. James, William. "The Dilemma of Determinism." *The Will to Believe and Other Essays in Popular Philosophy.* (1896). Libertarianism.
3. Hospers, John. "What Means This Freedom?" *Determinism and Freedom in the Age of Modern Science,* ed. Sidney Hook. New York: New York University Press, 1958, pp. 126–142. Hard determinism.
4. Foot, Philippa. "Free Will as Involving Determinism." *The Philosophical Review,* Vol. 66 (1957), pp. 439–450. A critique of the theory that moral responsibility requires determinism.

FOR FURTHER READING

Adler, Mortimer, *et. al. The Idea of Freedom.* Garden City, N.Y.: Doubleday, 1958.
Ayers, M. R. *The Refutation of Determinism.* London: Methuen, 1968.
Beardsley, Elizabeth L. "Determinism and Moral Perspectives," *Philosophy and Phenomenological Research,* 21 (1960), 1–20.
Bergson, Henri. *Time and Free Will.* New York: Harper & Row, 1962 (paperbound).
Berofsky, Bernard. *Determinism.* Princeton, N.J.: Princeton University Press, 1971.
——— (ed.). *Free Will and Determinism.* New York: Harper & Row, 1966. A valuable collection of writings from many sources.
Brand, Myles (ed.). *The Nature of Human Action.* Glenview, Ill.: Scott, Foresman, 1970 (paperbound). An anthology. A basic issue: can sufficient explanations of human actions be given by references to causes?
Campbell, C. A. *In Defense of Free Will.* London: Allen & Unwin, 1967. A collection of essays by a prominent proponent of libertarianism.
———. "Is 'Free Will' a Pseudo-Problem?" *Mind,* 60 (1951), 441–465.
———. *On Selfhood and Godhood.* New York: Humanities Press, 1957.
Cranston, M. *Freedom—A New Analysis.* London: Longmans, Green, 1953.
Dworkin, Gerald (ed.). *Determinism, Free Will and Moral Responsibility.* Englewood Cliffs, N.J.: Prentice-Hall, 1970 (paperbound).
Eddington, A. S. *The Nature of the Physical World.* Ann Arbor: University of Michigan Press, 1958 (paperbound), Chap. 14.
Edwards, Jonathan. *Inquiry Concerning the Freedom of the Will,* ed. by Paul Ramsey. New Haven, Conn.: Yale University Press, 1957.
Ezorsky, G. (ed.). *Philosophical Perspectives on Punishment.* Albany:

[1]*Concise Readings in Philosophy,* Part VIII.

State University of New York Press, 1972. Classical and contemporary selections.

Farrer, Austin. *The Freedom of the Will.* New York: Scribner, 1960.

Fingarette, Herbert. *The Meaning of Criminal Insanity.* Berkeley: University of California Press, 1974 (paperbound).

Flew, Antony. *Crime or Disease?* New York: Harper & Row, 1973. An examination of the concept of mental illness as it relates to the legal and moral issues raised.

Foley, R. "Compatibilism," *Mind,* 87 (1948), 421–428. Defends soft determinism (compatibilism) by means of a careful analysis of the meaning of "able to do otherwise."

Frankfurt, H. "Alternate Possibilities and Moral Responsibility," *Journal of Philosophy,* 65 (1969), 829–839. Argues that ability to do otherwise is not a condition of being morally responsible.

Franklin, R. L. *Freewill and Determinism.* London: Routledge and Kegan Paul, 1968.

Glover, J. *Responsibility.* London: Routledge and Kegan Paul, 1970. Defends soft determinism.

Halverson, W. H. "The Bogy of Chance," *Mind,* 73 (1964), 567–570.

Hampshire, Stuart. *Freedom of Mind and Other Essays.* Princeton, N.J.: Princeton University Press, 1971. Favors "free will."

Honderich, T. (ed.). *Essays in the Freedom of Action.* London: Routledge and Kegan Paul, 1973. Contemporary sources.

Hook, Sidney (ed.). *Determinism and Freedom in the Age of Modern Science.* New York: New York University Press, 1958.

Hospers, John. "Free-Will and Psychoanalysis," in W. Sellars and J. Hospers (eds.). *Readings in Ethical Theory.* New York: Appleton-Century-Crofts, 1952.

Hume, David. *A Treatise of Human Nature.* Many editions. See Book II, Part III.

Laird, John. *On Human Freedom.* New York: Hillary House, 1947.

Lehrer, Keith. "Can We Know that We Have Free Will by Introspection?" *The Journal of Philosophy,* 57 (1960), 145–157.

MacMurray, John. *The Self as Agent.* New York: Humanities Press, 1957.

Matson, W. I. "On the Irrelevance of Free-Will to Moral Responsibility," *Mind,* 65 (1956), 489–497.

Nathan, N. M. L. "Compatibilism and Natural Necessity," *Mind,* 84 (1975), 277–280. A critique of Glover's defense of soft determinism (see above).

O'Connor, D. J. *Free Will.* London: Macmillan, 1972. An introductory discussion of the problem.

Pears, D. F. (ed.). *Freedom and the Will.* New York: St. Martin's Press, 1963.

Pike, N. "Divine Foreknowledge, Human Freedom and Possible Worlds," *Philosophical Review,* 86 (1977), pp. 209–216. A defense of the thesis of his 1965 article (see below) against a critique by Alvin Plantinga (see below).

Pike, N. "Divine Omniscience and Voluntary Action," *Philosophical Review,* 84 (1965), 27–46. Argues that if God (as traditionally conceived) exists, no human actions are free.

Rankin, K. W. *Choice and Chance: A Libertarian Analysis.* Oxford: Basil Blackwell, 1961.

Rashdall, Hastings. *The Theory of Good and Evil.* Oxford: Oxford University Press, 1924, Book III, Chap. III.

Rolston, H., III. "Schlick's Responsible Man," *Philosophy and Phenomenological Research,* 36 (1975), 261–267. A critique of Moritz Schlick's soft determinism.

Schlick, Moritz. *Problems of Ethics,* trans. by David Rynin. Englewood Cliffs, N.J.: Prentice-Hall, 1939 (originally published in German in 1931), Chap. 7.

Sidgwick, Henry. *The Methods of Ethics.* 7th ed., rev. by Constance Jones. Chicago: University of Chicago Press, 1962.

Skinner, B. F. *Beyond Freedom and Dignity.* New York: Knopf, 1971. A famous psychologist argues that the concept of free will has adverse social consequences and offers an alternative approach to various social problems.

—————. *Science and Human Behavior.* New York: Macmillan, 1953, Chap. 1.

Smart, J. J. C. "Free Will, Praise and Blame," *Mind,* 70 (1961), 291–306.

Stebbing, L. S. *Philosophy and the Physicists.* New York: Dover, 1958 (paperbound).

Stevenson, C. L. *Ethics and Language.* New Haven, Conn.: Yale University Press, 1960 (paperbound), Chap. 14.

van Ingwagen, P. "Ability and Responsibility," *Philosophical Review,* 87 (1978), 201–224. A critique of Frankfurt's thesis (see above).

Walter, E. "Is Libertarianism Logically Coherent?" *Philosophy and Phenomenological Research,* 38 (1977–1978), 505–513. Argues that libertarianism is "not a logically possible state of affairs."

Watson, G. "Free Agency," *The Journal of Philosophy,* 72 (1975), 205–220. An attempt to elucidate some key concepts.

Wilson, John. "Freedom and Compulsion," *Mind,* 67 (1958), 60–69.

Young, R. *Freedom, Responsibility and God.* London: Macmillan, 1975. Defends a soft determinist view.

PART IX

FREEDOM
AND AUTHORITY

35

SOCIETY AND THE INDIVIDUAL

As John Donne once said, no man is an island. We are born into a world that has been shaped and molded by those who lived before us. We live our entire lives surrounded by other human beings whose individual and collective wishes impinge upon us in innumerable ways. During our formative years, we are surrounded by parents, teachers, and other adults who make every effort to mold us, to fit us into the society into which we have been born. We are taught to speak its language, adopt its customs, espouse its values—so that they become our language, our customs, our values. We are all members of human society; we cannot, even by the most bizarre efforts imaginable, totally depart from its influence. As in childhood, so in adulthood, society presents us with a variety of authorities whose commands we are expected to obey.

The Concept of Authority

What does it mean to say that someone is an "authority"? Evidently, it can mean either of two things: (a) it might mean that that individual possesses specialized knowledge in some particular area, that he or she is an "expert" on some subject; or (b) it might mean that he or she has the right to control, to some extent, the behavior of others.

There is no mystery about the former concept of authority. One becomes an authority in this sense by learning more about a given subject than is known by most other people. Such an authority does, indeed, claim that others ought in general to believe what he or she says when speaking in the field of claimed expertise. The basis for this claim is that the person in question has investigated the field more thoroughly than most others and, hence, is in a position to speak about the relevant facts on the basis of knowledge that they do not possess. Theoretically, any of us can become an authority on any subject we choose, provided only that we pursue our inquiries to the point where our knowledge of that subject greatly surpasses that of most of our contemporaries.

But what does it mean to be an authority in the sense of having "the right to control, to some extent, the behavior of others"? This definition does not take us very far because it defines one puzzling word, "authority," in terms of another equally puzzling word, "right." It is no better than if we had said, " 'Authority,' in the second sense, means the authority to control, to some extent, the behavior of others." Clearly, that is not very helpful.

Let us consider a hypothetical case in which we would be inclined to say that someone is an authority in the second sense. Consider, for example, a judge in a court of law. When exercising the office rather than acting as a private citizen, a judge can do certain things that the general public cannot do: issue commands with the expectation that they will be obeyed ("Silence in the court!" "Proceed with the examination!" and the like); invoke force to compel obedience to commands; make decisions (or, in some cases, participate in making decisions) about the guilt or innocence of persons charged with unlawful conduct; and impose penalties upon those who are judged to be guilty. The judge exercises authority as a judge precisely by doing these things that a private citizen could not do. In saying that a judge has the authority to do these things, what are we saying? That he or she has the right (that word again) and the power to control the behavior of others.

Suppose that in place of a judge on the bench we imagine these same prerogatives being exercised by the acknowledged leader of a small gang of thieves. An acquaintance of one of the gang members is suspected of tipping off the police about the gang's latest job, in which two members of the gang were apprehended. He is "brought to trial" before the gang, and the leader does the very things the judge was said to do when exercising judicial authority. He issues commands with the expectation that they will be obeyed ("Lefty, stand up!"); he invokes force to compel obedience to his commands ("Shorty, give Lefty's arm a twist and see if you can't make him a little more cooperative"); he decides that Lefty is "guilty"; and he imposes a penalty that will be enforced ("Be permanently out of town in one hour or you'll end up in the river"). We would not, in such a case, say that the gang leader was exercising "authority." Why not? Because, although he has the power, he does not have the right to act as he did.

We are in a dilemma. It appears that we can distinguish between a judge in a court of law (who is an authority in the required sense) and a gang leader who behaves in a judgelike way (but is not an authority) only by saying that the judge has the power and the right to act in a certain way, whereas the gang leader has only the power. What, then, is a "right"?

Let us try this: a right is an opportunity to act (or to refrain from acting) in some specified way, which opportunity is guaranteed by law or by the general consent of the community. What distinguishes the situation of the judge from that of the gang leader is that only the judge's exercise of power is sanctioned by the will of the community as expressed in the laws defining those powers. The judge is an authority by virtue of the fact that he or she exercises *legitimate* (according to law) power, whereas the gang leader's power has no such sanction.

If we accept this definition of "right," our definition of "authority" begins to make some sense. An "authority" is one who has the right (as defined above) to control, to some extent, the behavior of others and the power to enforce that control. Right + Power = Authority *whenever the right in question is the right to control the behavior of others.*

The exercise of authority involves, therefore, a limitation upon the freedom of the individual who is subject to that authority. If a police officer on traffic duty exercises his or her authority to tell me when I may and may not proceed through an intersection, or how fast I may drive, then my freedom to proceed through the intersection when I want to, or to drive at whatever speed I wish, is being curtailed accordingly.

The Authority of Society

Every society exercises some degree of authority over its citizens. It does this by passing laws that all citizens are expected to obey, and by imposing penalties upon those who do not obey these laws. The paradigm examples of "authorities" are, indeed, those who are charged with the responsibility of enforcing the law, trying those accused of breaking the law, and punishing those subsequently adjudged guilty.

The philosophical question to which we shall be addressing ourselves in this section is this: On what grounds, if any, does society have the authority to restrict the freedom of the individual to do as he or she pleases? Society, we have said, exercises authority over its citizens. What is the source of this authority? What, if any, is the justification for society's exercise of authority over its citizens?

It will be readily acknowledged, I suppose, that this question has considerable relevance for the contemporary political situation in the United States and, indeed, throughout the world. Self-proclaimed "revolutionary" groups have arisen in various places, claiming that they are subject to no law except revolutionary law, no authority except revolutionary authority. Planes are hijacked, property is destroyed, people are executed, all in the name of this or that revolutionary cause. Those who perform these acts contemptuously dismiss existing law, the police, the courts, and the will of society as an oppressive rule that has no legitimate authority over them.

The question has, however, been discussed by philosophers for many centuries. Plato deals with it in *The Republic,* and Aristotle in *Politics.* It is, in some ways, the central question in political philosophy. Let us look briefly at the principal ways in which it has been answered.

Four Alternatives

It is possible to argue, first, that the laws of society have the force of law because (or insofar as) they are sanctioned by natural law. This view, called the *natural-law theory,* holds that there are certain fundamental principles of right and justice that human reason can discern by attending carefully to the propositions asserting those principles. Such a principle is expressed, for example, in the proposition "The needless destruction of human life is evil." This proposition, according to the theory, cannot be proved, nor does it need to be: any right-thinking person will, upon reflection, acknowledge its truth. Laws prohibiting murder, then, are derived from this principle. Society's right to restrict the freedom of its citizens (for example, to prohibit the taking of another human life) is based on its perception of what is right, that is, on its perception of what is prescribed or prohibited by eternal and immutable natural laws.

A second alternative is what is called the *social-contract theory,* according to which each citizen of the state, by virtue of accepting the benefits of an ordered society, gives tacit consent to the government that maintains that order. Each citizen is, so to speak, agreeing with every other citizen to accept certain limitations on his or her own freedom in order to secure the greater security that is thereby made possible. This view was initially advocated by such theorists as Thomas Hobbes (1588–1679), John Locke (1632–1704), and Jean Jacques Rousseau (1712–1778), and was strongly influential in the thinking of the framers of the American Constitution.

One can also defend the legitimacy of certain restrictions on the freedom of individuals in society according to the theory of *social utilitarianism.* According to this theory, the natural function of government is to promote the general well-being of its citizenry, to secure the greatest happiness for the greatest number. The justification for restricting, by law, the freedom of each individual to do as he or she pleases is that such restriction will tend to promote the general welfare. It is a corollary of this view that any restriction of freedom that cannot be shown to actually promote the general welfare is unjustified.

A fourth alternative is to assert that there is no justification for society's restriction of the freedom of its individual members. This view, known as *theoretical anarchism,* asserts additionally that although society has no authority to impose itself on its members, it does so nonetheless because it has the *power* to do so and because it perceives a practical necessity to do so. What society calls "authority" is, therefore, merely superior power—whether it be wielded in the name of monarchy, or oligarchy, or even majoritarian democracy. Civil authority is always merely *de facto*, never *de jure*.

These, then, are the principal ways in which the question of the justification of society's restriction of individual freedom may be answered. Let us now consider in some detail the arguments that may be urged in support of each.

STUDY QUESTIONS

1. What are the two senses of "authority" distinguished in this chapter? Are you satisfied with the definition of "authority" offered on p. 275? If not, how would you improve on it?
2. Is a philosophy instructor an authority and, if so, in what sense?
3. What exactly is the question about authority that is posed in this chapter? List all the ways of answering this question that seem to you to have at least some measure of plausibility.
4. Do you think it is the case that any right-thinking person will, upon reflection, agree that "the needless destruction of human life is evil"? What apparent relevance does your answer have for the question at issue?
5. What is your present opinion regarding the question posed in this chapter?

36

THE NATURAL-LAW THEORY

The question before us is, What is the justification for society's exercise of authority over its citizens? I shall argue that this authority is justified insofar as the laws through which society exercises its authority are derived from natural law. I shall, in short, defend the natural-law theory.

The Theory

The natural-law theory involves the following claims: (a) there are some basic and unchanging principles of right and justice that ought to govern the affairs of society; (b) these principles can be known by us; and (c) laws have the force and authority of law insofar as they are derivable from these principles.

No one has, to my knowledge, ever attempted to codify all the basic principles of right and justice that together make up the natural law, but it is not at all difficult to produce numerous examples. The preceding chapter gave one example: the needless destruction of human life is evil. Many such principles are stated in the Universal Declaration of Human Rights adopted by the General Assembly of the United Nations, such as "All human beings are born free and equal in dignity and rights" (Article 1); "Everyone has the right to life, liberty and security of person" (Article 3); and "Everyone has the right to own property alone as well as in association with others" (Article 17 [1]). Additional examples could easily be given, but these will suffice.

Two things should be noted about these principles. First, they are fundamental in the sense that they apply to all people at all times, and in all circumstances. Any society that did not attempt to embody these principles in its laws would be regarded by all decent people as degenerate and inhuman. Second, these principles are not capable of being *proved.* If anyone is so base as to assert that some people are entitled to greater dignity than others (*contra* Article 1), or that there is nothing wrong with arbitrarily depriving some people of their life or liberty (*contra* Article 3), there is no way in the world that you can prove that person wrong. If he or she professes not to believe such a principle, the best that you can hope for is that he or she will consider it more carefully and by so doing come to see that it is true.

Unprovable though these principles are, however, they can be known because they are self-evident. They are, so to speak, laws that nature has inscribed upon the heart of every human being. We *know* that every human being has a right to life, liberty, and security of person—whether that person is an American, a Russian, an Indian, or some other nationality, and whether or not that right is actually guaranteed by the laws of that particular country. "We hold these truths to be self-evident," said the authors of the American Declaration of Independence. The advocates of the natural-law theory take this to be the status of all the fundamental principles of right and justice.

In saying, then, that laws have the force and authority of law insofar as they are derivable from these principles, I am saying, quite simply, that laws are valid and worthy of obedience insofar as they embody these principles. As St. Thomas Aquinas said, "Every human law has just so much of the nature of law as it is derived from the law of nature. But if in any point it departs from the law of nature, it is no longer a law but a perversion of law."[1] The basic principles of right and justice contained in the natural law are principles to which every person ought to be subject. The "oughtness" of the laws of any society derives from this source. Government is, so to speak, nature's surrogate in ordering the affairs of human society according to nature's laws.

In asserting that valid laws are derivable from natural law, I do not mean to be asserting that every particular valid law can be rigorously deduced from natural law by a series of valid syllogisms. The principle that every person has a right to security of his or her person, for example, justifies, in general, the limiting of the speed of automobiles in populated areas, but you cannot strictly conclude from this (and other relevant propositions) that the maximum allowable speed on Third Avenue between Apple Street and Cherry Boulevard should be exactly twenty-five miles per hour. Whoever is responsible for establishing speed limits has to exercise judgment in a matter such as this; that person might reasonably settle on any of several speeds as the one to be regarded as the "legal limit." Such a law, nonetheless, "embodies the principles" of natural law and is, therefore, a valid law.

---

[1]St. Thomas Aquinas, *Summa Theologica,* I–II, ques. 95, art. 2, in Anton C. Pegis (ed.), *Basic Writings of St. Thomas Aquinas* (New York: Random House, 1945), vol. II, p. 784.

This, then, is the natural-law theory with respect to the justification of society's curtailment of the freedom of the individual citizen. Let us turn now to a consideration of the principal arguments that may be given in support of this theory.

Just and Unjust Laws

Consider, in the first place, that if there were no natural law, it would follow that there would be no criterion for distinguishing between just laws and unjust laws. As Plato said, "What is to be the standard of just and unjust is the point at issue."[2] Were it not for the natural law written in the hearts of people, human beings would be without any moral basis for opposing tyranny. Legislators could enact laws to further their own interests and those of their friends, and the hapless citizens whose interests were violated by these laws would have no recourse to a higher tribunal. They could not appeal to the conscience of humanity, but would be powerless victims whose only hope for redress would be in overthrowing those in power.

But, in fact, we *do* distinguish between just and unjust laws. We recognize, for example, that the federal Fugitive Slave Law of 1793, which allowed slave "owners" to capture and retrieve slaves who had sought freedom in other states, was a profoundly unjust law because it violated the basic principle that every human being has a right to personal freedom, that compulsory servitide—slavery—is morally wrong. The Fugitive Slave Law, though it was the law of the land for many years, did not have the force of law because it was inconsistent with the natural law and was, therefore, repugnant to the moral sense of good people everywhere. Were it not for our common awareness of such a "higher law," we could not make such a judgment.

We recognize, then, that laws subjecting people to arbitrary arrest, or arbitrary seizure of their property, or unnecessary limitations on their freedom, are unjust laws. They are unjust whether or not they are consistent with the constitution (if there is one) of the country in which they hold sway, and notwithstanding the fact that they may have the majority or even unanimous approval of the lawmaking agency or of the population of that country. And the principle on which we pronounce them unjust is that they are inconsistent with the unwritten natural law that binds the consciences of all people everywhere.

The Treatment of Aliens

A second argument that may be adduced in support of the natural-law theory is that aliens are held to be punishable if they break a just law

---

[2]Plato, *Laws*, IV, in *The Dialogues of Plato*, trans. B. Jowett (New York: Random House, 1937), vol. II, p. 485.

of a country other than their own, even though the lawmaking agency of that country has no legal mandate to control their behavior. The British Parliament, for example, has no power to make laws governing the behavior of anyone except citizens of Great Britain. Yet we freely grant that an American citizen who commits, say, theft or murder in Great Britain is rightly punished for that crime according to British law. It is as if nature had assigned to each sovereign state the task of enforcing the natural law on all who happen in the course of their lives to come within the geographical borders of this or that state. It is, in the last analysis, the conscience of mankind that renders a verdict when a judge or a jury decides a case. Were it not for the universal applicability of the natural law, individuals would leave the reign of law whenever they left the country whose laws they are, as citizens, legally bound to obey.

Moral Legislation

The natural-law theory is supported by yet another line of reasoning —that natural law provides the only justification for many laws of the civilized nations of the world. Consider, for example, laws governing the distribution of pornographic material. It is hard to make a convincing case for the view that a substantial public interest is involved in this matter. If some people want to pay money to look at lewd pictures, or to read about the sexual exploits of others, the rest of society is not at all affected. Why, then, does society pass antipornography laws? On what basis can it justify this restriction of the freedom of those who would produce and sell pornography? On the basis that the proliferation of smut and the encouragement of lust are contrary to what most human beings perceive as good and right—contrary, in other words, to natural law.

Consider another example. Suppose that some individual, contrary to the practice of all civilized people, chose to go about in public (weather permitting) without any clothes. Such a person would most certainly be arrested for indecent exposure and either jailed or committed to a mental institution. On what grounds? On the grounds that such behavior is contrary to what civilized people regard as decent and right. Take away natural law and you must take away much of the moral legislation that governs the everyday life of all of us.

Our Knowledge of Natural Law

In appealing to natural law as the ultimate source of the authority of the actual laws under which human beings live, I do not mean to be implying that our knowledge of natural law is either complete or infallible. The training of the conscience of mankind is clearly a long and laborious process, and I would be the first to admit that we undoubtedly have a long way to go before we can plausibly claim that we have fully comprehended the content of the natural law. Our knowledge of the natural law, like our knowledge of the laws governing the physical universe, is incomplete and subject to error. But in neither case is our partial ignorance a reasonable excuse for ignoring or denying that portion of the whole that we clearly understand. Our legislators must legislate according to their understanding of what is good and right, just as our engineers must design our transportation and communication systems on the basis of their present understanding of the relevant physical and chemical laws.

Legislators, then, are not free to enact as law anything that might happen to suit their fancy or private interests. In a constitutional democracy they are, of course, bound by the constitution. But even in a country where there is no constitution defining the limits of legislators' authority, legislators are bound by the authority of an unalterable natural law to which all people are subject. When they are considering a piece of proposed legislation, they must continually ask, Is this right? Is it just? Does it protect the fundamental human rights of our citizens? Does it promote the common good? And to answer these questions, they must look not to the constitution, for that is at best an incomplete summary of the basic principles of right and justice, but to the natural law itself. The law that they enact will have the force of law and will be binding upon the behavior of the citizens only on the condition that it is grounded in the principles of natural law. To the extent that this is achieved, the law will commend itself to good people everywhere.

The Need for Written Law

But why, it might be asked, is written law even necessary if, as you say, the natural law is known to all? It is necessary, first, because although the natural law is *knowable* by all human beings, it is not equally *known* to all because not all have the interest or the patience or the time to attend to it. The patient consideration of the dictates of natural law, that is, the conceptualization of the truly good society, requires a concentrated effort for which few individuals have either the leisure or the sustained interest. Written law is necessary, therefore, in order that people may nonetheless be taught to live according to the precepts of the natural law.

Written law is necessary, second, in order to counterbalance the tendency of individuals, even though they may acknowledge what justice requires, to make exceptions in their own cases whenever the requirements of natural law come into conflict with their own self-interest. I may agree, for example, that citizens ought to pay taxes in proportion to their ability to pay, but I may selfishly desire that an exception be made in my own case because I would rather use my money to purchase something for myself. The written law, therefore, not only prescribes in detail how much a person in my circumstances must pay, but it prescribed penalties for nonpayment that are sufficiently severe to make it in my self-interest to do what the law requires. The natural law tells me, in general, what I ought to do; the written law, through its system of penalties, makes reasonably sure that I will do what the natural law requires.

In a world of perfectly reasonable and perfectly good human beings, no written law would be required. In such a world, everyone would know the natural law and would willingly do what it requires. But we must deal with the world as it is, accepting the fact that people are neither perfectly reasonable nor perfectly good. Hence, there is a need for written law notwithstanding the fact that the natural law is knowable by all.

STUDY QUESTIONS

1. List the three propositions that Natural-Law Theorist (NLT) says constitute the theory he is attempting to defend. Restate them in such a way as to demonstrate that you understand them.
2. Judging by the examples given in this chapter, what do you take to be the defining characteristics of a "natural law"? Can you produce additional examples that fit the definition?
3. "Were it not for the natural law written in the hearts of people, human beings would be without any moral basis for opposing tyranny." Attack or defend this statement.
4. What arguments does NLT use to support his theory? What is your opinion of the soundness of each?
5. Objection: if the natural law is "written in the hearts of people," there should be no need for written law. What is NLT's answer to this?

37

THE SOCIAL CONTRACT

It seems to me that Natural-Law Theorist (hereafter NLT) has not provided a satisfactory answer to the question concerning the justification for society's exercise of authority over its citizens. NLT's answer is that the laws through which society exercises this authority have the force of law insofar as they embody the principles of natural law, and that government is a kind of "surrogate for nature" in enforcing these laws. This view is then supported by a series of arguments, and NLT concludes by explaining why (in his view) written law is necessary despite the fact that the natural law is theoretically knowable by all.

I now want to show what is wrong with NLT's position and then expound what I believe to be the correct solution to this problem, namely, the social-contract theory.

Critique of the Natural-Law Theory

The crux of the difficulty with the natural-law theory is that even granting that there is a natural law knowable by all people, and that the mandates of written law derive their authority from natural law, the question as to why some individuals should have the right to enforce compliance with the law upon some other individuals remains unanswered. From the fact that some particular written law embodies the relevant principles of natural law, NLT simply assumes that whoever enforces that law upon his fellow human beings has the right to do so. But this surely will not do. The question is not, Ought everyone to obey the natural law? The question is, By what right does any group of people have the authority to compel others to act or refrain from acting in some particular way? Let it be granted that you and I and all individuals ought to obey the natural law. Whence comes the authority of policemen and judges and juries to compel us to such obedience? Why are we not all responsible for our own behavior?

Consider, for example, the matter of penalties. They are necessary, NLT tells us, in order to counterbalance the tendency of people to act in their own self-interest even when they know that such action is contrary to the requirements of natural law. I agree. But legislators invent these penalties on the assumption that they have the right to force compliance with the law. Whence comes this right? NLT has no answer.

It is interesting to note that NLT's arguments in support of his position are really arguments in support only of the proposition that there is a natural law. NLT is guilty of a *non sequitur.* From the arguments put forward by him, it does indeed follow that there is a natural law, but it does not follow that anyone in particular has the right to enforce that law upon fellow human beings. The fundamental question with which we are dealing remains to be answered.

The State of Nature

Let us imagine, now, a state of affairs in which no person or group of persons has assumed or been delegated the authority to enforce the natural law upon fellow human beings. Each individual, then, is responsible for his or her own behavior according to the natural law as he or she understands it. If he or she breaks the natural law, he or she is answerable only to his or her own conscience—with one important exception: if an individual's behavior results or threatens to result in injury to some other person or property, that person has a right to defend himself or herself and to demand reparation from the offender. Each individual, in this state of affairs, is judge and jury in any case in which his or her own interest is involved, and each must seek to enforce justice as best he or she can when it becomes necessary to render a judgment. Let us call this the state of nature, since it is the state in which nature places humankind pending some action on the part of human beings to create a different state of affairs.

What would it be like to live in this state of nature? It must be apparent, in the first place, that in such a state no one could be really secure, no one could ever be certain that some person or combination of persons stronger than oneself would not endanger one's life or property. If there is law (natural law) but no one to enforce the law, then the situation is almost as bad as if there were no law at all. Every person in the state of nature is potentially at war with every other person, and life is likely to be (as Thomas Hobbes once said) "nasty, brutish, and short."

Second, human beings living in the state of nature could not fail to observe that justice is rarely achieved, for self-interest will cause individuals always to favor their own side of the matter whenever they find it necessary to resolve a dispute. If I am judge and jury in any case in which my interest is involved, I am most assuredly going to make sure (if I can) that I get at least what is coming to me, and perhaps a little more. Since my opponent will be just as careful to watch out for his or her private interest, we shall, in all probability, end up fighting, and the decision will favor not the one having the greater justice but the one who is able to muster a superior force.

The question facing humanity in the state of nature, then, is this: How can we put an end to this war of all against all? How can we obtain a state of affairs in which there may be security of person, and where our disputes may be resolved not by force but according to the canons of justice?

The Social Contract

Government is humanity's solution to the problems inherent in the state of nature. It is as if the inhabitants of a certain region came together and—in exchange for the greater security and the increase in justice that would thereby result—agreed to delegate to some of their number the right to articulate and enforce the law. The right of each individual in the state of nature to enforce the natural law (so far as possible) in any case in which one's own interest is involved is thus given over to government when this contract to put an end to the state of nature is entered into. Every legitimate government is, at root, founded on such a social contract.

In saying that all government derives its authority from a certain authority originally held by the individual, I am not, of course, suggesting that as a matter of historical fact all existing governments came about in just this way. We are discussing political philosophy, not governmental history. I am saying that the theoretical basis for the authority of government lies in the will of the governed to avoid the insecurity and injustice of the state of nature. Whether, as a matter of historical fact, such a state ever existed is not at issue, nor is it relevant to our discussion.

Every individual who accepts the benefits of government—the protection of its laws, the greater security that results from government under law—tacitly consents to the social contract upon which that government rests. When people are born into a situation in which they live under law (as all of us are), then their allegiance to the government (that is, their consent to the social contract) is simply taken for granted unless they declare otherwise. If they emigrate to a foreign country, they must formally swear allegiance to this new land: they must, so to speak, explicitly affirm that they wish to become a party to the social contract that binds together the people whom they are adopting as their countrymen.

Supporting Arguments

The first argument that I would put forward in support of this theory is that it provides an inherently plausible account of why some individuals (those who govern) have the authority to enforce the law upon others (those who are governed). The social-contract theory, unlike the natural-law theory, does not sidestep the central issue in this dispute. To the question, What is the justification for society's exercise of authority over its citizens? the social-contract theory replies: this authority is derived from the antecedent right of each individual to enforce the natural law in defense of one's own interests. The social contract is the theoretical precondition of the authority of society, through its legally constituted government, to enforce the law equally upon all.

I would argue, second, that this theory is consistent with the widely held view that the right to govern derives from the consent of the governed. The Universal Declaration of Human Rights explicitly states, as a matter of fact, that "the will of the people shall be the basis of the authority of government" and that "this will shall be expressed in periodic and genuine elections which shall be by universal and equal suffrage and shall be held by secret vote or by equivalent free voting procedures" (Article 21 [3]). Through the voting process the people are reaffirming the contract by which they are constituted a body politic and are deciding who shall exercise the authority they have delegated to the holders of various offices.

Third, the social-contract theory is consistent with the general view that the responsibility of government is to resolve internal disputes, to protect from external danger, and to promote the common good. It is consistent with the views of most civilized people regarding both the *scope* and the *limits* of the authority of government.

What is the scope of government's authority according to the social-contract theory? Its authority must be exactly sufficient to solve the problems inherent in the state of nature. It must, therefore, resolve disputes among individuals. This it does by (a) developing a body of law clarifying the rights and duties of each individual (the legislative function), (b) enforcing those laws (the executive function), and (c) adjudicating cases in which some individual is alleged to have broken one of those laws (the judicial function). It must, further, promote the realization of true justice by passing and enforcing laws designed to assist the poor, the weak, and the helpless to achieve a decent life in a world in which they would otherwise be overwhelmed by those stronger and more richly blessed than they.

There are, however, definite limits to the authority of government. It has only such power as has been delegated to it in order to put an end to the perpetual conflict and injustice of the state of nature. The right to enforce the natural law is given over to government by the social contract. All other human rights are part of the natural heritage and remain in full force; they may not be abrogated by government.

Hence, government cannot legitimately subject individuals to arbitrary arrest, invade their privacy, confiscate their property, or do any of a long series of things that would constitute a breaking rather than an enforcing of the natural law.

We should not minimize the risk involved in handing over to a group of designated individuals the authority originally vested by nature in each individual. Government, any government, is a desperate solution to a desperate problem, and the risk involved is enormous. History is replete with horrible examples of people who have used the power of government for their own selfish gain and have squandered the lives and properties of their helpless subjects in the process. Unjust laws have been decreed, senseless and immoral wars have been fought, police powers have been exercised beyond all reasonable measure, and justice has been perverted in a thousand ways. Yet people cling to the necessity for government under law and seek a world in which "liberty and justice for all" shall become a reality. Why? Because they cannot tolerate a return to the certain injustice of the state of nature. The social contract is the bargain human beings must make with one another if they are to live together in a world where the interests of each individual are in potential conflict with those of all other human beings. Humanity's quest for a form of government that will make this a good bargain—the agonizing search for a government that will fulfill each person's longing for security and justice without itself becoming tyrannical—is one of the most poignant stories to be read in the pages of human history.

STUDY QUESTIONS

1. What is Social Contract Theorist's (SCT's) main objection to the natural-law theory? Is SCT right on this point?
2. What, exactly, does SCT mean by the "state of nature"? Does SCT seem to you to be describing an actual state of affairs that existed at some time in the past, or is the state of nature merely a logical construct?
3. What arguments does SCT use to support this theory? Do you find these arguments convincing?
4. "The social contract is the bargain human beings must make with one another if they are to live together in a world where the interests of each individual are in potential conflict with those of all other human beings." Does this imply that one might at some point conclude that it was a bad bargain, and revoke the contract? If so, under what circumstances?

38

SOCIAL UTILITARIANISM

Strictly speaking, the authors of the two preceding chapters have given but one answer to the question, What is the justification for society's exercise of authority over its citizens? That answer, precisely stated, is (a) the function of government, as the agent of society, is to enforce the "natural law," and (b) the authority to do this derives from a "social contract" by which the antecedent right of individuals to enforce the natural law, whenever their own interests are at stake, is given over to the governing body. Natural-Law Theorist (NLT) devotes his efforts to demonstrating that there is, in fact, such a thing as "natural law", which is a logical precondition of the theory. Social-Contract Theorist (SCT), building further on this foundation, argues in support of the "social contract" part of the theory. I think that this theory is wrong on all major points, and I am, therefore, compelled to attack the main theses of both NLT and SCT.

No Natural Law

First of all, the assertion that there is a natural law is, in my opinion, nothing but a holdover from the ancient view that there is "in the mind of God" a kind of plan for the government of His creation, an "eternal law" that is "natural" insofar as it is knowable by human reason unaided by divine revelation. St. Thomas Aquinas, whom NLT quotes with approbation, defines natural law in precisely this way. St. Thomas writes:

> ... The whole community of the universe is governed by Divine Reason. Wherefore the very Idea of the government of things in God the Ruler of

the universe has the nature of a law. And since the Divine Reason's conception of things ... is eternal, ... this kind of law must be called eternal ...

The rational creature ... has a share of the Eternal Reason, whereby it has a natural inclination to its proper act and end: and this participation of the eternal law in the rational creature is called the natural law ... It is therefore evident that the natural law is nothing else than the rational creature's participation of the eternal law.[1]

That the natural-law theory is an offspring of a theological view of ancient origin is not, of course, an argument against its validity. I would argue, however, that the theory loses much of its plausibility when divorced from that context. The natural affinity of natural-law theory is not with the social-contract theorists of the seventeenth and eighteenth centuries but with the divine-right theorists of an earlier day. It is understandable that NLT, as a child of the twentieth century, does not endorse the divine-right theory. It is even understandable that SCT, in an attempt to salvage the remnants of the medieval view, would appeal to a mythical "social contract" to fill the void left by the collapse of the view that the authority to rule is derived by appointment from the antecedent authority of God. But let us leave these historical considerations and consider the arguments by which NLT attempts to convince us that there is, in fact, a natural law.

NLT has argued, in the first place, that if there were no natural law, there would be no criterion for distinguishing between just and unjust laws. His argument is, then, an attempted *reductio ad absurdum* of the view that there is no natural law. My answer to this is that the alleged consequence does not follow. All that is required for individuals to distinguish between just and unjust laws is that they arrive at some common agreement on what is to count as just. Their opinions as to what is just and what is unjust are, in fact, constantly changing. To say that the current opinions regarding justice and injustice constitute a kind of reading of an immutable "natural law" is merely superfluous. "Just" is a word we use to describe laws that are to our liking, "unjust" a word to describe laws we do not like. The appeal to "natural law" in support of the view that a given law is just or unjust is nothing more than an attempt to invoke the pale shadow of a vanished deity to support an opinion that we hold on other grounds.

NLT's argument about the punishment of aliens, which was originally put forward by Locke,[2] is a puzzling one, and I am not at all clear about how it supports his position. In any case, I think he is simply

---

[1]St. Thomas Aquinas, *Summa Theologica*, I–II, ques. 91, art. 1, and ques. 91, art. 2, trans. by Fathers of the English Dominican Province (New York, Cincinnati, and Chicago: Benziger Brothers, 1910), pp. 10, 11.
[2]John Locke, *Two Treatises of Government,* 2d ed., ed. Peter Laslett (Cambridge, Eng.: Cambridge University Press, 1967), pp. 290–291.

mistaken in asserting that the legislative body in a given country has authority only with respect to the citizens of that country. A legislature's authority has, I should say, both a geographical and a citizen domain: it covers the relevant behavior of all people within a given geographical area (regardless of their citizenship) and the relevant behavior of its citizens (whether they are at home or abroad). We have yet to say how it comes by this authority, but the fact that legislatures and other governmental agencies do exercise such authority does not seem to me to support the natural-law theory in any way.

NLT's third argument—that without natural law a good deal of "moral legislation" would be found to be without justification—is correct as a simple assertion, but the assertion does not, in fact, support the natural-law theory. Rather, it supports the view that many laws now on the books have no justification and ought to be repealed. In short, I accept the consequence of this attempted *reductio,* but I deny that it is absurd. Laws of this type, in my opinion, are unjustified attempts to meddle in the private affairs of individuals. They are all in the same category as the notorious "blue laws" of colonial New England, which forbade Sunday indulgence not only in drinking and dancing but even in honest work. The view that there is a theoretical justification for governmental authority does not necessarily commit one to the defense of everything that governments do and have done under the guise of legitimate authority. NLT, in my opinion, is not sufficiently sensitive to the need for assigning definite limits to the authority of government over the lives of individual citizens.

There is, moreover, a decisive consideration that may be urged against the idea of natural law, namely, that there are no criteria for determining when an assertion is or is not a "part" of the natural law. NLT concludes from this that the natural law is known directly; I conclude that it is not known at all, for the very good reason that it does not exist. To decide whether a piece of proposed legislation ought to be enacted, the legislator must look, not to some mysterious natural law written, presumably, in heaven, but to the probable consequences of that legislation. I shall return to this point later in this essay.

No Social Contract

The idea of a social contract is no less a fiction than is that of natural law. Indeed, SCT seems almost to recognize this when he tells us that he is not suggesting that "as a matter of historical fact" actual governments were created in just this way. What SCT seems to be arguing, then, is that the idea of social contract is a *useful* fiction: it is a vivid way of stating what he considers to be the correct theory about the ultimate ground of the authority of government. I do not wish to quarrel with his use of the concept "social contract" as a mere literary device, however; my quarrel is with the theory itself.

What the social-contract theory comes down to, once isolated from the twin fictions of an imaginary "state of nature" terminated by an imaginary "social contract," is (a) the idea that individuals have an antecedent natural right to enforce the natural law whenever their own interests are at stake, and (b) the idea that they voluntarily hand this right over to the government they create in order to secure certain benefits such as greater security, justice, and so forth.

This theory is wrong, first of all, because it presupposes the existence of a natural law that is either nonexistent or unknowable. It is wrong, second, because it presupposes the existence of "rights" prior to the enactment of any law, which is a contradiction in terms. SCT would, I think, accept the definition of "right" given in Chapter 35: "an opportunity to act (or to refrain from acting) in some specified way, which opportunity is guaranteed by law or by the general consent of the community." He thinks he can talk about "natural rights" because he thinks the opportunities pertaining to those rights are guaranteed by natural law. But without natural law there are no natural rights; hence, there is nothing for individuals to hand over to the government that they create. Rights are created by the enactment of law, which presupposes the existence of a lawmaking agency that, according to the social-contract theory, comes into being only as a result of the social contract. Without natural law, the social-contract theory collapses.

An Alternative Proposal

In dealing with the question of the justification of the authority of society to limit the freedom of individual citizens, it is important that we be clear about precisely what question we are asking. Our question is not (as my opponents appear to have assumed) equivalent to the question, Who originally had the authority that we now see being exercised by government, and how did government get this authority from them? The authority of government, insofar as it can be justified, is justified not by its *origin* but by its *ends.* Government is a creature of society, a social institution. Like any social institution it is good insofar as it accomplishes the purposes for which it was created.

Why do people create governments? Chiefly, in my opinion, for purposes of self-protection. What all people desire is an opportunity to live their own lives, to do as they please, without interference from anyone else—in short, to be perfectly free. The trouble is that in a world where everyone is free to do as he or she pleases, to pursue his or her own self-interest without regard for the interests of anyone else, everyone would be involved in perpetual conflict with everyone else. We need government, therefore, to protect ourselves against others. In order to secure a situation in which all of us—the weak as well as the strong—shall have an opportunity to live our lives without the constant fear of attack by others, we need a system of restraints that each of us accepts on the condition that everyone else accepts those same restraints. It is the business of government to make those rules and to enforce them in such a way that it becomes in the self-interest of everyone to obey them. The exercise of governmental authority is justified insofar as it protects each individual member of society from the evils that might be inflicted by others were they not restrained by law.

Two important corollaries of this theory should be noted. The first is that the scope of government's authority is limited to those areas in which unregulated behavior is likely to do harm to someone else. Government has no business meddling in the private affairs of individuals, or restraining them in any way, except when such action is necessary to protect the rest of society from some probable harm. If a man wishes to drive sixty miles an hour through a heavily populated area, government has a right to restrain him; if he wishes to wear his hair at shoulder length, that is his own private business—however much the majority may disapprove.

The second corollary is that no particular type of government is a priori better than any other type. In one situation, a monarchical type may be best; in another, a democracy may be best; and in yet another, a military dictatorship may be most effective. The "best" in each case is defined as that type that is most effective in accomplishing the purpose for which government exists, that is, the protection of the members of society from the harm that would result if everybody were permitted to do as they pleased.

I would suggest that an appropriate name for this theory of the authority of government is social utilitarianism. It finds the justification of governmental authority in governments' securing the social ends that make it desirable that there be some government rather than none at all.

Supporting Arguments

In support of this position I would argue, first, that it justifies the exercise of governmental authority in the only way that any social institution can be justified, namely, by reference to its consequences. How do we judge whether an educational system is good? Clearly, we judge it by its consequences: we observe the quality of its graduates. How do we judge the practice of medicine? By the consequences: we observe the degree of success that physicians have in restoring to health those who are ill. So with government: its "justification" lies in its consequences, by which I mean that it justifies its existence to the degree that it succeeds in creating a situation in which every citizen is able to pursue his or her own interests so long as those interests do not impose harm on others.

I would suggest, second, that this defense of the authority of government is exactly consistent with the way in which individual pieces of proposed legislation are justified by their supporters. It is absurd to suggest that legislators "look to the natural law" in trying to decide whether a given piece of proposed legislation ought to be enacted. Legislators should not waste their time gazing into the empty lawbook of nature—nor do they. They should, and do, attempt to assess the probable consequences of the law they are proposing to enact. All argument about the wisdom or unwisdom of a proposed law is concerned with its probable consequences, and that is exactly what we should expect given the account of the authority of government I am proposing here.

Last, the utilitarian account of the authority of government provides a usable criterion for determining when government is and when it is not exercising its authority in a defensible way. When the intent of legislation is to eliminate some actual or potential evil, the exercise of governmental authority is justified. When, however, the intent is to impose on an unwilling minority the private preferences of the majority, or even of the lawmakers themselves, the exercise of the power of government has no justification whatsoever. Insofar as the behavior of an individual, however unconventional or unusual it may be, imposes no harm on others, government has no legitimate reason to interfere. The "rights" of the individual, properly understood, mean just this: the presumed freedom of every person to do as he or she pleases so long as those actions do not inflict harm on others. Government preserves such rights not by passing laws but by refraining from passing laws in areas where no substantial public interest is involved.

STUDY QUESTIONS

1. "All that is required for individuals to distinguish between just and unjust laws is that they arrive at some common agreement on what is to count as just." Is this correct? Defend your answer.
2. Why, according to Social Utilitarian (SU), is it a contradiction in terms to assert that people have rights prior to the enactment of any law?
3. What does SU say is the scope of the authority of government? Do you agree?
4. What arguments does SU offer in support of his theory about the authority of government? Do you find these arguments convincing?

39

THEORETICAL ANARCHISM

I want to distinguish *theoretical* anarchism, the position that I represent, from two other positions with which it is easily confused. The first, *militant* anarchism, is not so much a theory as a political posture. To be a militant anarchist is to be committed to the overthrow of existing government without regard to the practical consequences and with no intention of supporting some new government that might be established in its place. Militant anarchists may admit, for example, that in the absence of all government there would be widespread chaos, but they would say, "Nonetheless, we prefer that situation to the present one in which all these bureaucrats presume to tell us what we can and cannot do. We are willing to live in the midst of chaos in order to be truly free."

The second position, which I shall call *naïve* anarchism, holds that in the absence of governmental authority not only would chaos not result, but, on the contrary, there would be a greater realization of both freedom and order than there is under any form of government. Naïve anarchism takes an extremely optimistic view of human nature, for it maintains that in a society without governmental authority people would, in fact, limit their own desires in such a way that they would not be in perpetual conflict with one another.

In contrast to these two positions, theoretical anarchism is simply the view that although society may exercise authority over its citizens as a matter of practical necessity, there is no theoretical justification for such authority. I cannot, of course, be expected to bring forward affirmative arguments in support of this position. Theoretical anarchism is not a theory about the justification of the authority of government. Rather, it is the dilemma in which you find yourself when you discover that none of the theories on this question really answer the question. The only arguments available in support of theoretical anarchism are the arguments demonstrating the inadequacy of all attempts to justify governmental authority.

Social Utilitarianism

I am almost inclined to argue that Social Utilitarian (SU) is on my side in this dispute, since he does not, in fact, offer a theoretical justification for governmental authority. What he offers instead is a *practical* justification: governmental authority is desirable because it is a necessary means to the desirable end of protecting society from the evils that would result if everyone were free to do as he or she pleases. And since it seems clear to anyone except a naïve anarchist that society would be in even more serious trouble than it is were it not for the restraining hand of government, SU appears to win an easy victory without even entering into the intellectual puzzles that seem to me to be so unsoluble.

Let me say forthrightly that, in my opinion, SU has not offered a wrong answer: he has simply answered the wrong question. The question to which NLT and SCT addressed themselves—the one to which I wish I could find an answer but cannot—is this: *By what right* do some people (governors, legislators, police, judges, and the like) exercise coercive authority over the rest of society? I know as well as SU that certain goods are achieved through the agency of governmental authority. Indeed, NLT and SCT are equally clear about this. But the question still remains: Where does government get the authority to do what needs to be done in order to secure these goods? How is authority constituted in a world in which nature appears originally to have made us political equals? To this question SU gives us no answer at all.

The Social-Contract Theory

The social-contract theory at least has the merit of being an honest effort to solve the problem with which we are dealing. In many ways it is very attractive. Indeed, I think the theory can be stated in a more persuasive form than SCT has offered and in a way, moreover, that completely escapes SU's criticisms of the theory as put by SCT. I want to present this restatement, because I think it provides the best hope we have of finding a solution to this vexing problem. I shall then give my own reasons for rejecting the theory even in this purified form, as a consequence of which I find myself compelled to be an "agnostic" in political philosophy—a theoretical anarchist.

The form of the social-contract theory that I have in mind is this: quite apart from any theory about natural law, which SU rightly criticizes, it seems evident that in the absence of any civil authority, individuals would constantly have to defend themselves against the aggressive behavior of other human beings. We could imagine, then, a group of individuals in this "natural condition" getting together and saying, "Let's put an end to all this fighting among ourselves. Let's draw up some rules—we'll call them 'laws'—and let's appoint somebody to make sure that we all behave the way the laws say we should." This, I am suggesting, would be a kind of social contract—without the cumbersome doctrine of natural law that renders the whole theory suspect. Each subsequent individual, as in SCT's account, tacitly enters into the contract by accepting the benefits that are secured by government: no natural law, no natural rights, nothing but a "deal" made by a group of human beings who mutually agree to stop making war so that they can get on with other, more interesting, pursuits. Does this not give us the justification we have been seeking? Unfortunately, no. Let me explain why.

First, it assumes the explicit assent of each and every individual who is to be subject to the authority thus created—an impossible condition to realize in actuality. If some individual says, "I choose not to enter into the contract; I prefer to do as I please and defend myself as necessary," he or she is precisely the individual who would be singled out (if that person does what he or she says) for punishment under the law. If the whole human population consisted of only ten persons, it would require the consent of all ten to establish the state. If one dissents, the question remains: *By what right* do the other nine presume to coerce that person against his or her will? A cynical answer suggests itself: not by right but by power.

There is a second difficulty. Suppose that, after a time, one of the original parties to the agreement decides that it was a bad bargain and announces that he is pulling out. What is to prevent him from doing this? Must we say that his original decision to enter into the contract is irrevocable? That is not convincing. If he entered into the contract on grounds of self-interest, then, on those same grounds, he should be able to terminate it. But this means, in actuality, that any individual who concludes that his or her self-interest would be best served by breaking the law should be free to do so—and by so doing to terminate his or her participation in the social contract—in which case the civil authorities would cease to have any right to take action against him. In other words, the social contract establishes the authority of government *except when it is really needed.* In precisely the cases where it would like to exercise legitimate authority, all it has is naked power.

Then there is the problem of the second and subsequent generations, who *ex hypothesi* were not original parties to the contract but are, so to speak, born into it by virtue of being descendants of the original covenanters. Their theoretical case is even stronger than that of the founding father who decides he wants to terminate the contract, since they have never explicitly assented to the bargain and cannot with any degree of plausibility be said to have made an "irrevocable" commitment. By what right does the government established by their parents presume to govern them? Why should they obey a government in whose founding they had no part, and to whose authority they have never explicitly assented?

The social-contract theory justifies the authority of government only insofar as the governed consent to that authority. Those who do not consent become merely the victims of superior power. It may be prudent for them to do what the law requires, but the *right* of government to restrict their freedom has in no way been established.

The Power of Government

The truth of the matter seems to me to be this. Wherever the human species has appeared, some members have succeeded in gaining the power to compel obedience, to rule. Their wishes have been the law, their decisions the decrees of justice, their arms the means of enforcing compliance. They have been obeyed not because they had any right to be but simply because they had the power to ensure that they were. What is called "the duty of obedience" to one who exercises "legitimate authority" is nothing but the habit of bowing to the superior power of one who has assumed the role of ruler. The ruler may, in time, be compelled to share that power with some other powerful individuals (resulting in an oligarchy), or even with the people themselves (producing some form of democracy); yet the power of government, by whomever it is exercised, remains what it was in the beginning: naked power. The difference between a judge and the leader of a band of thieves is just this: the judge has more constituents.

I do not conclude from this that government is in general a bad thing, or that society would be better off in the absence of government. I think those theorists are right who say that in the absence of government, people's aggressive and acquisitive tendencies would create a situation of danger and chaos—a "state of nature," as SCT calls it—in which none of us would willingly choose to live. Even bad government is better than no government at all. The practical challenge, as I see it, is to achieve the security and order that we expect our civil authority to provide without creating a monster that seeks to dominate every aspect of our lives.

Having said this, however, I do not pretend that I have solved the theoretical problem of the rationale for the authority of government. That problem, in my opinion, has no solution. The authority of government has no higher sanction than the will of some to impose upon all some particular kind of order. If we accede to such authority, as most of us do, it is not because we think its claim to legitimacy has been established. It is simply because as a practical matter we acknowledge the need for civil authority in a society that consists of people like us.

STUDY QUESTIONS

1. Theoretical Anarchist (TA) distinguishes three types of anarchism. Are the distinctions clear? Is it logically possible to be both a theoretical anarchist and a militant anarchist? both a theoretical anarchist and a naive anarchist? Explain.
2. "SU has not offered a wrong answer: he has simply answered the wrong question." Is this correct?
3. How does TA's formulation of the social-contract theory differ from that contained in Chapter 37?
4. Summarize TA's objections to the social-contract theory. Do you find them convincing? Can you defend the theory against these objections?

CORRELATED READINGS[1]

1. Aquinas, St. Thomas. "Four Kinds of Law." *Summa Theologica,* First Part of the Second Part, Question 91, Articles 1–4. The natural-law theory.
2. Rousseau, Jean Jacques. "The Social Contract." *An Inquiry into the Nature of the Social Contract* (1791), Chap. V–VIII. A classic statement of the social-contract theory.
3. Mill, John Stuart. "The Utilitarian Basis of Authority." *On Liberty* (1859), Chap. 1. Social utilitarianism.
4. Pitkin, Hanna. "Obligation and Consent." *The American Political Science Review,* vol. 60 (1966), pp. 39–49.
5. Wolff, Robert Paul. "Beyond the Legitimate State." *In Defense of Anarchism.* New York: Harper & Row, 1970, pp. 69–82. Theoretical anarchism.

FOR FURTHER READING

Aristotle. *Politics.* Many editions. See especially Book VII.
Beran, H. "In Defense of the Consent Theory of Political Obligation and Authority," *Ethics,* 87 (1977), 260–271.
Barry, Brian. *Political Argument.* New York: Humanities Press, 1965.
————. *The Liberal Theory of Justice: A Critical Examination of the Principal Doctrines in "A Theory of Justice" by John Rawls.* New York: Oxford University Press, 1973.
Berlin, Isaiah. *Four Essays on Liberty.* New York: Oxford University Press, 1969 (paperbound).
Bosanquet, Bernard. *Philosophical Theory of the State.* London: Macmillan, 1920.
Brown, D. G. "Mill on Liberty and Morality," *The Philosophical Review,* 81 (1972), 133–158.
Cohen, Carl. *Democracy.* Athens: University of Georgia Press, 1971. A comprehensive analysis.
Crocker, L. G. *Rousseau's Social Contract.* Cleveland, Ohio: Cleveland Press of Case Western Reserve University, 1968.
d'Entreves, A. P. *Natural Law.* London: Hutchinson, 1951.
Feinberg, Joel. *Social Philosophy.* Englewood Cliffs, N.J.: Prentice-Hall, 1973 (paperbound).
Fuller, Lon L. *The Morality of Law.* New Haven, Conn.: Yale University Press, 1964. Deals with the status of law and its relation to moral rules.
Gierke, Otto. *Natural Law and the Theory of Society.* New York: Cambridge University Press, 1934.
Gilson, Etienne. *Medieval Universalism and Its Present Value.* New York: Sheed and Ward, 1937.
Gough, J. W. *The Social Contract.* 2nd ed. Oxford: Clarendon Press, 1957.

Grimsley, Ronald. *The Philosophy of Rousseau.* London: Oxford University Press, 1973 (paperbound). Includes an examination of social-contract theory.

Hart, H. L. A. *The Concept of Law.* New York: Oxford University Press, 1961.

—————. *Law, Liberty and Morality.* New York: Random House, 1963. Three lectures regarding "the proper scope of criminal law."

Hobbes, Thomas. *Leviathan.* Many editions. Originally published in 1651. See especially Part I, Chaps. 13–15.

Hobhouse, L. T. *The Metaphysical Theory of the State.* New York: Macmillan, 1918.

Hutchins, Robert M., *et al. Natural Law and Modern Society.* Cleveland, Ohio: World, 1963.

Kaplan, Abraham (ed.). *Individuality and the New Society.* Seattle: University of Washington Press, 1970.

Levine, A. "A Conceptual Problem for Liberal Democracy," *The Journal of Philosophy,* (75) (1978), 302–308.

Lewis, H. D. "Freedom and Authority in Rousseau," *Philosophy,* 53 (1978), 353–362.

Locke, John. *Two Treatises of Government.* Many editions.

McPherson, Thomas. *Political Obligation.* London: Routledge and Kegan Paul, 1967. Reviews and criticizes several theories as to the basis for civil authority.

Maritain, Jacques. *The Rights of Man and Natural Law.* New York: Scribner, 1945.

Melden, A. I. (ed.). *Human Rights.* Belmont, Calif.: Wadsworth, 1970 (paperbound). Contains classical and contemporary selections as well as such documents as the Universal Declaration of Human Rights.

Montesquieu, Charles de. *Spirit of the Laws,* trans. by Thomas Nugent. New York: Hafner, 1949.

Nagel, Thomas. "Rawls on Justice," *The Philosophical Review,* 82 (1973), 220–234.

Negley, Glenn. *Political Authority and Moral Judgment.* Durham, N.C.: Duke University Press, 1965. Critique of several theories regarding the basis of civil authority.

Nozick, R. *Anarchy, State, and Utopia.* New York: Basic Books, 1974. A thoughtful and witty presentation of a social-contract theory on the basis of which the author defends the authority of what he calls a "minimal" state.

Popper, Karl R. *The Open Society and Its Enemies.* Princeton, N.J.: Princeton University Press, 1950.

Rawls, John. *A Theory of Justice.* Cambridge, Mass.: Harvard University Press, 1971 (paperbound). A contemporary classic. Draws from social-contract tradition.

Russell, Bertrand. *Authority and the Individual.* New York: Simon and Schuster, 1949.

Sen, A. K. *Collective Choice and Social Welfare.* San Francisco, Calif.: Holden Day, 1970, Chap. 6.

—————. "The Impossibility of a Paretian Liberal," *Journal of Political Economy,* (78) (1970), 152–157.

Tassi, A. "Anarchism, Autonomy, and the Concept of the Common Good," *International Philosophical Quarterly,* 17 (1977), 273–283. A critique of anarchism.

Taylor, Richard. *Freedom, Anarchy, and the Law: An Introduction to Political Philosophy.* Englewood Cliffs, N.J.: Prentice-Hall, 1973 (paperbound).

Weil, Simone. *Oppression and Liberty,* trans. by Arthur Wills and John Petrie. Amherst: University of Massachusetts Press, 1973.

Wild, John. *Plato's Modern Enemies and the Theory of Natural Law.* Chicago: University of Chicago Press, 1953.

PART X

THE HIGHEST GOOD

40

THE STRUCTURE OF ETHICAL THINKING

It is an interesting and perhaps important fact about us human beings that we regularly appraise our own behavior and that of others in moral terms. Some behavior is appraised positively: an act is said to be good, or noble, or generous, or right; its enactor, benevolent, kind, humane, virtuous. And some behavior is appraised negatively: an act is said to be evil, or vile, or selfish, or wrong; its enactor, malevolent, bestial, inhumane, corrupt. People cannot escape involvement in a moral community. Their lives are enveloped by what we may call "the moral sphere."

The Moral Sphere

What distinguishes that kind of behavior which we consider subject to moral appraisal? What are the defining characteristics of the moral sphere?

First, it is apparent that it is only *human* behavior that we appraise in this way. Until astronauts landed on the moon, we did not subject anything that ever happened there to moral appraisal. Again, we do not apply terms of moral appraisal to the behavior of animals or insects. We do not criticize the mating practices of antelopes, or the predatory habits of leopards, or the "slave" systems of ants or bees. Only human beings and their behavior are called good or bad, right or wrong, virtuous or vicious.

Second, it is only human behavior involving *choice* that we regard as appropriately subject to moral judgments. We assume, when we ascribe praise or blame to some particular human behavior, that other alternatives were available to the person whose behavior is being judged. We neither praise nor blame a person for doing something if we believe that, under the circumstances, it was the only thing he or she could have done.

Third, even when choice is involved, not all instances of human behavior belong to the moral sphere. Under ordinary circumstances, for example, my decision to have juice and cereal for breakfast rather than eggs and toast has no moral significance. (Of course, we can imagine a set of unusual circumstances in which this choice would have moral significance—if, say, another person and I were both on the verge of starvation, a single serving of each kind of breakfast was available, and the other person was seriously allergic to eggs, whereas I was not.) The third defining characteristic of the moral sphere is, then, that some *moral rule or principle* is relevant to the behavior in question: there is something that a human being in a given situation ought or ought not to do, some choice that ought or ought not to be made, simply by virtue of the fact that he is a human being in those particular circumstances. It would be morally wrong for me to contribute knowingly to the demise of my allergic friend by eating the cereal that could sustain that person's life when another alternative is available to me. Why? Because I have a moral obligation to preserve human life when I can. The generalized version of this idea—that one ought to preserve human life when one has the opportunity—is an example of a moral rule or principle.

Normative Ethics

All of us, then, act in ways that are or may be subject to moral appraisal, and all of us make moral judgments about the behavior of others. In clear-cut cases, we make these judgments without difficulty: we praise a person who risks his or her life to prevent a homicide or who rushes into the flames to rescue a child. In such cases, we judge almost instinctively, as if there were no reasoning involved.

In other cases, however, our moral judgments are more problematic. Is mercy killing ever morally defensible, and if so, under what circumstances? Is conscientious objection morally superior to being a soldier? Are some wars morally defensible and others not? Was it or was it not morally right for the United States to drop atomic bombs on Hiroshima and Nagasaki? In such cases, we tend to be less certain about our answers, and we often disagree with one another in the answers we give. When we do disagree, we appeal to relevant general principles of right and wrong and try to show that the position we hold is consistent with those principles.

Normative ethics is an attempt to answer the question, What kinds of things really are right and wrong, and why? The aim of the ethical theorist is to introduce order and consistency into our ethical beliefs and to relate them, if possible, to some universal principle or principles from which they supposedly derive their validity as rules for the guidance of our behavior. If I ought to help old Mrs. Jones cross a busy intersection when I see her standing there apprehensively, it must be because there is some rule or principle that prescribes what a moral agent ought to do and in terms of which I will be appropriately praised or blamed for what I do or fail to do. If I also ought to attempt to rescue a child who is drowning, the same reasoning applies. The ethical theorist asks, What is it that these two cases, and hundreds of others that might be mentioned, have in common? Is there not some general principle that governs these and all other cases of moral obligation? To ask and attempt to answer such questions is to engage in the peculiar sort of inquiry called normative ethics. To exhibit a set of ethical beliefs as a coherent system deducible from one or more general principles is to construct an ethical system.

Two Types of Ethical Thought

The efforts of philosophers to introduce order and consistency into our thinking about the moral sphere have resulted in two general types of ethical systems.

The first type may be termed *teleological.* The moral value of any act, according to this type of theory, consists in the tendency it has (or is intended to have) to produce a good or bad result. Some things are intrinsically good, and other things are good or bad depending on their tendency to promote or to hinder that which is intrinsically good. If health is considered intrinsically good, for example, then the praiseworthy character of certain acts (giving food to the hungry, medical care to the ill, and the like) and the blameworthy character of other acts (knowingly selling or serving contaminated food) can be understood in terms of their relation to this good. Everything that is morally praiseworthy, according to this type of theory, is so because of its tendency to realize that which is intrinsically good: the intrinsically good is the end (*tèlos*), or goal, toward which all behavior having moral value is aimed. We shall return to a further consideration of this type of ethical system shortly.

Not all ethical theorists are convinced, however, that the whole moral sphere can be understood in terms of the relation of various acts to whatever may be said to be intrinsically good. Some acts, say these theorists, are obligatory in themselves, quite apart from any tendency they may have to produce an intrinsically good result. It may be argued, for example, that people have a moral obligation under virtually any set of conceivable circumstances to tell the truth or to keep a promise, whether or not they believe that by so doing they will promote the realization of the intrinsically good. Some acts are "morally right" in and of themselves; they are not right merely by virtue of their tendency to realize some other good. Ethical systems that attempt to understand the moral sphere along these lines are variously termed *formalist* or *deontological* theories.

The Summum Bonum

Among many philosophers who have attempted to understand the moral sphere in teleological terms, a much discussed question has been, What is humanity's *summum bonum*—the highest good? Some human "goods" are obviously good solely because of their instrumental value. Medicine, for example, is good only because of its value in producing health. Very well, let us then consider health. Why is it good? If we say that health is good because it is a precondition of being able to engage in enjoyable activity, then it too is an instrumental good (though it may also be an intrinsic good). Well then, why is enjoyable activity good? Is it instrumentally good in that it contributes to the realization of some higher good? If so, where does this process come to an end? What is humanity's "highest" good? What is that good that (a) is worthy of being desired in and of itself, (b) is not instrumentally good, and (c) is the cause of the goodness of other things insofar as they contribute to its realization?

Note that our question is open-ended. It can logically be answered in an infinite number of ways, though few of the answers would be likely to appear plausible. Let us look briefly at a few of the answers that have seemed sufficiently credible to win the support of at least some philosophers.

Some Possible Answers

It can be plausibly argued that *pleasure* is the highest human good, indeed, that it is the only thing that is good in and of itself. This view is called *hedonism* (from the Greek *hedone,* meaning "pleasure"). One of its earliest and best-known advocates was the Greek philosopher Epicurus (341–270 B.C.), who wrote:

> We recognize pleasure as the first good innate in us, and from pleasure we begin every act of choice and avoidance, and to pleasure we return again, using the feeling as the standard by which we judge the good.[1]

Some critics of hedonism contend that such a view treats people as if they were lower animals, merely sensuous beings. The truth is, they say, that the uniqueness of human beings consists in the fact that they are rational beings. The highest human good, therefore, is not pleasure—which may, indeed, be the highest good of a pig or a dog—but *activity according to reason.* This view we shall call *rational eudemonism* (from the Greek *eudaimonia,* meaning "happiness"). It was first advocated by Aristotle (384–322 B.C.), the great Greek philosopher and tutor of Alexander the Great.

Some ethical theorists have concluded that there is no one thing that is humanity's highest good, but that several things are worthy of

---

[1]Epicurus, "Letter to Menoeceus," in Whitney J. Oates (ed), *The Stoic and Epicurean Philosophers* (New York: Random House, 1940), pp. 31–32.

being desired for their own sakes and that the highest good consists in realizing as many of these intrinsic goods as possible. This view, advocated by a number of philosophers, we shall call *ethical pluralism.*

It seems evident, finally, that religious claims have some bearing on the question concerning the highest good. We shall, therefore, consider the view that humanity's highest good consists in a state of affairs that is incapable of being fully realized in this life, that the ultimate fulfillment of humanity's deepest needs and longings lies beyond the temporal sphere. This view, which we shall call *theological eudemonism,* has been advocated (with numerous differences in detail) by many philosopher-theologians, including St. Augustine (A.D. 354–430) and St. Thomas Aquinas (A.D. 1225–1274).

Although these four are the answers that have been given most frequently to the question we are now considering, it is obvious that they do not, by any means, exhaust the possibilities. We shall, however, limit our consideration to these four, beginning with some of the arguments that may be adduced in support of hedonism.

STUDY QUESTIONS

1. What are suggested in this chapter as the defining characteristics of the moral sphere? Do you agree with this definition? Can you think of an example of human behavior that you would regard as being appropriately subject to praise or blame that does not fall within the moral sphere as so defined? Can you think of any example of behavior that fits this definition, but which you would exclude from the moral sphere?
2. What is normative ethics?
3. What precisely is the difference between teleological ethics and deontological (or formalist) ethics?
4. Precisely what are you asking when you ask, What is the highest human good? Rephrase the question in a way that you think exhibits more clearly the point of the question.
5. In addition to those suggested in this chapter, can you think of any plausible answers to the question, What is the highest human good?

41

THE CASE FOR HEDONISM

Critics of hedonism seem to have rather consistently exhibited a perverse determination to misunderstand and misrepresent what its advocates are trying to say. The reason for this, I suppose, is that there is a simple-minded line of reasoning that appears to lead from the assertion "Pleasure is the highest human good" to the assertion "The highest rule of morality is, Enjoy yourself!" Since it seems obvious to everyone, including hedonists, that the injunction to enjoy oneself is not a promising starting point for ethics, it is lightly concluded that the fundamental axiom of hedonism—that pleasure is the highest good—is mistaken.

In order to rid our consideration of hedonism of this spurious reasoning, I propose that we begin our deliberation at a somewhat different point. Let us suppose that you and I are engaged by a very wealthy man to look after the raising of his children. His instructions to us are as follows: "The care of my children is entirely in your hands. You are to spare no effort and no expense to assist them in every possible way to achieve the very best life of which they are capable. Everything that would be for their good you are to provide; everything that would be for their evil you are, so far as possible, to omit from their experience. I leave it to you to judge what would truly be for their good and what would not."

If we are to carry out these instructions, we have some important decisions to make. We must decide what really is good—indeed, what really is best—for our charges. On what principle shall we decide? I say on the pleasure principle and would like to persuade you to agree with me.

When I assert that pleasure is the highest human good, I am *not* asserting that sensuous gratification is the highest good. People are not pigs. The highest good consists in the optimum realization of the pleasures of which people are capable. People are capable, to be sure, of pleasures of sensation, and such pleasure is most certainly to be preferred to pain. But people are also capable of what may be termed the "higher" pleasures. They are capable, for example, of experiencing intellectual pleasure, by virtue of which knowledge is a great human good. They are capable of experiencing pleasures of feeling and imagination, by virtue of which they perceive poetry, music, painting, and the other products of the visual and performing arts as goods. They are capable of experiencing pleasure in the very act of serving a human need, by virtue of which the moral sentiments acquire for them an intrinsic value all their own. The highest good for human beings is *human* pleasure. What is pleasurable for human beings, and, therefore, good for human beings, is different from what would be pleasurable for a creature with more limited capacities.

Pleasure is an experience, a state of being, that occurs whenever an awakened desire is satisfied. There is pleasure in eating food when you are hungry and in drinking a glass of cold water when you are thirsty. There is pleasure also in beholding a beautiful sunset when inspired by a love of beauty, and in mastering a theorem when stimulated by a hunger for knowledge. Any good thing that you or I can do for any other human being will be, must be, a contribution to that person's pleasurable experience. To say that an act of such and such a kind is morally good or right is to say that it is the sort of act that on the whole tends to enhance human pleasure. You see, then, how far we hedonists are from asserting that the first principle of ethics is "Enjoy yourself!" Such a principle cannot be derived from anything I have said and is, in fact, as repugant to me (as a moral principle) as to any other ethical theorist.

Two questions now need to be clearly distinguished. The first is, What is the highest human good? I have replied that pleasure (as defined above) is the highest good. A second and very different question is, About whose good ought I, as a moral agent, to be concerned? To this question, I would reply that I ought to be concerned about the good (the pleasure) of all people, myself included. To be concerned exclusively about my own good (my own pleasure) would be sheer selfishness and would, therefore, be deserving of moral disapproval. To be as concerned about the good (the pleasure) of others as about my own is the essence of morality and is summed up in the admonitions "Do unto others as you would that others do unto you" and "Love your neighbor as yourself."

Supporting Arguments

The assertion that pleasure is the highest good is not capable of strict and conclusive proof. Its probability can, however, be established by two persuasive arguments.

To say that something is the highest human good implies that it is worthy of being desired for its own sake. The intrinsic desirability of pleasure is rendered highly probable, it seems to me, by the fact that it is universally desired. That something is visible is indicated by people's actually seeing it. That something is audible is shown by people's actually hearing it. In like manner, I would suggest, the desirability of pleasure is evident from the fact that people actually desire it.

This argument is not weakened at all by examples of individuals who have freely subjected themselves to experiences that they fully expected to be more or less painful. Consider a mother who permits one of her kidneys to be transplanted into the body of her daughter, whose kidneys had been removed because of disease. Is this woman demonstrating that she prefers pain to pleasure? Surely not. She demonstrates only that she is willing to suffer pain in order that her child may have an opportunity to experience the pleasures of a normal life. Her pain is chosen not for its own sake but for the sake of the pleasure she might give to someone she loves. Every instance of pain freely accepted that I can think of can be understood in the same way: as a means to the enhancement of some human pleasure that is valued for its own sake.

Second, the assertion that pleasure is the highest good is broadly supported by the fact that it renders intelligible the moral rules and principles by which most people agree we ought to try to live. Why is it morally wrong to steal? Because human pleasure is enhanced when people respect each other's property rights. Why is it morally wrong to lie? Because life proceeds more serenely, more happily when people can be counted on to tell the truth. Why is it virtuous to feed the hungry, to visit the sick, to comfort the bereaved, to aid the destitute? Because in doing these things we are assuaging human pain and enhancing human pleasure. Hedonism, then, merely makes explicit the principle that has unconsciously guided the conscience of humanity through the thousands of years in which the moral code by which most civilized societies live has been developing. The explicit assertion of this principle makes possible the further development of the moral code as society moves rapidly into a new era in which the rules of the past may be insufficient to guide us in resolving the problems that we are likely to encounter.

Qualities of Pleasure

Let us now return to the point where we began: the task of providing for the children of our wealthy employer "everything that would be for their good" and shielding them from "everything that would be for their evil." How shall we proceed? What pleasures shall we teach them to enjoy? What pains shall we seek to eliminate from their experience?

We shall, of course, provide adequately for their physical needs: food, shelter, clothing, and the like. We shall let them feel the warmth of the sun on a summer day and the refreshing coolness of a stream when they are old enough to swim. We shall employ the best medical knowledge available to protect them from disease and to heal them when they are ill.

But clearly, if we are to provide "everything that would be for their good," we must do much more than this. We must awaken in them the higher faculties, the uniquely human desires, in order that they may experience the sublimer pleasures that human beings alone, so far as we know, are capable of enjoying. We shall attempt to awaken their thirst for knowledge, to make them curious about themselves, their world, and other human beings. Then, we can guide them toward the discovery of answers in order that they may experience the incomparable pleasure of learning.

We shall also attempt to awaken in our young charges a love for beauty, so that they may experience the sublime pleasures of art, music, sculpture, and nature itself. We shall expose them to mountains and oceans and sunsets, to the paintings of the masters, to the mighty symphonies of Beethoven and the exquisite music of Mozart, to architectural creations of exceptional beauty, to theater, cinema, and dance. We shall cultivate in them a taste for beauty in form and movement, an aesthetic sense that will provide them with immeasurable pleasure throughout life.

We shall, finally, attempt to awaken in them a moral sense, a natural preference for good and an abhorrence of evil. We shall teach them to desire the pleasure of all human beings, indeed, of all sentient creatures, and shall attempt to inculcate in them that natural kindness and generosity of spirit that is the essence of virtue. We shall not, certainly, seek to make of them either ascetics or grim moralists. But we shall teach them to value the pleasurable experience of every creature, and especially of every human being. We shall teach them, when the occasion demands it, to forgo some pleasure themselves in order that some greater or rarer pleasure may be experienced by others.

"That all sounds very lovely," someone may say, "but let me ask a practical question. If pleasure is the highest human good, why do you not simply maximize the *quantity* of pleasure for your young charges and stop worrying about the *quality*? If money were the highest good, it would make no difference whether one got it in fives, tens, or hundreds; only the total quantity would be relevant. Why not with pleasure?"

To this question, I would reply as follows: no person would be willing to exchange the higher faculties—the capacities to experience intellectual and aesthetic and moral pleasure—for any quantity whatsoever of merely sensual pleasure. Promise a person every variety of sensual pleasure, in any quantity imaginable, on the condition that he or she cease to be a human being and become a lower animal, and that person will refuse it. Why? Because, in fact, people do value some pleasures above others and are, on occasion, willing to endure a fair amount of physical discomfort for the sake of securing some of the higher pleasures. All pleasure, *qua* pleasure, is good and worthy of being desired; but in the judgment of those who have experienced a wide spectrum of pleasures (and they alone are competent to judge), some forms of pleasure are more valuable, more worthy of being desired, than others.

Our problem as tutors, then, is not merely to maximize the quantity of pleasure for our charges, but to orchestrate the variety of pleasures in such a way as to guide them toward a truly satisfying life. This, admittedly, is no easy task, for there is danger of imbalance in many directions. We do not want them to become sensualists, or esthetes, or arid intellectuals, or rigid moralists: we want them to become well-rounded human beings, sensitively balancing the various forms of pleasure in their own experience and seeking to further a similar balance in the lives of others.

Let me conclude by underscoring the point with which I began. The greatest problem that we hedonists have to face is that our position is often misrepresented in such a way as to make it into something that no person with any sense of human dignity would espouse. This is usually done by defining pleasure in purely sensual terms and then suggesting that according to hedonism each individual should be concerned only about his or her own pleasure (so defined). But this, I repeat, is a gross parody of hedonism. Hedonism is, indeed, the view that pleasure is the greatest human good. But hedonists affirm that what is pleasurable for human beings is different from that which is pleasurable for a lower animal, because human beings are capable of enjoying a richer variety of pleasures. If moral virtue consists in desiring what is good for all people and doing what will tend to achieve it, then from a hedonist's point of view a moral agent must desire and work for human pleasure in all its various forms.

STUDY QUESTIONS

1. What exactly is pleasure? Write your own definition, then compare this with the definition in a dictionary.
2. "Any good thing that you or I can do for any other human being will be, must be, a contribution to that person's pleasurable experience." Do you agree? If you do agree, does that settle the issue for you—that is, does it follow that pleasure is the highest human good?
3. "The assertion that pleasure is the highest good is not capable of strict and conclusive proof." Do you agree? In general, how would you go about trying to support the claim that x (pleasure, or what-have-you) is the highest good?

4. Objection: If pleasure is the highest human good, then the more pleasure there is, the more good there is, regardless of the *quality* of pleasure involved. Do you agree?

5. Suppose that someone experiences pleasure in torturing animals. Is the pleasure good? Is the activity of torturing animals right? How might Hedonist respond to these questions?

42

A LIFE OF REASON

I want to begin my contribution to this discussion by reintroducing the beautiful word "eudemonia" from Chapter 40. It is usually translated as "happiness," but it means much more: literally, "having a good spirit"; connotatively, "good fortune," "fulfillment," "a rich destiny." Eudemonia is that for which one would exchange all that one has. It is the pearl of great price, the goal and desire of every human being.

It is a mere tautology to say that the highest human good is to achieve eudemonia. The question is, In what does humanity's eudemonia consist? Hedonist tells us it consists in the experience of pleasure. I think he is mistaken in this assertion, and I shall attempt to show why.

Critique of Hedonism

Let us look first at Hedonist's reasoning. The intrinsic desirability of pleasure is evident, he says, from the fact that it is universally desired. For just as something is visible by virtue of the fact that people actually see it, and audible by virtue of the fact that people actually hear it, so a thing is desirable by virtue of the fact that people desire it. Ergo, he concludes, pleasure is desirable.

This reasoning is altogether specious; indeed, it is nothing more than a play on words. To say that something is visible or audible is to say that it is *capable* of being seen or heard. To say that something is desirable, on the other hand, is to say that it is *worthy* of being desired. "Desirable" is like "despicable" and "lovable, " not like "visible" and "audible." That people desire something does not at all tend to show that it is truly desirable, that is, that it is *worthy* of being desired. It only shows that it is desired.

I must also take issue with Hedonist's attempt to square his assertion that pleasure is the highest human good with the idea that some forms of pleasure are more desirable than others by virtue of their higher quality. On the premise that pleasure is the highest good, what can "higher quality" possibly mean? It can only mean, it seems to me, "more pleasurable": it can be of a higher quality only in the way that a ten dollar bill is of a higher quality (if you want to put it that way) than a one dollar bill. And if people are criticized for neglecting their intellectual and aesthetic and moral development for the sake of being pure sensualists, they could, on Hedonist's premise, convincingly defend themselves by arguing that they find sensual pleasure *more pleasurable* than other kinds. I know that Hedonist does not want to say this; indeed, his theory about "qualities of pleasure" is intended precisely to avoid this conclusion. My point is that he cannot have it both ways. If pleasure is the highest good, then one pleasure can be "higher" than another only by virtue of being more pleasurable. If various forms of pleasure differ in quality, then they must differ by virtue of some component other than pleasure itself, and in that case pleasure is not the highest human good.

That Hedonist's argument contains some specious reasoning does not, of course, prove that he is mistaken in his assertion that pleasure is the highest good. Good theories are sometimes supported with bad reasons, and in such cases we must be wise enough to look beyond those bad reasons and consider the theory on its own merits. Let us now do this with Hedonist's theory. Let us forget his faulty reasoning and consider directly whether or not pleasure is the highest human good. I shall, of course, argue that it is not.

First, imagine a person enjoying, to a high degree and throughout a long life, all the pleasures that Hedonist has described—sensual pleasures, intellectual pleasures, aesthetic pleasures, pleasures of every conceivable kind. According to Hedonist's theory, this person would have achieved the highest good and should wish for nothing more. But let us suppose something more about this person. Though this person possesses an abundance of pleasure at every moment, he or she does not possess memory, so he or she cannot remember experienced pleasure in the past. Moreover, though this person is experiencing immense pleasure moment by moment, he or she is not *conscious* of experiencing pleasure, not able to anticipate future experiences of pleasure. This person, in short, lacks those faculties by which he or she could be conscious of experiencing pleasure. Would we really say that the person was realizing the highest good? We would not. But if pleasure is the highest human good, we clearly should.

"Well," Hedonist may say to us, "you are just nitpicking. Any reasonable person must know that when I say that pleasure is the highest good, I mean that the *consciousness* of pleasure is the highest good.

Certainly, I don't mean to assert that pleasure, apart from the consciousness of pleasure, is good." Very well, let us accept this revision of Hedonist's theory. It still does not stand up under close scrutiny.

Imagine now that a person has been put to sleep with an anesthetic, and that all necessary arrangements have been made to take care of normal bodily processes—supplying food and water, getting rid of bodily wastes, and so forth. In addition, since medical science is at an advanced stage, the brain is artificially stimulated in such a way that the person has the consciousness of experiencing, to a very high degree, all the pleasures that Hedonist describes as constituting the highest human good. The person experiences every imaginable form of sensual pleasure, every form of aesthetic pleasure, and the highest reaches of intellectual ecstasy. And let this experience of sheer ecstasy, unadulterated by any consciousness of pain, go on and on and on. Let it continue forever. Would we say that this person is an example of someone who was realizing the highest good? We would not. Yet, if the consciousness of pleasure were the highest good, we should assent to this.

Or consider this: If pleasure, or the consciousness of pleasure, were the highest human good, then the best of all possible worlds would be one in which half the people on earth were sadists and the other half masochists. There would, certainly, be a great deal of pleasure in such a world—much more, presumably, than there is now—but I for one would not call it a better world. Yet, if I were to accept the thesis that pleasure is the highest good, I would be obliged to applaud such a world.

Hedonism, then, is not an acceptable theory about what constitutes the highest human good. Let me present an alternative view.

Rational Eudemonism

Suppose that we ask what constitutes the highest good of a fish. It is apparent that the eudemonia of a fish would be that state of affairs that would enable the fish to do those things that nature has equipped it to do, most prominently, swimming, an activity in which the fish expresses its uniqueness as a fish. In order to identify the highest good of any species of living thing you have first to identify what it is about that species that is unique; for the highest good of any creature is that activity or state of affairs in which it is, so to speak, fulfilling its unique destiny, realizing its unique purpose for being.

What, then, is unique about human beings? Their capacity for growth and reproduction they share with all other living things, plants as well as animals. Their capacity to experience sensation (sight, hearing, touch, taste, smell) and to move about (locomotion) they share with all the animals. That which is unique to humans is not to be found in these areas. People differ from every other species of living thing by virtue of their reason. Human beings, alone, are able to seek and to know truth, though admittedly they often fall into error in their quest for truth. This capacity to exercise reason, then, to seek understanding, knowledge, science, wisdom, is humanity's unique endowment.

The *highest* human good, then, must consist in the exercise of the highest human faculty. People have, to be sure, many lesser goods— food, companionship, pleasurable sensations, and the like. But the highest good, that in which humankind's eudemonia essentially consists, is the right exercise of the rational faculty.

In addition to seeking knowledge, however, it is the function of human reason to instruct us regarding what is good and right. Thus, we are exercising our rational faculty not only when we are searching for or contemplating truth, but also when we are acting according to what reason tells us is good and right. Consequently, we arrive at the view that the highest human good consists in *activity according to reason,* eithe : in the quest for truth or in practical activity according to the moral dictates of reason.

I freely admit that this high goal of always acting according to reason is rarely achieved by human beings. For there is in all of us, as every serious student of the human psyche from Plato to Sigmund Freud has told us, a powerful irrational element that seeks expression in those very actions that we have said are supposed to be controlled by reason. Indeed, the sharp difference between Hedonist's position and my own is vividly illustrated at this point; for Hedonist is bound to say that insofar as the expression of libido is pleasurable it is good, whereas I affirm that insofar as it leads to behavior that is not in accordance with reason it is bad. People progress toward their highest good not by following the path of least resistance (which hedonism would appear to counsel them to do) but by striving—sometimes heroically—to bring their various drives and appetites under the control of a disciplined reason. This may not always be maximally pleasurable, for there is undoubtedly pleasure in the fulfillment of an awakened desire and disappointment in its denial, but it is the way to eudemonia.

We have noted that the view that there are various qualities of pleasure, and that the "higher" pleasures are to be preferred to the "lower" pleasures, is not consistent with the basic thesis of hedonism that pleasure constitutes the highest good. I would now suggest that the assertion that there are "qualities of pleasure," which does appear to be correct, can best be understood in conjunction with the theory I am defending here. For to say that one sort of pleasure is higher than another means, I suggest, that there is more reason in it. A child's delight in playing in the snow is surely as innocent as any pleasure imaginable, but it is of a lower order of pleasure because there is little reason in it. The pleasure of a student of physics in finally mastering relativity theory is of a higher order of pleasure because there is much reason in it. The scale according to which we rank pleasures as being higher or lower is the scale of reason.

In affirming that activity according to reason is the highest human good, I am not denying that pleasure is *a* good. On the contrary, I hold that pleasure may be a very high-level good, and that it is worthy of being desired insofar as it does not detract from the pursuit of this highest good. We should aim, it seems to me, at being rational beings, at realizing in practice the goal of activity according to reason; it will then follow, as a natural concomitant of such a life, that we will experience such pleasures as are good for us.

STUDY QUESTIONS

1. What is Rational Eudemonist's objection to Hedonist's claim that pleasure is desirable because it is universally desired? Who is right on this point?
2. "If various forms of pleasure differ in quality, then they must differ by virtue of some component other than pleasure itself, and in that case pleasure is not the highest human good." Do you agree?
3. Rational Eudemonist presents two *reductio ad absurdum* arguments to show that pleasure is not the highest human good. Do they succeed? How might Hedonist defend himself?
4. How does Rational Eudemonist support his claim that the highest good consists in activity according to reason? Do you find his argument convincing?

43

ETHICAL PLURALISM

Discussions about the summum bonum often seem to me to confuse several questions. I want to preface what I have to say on the subject of the highest good by distinguishing the several questions that are sometimes discussed almost interchangeably, and by indicating which of these questions I shall be answering in the remainder of this essay.

Four Questions

In asking, What is the highest human good? it is possible, first, to be asking for a description of the best conceivable state of affairs for human beings. In answer to this question we might posit, for example, a world in which the temperature at ground level is always 72° Fahrenheit, where no illness or suffering of any kind ever occurs, where people remain youthful forever, and so on. Such a description might even be of some practical value in defining a remote ideal toward which our efforts in the real world might fruitfully be directed, but it would not be a description of "the highest human good" in the sense in which I shall be discussing it.

Second, this question could be construed to mean, What is the best possible state of affairs for human beings, the laws of nature being what they are? In this case, we would have to describe a kind of ideal society in which all the remediable ills of society as we know it are somehow cured. Plato, in the *Republic,* and Thomas More, in *Utopia,* tried to do this; but it is not the question I shall be discussing.

A third possible meaning of the question concerning the highest human good is this: Of the various good things that people may for various reasons desire, which are the most worthy of being desired for their own sakes? What are the principal intrinsic goods for human beings? I shall be addressing myself to this question shortly.

The fourth way in which the question may be construed is as follows: Of the various things that are worthy of being desired for their own sakes, which *one thing* is most worthy of being desired? This question assumes that there is a multiplicity of things that are intrinsically good, but that one of them is so much better than the others that it should be desired even at the cost of losing the other, and lesser, intrinsic goods. I shall have something to say on this point also in what follows.

Of these four questions, it seems to me that Hedonist has addressed himself to the third and Rational Eudemonist to the fourth. Hedonist has argued that pleasure alone is intrinsically good and worthy of being desired for its own sake, and that whatever else is good for human beings is good only insofar as it is productive of human pleasure. Rational Eudemonist, on the other hand, has conceded that pleasure is *a* good, perhaps even an intrinsic good, but has argued that another intrinsic good—activity according to reason—is the *highest* intrinsic good for human beings, that is, the intrinsic good most worthy of being desired.

In order to defend my position against both Hedonist and Rational Eudemonist, therefore, I am obliged to reply to these two questions. Against Hedonist I shall argue that pleasure is only one of several intrinsic goods for human beings; and against Rational Eudemonist I shall argue that the highest good consists, not in the maximum realization of some one intrinsic good to the possible exclusion of all others, but rather in the maximization of all.

A Word About Method

It is notoriously difficult to argue for or against any theory about what things are intrinsically good and worthy of being desired as ends in themselves. Hedonist frankly admits that he cannot provide a "strict and conclusive proof" of his position. Rational Eudemonist does not even try. The method that seems to me most appropriate is what I shall call the method of imaginative isolation. Let us suppose that we are trying to decide whether x is intrinsically good. We then imagine a universe in which x is absent, and then another that is identical in all respects except that x is present. We then ask, Does the presence of x in the second case provide a reason for preferring the second universe over the first? If the answer is affirmative, x may be presumed to be intrinsically good; if the answer is negative, we conclude that x is not intrinsically good.

Pleasure

If we now apply this method to the case of pleasure, we shall not be surprised to discover that pleasure is, indeed, an intrinsic good. If we were to imagine, let us say, one universe in which sentient beings are always in pain and another identical in all respects except that sentient beings consistently experience pleasure, we would say without hesitation that the second universe is preferable to the first. In saying this, we would be acknowledging that pleasure is intrinsically good.

However, not all pleasure is intrinsically good. For let us suppose that some great tragedy occurs—a hurricane, for example, that results in great loss of human life—and that someone contemplates this awful tragedy *with pleasure.* Surely, we would say, a universe in which tragedy produces sorrow is better than one in which it would produce pleasure, because pleasure of this kind is *not* good. Or suppose that someone experiences pleasure in doing some reprehensible act: a universe that lacked *such* pleasure, we want to say, is to be preferred over one that contains it.

These exceptional cases raise a difficult question: If we assent to the proposition that, on the whole, pleasure is good and worthy of being desired, precisely why do we object to its occurrence in these cases? The answer would appear to be that it is not to the pleasure as such that we object, but to pleasure caused by something intrinsically bad. All other things being equal, we prefer a universe where sentient beings experience pleasure to one in which they experience neither pleasure nor pain; but we should prefer the latter universe to one in which some sentient beings experience pleasure in contemplating the suffering or death of others.

The result of our analysis appears to be, then, that pleasure is good except in those cases in which it is caused by something that is intrinsically bad.

Knowledge

By using the same method we shall find that *knowledge* also is intrinsically good. Imagine a universe in which there is a definite quota of pleasure but no knowledge, and another in which there is an exactly equal quantity of pleasure but, in addition, widespread knowledge of the laws of nature and of human society. We would unhesitatingly choose the latter. And note that we do not (as Hedonist might argue) value the knowledge because of the pleasure it gives, for according to our hypothesis, the amount of pleasure in the two cases is exactly equal. It is clear, therefore, that we value the knowledge for its own sake.

Are there exceptions in the case of knowledge, as we discovered there were in the case of pleasure? It would seem so. Certainly, most of us would feel obliged to conceal from a young child information that might be hurtful or acutely embarrassing—that its mother had abandoned it, for example, or that its father was a criminal. Eventually, we realize, the child should know even these painful truths, but while the child is young and possibly capable of severe emotional damage, we would probably feel obliged to "protect" the child from this knowledge. Again, in the case of a person of any age who is very ill, we can easily imagine information that we might decide to withhold on the ground that knowledge of it would (we think) only aggravate the condition or add mental torture to the pain the person is already suffering.

The generalization to which these considerations bring us is that knowledge is good except when it would lead to consequences sufficiently bad to outweigh the good. Perhaps, we could even say that knowledge is always good; but there are cases in which this good cannot be realized without simultaneously realizing an evil of such magnitude that the good comes as a poor bargain.

Moral Virtue

At this point, I do not wish to split hairs about the exact definition of moral virtue, but I cannot avoid mentioning it if my list of intrinsic goods is to be at all complete. By moral virtue, then, I mean what I think is just the common and accepted meaning of this phrase, namely, those qualities of character that predispose someone to act kindly toward other people and, in general, to behave in ways that the individual considers good and right.

Now it seems clear to me that such qualities of character and the actions in which they are expressed are intrinsically good. Again, we apply our method of imaginative isolation. Consider a world that contains a definite quantity of pleasure and knowledge but no moral virtue, and consider another universe containing exactly the same amount of pleasure and knowledge but moral virtue as well. We would, I think, unhesitatingly choose the latter. If so, it is clear that we regard moral virtue as something that is good in itself apart from its consequences. Moreover, it seems to me that in this case the conclusion holds without exception: I can think of no case in which we would be inclined to say that it would be better for virtue not to exist because of its allegedly bad consequences.

Other Intrinsic Goods

Are there other things that, by a further application of the method of imaginative isolation, might be identified as intrinsic goods? I find it difficult to answer this question with any degree of confidence. Other candidates suggest themselves: justice, creativity, optimism, freedom, even life itself. But certain of these, I think, are reducible to some combination of the intrinsic goods we have already identified, and others appear to be merely instrumental goods. In any case, I am not willing to say flat out that pleasure, knowledge, and virtue are the only intrinsic goods for human beings, but I am unable, at this time, to extend the list any further myself. If imaginative isolation can identify other intrinsic goods, then so be it: it does not affect my argument in the least.

The Highest Human Good

Is some one of these intrinsic goods more worthy of being desired than others? Many philosophers would answer this question in the affirmative. Hedonist, for example, elevates pleasure to the highest level and treats all other goods merely as means to the production of pleasure. Rational Eudemonist, by elevating activity according to reason to the highest rank, ends up with a definite order of preference: knowledge, then virtue, then pleasure. So far we have not heard in this debate from anyone who holds that virtue is the highest good, but we are reminded of the words of Socrates at the end of the Apology: "When my sons are grown up, I would ask you, O my friends, to punish them; and I would have you trouble them, as I have troubled you, if they seem to care about riches, or anything, more than about virtue ..."[1]

If pleasure, knowledge, and virtue are, indeed, all intrinsic goods, it seems plainly foolish to elevate any one of them to the position of the *summum bonum* to the possible exclusion of the others. These three are related not as superordinates and subordinates but as coequal goods worthy of being desired by all people. Our eudemonia consists not in being a mere pleasure seeker, nor in being an arid intellectual, nor in being a grim moralist: our eudemonia consists in being a human being. Insofar as we are intellect, our eudemonia consists in the acquisition of knowledge; insofar as we are will, in the cultivation of virtue; insofar as we are feeling, in the experience of pleasure. Our *summum bonum* is to realize so far as possible every intrinsic good, in such balance and proportion as our natural endowments and circumstances may permit.

STUDY QUESTIONS

1. What are the "four questions" that Pluralist attempts to distinguish on pp. 321–322? Is he right in saying that "Hedonist has addressed himself to the third, and Rational Eudemonist to the fourth"?
2. What is "the method of imaginative isolation"? How is it supposed to be useful in the discussion of the present issue?
3. List the things that Pluralist identifies as intrinsic goods. Do you

---

[1]Plato, *Apology,* in *The Dialogues of Plato,* trans. B. Jowett (New York: Random House, 1937), vol. I, p. 423.

agree that these are intrinsic goods? Would you add anything else to this list?

4. What is Pluralist's final answer to the question, What is the highest human good? Do you agree with him?

5. Suppose that Pluralist had an opportunity to obtain either one (but not both) of two intrinsic goods. On what basis, if any, could the choice of one over the other be made?

44

THEOLOGICAL EUDEMONISM

I enter this debate as a modern advocate of a view that has a long and distinguished history. In the Greco-Roman world, it vied successfully with several of the theories set forth in preceding chapters, and it was, for centuries, the universally accepted opinion regarding the highest human good. In recent years, however, this view has been abandoned by many people in favor of one or another of the alternative theories. I remain convinced, however, that it is the correct view and propose to present it as convincingly as I am able.

Some Generalizations

Let me begin by making some generalizations that seem to be warranted on the basis of the foregoing discussion. First, all parties to the debate appear to be agreed that the highest human good consists in the fulfillment of our deepest longings and desires. Human beings are, so to speak, "unfinished" creatures. They long for completeness, for fulfillment, for the satisfaction of their desires. The assertion that pleasure, or knowledge, or virtue, or all these together, constitutes the highest human good really means that the realization of whichever of these is proposed will satisfy our deepest needs and cause us to experience completeness. If it does not, then what is being proposed is not, in truth, humanity's *highest* good but merely, at best, some lesser good.

It follows, therefore, that any view about the *summum bonum* presupposes some judgment about humanity's deepest needs, some judgment about what it would take to render human beings truly complete. If you really believe that all that human beings lack in order to be truly complete is a goodly quantity of pleasurable experiences of various sorts, then (and only then) are you justified in adopting hedonism; and so on for any other proposal that may be put forward.

Let us, then, ask the crucial question about each of the theories advanced thus far. Would an immense quantity of pleasurable experiences satisfy the deepest longing of the human heart? Clearly not. Would an immense amount of knowledge satisfy this longing? No. Would any amount of pleasure, knowledge, and virtue give people the completeness that they crave? It would not. These are goods, to be sure, but none is the *highest* human good. Our search must continue.

An Alternative View

Suppose that we press our search by asking the question, *Why* do human beings experience this incompleteness, this longing that cannot be satisfied by any imaginable quantity of pleasure, knowledge, or virtue? The answer, I would suggest, is that *human beings are separated from that to which they essentially belong, and so long as that condition remains, they are restless and unfulfilled.* To understand what it is that constitutes the highest human good, we need first to understand the depth of the human predicament.

To say that human beings are separated from that to which they essentially belong is to say that they are "out of harmony" with themselves, with their world, and with God. They experience conflicts *within themselves*—conflicts between the call of duty and the lure of desire, between the drive toward individuality and the desire to conform, between the longing for solitude and the need for companionship. They experience conflict with *other human beings*—with people who seem "strange" to them because they are of a different race, a different nationality, a different economic or social class, a different faith, a different culture. And they experience conflict with God, whose very existence seems doubtful to them, whose authority they resent, whose laws they hate, and whose nature they cannot comprehend. Let us call this situation *estrangement.* It is the universal human condition, the tragic predicament of fallen humanity.

If estrangement is the ultimate reason for the restless hunger of the human heart, then clearly the highest good is that state of affairs in which estrangement is overcome and human beings are restored to a harmonious relationship with themselves, with their world, and with God. Such a state of affairs is called "salvation." *Humanity's highest good consists in the reconciliation of that which is estranged, in the healing of broken relationships, in salvation.* Nothing short of this will ultimately satisfy the deepest longings of the human spirit.

Please note that in affirming that the highest good consists in salvation, I am at present talking about a this-worldy process, a good that is attainable in some degree here and now. The reconciliation of that which is estranged, the healing of that which is broken, is a process that is going on in the world here and now, a process that we enter into whenever we participate in the overcoming of enmity, conflict, and strife.

Indeed, if some of my readers find the term "salvation" too loaded with other connotations to convey the meaning I am trying to express, I suggest that they simply substitute the term "peace." Augustine once wrote (and note how he speaks to each of the elements of estrangement enumerated above):

> The peace of body and soul is the well-ordered and harmonious life and health of the living creature. Peace between man and God is the well-ordered obedience of faith to eternal law. Peace between man and man is well-ordered concord ... The peace of all things is the tranquility of order.[1]

"The peace of all things"—that, I submit, is the state of affairs that all human beings desire above every other good. To the extent that such peace is achieved, we reach our highest good. To the extent that it is not, we remain restless and dissatisfied.

Can this state of affairs be achieved in this earthly life? The answer would appear to be, Yes, in some degree. The faith by which Western civilization lived for many hundreds of years speaks of a God who with infinite love and patience seeks to reconcile to Himself a creation that has turned its back on Him. Insofar as God's creatures learn to love Him above all things, the "tranquility of order," of which St. Augustine speaks, is restored. For the *dis*order that plagues our world is a consequence of our misdirected love—a consequence of loving the creature more than the Creator. In response to God's love, however, our love can be redirected, and we can begin to experience the wholeness, the peace, the tranquility, that we and all creatures would experience in its fullness if "the peace of all things" were fully achieved.

The Eternal Dimension

Every human life, then, is a quest for salvation, though salvation is sometimes wrongly sought in ways that only deepen estrangement. But every human life, however much it may experience reconciliation, falls short of a complete realization of the *summum bonum,* inasmuch as no one life can experience the perfection of salvation apart from "the peace of all things."

The full realization of the highest human good—the final reconciliation and peace of all things—lies, therefore, beyond this present life in a life of eternal blessedness. Indeed, every fundamental desire of the human spirit cries out for a fulfillment that cannot be completely achieved in this life.

---

[1]St. Augustine, *The City of God,* XIX, xiii, in Whitney J. Oates (ed.), *Basic Writings of St. Augustine* (New York: Random House, 1948), vol. 2, p. 488.

As intellectual beings, people have an insatiable desire to know the truth. This is evident not only from our own experience of taking great delight in achieving some new understanding, but also from observing that many people spend their entire adult lives in pure research, with little or no thought to any possible practical consequences of their hard-won knowledge. As Aristotle remarked, "All men by nature desire to know";[2] this desire to know is not satisfied by any quantity of learning that may be achieved in this life.

As moral beings, we also desire to live rightly, to do what is good and just, and to refrain from doing wrong—in short, to achieve the perfection of virtue. But this desire, however great its achievement by the noble few, is never fully satisfied in this life. Selfish desires, the lusts of the body, ignorance and frailty, conspire to prevent us from achieving moral perfection. That perfection, if it is ever to be achieved, must await another life.

There are, further, certain goods that we all desire as members of human society: among other things, honor and appreciation for the good that we have done; reputation among our fellows; and such riches as may enable us to be comfortable and secure as we face an uncertain future. Regardless of the magnitude of its realization, our desire for these goods is never fully satisfied in this life.

There is also in us, as Hedonist has emphasized, a desire to experience pleasure; indeed, so intense is this desire in some of us that we race from pleasure to pleasure, believing that if only we could experience a sufficient quantity and variety of pleasures, our restless hearts really could be quieted. But from every such venture, however great the momentary ecstasy, we return to the world of reality to find that the void still remains and the spirit is still unsatisfied.

There is in us, finally, as Spinoza has beautifully put it, a desire to "persevere in our being . . . [through] indefinite time."[3] We do not want our life to come to an end, and we demonstrate this by taking all sorts of measures to protect ourselves from danger and to guard our health. Yet, we know that this earthly life will eventually come to an end.

There is, to be sure, a kind of earthly happiness in such satisfaction of these several longings as we are able to secure in this life. But over all our futile searching for a paradise on earth stand those haunting words of St. Augustine in the opening chapter of *The Confessions:* "Thou has formed us for Thyself, and our hearts are restless till they find rest in Thee."[4] The highest human good, our true eudemonia, can be achieved only in a preliminary and fragmentary way in this life. Its perfection must await that life of eternal blessedness that God desires to give to all His children.

---

[2]Aristotle, *Metaphysics,* I, i, in Richard McKeon (ed.), *The Basic Works of Aristotle* (New York: Random House, 1941), p. 689.

[3]Benedict de Spinoza, *Ethics,* part III, prop. VI and VIII, in John Wild (ed.), *Spinoza Selections* (New York: Scribner, 1930), pp. 215, 216.

[4]St. Augustine, *The Confessions,* I, i, in Oates (ed.), *op. cit.,* vol, I, p. 3.

What do we mean by a life of eternal blessedness? First and foremost, we mean a life in which our estrangement is *totally* overcome and we are restored to a harmonious relationship with ourselves, our world, and God. In such a life, every good that we desire is achieved in its fullness. Our desire for knowledge is fully satisfied, for all that we are capable of knowing is known completely and without error. Our quest for virtue reaches its goal, for our characters at last reach the perfection that forever eludes us in our present life. Our desire for honor, fame, and wealth is fulfilled insofar as it is good for us and extinguished insofar as it is not. In this life of which I speak, we shall experience pleasure of such purity and such permanence as we never dreamed of in this life. Finally, we shall no longer have to labor under the depressing knowledge that sooner or later our life will come to an end, for we shall have the blessed certainty that it will continue forever. Such a life, and nothing less than this, would constitute the true happiness, the eudemonia, the ultimate fulfillment, of a being whose needs and longings are what we know our own to be.

A Choice

If we grant that human beings really do have the needs and longings that I have enumerated, and that their highest good does not consist in anything attainable in this life, then there are three alternatives among which we must choose. First, we may assert that eternal happiness is a real possibility, in which case we should spare no effort to attain such a life. Or, second, we may conclude (as many evidently have) that eternal life is not possible, and that there is no chance of ever being truly and completely happy. If we accept this position, the practical alternatives are (a) to attempt to stifle our desires, since they cannot be satisfied (this is Stoicism), or (b) to sullenly accept some limited set of attainable goods as the best we can hope for. It is no accident, I think, that the prevailing ethic of our time is a strange mixture of Stoicism and a very superficial hedonism.

Given these three alternatives, in any case, I do not hesitate to adopt the first and to assert that eternal happiness is a real possibility. In the remainder of this essay, I want to offer some persuasive reasons in support of this view.

Supporting Arguments

I am impressed, first, by the fact that for every natural appetite there is a corresponding way by which that appetite is naturally satisfied. For the appetite of hunger there is food, for thirst there is drink, for sexual desire there is sexual intercourse, for loneliness there is human companionship, and so on. Consequently, it is inconceivable to me that nature should have endowed us with a set of appetites if there were no way for them to be satisfied. If our hunger for eternity—the deepest hunger of all—should turn out to be the one hunger for which there is no satisfaction, it would be a cruel trick indeed. Thus, it seems probable that a state of eternal blessedness, in which this longing would be fully satisfied, is a real possibility.

Next, I call your attention to the fact that human beings are "over-endowed" if this life is the only life for which they were intended. The evolutionary process has, in general, equipped each organism with just those qualities that it needs to survive in the struggle for life. Human beings, however, are a remarkable exception. Their capacity for abstract knowledge, their moral aspirations, their love of beauty, their spiritual ideals, go far beyond what is needed to secure their mere earthly survival. These endowments mark human beings as creatures destined for higher things—destined, indeed, for a life of eternal blessedness.

I appeal also to what I shall call the "presentiment of immortality" in the souls of virtually all people, ourselves included. The great spiritual leaders of mankind—Socrates and Plato and Kant, Buddha and Jesus and Mohammed, St. Augustine and St. Thomas Aquinas and countless others—have spoken unashamedly of this sense of immortality; their words express the hopes and feelings of the great majority of the human race. It is not unreasonable to hold that the sentiments expressed with such unanimity by those whom we revere as the greatest and holiest of men express a genuine insight into the true destiny of the human spirit.

There is even some straightforward empirical evidence in favor of human immortality as the result of research that has been done in the area of parapsychology. Numerous cases are on record of persons who have apparently conversed with deceased loved ones or acquaintances and, in the course of these conversations, have secured information they could not have received from any other sources. The number of qualified researchers working in this area is, unfortunately, small, because parapsychology does indeed regard as possible some things that are unpalatable to the typical contemporary scientific mind. The evidence in support of the theory that the soul survives the death of the body is growing, however, and this theory is, of course, an essential part of the view that eternal life is a real possibility.

One further argument in support of human immortality may be suggested. If God exists, and if (as theism asserts) He loves His creation, then it is not unreasonable to assume that He desires and will provide for the preservation and happiness of human beings, the crown of His creation. If we are in doubt about the existence of God, then we have to resolve that question before we can decide on the merit of the present argument. If we believe in the existence of God, then a belief in human immortality seems more plausible than disbelief.

I acknowledge, however, that the evidence of these arguments is inconclusive: we cannot know with certainty that we shall or shall not survive death. We must, therefore, as Blaise Pascal said, wager one way or the other. It makes supremely good sense, I think, to wager on the possibility of an eternal life in which our every need and longing shall be fully satisfied. To do so gives to this present life a quality, a meaning, and a perspective that make it a much richer adventure than it otherwise would be. We may never succeed in making this world a paradise, but we need the concept of paradise in order that the ideal of the perfect life may ever be before us, and that we may endure with tranquility the sorrows and disappointments that beset us as we make our way through life. If, in wagering on a future life, we should turn out to be mistaken, we shall still be the gainers by virtue of the richness lent to this life by the hope of another. And if we are right, we shall in due time experience in reality that eternal happiness in which our deepest longings and desires are at last fully satisfied.

STUDY QUESTIONS

1. "All parties to the debate appear to be agreed that the highest human good consists in the fulfillment of people's deepest longings and desires." How would Hedonist be likely to respond to this statement? Pluralist?
2. "Human beings are separated from that to which they essentially belong." What, exactly, does this mean?
3. What exactly is the proposal of this chapter concerning the highest good? To which of Pluralist's four questions does this theory appear to be addressed?
4. "If we grant that human beings really do have the needs and longings that I have enumerated, ... then there are three alternatives among which we must choose." Do you agree? Do you agree with the "if" clause? What are the "three alternatives"? Are there others?
5. What arguments are offered in support of the view that "eternal happiness is a real possibility"? Do you find these arguments persuasive?
6. "It makes supremely good sense ... to wager on the possibility of an eternal life in which our every need and longing shall be fully satisfied." Does it?

CORRELATED READINGS[1]

1. Aristotle. "Activity According To Reason Is the Highest Good For Man." *Nicomachean Ethics,* 1097 a 15–1100 a 10.
2. Epicurus. "Pleasure Is the Highest Good." *Letter to Menoeceus.* A succinct statement by a philosopher whose name is virtually a synonym for hedonism.
3. Epictetus. "Tranquility Is the Highest Good." *The Manual of Epictetus,* Selections 1, 5, 8, 9, 11, 12, 14.
4. Augustine of Hippo, St. "Man's Ultimate Happiness." *The City of God,* Book XIX, Chap. 4. Theological eudemonism.
5. Mill, John Stuart. "In Defense of the Pleasure Principle." *Utilitarianism,* Chap. II. Another statement of hedonism.
6. Ross, William David. "A Plurality of Intrinsic Goods." *The Right and the Good.* New York and London: Oxford University Press, 1930, pp. 134–141.

FOR FURTHER READING

Aquinas, St. Thomas. *Summa Contra Gentiles.* Many editions. See Book III, Chaps. 25–37, 48, 60–63.

Augustine, St. *The Morals of the Catholic Church.* Many editions. See Chaps. 1–14.

Bennett, Jonathan. *Rationality: An Essay Towards an Analysis.* New York: Humanities Press, 1964.

Bentham, Jeremy. *An Introduction to the Principles of Morals and Legislation.* Several editions. See especially Chaps. 1, 2, 4, 10. Of interest especially because of its description of the "hedonistic calculus."

Broad, C. D. *Five Types of Ethical Theory.* New York: Humanities Press, 1956.

DeWitt, N.W. *Epicurus and His Philosophy.* Minneapolis: University of Minnesota Press, 1954.

Ewing, Alfred C. *The Definition of Good.* New York: Macmillan, 1947.

Gosling, J. C. B. *Pleasure and Desire: The Case for Hedonism Reviewed.* Oxford: Clarendon Press, 1969.

Jones, H. "Mill's Argument for the Principle of Utility," *Philosophy and Phenomenological Research,* 38 (1977–1978), 338–354. A critique of Mill's arguments in support of his central thesis.

Lucretius. *On the Nature of Things.* Many editions. See Books III and IV. A well-known statement of the hedonistic view by an ancient admirer of Epicurus.

MacKinnon, D. M. *A Study of Ethical Theory.* London: A. and C. Black, 1957.

---

[1]*Concise Readings in Philosophy,* Part X.

Moore, G. E. *Principia Ethica.* Cambridge, Eng.: Cambridge University Press, 1903. Chap. 3 is a detailed critique of hedonism; Chap. 6 is a statement of the pluralistic view.

Murdoch, Iris. *The Sovereignty of Good.* New York: Schocken Books, 1971.

Passmore, John. *The Perfectibility of Man.* New York: Scribner, 1971.

Plato. *Philebus.* Many editions. Difficult reading, but of great interest for its critique of hedonism and its advocacy of a pluralistic view.

Ross, W. D. *Foundations of Ethics.* London: Oxford University Press, 1939.

Stocks, J. L. *Aristotle's Definition of the Human Good.* Oxford: Basil Blackwell, 1919.

Tsanoff, Radoslav A. *The Moral Ideals of Our Civilization.* New York: Dutton, 1942.

PART XI

THE LANGUAGE
OF MORALS

45

THE CENTRAL PROBLEM
OF METAETHICS

Anyone who is old enough to be reading a book on philosophy has certainly learned to use "the language of morals" with some facility, and probably uses it more or less unconsciously almost every day. We read of an act of cruelty and say, "How terrible!" Or we learn of an act of unusual kindness and say, "How nice!" We say that slavery and racial discrimination are "wrong," and that helping human beings to realize their potential is "right." We say that some things are "good" and other things are "evil," some acts are "right" and some are "wrong."

Not only do we use this kind of language; we also sometimes *disagree* with one another about what things really are good or bad, right or wrong. Indeed, we sometimes try to persuade those who disagree with us on an ethical matter that their opinion is mistaken. The current debate that is raging over the abortion issue, for example, is basically a case of ethical disagreement. The parties to the debate are disagreeing not about the empirical facts but rather about what *moral* appraisal (good, bad, right, wrong) is appropriate in light of those facts.

In using the language of moral appraisal, and in disagreeing with one another about moral issues, we assume, obviously, that we are using language meaningfully. Ethical discourse, then, has some kind of meaning. But exactly how is such discourse meaningful? *How are we using language when we say of something in a moral sense that it is good or bad, right or wrong?* This is the problem with which we shall be concerned in the present section.

Normative Ethics and Metaethics

Note that the problem just formulated is not the sort of question that concerns normative ethics. Normative ethics, we have said (see Chapter 40) deals with substantive ethical issues—for example, with what things really are intrinsically good, or what things are morally right or wrong, and why. Here, we are concerned with the language in which we express our opinions on such issues. We are asking not about what *is* intrinsically good, but about what it means to *say* that something is intrinsically good; not about what *is* good or bad, right or wrong, but about what it means to *call* something good or bad, right or wrong.

The generic name for inquiries that have as their object the language of moral appraisal is *metaethics*. The raw material with which the metaethicist is concerned is the actual language that people use when they make moral judgments. The objective of metaethics is to produce a correct description of that language—to elucidate what is really being said when people say things like "Albert Schweitzer was a good man," or "The infliction of needless pain is morally wrong."

Suppose that after studying this matter for some time, one finds that one is in genuine doubt about the meaning of such language. Ought one then to stop using "moral predicates" altogether? Certainly not, unless one is prepared to abdicate concern for many of the major problems that we as individuals and as a society must face in the years immediately ahead. Just as one can speak a language without knowing all the grammatical rules that govern that language, so one can use the language of moral appraisal without having a correct metaethical theory about that language. If all ethical discourse were to be prohibited until metaethics had completed its work, metaethics would have no subject matter upon which to begin. The business of metaethics is to describe how people do use the langauge of moral appraisal, not to prescribe how they may use it.

The Options

All language appears to serve four principal functions: to request information (the interrogative function), to convey information (the informative function), to direct behavior (the directive function), and to express feeling (the expressive, or emotive, function). If this is so, then ethical discourse must also be reducible to one or more of these functions, or types of discourse.

It seems obvious that ethical discourse does not serve an interrogative function. However, it may be a species of informative language. Many metaethicists are agreed that it is. But, if so, what information does it give? Here opinions vary, with at least four different answers having been proposed.

Some philosophers hold that to apply a moral predicate to the appraisal of something is to assert the presence or the absence of a certain empirical quality or qualities in the thing being appraised. It may be said, for example, that to call an act "praiseworthy" or "good" is to say that it is productive of pleasure, and the question of whether or not an act is productive of pleasure is obviously an empirical question. Or it may be said that to call a certain form of conduct "good" is to say that it is characteristic of those beings who have proceeded the farthest or the highest along the evolutionary path, and this assertion, if spelled out in some detail, is also capable of being determined empirically. We shall call this view, which is developed in Chapter 46, *ethical naturalism.* It is also sometimes called *naturalistic objectivism.*

Other philosophers hold, however, that ethical discourse is informative in the sense that it asserts the presence or absence of some *non*-natural quality in the thing being appraised. This was the view of G. E. Moore, who said:

> If I am asked, What is good? my answer is that good is good, and that is the end of the matter. Or if I am asked, How is good to be defined? my answer is that it cannot be defined, and that is all I have to say about it . . . My point is that "good" is a simple notion, just as "yellow" is a simple notion; that, just as you cannot, by any means, explain to anyone who does not already know it, what yellow is, so you cannot explain what good is.[1]

This position, which is developed in Chapter 47, is variously called *nonnaturalistic objectivism* or, more commonly, *intuitionism.* The reasons for calling it the former are evident when one compares it with its "naturalistic" counterpart. The reason for calling it "intuitionism" is that since the quality in question is, according to the theory, nonnatural, it is not subject to empirical investigation and must, therefore, be intuited, that is, rationally discerned. (The term "intuition," as used by philosophers, does not mean what it means in the everyday expression "a woman's intuition." It means, rather, direct apprehension, or rational discernment: it denotes the act by which, according to rationalists, the intellect directly grasps some truths. See Chapter 4 for a fuller exposition of the rationalist thesis.)

It may be, however, that ethical discourse is informative in a quite different way. It may be that "moral judgments," as they are called by some philosophers, convey information not about the object or the act being judged but about the likes or dislikes of (a) the person making the judgment or (b) some group of people for whom that person speaks or to whom that person has reference in making the judgment. Such views are called *subjectivist,* and depending on whether it is (a) the speaker's likes or dislikes or (b) the likes or dislikes of some group for which that person speaks or to which that person has reference, you

---

[1]G. E. Moore, *Principia Ethica* (Cambridge, Eng.: Cambridge University Press, 1959; originally published 1903), pp. 6–7.

have, respectively, *private subjectivism* (Chapter 48) and *cultural relativism* (Chapter 49).

Note that these four theories have one important feature in common, namely, the belief that a moral appraisal is a truth claim, that it asserts that something is the case. According to all these theories, therefore, moral appraisals are capable of being true or false. To know that a given moral appraisal is true or false is, according to these theories, to know that something is or is not the case; thus, it is proper to speak of these as *cognitivist* theories.

It is possible, however, that ethical discourse is not informative of anything at all—that, instead, it is to be understood as a species of directive or expressive discourse. Theories affirming such a position are termed *noncognitivist,* with *emotivism* viewing ethical discourse as expressive and *imperativism* viewing it as directive. Both theories are discussed in Chapter 50.

To summarize: On the assumptions (a) that all language serves either an interrogative, an informative, a directive, or an expressive function, and (b) that ethical discourse obviously does not serve an interrogative function, we arrive at the following list of metaethical theories, each of which constitutes an answer to the question posed at the beginning of this chapter:

I. Cognitivist Theories
    A. Objectivist Theories
        1. Ethical Naturalism (Naturalistic Objectivism)
        2. Intuitionism (Nonnaturalistic Objectivism)
    B. Subjectivist Theories
        1. Private Subjectivism
        2. Cultural Relativism (Societal Subjectivism)
II. Noncognitivist Theories
    A. Emotivism
    B. Imperativism

We cannot state with certainty, however, that the theories we have just enumerated constitute all the possible ways of answering the question about the meaning of ethical discourse. This is true for at least two reasons. First, we cannot be sure that the four "functions of language" from which our analysis began are the only functions that an exhaustive study of language might reveal. Should some other function be identified, it is possible that a case could be made for the view that ethical discourse is a species of that function of language. Second, the specification of subtypes within each of the functions listed above is by no means exhaustive. Language is capable of being informative, directive, and expressive in an immense variety of ways, and the theories listed identify only the particular ways that have commended themselves to philosophers as being the most plausible ways of construing ethical discourse.

All that can be claimed for the above classification, then, is that it is a reliable road map for one who is just beginning to learn his or her way around in the province of metaethics. It identifies six neighborhoods (to continue the metaphor) where all writers on metaethics currently reside, but, like any map, it omits a great deal of interesting detail. After one has become familiar with the province, the road map can perhaps be discarded, and one can then begin to explore more carefully the neighborhood or neighborhoods that seem to offer the most promising sites for the construction of a metaethical home.

STUDY QUESTIONS

1. State whether you agree or disagree with the following assertions, and defend your opinion.
   a. Moral appraisal language occurs more or less frequently in the everyday conversation of most adult human beings.
   b. People sometimes disagree on ethical matters.
   c. People sometimes present rational arguments to persuade other people to change their ethical views.
   d. Moral appraisals have some kind of meaning.
   e. Some ethical issues are issues that most people regard as important.
   f. It is possible to have an opinion on an ethical matter.
   g. It is possible to be mistaken in one's opinion on an ethical matter.
2. What do you understand to be "the central problem of metaethics"? Does this seem to you an important problem? What bearing, if any, does it have on such matters as the controversy over the morality of abortion, or the legitimacy of the feminist demand for equal rights?
3. What do subjectivist theories regarding the meaning of moral appraisals have in common with objectivist theories? What is it that distinguishes them? What is the difference between ethical naturalism and intuitionism? between private subjectivism and cultural relativism? between private subjectivism and emotivism?
4. Why is it impossible to conclude with certainty that one has surveyed all the possible answers to the question posed in this chapter?
5. What is your present opinion on the matter? What is the source of this opinion?

46

ETHICAL NATURALISM

Ethical naturalism, or naturalistic objectivism, is the view that moral sentences—both those employed in everyday moral judgments and those employed by writers on normative ethics—are reports about the presence or absence of certain natural qualities in persons, acts, or states of affairs. They are, accordingly, translatable, without loss of meaning, into sentences that do not employ any of the so-called moral predicates (good, bad, right, wrong, and so forth).

Since different definitions of the key moral predicates are compatible with the central features of ethical naturalism, I shall begin my defense of this position by indicating what all its adherents hold in common and on what point they differ. I shall then go on to elaborate the particular version of ethical naturalism that I hold to be correct.

First, I want to make it clear that we who hold this theory, or any metaethical theory, are not offering an arbitrary verbal definition of key ethical terms, nor are we making a recommendation about how people generally *ought* to use these terms. Our claim is that the structure of language allows only certain ways in which a sentence can have meaning. Ethical naturalism is a theory about which of these ways correctly describes the particular kind of meaning that moral sentences have.

All ethical naturalists hold in common three interrelated views with respect to moral sentences (that is, sentences expressing what are commonly called moral judgments). These views are as follows:

a. to say that something is good or bad, right or wrong, is to say that it has, or does not have, certain empirically ascertainable qualities;

b. moral sentences, like all informative sentences, are either true or false;
c. questions about the truth or falsity of such sentences are theoretically resolvable by straightforward empirical means.

These three points constitute the defining characteristics of ethical naturalism. Anyone who holds this position must, therefore, be prepared to show that moral sentences do, in fact, exhibit these features.

There should not be any disagreement over the method by which this matter must be resolved. Since a metaethical theory deals with the meaning of moral sentences, we must always look to the actual judgments that people make: the theory must conform to real usage. To ask for the meaning of "good" in its moral sense is to ask for a definition of that term as used by ordinary people and ethical theorists when they frame what we call "moral judgments." If we lose sight of this—if we depart from actual usage—we are bound to get lost in a never-never world of arbitrary definitions.

Having covered the areas of unanimity among ethical naturalists, we now come to the single point on which they disagree: just *which* qualities it is whose presence or absence is being asserted when something is judged to be good or bad, right or wrong. If, for example, someone says that "good" means "conducive to the development of socialism," or "conducive to the further evolution of humanity," that person is expressing a naturalistic view, but in my opinion a mistaken naturalistic view. I shall not take time, however, to survey the various proposals that have been made by ethical naturalists on this point, but shall proceed directly to an exposition and defense of my own view. If I succeed in presenting a convincing case, then it will follow that ethical naturalists who disagree with me on this point, as well as metaethicists who hold fundamentally different views about the logic of ethical discourse, are mistaken.

The Meanings of "Good"

If any one term may be said to be of central importance among the moral predicates, that term is "good." Unfortunately, this term has so many meanings in both ethical and everyday usage that we shall have to analyze it carefully in order to see its significance in ethical thinking.

The most important moral sense of "good" is as the antithesis of "evil." All the other moral predicates are definable in relation to "good" and "evil," as I shall shortly attempt to show. But first, we must distinguish some other senses of "good" to avoid later confusion.

There is a completely *non*moral sense of "good" meaning the opposite of "poor." We speak, for example, about good knives and poor knives, about good watches and poor watches, about good runners and poor runners. In such cases we mean, apparently, "conforming to (good) or failing to conform to (poor) the criteria appropriate to the assessment of such items." A good knife is, among other things, one that cuts well, a good watch, one that keeps accurate time, and a good runner, one who runs swiftly. A poor knife, or watch, or runner is one that does not meet these criteria. "Good" in this sense is not a moral predicate at all and must not be confused with "good" in its centrally important moral sense as the opposite of "evil."

There is still another sense of "good," however, in which it is the opposite of neither "poor" nor "evil" but of "bad"; and in this sense it usually is a moral predicate. (Not always, however: we talk about good and bad pitches in baseball, good and bad shots in basketball, and we clearly do not, in such cases, intend to make a moral judgment.) I shall speak of "good" in this sense as the *secondary* sense of "good" and of "good" when it stands opposed to "evil" as the *primary* sense of "good."

In this secondary sense, there are four classes of things that we call good (or bad): people, certain of their mental acts (thoughts, intentions, desires, purposes), their overt acts, and the products of their overt acts (governments and other manmade institutions). I am unable to think of anything else that we would call good or bad in this clearly moral sense except in a metaphorical way. To say that something is good in the secondary sense is to say that it promotes, or tends to promote, what is good in the primary sense. "Good" as opposed to "evil" means "*intrinsically* good"; "good" as opposed to "bad" means "*instrumentally* good." This is the reason for calling the latter a secondary, or derivative, sense of "good."

All other moral predicates can be defined in relation to "good" in the primary sense. My "duty," for example, is to do what I ought to do, all things considered. "Duty" and "what I ought to do" are synonymous expressions; and what I ought to do is the act that, among all the things I might do, will have the greatest tendency to promote what is good in the primary sense. Any act that tends to promote what is intrinsically good is to that extent *right;* any act that tends to hinder the achievement of what is intrinsically good, or to promote what is intrinsically evil, is to that extent *wrong.* An act that has no tendency to promote either good or evil is *morally indifferent.* It is evident, therefore, that "good" in the primary sense of "intrinsically good" is the key concept in our ethical thinking.

The Primary Meaning of "Good"

The crucial question that we must ask in metaethics, therefore, is, What is the meaning of "good" in the primary sense? To this question, the correct answer, as I conceive it, is "pleasurable for human beings." This is what we *mean* by calling something "good" in the primary sense; everything else that depends on the disposition and choices of people is good or bad, right or wrong, praiseworthy or blameworthy, insofar as it tends to promote or to hinder the achievement of human pleasure.

Perhaps the best way to demonstrate the truth of what I am stating is to consider a hypothethical case in which two people are disagreeing about whether or not a certain proposed course of action is "right," say, the using of tear gas to quell a riot. *A* thinks it would be wrong to use it; *B* thinks it would be wrong *not* to do so.

How might either party attempt to support his or her view? The best way would be to indicate the probable results of the proposed action. *A* might argue, "If tear gas is used, the rioters will retaliate by using firearms, and the situation will be even worse than it is now. So far, all we have to worry about is a small riot; the course you are proposing could turn it into a civil war." *B* might argue, "I think you are mistaken. Tear gas has been thoroughly proven as an effective means of controlling riots, and it should be used immediately. The longer this situation is allowed to remain out of control, the greater is the danger of its turning into a civil war—the very thing you fear. I say tear gas should be used without delay."

It should be noted that both *A* and *B* are agreed that the "right" course of action is the one that will have the greatest tendency to promote human well-being, or what comes to the same thing, to prevent human suffering. If *A* were to become convinced that the result of using tear gas would be as *B* says, he would on his own premises have to concede that the proposed action is indeed right; and if *B* were to become convinced that the result would be as *A* describes it, she would have to concede to *A*. The argument of both assumes that what is right or wrong in the case in question can be decided only by attempting to calculate the human consequences.

The same point can be reinforced in another way. Suppose that a third party, *C*, enters the dispute. "I agree with *B*," says *C*. "I think tear gas should be used—although I agree with *A* that it will probably lead to civil war. Nonetheless, even though it will cause suffering for many people, I think it is the right thing to do." *A* and *B*, surely, would be equally astonished by such a statement. They could only ask, "What on earth does *C mean* by 'good'?" Obviously, *C* does not mean by "good" what most people mean by it, which is "that state of affairs, among the options available to us, in which the maximum of human pleasure and the minimum of human suffering are achieved." If this meaning is not assumed, the whole context in which the dispute was carried on is destroyed, and the dispute itself becomes unintelligible.

Let us consider a second example. Most people would agree, I think, that the excessive drinking of alcoholic beverages is morally wrong (if there are some who disagree, it makes no difference to the argument). Those who do take this position do so because of certain well-known consequences: excessive drinking is injurious to one's health; it is a frequent cause of automobile accidents; it can deprive a family of many of the conveniences and even the necessities of life (because of its cost, by causing the loss of one's job, or both); it poisons human relationships by making people who are normally pleasant and kind become belligerent and cantankerous; and so on. These consequences, it is evident, are all descriptions of some adverse effect that the act or habit in question has, or tends to have, on human beings. If the excessive drinking of alcoholic beverages did not have these consequences, as the drinking of water in any quantity apparently does not, we would not regard it as wrong, and "drunkenness" would not be a term of moral disapprobation. Thus, it seems clear that it is human pleasure that is regarded as intrinsically good, and that everything else is regarded as being good or bad insofar as it tends to promote or to hinder that end.

One could continue to give examples indefinitely, but it hardly seems necessary. Consider any example you wish and you will discover that anything that people commonly assess in moral categories —people, their thoughts, dispositions, intentions, or acts—lends itself to such appraisal solely by virtue of its assumed tendency to promote or to hinder human pleasure. If we could know (a) what state of affairs would achieve the absolute maximum of human happiness together with a minimum of human suffering, and (b) what acts would have the maximum tendency to promote that state of affairs, we should have no difficulty in deciding in any particular case what is the right thing to do. The moral dilemmas that we face are due to our ignorance not of what "good" means, but of what to do in order to achieve that ideal state of affairs in which the maximum of human pleasure and the minimum of human suffering are realized.

When I say that a moral judgment consists in the assertion that some empirically ascertainable qualities are or are not present in the thing being judged, I do not mean that these qualities are precisely ascertainable in the way that, say, the presence or absence of sodium chloride in a solution would be. I do mean, however, that there is nothing over and above the empirical facts to which we must attend in order to decide whether the judgment in question is true or false. The problematic character of many moral judgments is due, not to the supposed fact that "goodness" consists in some odd nonempirical quality, but to the fact that such judgments often involve suppositions— even conjectures and guesses—about the probable results of this or that action. Such uncertainty will persist until we are able to calculate much more precisely the human consequences of alternative courses of action.

The chief reason that this account is not as obvious to most people as might be expected (in view of the fact that they handle the language of moral appraisal without difficulty almost every day of their adult lives) is that most of us are taught moral principles in a way that does not clearly exhibit their relations to human pleasure. We are taught as children that certain kinds of things (like slapping or biting other children, or taking things that belong to them, or telling lies) are "naughty," and that certain other kinds of things (like paying compliments, helping people in need, or visiting the sick) are "nice." If we reflect on the many rules that we have learned in this way, we may be puzzled and tempted to look for some odd quality that gives these rules their "obligatory" character. What we fail to understand if we think in this way, however, is that the rules have been formulated precisely because they specify some of the most common ways in which human pleasure can be enhanced and human suffering minimized. To see moral principles in this light is to rid them of the purely arbitrary character they sometimes seem to have, and to exhibit them as legitimate rules of behavior for anyone who desires to know and to do what is morally right.

The Truth or Falsity of Moral Sentences

I said earlier that anyone who holds the naturalist view must be prepared to show that moral sentences are true or false and that their truth or falsity is ascertainable by empirical means. Let us now consider these features as they apply to what might be thought to be a difficult case for an ethical naturalist to account for: one in which a particular person—Joe Doakes, say—is said to be (in the moral sense) "a good person" or "a good man."

Is there any evidence that would count against the statement "Joe Doakes is a good man"? Yes. If we were to learn that Joe is a heavy drinker, or that he commonly mistreats his wife and children, or that he is habitually careless in his work, or that he does not get along well with most people, we would be inclined to regard the statement as false. To say that Joe Doakes is a good man is to say that, for the most part, he acts in ways that are not compatible with those just described. The difference between these two kinds of behavior—what makes one type of behavior "good" and the other "bad"—is precisely the tendency of each to promote or to hinder human pleasure.

But the means for determining which of these ways is descriptive of Joe's behavior are clearly empirical. We must watch him to see how he behaves and listen to what other people say about his behavior. It is on that basis that we make up our minds. If Joe is like most of us, it is quite certain that he is neither unambiguously good nor unambiguously bad: sometimes he acts in ways that promote human pleasure and sometimes in ways that decrease it. It is the facts about Joe's actual behavior that determine whether and to what extent he is truly described as "good" or "bad." These facts are ascertainable only by the empirical method of first- and second-hand observation of his behavior. Ergo, moral sentences are true or false, and confirmable or disconfirmable, by empirical means.

STUDY QUESTIONS

1. True or false: A number of mutually incompatible theories belonging to *normative ethics* could be correctly described as "naturalistic" theories. Why or why not?

2. True or false: Ethical naturalism is just another name for hedonism. Explain.

3. What does Ethical Naturalist (EN) say is "the method by which this matter must be resolved"? Is he right? How do you determine what method is appropriate? Is it implicit in the question that is being asked, or is it determined in some other way? Can you think of any reason why any of the parties to the dispute might object to this method?

4. Do you think EN is on the right track in distinguishing three meanings of "good"? Suppose that he is right. Does this substantiate his main thesis? Does he claim that it does?

5. Is EN right in saying that the statement "Joe Doakes is a good man" can be refuted by empirical facts? How does this argument affect EN's case?

6. Summarize EN's arguments in support of his position. Can you think of any arguments against it?

47

INTUITIONISM

There are two kinds of hedonists: those who affirm that "good" just *means* "pleasurable" or "conducive to happiness" and those who maintain that whatever "good" means, pleasure (or happiness) is the only thing to which it applies. We might call these positions, respectively, *analytic* hedonism and *synthetic* hedonism, since according to the former the statement "Pleasure is good" is an analytic statement and according to the latter it is a synthetic one.[1] Both forms of hedonism, I am convinced, are mistaken; but analytic hedonism is by far the more seriously in error of the two. And Ethical Naturalist, unfortunately, is an analytic hedonist.

Nevertheless, much of what Ethical Naturalist has said appears to me to be both true and valuable. He is quite right, for example, in distinguishing three meanings of "good" (the nonmoral sense and the instrumental and intrinsic senses of moral goodness). He is also right in his contention that most (though not all, in my view) other moral predicates can be defined in relation to the important concept of intrinsic goodness. But the crucial question for metaethics, as he himself says, is What is the meaning of "intrinsically good"? And on this question, I think he is profoundly mistaken.

The Open-Question Test

There is a simple test, which I shall call the open-question test, by which we can easily assess the accuracy of any proposed definition.

---

[1]See Glossary for further clarification of the terms "analytic" and "synthetic." See also the discussion on pp. 28–29.

Let us call a word for which a definition is being proposed the *definiendum* and the definition that is proposed the *definiens*. If we ask a question of the form, Are all (definiens) really (definiendum)? it is evident that if our definition is accurate, we shall not be putting a significant (or open) question; and if our definition is not accurate, we shall. Suppose, for example, that I define "bachelor" as (a) an unmarried male and as (b) an unmarried adult male human being. If I apply the test, it is clear that in the one case I do have an open question, and that in the other case I do not. If I ask, Are all unmarried males bachelors? I have an open (significant) question to which the correct answer is No, because preadult human males and nonhuman males of any age are unmarried males who are not bachelors. But if I ask, Are all unmarried adult male human beings really bachelors? it is equally evident that I am not asking an open, or significant, question; for the briefest reflection makes it clear that the definiens is what I mean when I use the term "bachelor."

If, now, we apply the test to Ethical Naturalist's proposed definition of "intrinsically good," it is clear at once that this definition will not do. For the question, Are all instances of human pleasure really good? is an open question, to which it is highly unlikely that an affirmative answer would be correct. Consider a few examples. Is it plausible to maintain that the enjoyment that a young boy might get out of torturing a frog (or some other sentient creature), or the pleasure that a sadist might get out of tormenting another human being (even if his happiness should exceed his victim's suffering), or the perverted pleasure of a masochist who allegedly enjoys being punished, are good? Clearly not. If we judge human pleasure to be good, the reason is not that goodness simply *means* human pleasure, but rather that we discern that the quality denoted by the term "good" is present in most, but not all, instances of human pleasure. It is this insight that we express in our synthetic judgment, "Human pleasure, by and large, is good."

There are, as Ethical Naturalist has pointed out, a number of rival theories of the naturalist type, and space obviously does not permit us to list them and apply our test to each of them in turn. The hedonist version of this theory, however, is by far the most plausible. Since it fails to pass the open-question test, we may be confident that any other theory of this type would also fail.

Refutation of Hedonism [2]

The inadequacy of hedonism can be demonstrated apart from the open-question test, which, it is to be noted, shows the incorrectness only of analytic hedonism. The arguments that I shall now put forward demonstrate the inadequacy of hedonism in both its analytic and synthetic forms. Our discussion will require a brief venture into the

---

[2]See also Chapter 42, pp. 316–318.

domain of normative ethics in order to present more clearly what I consider to be the correct metaethical theory.

The incorrectness of hedonism is evident, first, from the fact that there are many things other than pleasurable states of mind that we regard as being intrinsically good. W. D. Ross has shown, for example, that (a) virtuous disposition and action, (b) the apportionment of pleasure and pain to the virtuous and vicious respectively, and (c) knowledge and right opinion are *intrinsic goods*, and that they cannot be reduced to pleasurable states of mind or to acts tending to increase the sum of human pleasure.[3] A universe in which these things occur—quite apart from any consideration of the balance of human pleasure that they may or may not produce—is intrinsically better than a universe in which these things do not occur. We have only to contemplate the two states of affairs, assuming the quantity of human pleasure to be equal in the two cases, to see that this is so.

The same conclusion, however, may be established in another way. There are some instances of human pleasure that, if we suppose them to occur, reduce the total quantity of goodness in the universe. Suppose, for example, that *A* suffers great misfortune; and suppose that *B*, who has long been jealous of *A*'s earlier good fortune, contemplates *A*'s misfortune *with pleasure.* Certainly, in this case, the quantity of pleasure in the universe is greater than it would be if *B* did not react in this way to *A*'s misfortune; but it is equally clear that *B*'s responding in this way is not a good but an evil. Indeed, it would be better under these circumstances if there were less pleasure in the universe, for there would be more good in the universe if *B* were sorrowful instead of happy. It seems obvious, therefore, that goodness is not simply identical with pleasure, and that not all instances of human pleasure are good.

The inadequacy of hedonism can also be exhibited by the following *reductio ad absurdum* argument. If human pleasure were the only thing that is instrinsically good, and if the amount of good in the universe depended entirely on the amount of human pleasure, then a universe in which there was but one individual who experienced a moderate quantity of pleasure *forever* would be intrinsically better than one in which a finite number of individuals experienced pleasure in whatever degree for any finite length of time. But we obviously do not think this to be the case. Even if we were persuaded that some one person could be made to experience moderate pleasure forever (thus producing an infinite quantity of pleasure and, *ex hypothesi*, goodness in the universe), we would not, if it were necessary, approve of the annihilation of all other human beings in order to achieve this, although, according to the hedonist hypothesis, their pleasure would be of a merely finite quantity and therefore inferior to that of our hypothetical eternal individual. Since we cannot draw the conclusion

---

[3]W. D. Ross, *The Right and the Good* (Oxford, England: Clarendon Press, 1930), Chap. 5.

that would follow from the hedonist theory, it is evident that the hedonist theory is false.

The Indefinability of "Good"

We have been speaking—without any misgivings about the meaningfulness of what we have been saying—about a variety of things (states of mind, acts, states of affairs in the universe, and the like) that we would or would not call good. We have said that, contrary to the claim of ethical hedonists, we do not mean simply "pleasurable" when we call something good (analytic hedonism), nor is it only pleasure that we regard as being good (synthetic hedonism). What, then, do we mean when we call something good? The correct answer to this question, I think, is the one given by G. E. Moore: we mean good, and nothing else. "Everything is what it is, and not another thing."[4] We can, indeed, find other words to denote the quality that we commonly denote by the word "good"; we can use the German word *gut*, or the French *bon*, or even the English phrase "worthy of being valued in and of itself"; but that which we denote in these various ways is a simple, indefinable, nonnatural quality whose presence in a person, act, or state of affairs is what warrants our calling it good.

"Good" is indefinable because it is a simple concept. In order to define a concept, it is necessary that that concept be complex, that it be composed of simpler concepts. One can define "daffodil," for example, as "a yellow flower of the genus *Narcissus*" because its various elements—being yellow, being a flower, and being of the genus *Narcissus*—are all constituent parts of the complex concept of a daffodil. Of these constituent elements, "flower" and "genus *Narcissus*" can also be defined. But, as Moore pointed out, "yellow" cannot be defined (except, of course, in the sense that one can point to examples of yellow objects) because it is a simple concept. All definitions must ultimately be built up out of such concepts, for the process of defining concepts by pointing to the elements of which they are composed cannot go on indefinitely: at length, we must come to those elements that, like "good" and "yellow," are simple, and therefore indefinable.

"Good," like "yellow," is a simple and indefinable concept. But the quality it denotes, unlike the quality denoted by the term "yellow," *is not a natural quality*. By this I mean, simply, that the goodness of a person, act, or state of affairs is not something that can be perceived by the senses; it must be *rationally discerned*, or *intuited*, if it is to be apprehended at all.

Let us consider again the illustration of the person who contemplates with pleasure the misfortune of another human being. There is

---

[4]Bishop Butler, quoted by G. E. Moore on the title page of *Principia Ethica* (Cambridge, Eng.: Cambridge University Press, 1959, originally published 1903).

no question here of the probable effects of *B*'s malice: we can well imagine that *A* is already dead, or that *B* expired shortly after entertaining unkind thoughts about *A*'s misfortune, and still we would judge that *B*'s malice was evil. But how do we know this? Certainly, it is in virtue of the supposed facts that we render our judgment; but our judgment that "*B*'s pleasure in *A*'s misfortune is evil" is not simply a confused way of reporting that *B* did in fact entertain feelings of pleasure in contemplating *A*'s misfortune. It is a judgment about the *moral significance* of those facts. And this judgment rests, not on the perception of some additional natural qualities or some supposed tendency of *B*'s act (of contemplation), but on our direct intuition of the evilness of the act itself.

Consider a second example. *X* has borrowed a sum of money from his wealthy friend *Y* and has promised to repay him on a certain date. The date arrives and *X*, being a man who keeps his word, repays the loan. Although hardly an instance of moral heroism, this is, I presume, an act on which we would without hesitation pronounce a favorable judgment. Since it is an instance of promise-keeping, and promise-keeping is something that we regard as a moral duty under normal circumstances, the act in question is judged to be good. But note that no calculation of the probable consequences of alternative possible courses of action is involved in this judgment. Indeed, it is highly likely that the same sum of money given to a poor family would produce more human pleasure than it would if returned to the bank account of *Y*. But the calculation of consequences is not relevant in this case: *X* has contracted a duty in making a promise to *Y*, and that duty takes precedence over all but the most unusual of circumstances. We judge, therefore, that *X*'s act of returning the money on the date promised is good.

What are we saying, then, when we say, "This act is good," and on what basis? Clearly, we are not saying that *X*'s act is the one that, of all the alternatives available to him, has the greatest tendency to increase the sum of human pleasure. Indeed, we can be quite sure that this is not the case. We are saying that *X*'s act, as an instance of promise-keeping, is good, and that is all that we are saying. Our basis for saying this is not that we perceive some empirical facts in addition to those that make us call this act an instance of promise-keeping, but simply that we apprehend such an act as being good.

There is, I realize, a widespread tendency among philosophers today to reject intuition, or direct rational insight, as a mode of acquiring knowledge and to insist that the only knowledge available to us must come by empirical means. This bias against rational insight explains, I think, the recent flurry of activity in the empiricist camp to find some way to account for our knowledge of ethical truths and our ability to make valid moral judgments, without admitting these as instances of rational, or nonempirical, insight. But the effort is doomed to failure. Even our judgment that human pleasure is, on the whole, good, is a synthetic judgment that we could not make apart from our direct apprehension that the quality of goodness is in fact present in most but not all instances of human pleasure. It is this apprehension, and this alone, that allows us to distinguish between those instances of human pleasure that are good and those that are not. What is apprehended, in such cases, is not "another thing" but *goodness itself.*

If this view is correct, any attempt to define "good" in terms of some natural quality or combination of natural qualities is mistaken: it confuses the nonnatural quality designated by the term "good" with something else that it is not. I propose, following Moore, to call this particular kind of mistake the *naturalistic fallacy.* It is a fallacy because it is an error in logic, and it is naturalistic because it is the specific error of confusing a natural quality with a nonnatural quality. It is this fallacy, which exists regardless of the set of natural qualities proposed as a definition of "good," that is effectively exposed by the open-question test. Many writers on ethics, as Moore has shown, have been guilty of it.

A Word About Moral Duty

Earlier I stated that I am not in complete agreement with Ethical Naturalist's suggestion that all other moral predicates can be defined in relation to the centrally important concept "good". My chief misgivings on this score concern the concept "moral duty." I do not think it is correct to say, as Ethical Naturalist does, that someone's moral duty is always to do the act that, of all the alternatives available, will produce the greatest total increase of good in the world. I think some acts have an obligatory character quite apart from their supposed consequences. But first I want to make a preliminary observation about moral duty that may be of some help in clearing up this rather elusive concept.

In order to make intelligible the commonplace fact that a person can be mistaken about what his or her moral duty is in a given situation, it is important to distinguish between (a) objective duty and (b) apparent duty. "I believe it is my duty to do thus and so" is an intelligible statement, and its intelligibility rests on the assumption that what I *believe* to be my duty may be different from what really *is* my duty.

It is certainly evident that we cannot possibly know which of the many things that we might do at any moment will, in fact, produce the greatest increase of good in the world, so if this is what Ethical Naturalist means, his view would entail that we never know what our duty is. And this, I think, is absurd. We must, then, interpret him to mean that we ought always do that act which *we believe* will produce the greatest increase of good in the world. In other words, we must construe his remark as applying not to our objective duty but to our apparent duty. But even then, his view does not stand up; for what I believe to be my duty on many occasions is not at all the act that I believe is likely to produce the greatest increase of good in the world, all things considered. Neither objective duty nor apparent duty, therefore, seems to be definable in relation to "good."

The "obligatory" or "dutiful" character of certain kinds of acts is a quality of those acts that must be rationally discerned in the same way that the goodness of certain states of affairs must be rationally discerned. There are, as Ross has pointed out,[5] various kinds of duties— duties of fidelity (telling the truth, keeping promises), duties of reparation (making amends for wrongful acts), duties of gratitude (expressing thanks for favors done by others), duties of justice (assisting the needy), duties of beneficence (relieving suffering), and so on. No doubt we sometimes err in thinking a particular act to be our duty when it is not, just as we sometimes err in judging a given state of affairs to be good when it is not; for our knowledge of moral truths is not infallible. But our knowledge of moral truths, insofar as we have such knowledge, is nonempirical. The qualities that we judge when we make a moral judgment—both the goodness of good things and the obligatoriness of acts that are our duty—are nonempirical, or nonnatural, qualities.

STUDY QUESTIONS

1. What is the open-question test? Can you think of any examples in which the test fails to prove what Intuitionist says it proves?
2. What distinction does Intuitionist make between "analytic hedonism" and "synthetic hedonism"? What is the relationship between hedonism of these two types and ethical naturalism? How does Intuitionist attempt to refute hedonism of both types?
3. Would it be logically consistent for a person to be both (a) an intuitionist and (b) a synthetic hedonist? Explain.
4. Consider carefully Intuitionist's examples of moral judgments. Does he convince you that they *cannot* be construed in the way that Ethical Naturalist would have us construe them? Does he convince you that they should be construed in the way he proposes? Try his proposal with a few examples of your own.
5. How does Intuitionist analyze moral duty? Would it be logically possible for Intuitionist to agree with Ethical Naturalist's analysis of moral duty?

---

[5] W. D. Ross, *op. cit.*, Chap. 2.

48

PRIVATE SUBJECTIVISM

Neither of the two preceding theories constitutes a truly adequate account of the logic of moral discourse. Each of them, it seems to me, explains some of the facts about the language of morals and leaves certain other facts unexplained. Let us try to separate truth from error in the foregoing accounts, and let us proceed from there to develop a theory about the logic of moral discourse that is adequate to *all* the relevant facts.

Ethical Naturalist has affirmed the following propositions:

a. The term "good" has three distinguishable meanings: a primary moral meaning (good as opposed to evil), a secondary moral meaning (good as opposed to bad), and a nonmoral meaning (good as opposed to poor).
b. The most important concept for understanding the logic of moral discourse is "good" in its primary moral sense.
c. All other moral predicates are definable in terms of this concept.
d. The meaning of "good" in this primary sense is "pleasurable for human beings."
e. Moral judgments are, therefore, true or false.
f. The truth or falsity of moral judgments is theoretically ascertainable by straightforward empirical means.

Of these six propositions, Intuitionist has agreed, explicitly or by implication, with propositions *a, b,* and *e,* and has disagreed with the other three. In place of the propositions that he rejects, Intuitionist has offered the following:

g. The term "duty," at least, is not definable in terms of "good" in the primary sense.

h. The term "good" in the primary sense denotes a simple nonnatural quality, and by virtue of its simplicity is undefinable.

i. The truth or falsity of moral sentences is ascertainable by nonempirical means (intuition).

Of these nine propositions, I think we can, without further ado, simply accept propositions *a, b, e,* and *f*. My reasons for holding propositions *e* and *f* to be true are, however, quite different from those given by Ethical Naturalist, as will shortly be apparent. (I do think that moral sentences consist in the assertion—rather misleading—of some commonplace facts. I am, therefore, bound to hold that the two propositions in question are true.) I have no wish to enter into the side argument between Ethical Naturalist and Intuitionist about whether or not "duty" is definable in terms of "good" in the primary sense, so I shall refrain from expressing myself on propositions *c* and *g*. I am inclined to doubt whether our moral concepts are as neatly organized into a coherent system as Ethical Naturalist has suggested; but I am even more certain that what we know when we know that something is our duty is not what Intuitionist says we know, nor do we know it in the way he says we do (proposition *f*). But this is, in any case, a small side issue, and I do not wish to commit myself to a definite position on it.

There are, then, three propositions among the nine that have been enunciated by my two predecessors—propositions *d, h,* and *i*—with which I definitely disagree. I propose to indicate briefly my reasons for rejecting each of them.

Let us consider first Intuitionist's claim that the truth or falsity of moral sentences is ascertainable by nonempirical means (proposition *i*). I disagree with this claim for two reasons. First, I hold that all our knowledge of synthetic truths arises out of experience: I am, in short, an empiricist. If there were some other convincing examples of synthetic truths that are known a priori—"intuited," as Intuitionist says —then we might, of course, entertain the possibility that the truth of moral sentences is also known in this way. But it has been amply demonstrated by many philosophers that the most plausible examples of such truths can be easily accounted for in a way that is consistent with empiricism.[1] Since this is the case, it seems unlikely that moral truths are an exception to the rule. Second, even if the correctness of the general thesis of empiricism be disallowed, it cannot be plausibly argued that moral truths are examples of synthetic truths that are known a priori. These truths do not exhibit the qualities of necessity and universality—or of self-evidence—that are alleged to be the hall-

---

[1]See Chapters 5 and 6 for a fuller explanation of empiricism.

marks of a priori knowledge. There is, admittedly, a certain oddness about moral sentences; but this oddness, as we shall see, is due to something quite different from the alleged fact that they are truths that are directly "intuited" as Intuitionist claims.

As for proposition *h,* it is sufficient to point out that if proposition *i* is rejected, proposition *h* must be rejected as well—or else we must draw the conclusion that we are in complete ignorance with respect to moral truths. I think that usually when we say that something is "good" or "right," we do know that what we are asserting is the case, though we are seldom explicitly aware of exactly what we are asserting. I, therefore, conclude that the theory that "good" denotes a simple nonnatural quality is incorrect.

Ethical Naturalist's thesis that "good" means "pleasurable for human beings" is inadequate in a number of ways. Intuitionist has pointed out, for example, that our judgment that a state of affairs is good, or that an act is right, does not vary exactly with the quantity of human pleasure supposed to be present; and I think that in this he is right. But the inadequacy of the theory can also be shown in another way. There is no valid argument by which we can, from premises containing no moral predicates, deduce a sentence that does contain a moral predicate. If Ethical Naturalist's thesis were correct, we ought to be able to argue as follows:

State X is a state of the universe in which there would be substantially more human pleasure than there is at present.
Act W is, of all the things I might do, the act that would be maximally conducive to the achievement of state X.

I *ought* to do act W.

Now it is apparent, I am saying, that we cannot validly argue in this way. The "ought" that appears in the conclusion is not deducible from the merely descriptive statements that constitute the premises of the argument, whereas according to Ethical Naturalist's thesis it should be. Moreover, insofar as we do feel that the conclusion is somehow appropriate to (even though not deducible from) those premises, it is because of another unexpressed premise—that one ought, on the whole, to do things that are conducive to human pleasure.

It seems to me, therefore, that the attempts of both Ethical Naturalist and Intuitionist to describe the peculiar logical structure of moral discourse must be regarded as failures. Moral predicates do not refer to either observable or unobservable qualities in the objects of which they seem to be descriptive. Hence, moral sentences are not informative in the sense of conveying some information about the object that is said to be good or bad, right or wrong. It remains to be seen, however, whether such sentences are not informative in another sense.

The Case for Subjectivism

An important fact about moral utterances, for which objectivist theories give no account whatsoever, is that they are always expressive of some attitude, either positive or negative, on the part of the person making the judgment. Some moral predicates, like "good," "right," "praiseworthy," and "virtuous," report what we may call a "pro-attitude"; others, like "evil," "bad," "wrong," "blameworthy," and "vicious," report an "anti-attitude." This fact about moral predicates and the sentences in which they are employed is a valuable clue to the logical structure of the language of morals, for it suggests that what we are saying when we call something good or bad, right or wrong, is that we have, or tend to have, a favorable or unfavorable attitude toward it. The real meaning of the statement "The infliction of needless pain is evil" is "I disapprove of the infliction of needless pain." Moral sentences, in short, are informative of the attitude of the person rendering the judgment, not of the qualities of the object being judged.

My point may be illustrated by considering the somewhat parallel case of food preferences. *A* says, "Rutabagas are good." *B* says, "I disagree: rutabagas are not good at all." On the surface of it, it looks as if *A* and *B* are engaged in a disagreement about whether rutabagas do or do not possess the quality of "tasting good." However, *A* and *B* are not really disagreeing about any empirical or nonempirical qualities of rutabagas at all. What *A* means by "Rutabagas are good" is "I, *A,* like rutabagas," and what *B* means by "Rutabagas are not good" is "I, *B,* do not like rutabagas." *A* and *B* have, then, different *attitudes* toward the taste of rutabagas, and their respective statements about the goodness or nongoodness of rutabagas are simply misleading ways of reporting their private tastes.

Moral sentences, I am suggesting, are misleading in exactly this way. Like statements about tastes, they look as if they are informative about the object that is said to be good or bad, right or wrong, but they are, in fact, informative only of the feelings, or attitudes, of the person making the statement. "Helping someone in need is praiseworthy" is like "Rutabagas are good," not like "Daffodils are yellow"; but the misleading character of moral sentences is less obvious than is that of sentences about food preferences.

There is one common, and at first sight quite plausible, objection to this view, namely, that on the theory proposed here it would seem that there is nothing to argue about in matters of ethical "disagreement," just as there is nothing to argue about if you like rutabagas and I do not: the most we can do is recognize that our tastes differ at this point, and that is the end of it. But, of course, people *do* argue about ethical matters, and they even cite empirical evidence to support their views. How, then, can this be accounted for in the subjectivist theory?

The answer is that (a) by and large people do tend to approve and disapprove of the same "ends" and (b) when they disagree, their disagreement is usually about the most effective means of achieving those ends. Ethical Naturalist's example of the two people who disagreed about whether it would be right to use tear gas in a certain situation is a case in point. The two did not disagree in what we may call their basic moral attitude: they both favored a restoration of order and regarded with disfavor the occurrence of a civil war. Their disagreement was only about the likely results of using the tear gas; because they held different opinions on this point, they held different attitudes toward the proposed action. Since empirical evidence is relevant to assessing the probable consequences of this or that course of action, the citing of evidence is appropriate in such circumstances.

As a general rule, significant disagreement on ethical matters is possible only if, and insofar as, the disputants tend to hold the same basic attitudes toward the same actual or imagined states of affairs. If they reach agreement about the facts but still persist in holding conflicting attitudes, there remains nothing that can be settled by rational argument.

"But surely," it may be objected, "people do disagree in their basic moral attitudes and even try to persuade others to agree with them." Granted. People seem to feel more strongly about their moral attitudes than they do about their food preferences (we do not talk, for example, about our "culinary convictions") and are generally unwilling to accept questioning of them. But the only methods by which anyone can persuade another to change basic moral attitudes are those not of rational argument but of nonrational persuasion: name-calling, intimidation, threats, and so on. This is probably why our language has words like "prude," "moral ignoramus," and the like.

Does this view lead to pessimistic conclusions about the possibility of achieving enough ethical agreement among people to make harmonious life possible? Not at all. To so conclude would be equivalent to a restaurateur's concluding that, since people's tastes differ, he might as well give up trying to develop a menu that will win the general approval of his customers. Fortunately, people, by and large, tend to approve and disapprove of the same kinds of things: that is why there is little disagreement with statements like "The infliction of needless pain is evil" or "It is good to help others who are in need." It is not the alleged objectivity of moral judgments but the substantial similarity of our basic moral attitudes that renders possible a reasonably harmonious society.

The Truth and Falsity of Ethical Statements

I have already stated that I agree with Ethical Naturalist's assertions that ethical statements are true or false, and that their truth or falsity is ascertainable by empirical means. Now I want to indicate why and in what sense I hold these assertions to be true.

Since, according to my view, ethical statements are reports about the speaker's attitudes, such statements are always either true or false:

they are true if the speaker really has the attitude that he or she claims to have and false if he or she does not. Moreover, the means by which we determine whether a person has the attitude he or she claims to have are straightforwardly empirical: introspection in the case of ourselves, and observation in the case of others. The evidence that Johnny does not like spinach is his behavior—the fact that he never voluntarily eats spinach, objects violently if told that he must eat some spinach, makes a face when a spoonful of spinach is put in his mouth, and so on. The evidence that people who say that honesty is good really do approve of honesty is that they pay their bills, do not take things that do not belong to them and, in general, behave in ways that are consistent with what is normally meant by the term "honesty."

It seems to be possible, incidentally, for people to be mistaken about their own attitudes and thus to make false ethical statements without any intent to deceive. At times, people can affirm general principles learned earlier in life, which may have been truly descriptive of their attitudes at that time, without realizing that their present attitudes (as judged by their behavior) are no longer what they formerly were. A person who has been taught that all drinking of alcoholic beverages is wrong, for example, may continue to say this on occasion even if he or she engages in moderate drinking and has no objection to others doing the same. There is, so far as I can see, no logical inconsistency in this; it is just that the general principle learned earlier in life is no longer truly descriptive of this person's present attitude.

Moral Attitudes and Objectively Descriptive Inferences

There is a sense, however, in which moral utterances are implicitly descriptive of the objects that are asserted to be good or bad, right or wrong. It is true, as Ethical Naturalist says, that if someone is said to be "a good man," we would be very surprised to learn that he is a poor husband and father, difficult to get along with, careless in his work, and so on; and this gives some credence to the view that the statement "Joe Doakes is a good man" is an assertion to the effect that Joe Doakes has certain qualities and does not have others.

That the assertion "Joe Doakes is a good man" is not as straightforwardly descriptive as this example makes it appear to be, however, is apparent from the fact that what we would regard as its "objective descriptive content" would vary considerably depending on whether we understood the statement to have been uttered by (a) the president of the local temperance union, (b) a fundamentalist minister, (c) oneself, or (d) the head of the Mafia. There are some "objective descriptive implications" in each case, but their precise character varies depending on the speaker. How can this be?

The correct solution to the puzzle, I would suggest, is as follows. What is sometimes called the descriptive content of a moral utterance is a result of an inference that we make from (a) what we know or suppose about the basic moral attitudes of the speaker in conjunction with (b) the particular statement that the speaker makes to the effect that so and so is good. We know, for example, that Mr. X, the head of the Mafia, generally approves of men who can rob a bank without getting caught, who always share their loot with the rest of the mob, and so on. If, then, Mr. X says "Joe Doakes is a good man," we infer that Joe Doakes is not a psalm-singing philanthropist but a man who exhibits the qualities that Mr. X is in the habit of commending. If we knew nothing about the attitudes of the speaker, we would be very much in doubt about what kind of a man Joe Doakes is, even though he is said to be a "good" man.

If, when we hear someone described as a "good" or "virtuous" person, we are not usually in doubt about what sort of person he or she is, it is not because "good" or "virtuous" directly mean such and such a combination of qualities, but because people by and large tend to favor certain kinds of qualities and behavior in other people. It is this fact that lends ethical naturalism whatever plausibility it has, and it leads us mistakenly to conclude that the primary meaning of moral utterances is their objective descriptive meaning. The variability of this descriptive meaning (depending on the basic moral attitudes of the speaker) makes it evident that this descriptive content is inferential rather than direct, and it is precisely the subjective theory of the primary meaning of moral utterances that enables us to account for this undeniable variability. I take this, therefore, as a most powerful confirmation of the correctness of the view here proposed.

STUDY QUESTIONS

1. What are the "three propositions" enunciated by one or the other of the two preceding writers with which Private Subjectivist (PS) feels obliged to take issue? With whom are you inclined to agree on each of these points? Why?

2. Is PS right in saying: "There is no valid argument by which one can, from premises containing no moral predicates, deduce a conclusion that does contain a moral predicate"? If he is right, is this fact damaging to ethical naturalism? Explain.

3. What exactly is PS's own view about the meaning of moral sentences? Do the examples he gives especially lend themselves to this kind of interpretation? Can you think of any examples that he might find it difficult to interpret in this way?

4. In what sense does private subjectivism maintain that ethical statements are capable of being true or false? How, according to this view, can the statement "The infliction of needless pain is evil" be contradicted?

5. What does PS mean by the statement that the "descriptive content" of ethical statements is inferential rather than direct? Do you think he is right?

49

CULTURAL RELATIVISM

The view of moral judgments presented in the preceding chapter represents a decided advance over the two objectivist theories introduced earlier. It seems clear that pro-attitudes and anti-attitudes are involved in an important way in the meaning of moral judgments. Any theory that fails to take account of this fact must be regarded as inadequate.

Some things about Private Subjectivist's proposal, however, strike me as being very strange. I shall point out what I consider to be certain oddities in this theory, features that demonstrate beyond a reasonable doubt that it is not the whole and correct answer to our problem. I shall then suggest a slight emendation by means of which the difficulties inherent in the private subjectivist view can be overcome.

Some Oddities of Private Subjectivism

If we were to adopt the private subjectivist theory, we would have to conclude that moral judgments are never false except in the very unusual instance in which the person making the judgment has made some mistake in assessing his or her own attitude; and this seems strange. Let us suppose that A and B are discussing the rightness or wrongness of r. A says, "r is right"; B says, "r is wrong." It would hardly be appropriate for A to say in this situation, "But B, you don't really disapprove of r, you do it all the time!" Even if A confronted B with evidence that he regularly had a pro-attitude toward r, this still would not make B withdraw his statement. We could imagine him replying, "I didn't say I *disapproved* of r, I said that r is *wrong*—

notwithstanding the fact that I, reprobate that I am, approve of it." And in saying this, *B* would not be talking nonsense.

This brings me to my second point. According to private subjectivism, it would be nonsensical (because self-contradictory) to say, "I approve of some things that are wrong," or "I disapprove of some things that are right." The self-contradiction is plain: "I approve of some things that are wrong" means, according to this theory, "I approve of some things that I do not approve of." But certainly, it is not self-contradictory to speak of approving of some things that are wrong. A theory that requires us to banish such statements to the realm of nonsense is somehow mistaken.

There is another type of statement that has a perfectly legitimate use in ordinary discourse that becomes nonsensical according to the private subjectivist view. Consider the statement, "We ought never to do anything that we believe to be wrong, even if we want to." Surely, this is a statement that would be very natural in certain contexts—in a treatise on normative ethics, for example—and we would have no difficulty in understanding it or, probably, assenting to it. But according to the private subjectivist view, this becomes a nonsensical statement because it means "I disapprove of people doing things that they disapprove of, even when they approve of them." Now the purpose of a metaethical theory is not to reform moral discourse but to explain it. Since we do have a use for statements such as this, and since private subjectivism does not allow that use, the theory surely needs some improvement.

Further, if the private subjectivist theory is correct, then it follows that treatises on normative ethics tell us nothing except the private likes and dislikes of their authors. This idea, to say the least, is a strange one. No doubt such great ethical theorists as Aristotle, St. Thomas Aquinas, and Immanuel Kant had their private likes and dislikes on moral questions, just as they presumably had their own peculiar tastes in food. But surely, it is not because of a purely biographical interest that we read Aristotle's *Nicomachean Ethics,* St. Thomas Aquinas's *Summa Theologica,* or Kant's *Critique of Practical Reason.* We read them because we expect these writers to help us understand, among other things, what we *ought* to approve of, what *really is* right or wrong, good or evil; and we should not be interested in such questions, or even be able to ask them, if moral appraisals expressed nothing but the speaker's private likes and dislikes.

Finally, it seems that part of the persuasiveness of Private Subjectivist's account results from a confusion of which he and many of his readers are probably not aware. I suspect that the most convincing feature of private subjectivism for many people is its apparent capacity to account for shifts in the "objective descriptive content" of ethical statements depending on who makes the statement. Private Subjectivist says we infer certain things about the object judged on the basis of what we know about the general likes and dislikes of the person making the judgment. What Private Subjectivist fails to note, however, is that when the statement "Joe Doakes is a good man" is made by, say, the head of the Mafia, it is no longer a *moral* judgment: it is a judgment employing "good" in a *non*moral sense, such as we find in the sentence "A Buick is a good automobile." When the head of the Mafia says that Joe Doakes is a "good man," he certainly does not mean that Joe is a paragon of virtue: he means that Joe is a good (effective) gangster, that he does well those things that the speaker expects a gangster to do. How, then, do we distinguish between the moral and the nonmoral uses of "good"? Actually, we distingush without diffi- culty: we recognize immediately, once our attention is called to it, that the statement about Joe Doakes by the number one man in the Mafia is not a moral judgment, whereas the same statement made by you or me normally would be. Private subjectivism fails to recognize this difference and is unable to account for it. Hence, we must look further for a metaethical theory that is adequate to all the relevant facts.

An Alternative to Private Subjectivism

The theory that I should like to offer is known as *cultural relativism*. Moral judgments, according to this view, are indeed reports about pro-attitudes and anti-attitudes (as they are according to the private subjectivist theory); but the attitudes that they purport to describe are not necessarily or exclusively those of the person making the judg- ment. Rather, they are those of some group with which the person identifies or has reference to in making that judgment. Basic moral attitudes, in short, are never simply the private attitudes of this or that individual. They are always the common attitudes of some community of which the individual is a part. Indeed, it is precisely the generality of such attitudes—their nonprivate character—that gives them the force of moral principles. Let us see how the features of moral dis- course that have proven to be so perplexing for the private subjectivist theory can be understood if we construe moral sentences in the way I am proposing.

What meaning can be allowed for the statements "I approve of some things that are wrong" and "I disapprove of some things that are right?" Both of these, as we have seen, are meaningless if we interpret them according to the private subjectivist theory. According to my view, however, they are perfectly intelligible statements. "I approve of some things that are wrong" means "I approve of some things that are not generally approved of by people whose opinions I ordinarily re- spect"; and "I disapprove of some things that are right" means "I disapprove of some things that are generally approved of by people whose opinions I ordinarily respect." As soon as we recognize that the approval or disapproval expressed in a moral judgment is not neces- sarily or exclusively that of the speaker but represents some "commu- nity" with which the person identifies, the apparent self-contradiction of such statements disappears.

There is a certain deliberate vagueness in the expression "gener- ally approved of by people whose opinions I ordinarily respect" that

I want to discuss briefly at this point. Considerable variation exists from one individual to another with respect to the "community" with which a person identifies, and, consequently, with respect to the opinions that person takes into account when making moral judgments. In every culture—especially in a self-consciously pluralistic culture such as our own—there are various subcultures that, in many cases, are the "communities" of which their members feel themselves to be a part. No one is just an American, or a Russian, or a Swede. A given American, for example, may be, at one and the same time, (a) an American, (b) a Catholic, (c) a Democrat, (d) a college professor, and (e) a member of the Society for the Prevention of Cruelty to Animals. Each of these "communities" may, on different occasions, be the one to which the person has reference when he or she calls something right or wrong, good or evil. Which community is relevant in a given case depends on the basic attitudes typical of each. For our hypothetical American it might vary depending on whether the topic under discussion is (a) the freedom of the press, (b) birth control, (c) the proper role of the federal government, (d) plagiarism, or (e) slaughterhouse procedures. It is to allow for this varying reference of moral judgments that I have used the phrase "generally approved of by people whose opinions I ordinarily respect," it being understood that *whose* opinions one respects varies greatly from one individual to another and even from one occasion to another (depending on what is being considered). "Morally neutral" would then mean "an object of neither pro-attitudes nor anti-attitudes in any of the communities whose opinions I tend to respect."

All the moral predicates are, I think, correctly construed as purported descriptions of the basic attitudes, positive or negative, of whatever community or communities the speaker has reference to in making judgments. "Ought," however, is not a predicate, and it is not definable in terms of community attitude. "Ought" is descriptive, rather, of the *expectations* of the community with respect to its members. To say "I ought to do such and such" is to say "It is expected of me by those whose good will I cherish that I do such and such." The meaning of the statement "We ought never to do what we believe to be wrong, even if we want to" is, therefore, rather complex. It means "It is expected of a person, by those whose good will he or she cherishes, that he or she refrain from doing the things they generally disapprove of, even if his or her personal inclination is to do them." This interpretation expresses exactly what we would understand a person to mean if he or she were to make the statement in question.

Cultural relativism also enables us to understand how people can make false moral judgments apart from the rather unusual circumstance in which they might be mistaken about their own attitudes. According to cultural relativism, a moral judgment is true if the people in the community to which the speaker has reference have the attitude attributed to them; it is false if they do not. It is quite natural that a person should occasionally be mistaken about the pro- and anti-attitudes of the members of his or her community with respect to some matter that the person may never have had an opportunity to discuss with them—especially since most people are simultaneously members of several communities. Thus, at this point too, cultural relativism appears to solve a puzzle that the private subjectivist theory leaves unsolved.

What, finally, is the content of treatises on normative ethics? Why are these works not the mere expression of the private likes and dislikes of their authors, as private subjectivism would have them be? The answer is that an ethical treatise is an attempt by one member of a community to assist the other members to clarify their moral attitudes, to eliminate any inconsistencies that may be present (to render them coherent), and to adopt certain additional attitudes consistent with those already held. Indeed, a daring and original ethical thinker may do even more: he or she may recommend adopting attitudes different from those currently held—in which case the person will be regarded by the community either as a great teacher or as an eccentric, depending on whether or not those recommendations are accepted.

This brings us to the final difficulty that we noted in connection with the private subjectivist theory: that no basis could be given for the difference we instinctively sense between moral and nonmoral meanings of "good." The question is, Why do we assume that the statement, "Joe Doakes is a good man," when spoken by the head of the Mafia, is not a moral judgment, when we assume that the same statement when spoken by someone else may be? I think the answer is as follows. The subculture to which the head of the Mafia has reference in calling Joe Doakes "a good man" is not a "community" in any meaningful sense of the word. It is only a group of men whose common bond is a parasitic relation to a community. If the head of the Mafia were to call Joe a good man in the *moral* sense of "good," he would have to have reference to the basic attitudes of the community, that is, to law-abiding society. And this, of course, would be tantamount to saying that Joe is quite unfit for service in the Mafia. Were he to call Joe a good man in the moral sense of "good," therefore, we could only construe it as an expression of his disapproval of Joe. ("Buy off Joe Doakes? Forget it. He's a *good* man, unfortunately.") However, if he says, "Joe Doakes is a good man," in an approving way ("You need somebody to help you on that Jones job? Take Joe. He's a good man."), we know immediately that what he is expressing is not a moral judgment at all but simply what we may call "goodness of function." (Compare: "You need another car for the Jones job? Take mine. It's a good car.")

Concluding Unphilosophical Postscript

It should be apparent that the view presented here not only solves the difficulties noted in the private subjectivist view but also retains everything that is most persuasive in that view. For example, the variability of the objective descriptive content of a moral judgment depending on who happens to utter it—a fact that is absolutely fatal to any objectivist theory—is easily explicable in terms of the different communities to which a given speaker may have reference (or, as we said before, in terms of the same speaker on different occasions or with respect to different topics). No doubt people's habits of approval and disapproval tend, on the whole, to coincide with those of the communities with which they identify. Therefore, from our knowledge of a person's general attitudes we can often infer directly the descriptive statements implied in that person's judgment that something is good or bad (in the moral sense). The fact remains that we can distinguish between people's private attitudes and their moral convictions, and our theory provides a basis for this distinction, whereas the private subjectivist theory does not.

There is one further feature of moral judgments, which none of the previous writers has mentioned, that is rather important. The discussion of it will require us to venture briefly into the realm of social psychology, however, and here I can only offer my comments as a layman's surmise, a "concluding unphilosophical postscript" to what I have already said.

The feature of moral judgments to which I refer is what might be called their "constraining" or "obligatory" character. Moral principles sincerely held seem to make a claim, to demand (but not force) obedience. Discussion of moral issues, accordingly, always seems to be a matter of unique importance: we are concerned about them "in the center of our being," so to speak.

The explanation of this fact, I suggest, is as follows. As social beings, our acceptance by the communities with which we identify is deeply important to us. Consequently, our conformity to the expectations of the community and our identity with the community by way of sharing its basic moral attitudes are also very important to us. We exist not as isolated individuals but as human beings in community with other human beings. The attitudes and expectations of the community thus impinge upon us, constrain us, make demands on us: it is this that gives us our sense of duty and obligation and our attitudes concerning right and wrong, good and evil, virtue and vice. Morality is a social phenomenon and we are social beings; therefore, moral questions, problems, and principles strike us as being among the most important matters with which we can be concerned.

STUDY QUESTIONS

1. List the objections that Cultural Relativist (CR) raises with respect to private subjectivism. Are these serious difficulties for the private subjectivist? Can you think of any way to defend private subjectivism against these objections?

2. What does CR offer as an alternative to private subjectivism? To what extent does this involve disagreement with Private Subjectivist's position?

3. What analysis does CR offer of the sentences that he earlier cited as being "nonsensical" if interpreted according to the private subjectivist theory? Are you satisfied with this analysis? Can you think of any moral sentences that CR might have difficulty in construing in a way consistent with his theory?

4. Do we know that the statement "Joe Doakes is a good man," spoken (in an approving way) by the head of the Mafia, is not a moral judgment? How? (If you are not satisfied with CR's account, devise one of your own.)

5. Would there be any inconsistency in being both a cultural relativist and a moral critic of one's own community or society? To what moral standard would such a person (qua critic) be appealing?

50

NONCOGNITIVISM

All the metaethical theories presented thus far assume that moral sentences are assertions. Ethical Naturalism construes moral sentences as assertions about the presence or absence of some natural quality (for example, pleasure-producing potential) in the act or state of affairs about which the alleged assertion is made. Intuitionism construes such sentences as assertions about the presence or absence of an alleged nonnatural quality (that is, goodness) in the judged object. Private subjectivism construes them as assertions about the attitudes of the asserter. And most recently we have heard from Cultural Relativist, who advises us to construe such sentences as assertions about the feeling of approval and disapproval on the part not of the speaker but of some group with which the speaker identifies or to which the speaker has reference in making his or her assertion.

The inadequacies of the first three of these theories have already been discussed. Cultural relativism is also inadequate in its own way, however, and I want to point out some of the most serious problems inherent in this view before going on to propose what I believe to be a more adequate alternative.

Critique of Cultural Relativism

First, when we "unpack" a moral sentence in the way that cultural relativism says we should, what we end up with is not a plausible account of the sentence with which we began. Consider, for example, the sentence (which one could readily imagine being uttered by a stern-voiced father) "Son, you ought not drive so fast." According to cultural relativism, the meaning of this sentence is roughly as follows:

"You commonly drive at speeds that are excessive and if you continue to do so you are apt to become involved in an accident; moreover, your mother and I, and many others whose opinions you normally respect, have feelings of disapproval toward your so doing." Now this, I am saying, is not a plausible account of what we mean by the moral sentence "You ought not drive so fast." And this conclusion can be reinforced by applying the relativist theory to additional examples.

Second, cultural relativism obliterates the distinction between the manners and the morals of a given culture. We are, in fact, able to distinguish between the moral standards of a group of people and their standards of etiquette; indeed, we are able to make that distinction even with respect to our own culture. We consider it bad manners to make uncouth noises while eating, for example, but we do not consider it immoral to do so. Yet in both cases, we have what might be described as "feelings of disapproval." If the sentence "X is wrong" means merely "The group of people whose opinions I normally respect disapprove of X," then we should not be able to make this distinction and, in fact, it should be correct to say (in our culture), "Eating noisily is morally wrong." Hence, it is clear that moral sentences cannot be satisfactorily construed in the way that cultural relativism urges us to construe them.

Finally, if moral sentences mean what cultural relativism says they mean, we should not be able to meaningfully ask the question, Are all the things that my cultural reference group approves really right, and are all things that they disapprove really wrong? But we *can* meaningfully ask this question—indeed, as we noted a moment ago, we can readily think of examples of things that are the object of general approval or disapproval that nobody would think of calling right or wrong. Thus, it is evident that "right" and "wrong" do not mean simply approval or disapproval by the appropriate cultural reference group.

Since all the theories that attempt to construe moral sentences as *assertions* of one kind or another have now been shown to be inadequate, it seems clear that our only alternative is to construe them as sentences of a very different kind—that is, as sentences that do not *assert* anything at all. Two such theories have been put forward in recent years, namely *emotivism* and *imperativism.* I shall cover emotivism only briefly, because I think it can be readily shown that it is not a promising alternative to the theories that have already been discussed. I shall then attempt to state the case for imperativism, which I believe to be the most plausible account of the meaning of moral sentences.

Emotivism

According to emotivism, the specifically moral character of moral sentences consists, not in the assertion that the speaker, or some group to which the speaker has reference, has certain feelings, but in a nondescriptive *expression of* those feelings. Moral words, insofar as they have a distinctively moral flavor, are not descriptive of either the object being "judged" or anybody's feelings: they are not descriptive at all. Grammatically, they have the status of an interjection. "You ought not drive so fast" means, roughly, "You commonly drive at excessive speeds: for shame!"

Emotivism acknowledges, however, that some moral sentences cannot be reduced to (a) a factual assertion ("You commonly drive at excessive speeds") plus (b) an expression of approval or disapproval ("for shame!"). A sentence like "Driving at excessive speeds is wrong," for example, has no factual meaning; its only meaning is, therefore, emotive, according to this view. It is as if someone said "driving at excessive speeds!" in a "raised-eyebrows" tone of voice, thus indicating his disapproval of the behavior in question. General moral sentences are neither true nor false according to the emotivist view. People who say, "Driving at excessive speeds is wrong," cannot be contradicted because they are not making an assertion. Anyone who appeared to be disagreeing with them would only be expressing a contrary attitude.

Many people have great difficulty understanding the difference between emotivism and the private subjectivist view. The difference can be stated as follows: according to the private subjectivist theory, moral sentences are informative sentences; according to emotivism, they are not. Or the difference can be expressed in this way: according to the private subjectivist view, moral sentences are always either true or false; according to emotivism, they are not. According to the private subjectivist view, the statement "Driving at excessive speeds is wrong" can be contradicted by the statement "You do not really disapprove of fast driving." According to emotivism, the utterance cannot be contradicted because it makes no assertion.

The difference between private subjectivism and emotivism is not over whether or not a person who utters a moral sentence has the feelings in question: both views assume that the person normally does. The question is, does the meaning of a moral sentence consist in an assertion by the speaker that he or she has such and such feelings, or is a moral sentence a nonreportive expression of those feelings? Private Subjectivist says the former, emotivism says the latter. The difference is subtle but important.

I do not wish to dwell at great length on the defects of the emotivist theory. It has been widely and soundly criticized since it was first put forward some years ago, and many of its early supporters have abandoned it in recent years. Rather I want to mention just three or four of the most serious objections that have been raised against the theory.

The emotivist theory does not do justice to the seriousness with which moral sentences are commonly uttered. Questions calling for moral appraisal and decision are frequently matters of great moment: the fates of people and nations are sometimes at stake. To say that the sentence "War is evil" means "Boo for war," or that the sentence "Bravery is good" means "Hurrah for bravery," is absurd. No doubt we frequently take ourselves too seriously, but we surely are not guilty of this when we say that our moral appraisals of war, of bravery, or of thousands of other things that we appraise in this way are important. The "boo-hurrah" theory offends us because it makes light of serious matters. For this reason alone, it deserves to be rejected.

Moreover, a number of odd and distressing consequences follow if we assume this theory to be true. For example, we can never be in error in making a moral "judgment," and from this it follows that neither blame nor remorse is ever appropriate. Moreover, according to this theory, there can never be a rational basis for an ethical appraisal or decision. And most distressing of all, it would follow that ethical disputes cannot be resolved by rational means: if individuals or nations cannot agree on some matter of importance, there is nothing to do but to fight it out until the strongest wins.

The issue resolves itself, really, to this: Are moral utterances rational or are they not? The unanimous answer of our whole Western ethical tradition, from Plato and Aristotle to Kant, Mill, Moore, and Ross, is that they are. The reply of the emotivists is that they are not. This is no trifling matter. If ethics can be rational, then moral progress —the gradual improvement of our moral principles by reflection and criticism—is possible; if not, such progress is not possible. Indeed, the very notion of "progress" becomes, in this theory, incomprehensible. Anyone concerned about the future of civilization would do well to ponder these consequences.

Let us look, then, at one final alternative, the noncognitivist meta-ethical theory known as imperativism.

Some Features of Directive Language

Rational beings employ language for a variety of purposes, only one of which is to convey information. Because so much of our use of language does consist in this informative function, however, conventional logic has dwelt almost entirely on the logical behavior of language so employed. But the directive function of language—the use of language to guide behavior—is an equally rational function.

The difference between these two kinds of language can be understood in terms of the differing types of questions to which each might be appropriate in framing an answer. We use language informatively only in instances where we presuppose a question of the form, What are the facts? or What is the case? We use language in its directive function only in instances where we presuppose a question of the form, What shall I do? To a question of the latter type, any statement of fact would be inappropriate; to a question of the former type, a moral appraisal would be equally inappropriate.

There are many different instances in which the function of the language used is quite evidently directive. Consider the following list: a typical verbal communication from a sergeant to his platoon; a recipe; assembly instructions for a child's toy; instructions from ground control to a team of astronauts; a teacher's remarks in preparation for an examination; a parent's word to a small child who is dallying after bedtime. All these are instances of language being used directively—to guide behavior.

Language used directively, like language used informatively, envisages a fairly specific state of affairs. "Johnny, go to bed" (directive), like "Johnny is going to bed" (informative), anticipates Johnny's going to bed in the very near future. Both utterances are about Johnny's going to bed, but what is said about Johnny's going to bed is different in the two cases. The directive sentence is addressed to Johnny, and it might be translated "Johnny's going to bed: do it!" The informative sentence is addressed to anybody who cares to listen, and it might be translated "Johnny's going to bed: it is occurring."

Language intended to serve a directive function is typically addressed to the person or persons whose behavior is to be guided. Some directives are intended for some one specific individual ("Johnny, go to bed!"). Others are intended for whoever may be in a position to benefit from them ("Tear on dotted line"). Some appear to be addressed to everyone; that is, they are intended to be universally applicable ("Do not take for yourself what belongs to another"). We shall return to this shortly.

The directive function, like the informative, is *sui generis*: neither can be reduced to, or derived from, the other. A given sentence may, of course, serve both functions ("Bring me the book that is lying on the dresser"), but the functions themselves may, nonetheless, be distinguished.

We cannot determine the intended function of a sentence simply by identifying its mood. Function depends on the intentions of the speaker, whereas mood does not. The sentence in parentheses in the preceding paragraph, for example, is in the imperative mood, but it is bifunctional. "Johnny, go to bed" and "Johnny, it is past your bedtime" may both serve a directive function, but the two sentences differ in mood.

Ethical Discourse as a Species of Directive Language

Let us return to ethical discourse and see how the foregoing reflections on the nature of directive language may help us to understand this common type of talk.

Most moral sentences are in the indicative mood. This may be one of the reasons why nearly all the earlier efforts to ascertain the status of moral sentences proceeded on the assumption that they must be understood as some subvariety of informative language. It is not at all inconsistent with this fact, however, to suggest that the function of moral sentences is to guide behavior—is, in short, directive.

Consider, first, the way in which children normally learn to use moral concepts. A typical instance is the following: Johnny accompanies his mother to the grocery store, and seeing some tasty-looking candy within reach, decides to help himself. Mother says, "No, Johnny, you must put that back. It is *wrong* to take something that belongs to someone else without paying for it." Three elements of this situation should be noted: (a) the moral sentence is uttered in a situation involving choice among alternative ways of behaving—a situation like many Johnny may be expected to encounter in the future; (b) the evident function of the moral utterance is to serve as a principle for the guidance of conduct—a rule that may help Johnny decide how to act in future situations of this type; and (c) the moral principle thus enunciated is universal in scope—it applies not only to Johnny but to everyone. It is chiefly this third characteristic that identifies it as a moral principle rather than a merely conventional rule.

Think for a moment about the kinds of situations in which we commonly employ moral talk: the same three features, it will be found, are always present. Moral principles, we might say, play a role among human beings analogous to the role of instinct in the behavior of animals. They serve as rules of conduct, guiding us in the multifarious choices that we are constantly called upon to make. Because moral principles are universal in scope, it is always appropriate to state them, even when we are alone. The fact that moral judgments are sometimes spoken in solitude (for example, "How noble!" or "How reprehensible!" uttered while reading) in no way invalidates the claim that the primary and normal function of such utterances is to guide behavior.

We may observe, finally, that for several reasons it is absolutely impossible for human beings to live without principles of this kind. First, our knowledge of the probable consequences of acting in this or that way is severely limited. We need general rules of conduct, embodying the accumulated wisdom of preceding generations, to guide our behavior in those situations in which we do not know how to calculate the likely consequences of various alternatives. Second, however extensive our knowledge of probable consequences may be, we require principles that will provide reasons for preferring one set of consequences over another. This would be true even if we were omniscient, knowing in precise detail what would be the short- and long-range consequences of each alternative before us. Finally, without such principles, we would not be able to accumulate practical wisdom and pass it on to our children. All learning, it must be remembered, involves generalization; it is only through generalizations that we escape the irrationality of sheer individuality. Moral principles are to the practical life what general truths are to the intellectual life. They are the generalizations that relate the particulars of experience, thus casting them into an intelligible pattern.

There is no danger that people will cease to have ethical principles as a consequence of this or that inadequate metaethical theory, no matter how widely such a theory may come to be held. There is danger, however, that widespread bewilderment about the meaning of moral utterances may lead to a weakening of their directive power, and thus to a chaotic situation in which the groping for new principles goes on without the benefit of the foundation of the old. It is necessary and important that these principles change, otherwise human beings would not be able to adjust to the constantly changing conditions in which they live. But if change is to be healthy, it must be orderly—a creation of the new by way of a modification of, and addition to, the old. This cannot occur if old principles are simply ignored or if they altogether lose their directive power. Hence, it is a matter of more than casual importance that their status be understood and their role duly respected.

STUDY QUESTIONS

1. Imperativist offers three arguments in opposition to cultural relativism. Summarize these arguments.
2. What, exactly, is emotivism? How does it differ from private subjectivism?
3. Summarize Imperativist's criticisms of the emotivist theory. Do these seem to you to be sound criticisms?
4. Summarize the "features of directive language" discussed by Imperativist. Do these features, in fact, distinguish directive language from informative language, as Imperativist apparently believes?
5. What arguments does Imperativist offer in support of his central thesis regarding the meaning of moral sentences? Do you find his arguments persuasive?
6. For what reasons, according to Imperativist, do we need moral principles? Is it possible to agree with him on this without accepting his main thesis?

CORRELATED READINGS[1]

1. Moore, George Edward. "The Meaning of Good." *Principia Ethica.* Cambridge, Eng.: Cambridge University Press, 1903, Chap. I. Intuitionism.

2. Blanshard, Brand. "In Defense of Naturalism." *The Impasse in Ethics—and a Way Out.* Berkeley: University of California Press, 1955.

3. Ayer, Alfred Jules. "Emotivism." *Language, Truth and Logic.* New York: Dover Publications, 1946, Chap. VI.

4. Toulmin, Stephen. "Ethics and Society." *An Examination of the Place of Reason in Ethics.* Cambridge, Eng.: Cambridge University Press, 1950, Chap. 10. Cultural relativism.

5. Mothersill, Mary. "Moral Knowledge." *The Journal of Philosophy,* Vol. LVI (1959), pp. 755–763. A critique of noncognitivist theories.

FOR FURTHER READING

Aiken, H. D. *Reason and Conduct: New Bearings in Moral Philosophy.* New York: Knopf, 1962.

Baier, Kurt. *The Moral Point of View.* Abr. ed. New York: Random House, 1965 (paperbound).

Blanshard, Brand. *Reason and Goodness.* New York: Macmillan, 1961.

Brandt, R. B. "The Emotive Theory of Ethics," *The Philosophical Review,* 59 (1950), 305–318.

————. *Ethical Theory.* Englewood Cliffs, N.J.: Prentice-Hall, 1959, Chaps. 7–11.

————. "The Status of Empirical Assertion Theories in Ethics," *Mind,* 61 (1952), 458–479.

Carter, C. L. (ed.). *Skepticism and Moral Principles.* Evanston, Ill.: New University Press, 1973. Contains Marcus Singer's criticisms of private subjectivism, cultural relativism, and emotivism.

Edel, Abraham. *Science and the Structure of Ethics.* Chicago: University of Chicago Press, 1961 (paperbound).

Edwards, Paul. *The Logic of Moral Discourse.* New York: Free Press, 1955 (paperbound), Chaps. 7–9.

Ewing, A. C. *Second Thoughts in Moral Philosophy.* New York: Macmillan, 1959, Chaps. 1 and 2.

Falk, W. D. "Goading and Guiding," *Mind,* 62 (1953), 145–171.

Feinberg, Joe (ed.). *Moral Concepts.* New York: Oxford University Press, 1970.

Frankena, W. K. "Moral Philosophy at Mid-century," *The Philosophical Review,* 60 (1951), 44–55.

---

[1]*Concise Readings in Philosophy,* Part XI.

Gewirth, Alan. "Meanings and Criteria in Ethics," *Philosophy,* 38 (1963), 329–345.

Hancock, Roger. "The Refutation of Naturalism in Moore and Hare," *The Journal of Philosophy,* 57 (1960), 326–334.

Hare, R. M. *Applications of Moral Philosophy.* Berkeley: University of California Press, 1972.

——————. *Essays on the Moral Concepts.* Berkeley: University of California Press, 1972.

——————. *Freedom and Reason.* New York: Oxford University Press 1963 (paperbound).

——————. *Practical Inferences.* Berkeley: University of California Press, 1972.

——————. *The Language of Morals.* New York: Oxford University Press, 1964 (paperbound).

Harman, G. "Moral Relativism Defended," *The Philosophical Review,* 84 (1975), 3–22. A lucid defense of cultural relativism.

Harsanyi, J. C. "Ethics in Terms of Hypothetical Imperatives," *Mind,* 67 (1958), 305–316.

Hudson, W. *Ethical Intuitionism.* New York: Macmillan, 1967. A short historical study of the intuitionist theory.

Kerner, George C. "Approvals, Reasons and Moral Argument," *Mind,* 71 (1962), 474–486.

——————. *The Revolution in Ethical Theory.* Oxford: Clarendon Press, 1966.

Ladd, John (ed.). *Ethical Relativism.* Belmont, Calif.: Wadsworth, 1973.

Mill, John Stuart. *Utilitarianism.* Indianapolis, Ind.: Liberal Arts Press, 1960 (paperbound).

Monro, D. H. *Empiricism and Ethics.* London: Cambridge University Press, 1967. Defends a subjectivist view.

Nielsen, K. "Does Ethical Subjectivism Have a Coherent Form?" *Philosophy and Phenomenological Research,* 35 (1974–1975), 93–99. Argues that it is not clear what it means to say that one is a "subjectivist" or an "objectivist" in ethics.

Nowell-Smith, P. H. *Ethics.* Baltimore, Md.: Penguin Books, 1954.

Perry, R. B. *General Theory of Value.* Cambridge, Mass.: Harvard University Press, 1926.

Prichard, H. A. *Moral Obligation.* New York: Oxford University Press, 1949, Chaps. 1, 2, 5.

Prior, A. N. *Logic and the Basis of Ethics.* New York: Oxford University Press, 1949.

Raphael, D. Daiches. *Moral Judgment.* New York: Hillary House, 1955, Chaps. 4, 7, 8.

——————. *The Moral Sense.* New York: Oxford University Press, 1947.

Ross, W. D. *Foundations of Ethics.* New York: Oxford University Press, 1939, Chaps. 2, 3, 11.

——————. *The Right and the Good.* New York: Oxford University Press, 1930, Chap. 2.

Sedgwick, Henry. *The Methods of Ethics.* 7th ed., rev. by Constance Jones. Chicago: University of Chicago Press, 1962, Chaps. 3, 8, 9.

Singer, M. G. *Generalization in Ethics.* New York: Knopf, 1961.

Smart, J. J. C., and Bernard Williams. *Utilitarianism: For and Against.* New York: Cambridge University Press, 1973. A debate between the two authors.

Stevenson, C. L. *Ethics and Language.* New Haven, Conn.: Yale University Press, 1960 (paperbound), Chaps. 1, 2, 4–6.

Stroll. A. *The Emotive Theory of Ethics.* Berkeley and Los Angeles: University of California Press, 1954.

Swinburne, R. G. "The Objectivity of Morality," *Philosophy,* 51 (1976), 5–20.

Taylor, Paul W. *Normative Discourse.* Englewood Cliffs, N.J.: Prentice-Hall, 1961.

Urmson, J. O. *The Emotive Theory of Ethics.* London: Hutchinson's University Library, 1968.

Veatch, Henry B. *For an Ontology of Morals: A Critique of Contemporary Ethical Theory.* Evanston, Ill.: Northwestern University Press, 1971. From a Thomist background.

Warnock, G. J. *Contemporary Moral Philosophy.* New York: St. Martin's Press, 1967. See also a critical review of Warnock's book by R. M. Hare in *Mind,* 77 (1968), 436–440.

Wellman, Carl. *Challenge and Response: Justification in Ethics.* Carbondale: Southern Illinois University Press, 1971.

————. *The Language of Ethics.* Cambridge, Mass.: Harvard University Press, 1961.

PART XII

AESTHETIC JUDGMENT

51

THE PROBLEM OF AESTHETIC JUDGMENT

The problem to which we now turn our attention is in the area of *aesthetics,* which might be loosely defined as theorizing about the fine arts. One can, of course, be a practitioner of a fine art—a painter, a sculptor, a composer—without engaging in serious theorizing about it or about fine arts in general. Moreover, the fact that someone is a practitioner does not necessarily qualify that person to theorize about the fine arts, any more than the fact that someone is not a practitioner *dis*qualifies that person from theorizing about them. It's like flying and studying the laws of aerodynamics, or exercising and researching the principles of exercise physiology: doing and theorizing about that doing are two different things.

Aesthetics begins with the fact that there exist among us certain products of human activity that are valued because they are in some unique way pleasing to the eye or ear. We call them works of art. In aesthetics we ask, and attempt to answer, certain questions that arise as we think about these objects, about the activities that brought them into being, and about the experience of those who view them (or, in the case of music, hear them).

If we begin to think seriously about the fine arts, a number of questions arise. What, exactly, is art? What characteristics must an object have in order to qualify as a work of art? Is art related in any way to the quest for truth? Can a work of art be true or false, or can it at least facilitate the acquisition of a belief that is true or false? Is it ever appropriate to assess a work of art in ethical terms, or is art completely nonmoral in character? Can a work of art be good or evil?

One of the most interesting questions that arises in aesthetics, however, concerns the nature of aesthetic judgment. That question is: Exactly what is one saying if one says that a work of art is good, or fair, or poor? This is the question that we shall be discussing in this section.

Clearly, there are some who claim special expertise in making such judgments—for example, art and music critics. Museums stake millions of dollars on the claim that some paintings and sculpture are significantly better than others. Symphony orchestras persist in playing the music of Mozart and Beethoven, Brahms and Tschaikowsky, but seem singularly disinterested in performing the latest exercises of beginning harmony students. Why? Are there some identifiable qualities present in some works of art that make them objectively better than some other works of art in which those qualities are not present? If so, what are those qualities, and how are they known? That is the issue we will be concerned with, here.

Let us call the quality by virtue of which something is said to be a work of art "aesthetic value." Let us then say that one work of art, A, is better than another work of art, B, provided that A possesses this aesthetic quality to a greater degree than does B. In addition, let us call one who claims the ability to assess such value (whether that individual is an art critic, a curator of a museum, or simply a private citizen) an "aesthetic valuator." Our problem might then be stated this way: Is it possible for an aesthetic valuator to know that something has aesthetic value, and if so, precisely what is it that that person knows?

Works of Art

It will be helpful for our further discussion of this problem if we make a distinction between (a) a purported work of art and (b) an acknowledged work of art. A *purported* work of art is something (anything) that is alleged by someone (anyone) to have aesthetic value. An *acknowledged* work of art is something (anything) that is generally regarded to have aesthetic value. Thus, a given object might, in accordance with these definitions, be successively (a) an object not regarded as a work of art (because no one claims that it has aesthetic value), (b) a purported work of art (because someone now claims that it has aesthetic value), and finally (c) an acknowledged work of art (because it comes to be generally regarded as having aesthetic value).

Theoretically, anything whatsoever that is created by a human being could be alleged by someone to have aesthetic value and to be, therefore, at least a purported work of art. Practically speaking, however, it is the products of the *fine* arts that are normally alleged to have aesthetic value. In the discussion that follows, therefore, we shall limit ourselves to examples drawn from the fine arts.

Within the fine arts one may distinguish two broad classes, namely, the visual arts and the performing arts. The visual arts include painting, sculpture, architecture, photography, print-making—all the art forms that attempt to create static (that is, unchanging) objects whose principal or only value is the aesthetic quality that they are alleged to possess. The principal performing arts are music, drama, and dance —art forms, it will be noted, whose "end product" in each case is not a static object but a "performance" of some sort by one or more human beings.

Literature seems to be in a class by itself: it is neither a visual art nor a performing art.

Note that in the case of the visual arts there is what might be called a direct relationship between the original artist and the individual who admires or appreciates the product of the artist's efforts, whereas in the case of the performing arts, a performer or group of performers stands between the original artist and the admirer/appreciator of that work. If I view Rembrandt's "Simeon" or Munch's "The Sick Child," the only human beings necessarily involved in the transaction are Rembrandt and myself, Munch and myself, the painter and the viewer. A picture, one might say, is its own performance. It is quite different, however, with a symphony, a play, an opera, or a ballet. In these cases, what the original artist has created is essentially a set of instructions for performers, and without their cooperation the work of art is not complete. The Bachs and Mozarts and Shakespeares of the world are, therefore, dependent on such people as conductors, singers, instrumentalists, actors, and numerous other people in a way that has no exact parallel in the visual arts.

The products of the performing arts share with those of the visual arts the important characteristic that their principal reason for being is their alleged aesthetic value. Their reason for being is not primarily to provide employment for curators or musicians, nor to adorn the walls of the homes of millionaires, nor to provide long-term capital gains for investors—although they may do all these things—but solely to embody the aesthetic value that they are alleged or acknowledged to have. Any other value that a work of art may have—monetary, decorative, or whatever—is quite incidental to the principal value by virtue of which it is said to be a work of art, that is, its aesthetic value. Aesthetic value has no essential relation to utility.

The moment one conceives of an object being created for some purpose other than to embody aesthetic value, one moves from the realm of the fine arts to that of the applied arts. We tend to speak of the practitioners of the applied arts as artisans or craftsmen rather than artists, but this distinction is not absolute. Indeed, one can imagine varying degrees of concern for aesthetic value on the one hand and utility on the other, and one can readily think of objects that one is tempted to call "works of art" notwithstanding the practical uses that the designers clearly had in mind in designing them. One thinks, for example, of such things as fine china or crystal, oriental rugs, some furniture, stained glass windows, even musical instruments. Indeed, the aesthetic value of some objects may, in time, come to predominate to such an extent that the object is no longer used for its utilitarian purpose, but is "put on display" as a work of art. This is clearly what is happening when people hang their oriental rugs on the wall, put their china and crystal on the mantle—and serve their guests on paper plates.

Theories of Aesthetic Judgment

Theories with respect to the nature of aesthetic judgment fall into two broad classes: objectivist theories and subjectivist theories. Objectivist theories hold that a statement claiming that something has aesthetic value is a factual assertion, a claim that the object in question has such and such a quality or group of qualities that justify the ascription of aesthetic value. Subjectivist theories hold that statements about aesthetic value are merely reports of the private preferences of some individual or group of individuals.

According to one type of objectivist theory, the assertion that something has aesthetic value is equivalent to the assertion that it is beautiful, and the assertion that it is beautiful is held to mean that it possesses in some degree the nonnatural quality "beauty." This view is called *aesthetic intuitionism,* and is described and defended in Chapter 52.

In direct and radical opposition to aesthetic intuitionism is a view known as *private subjectivism.* According to this view, the assertion that something has aesthetic value is merely an expression of the personal preference of the person making the assertion. Thus the statement, "The ceiling of the Sistine Chapel is a great work of art," is not, in fact, a statement about the ceiling of the Sistine Chapel. Rather, it is a statement about the aesthetic preferences of the person making the statement. It means, roughly, "I experience pleasure in viewing the ceiling of the Sistine Chapel." This view is the subject of Chapter 53.

Between intuitionism and private subjectivism lie a number of theories that might be (and in some cases have been) put forth as solutions to our problem. Consider the following simple diagram:

Objectivist Theories	Mixed Theories	Subjectivist Theories
A	B	C	D

If position A represents aesthetic intuitionism, and position D represents private subjectivism, one can readily see that a number of alternatives remain. Along the line AB would lie all the theories that hold that aesthetic judgments consist in the assertion that the object in question has such and such qualities—unity, coherence, originality, structure, balance, or whatever may be asserted to be the objective criteria of aesthetic excellence. Along the line CD would lie the theories that hold that aesthetic judgments consist merely in reports of the preferences of some individual or group of individuals—art/music historians, art/music critics, the artists themselves, or whoever. And along the line BC would lie the theories that find both objective and subjective elements in all aesthetic judgments.

The final chapter of this section will set forth one such "mixed" theory. According to this theory, the assertion that something has aesthetic value is indeed a claim that it has certain objective qualities (and to that extent it is an objectivist theory), but the fact that these particular qualities, rather than some other qualities, are appropriate criteria of aesthetic value is said to be related to the fact that we human beings are made the way we are. This view of aesthetic judgments is called *objective relativism* or the *cultivated taste* theory.

Thus, we have before us three theories regarding the status of aesthetic judgments: aesthetic intuitionism, private subjectivism, and objective relativism (the cultivated taste theory). Let us see what may be said in support of each.

STUDY QUESTIONS

1. Define the following terms: aesthetics; aesthetic value; aesthetic valuator; purported work of art; acknowledged work of art; visual arts; performing arts; fine arts; applied arts.
2. What, exactly, is the problem of aesthetic judgment? What do you think is the prevailing opinion on this matter? What is your opinion at the present time? What reasons can you offer in support of your opinion?
3. "A picture ... is its own performance" (p. 387). Is this true? Do the people who arrange an art show, for example, play a role similar to that of a performer of a play or a piece of music? Do poems require "performers"?
4. Explain the difference between objectivist and subjectivist views regarding the nature of aesthetic judgment. Does your own view on this question tend toward objectivism or toward subjectivism? Does it make sense to say that aesthetic judgment is partly objective and partly subjective?

52

AESTHETIC JUDGMENT AS THE DISCERNMENT OF BEAUTY

I ask each reader to call to mind a work of art that he or she greatly admires. Let it be a painting, a piece of sculpture, a poem, a musical composition—anything you wish so long as (a) you are quite familiar with it, (b) you consider it a work of art, and (c) you admire it greatly. I also ask you to keep that object clearly in mind as we proceed with our discussion.

With respect to the work of art that you are now contemplating, I ask: What makes it a work of art? Surely, it is clear that not every painting, not every piece of sculpture, not every poem, not every musical composition is worthy of being called a work of art. What is it, then, that qualifies some objects to be so designated? What distinguishes fine painting from doodling, sculpture from three-dimensional junk, poetry from doggerel, music from noise? That, in plain language, is the question that we are seeking to answer.

My answer is that an object is a work of art by virtue of the fact that it is beautiful, and to say that it is beautiful is to say that it possesses the quality of beauty. "Beauty" is the correct name for that which, in the preceding chapter, was called "aesthetic value," that is, the value by virtue of which an object is a work of art. The beauty of any beautiful object *is* its aesthetic value, and aesthetic value is greater or smaller in precisely the degree to which the object is more or less beautiful.

Beauty

What, then, is beauty? My answer is that *beauty* is beauty, and nothing else. Beauty is what it is: it is itself. It consists in no color or combination of colors, no shape or combination of shapes, no sound or combination of sounds: it is itself, unique, *sui generis*. That in which it is present is beautiful, that in which it is not present is not beautiful. It is as simple as that.

Beauty is that which all beautiful things have in common—landscapes, sunsets, paintings, poems, songs, symphonies, statues, cathedrals. Indeed, it is in all probability the *only* quality that these diverse objects have in common. Be that as it may, however, it is clear that it is by virtue of their possession of the quality of beauty that these things are said to be beautiful; and that, at the moment, is all that I am attempting to establish.

The status of beauty is like that of moral goodness (see Chapter 47): it is a simple, indefinable, nonnatural quality. Because it is simple— because it is one thing and not many—I cannot clarify the concept for you by specifying its constituent parts. Since it has no constituent parts, I cannot define it for you. And since it is nonnatural, that is, nonempirical, I cannot even point to it (as I can, for example, to redness, or smoothness, or oblongness) and say, "There, that is the quality that I am talking about."

Nonetheless, I wish to argue that beauty is a real existent, an objective reality in the world, and that it does not depend for its existence upon the perceptions or feelings of any percipient. So long as there are sunsets and birdsongs and starry skies, so long as Michelangelo's *Pieta* and Bach's *B Minor Mass* and Leonardo da Vinci's *Mona Lisa* continue to exist, beauty will continue to exist among us—whether or not we are able to recognize its presence. Beauty is a real quality of beautiful objects, as real as their shape, color, texture, size, weight, or temperature. It is the presence of beauty in an object, and that alone, that makes it possible to speak truly when we say, "That is beautiful."

The Discernment of Beauty

Unlike shape, color, texture, size, weight, or temperature, however, beauty cannot be perceived by our senses. We see shapes and colors and patterns, but we do not see beauty. We hear pitches and timbres, melodies and harmonies, but we do not hear beauty. Beauty is not the sort of thing that can be seen, heard, tasted, touched, or smelled— though objects in which beauty is present may, indeed, be sensed in all these ways.

How, then, do we discern the presence of beauty? Directly, by what is called *intuition*. The judgment that something is beautiful is a synthetic truth that is known a priori (see Chapter 4). We view a painting or a piece of sculpture, we observe a landscape, we listen to a musical performance, and—with the eyes and ears of the soul, so to speak—we discern the presence of beauty. It is this discernment that is expressed in the judgment, "It is beautiful."

Think, now, about the work of art that I asked you to call to mind at the beginning of this essay. Is it not true that it is in virtue of its *beauty* that you call it a work of art? And is it not also true that its beauty, while not unrelated to its observable (or, in the case of music, audible) characteristics, is something over and above those characteristics? Let us assume that the work of art that you have in mind is a painting. The painting, then, has certain observable characteristics: certain colors, a certain composition, a certain measure of lifelikeness, and so on. Moreover, it has a certain subject matter, a certain shape, and a certain size. All these things are observable. But the *beauty* of the picture, in what does it consist? In these characteristics? No. Its beauty is something else that exists in, with, and under these observable characteristics. It is this and this alone that makes it beautiful, this and this alone that gives it aesthetic value.

Now it may well be true—indeed, I think it is true—that beauty is normally accompanied by other characteristics that *are* empirically observable. In the visual arts, for example, beauty seems always or nearly always to be accompanied by such empirical qualities as unity, balance, and proportion. In the case of music, it seems to me that beauty is normally accompanied by one or more of the following: ordered structure, grace of melody, harmonic complexity, ultimate resolution (the piece comes to a recognizable end). And yet, beauty is not simply the sum of these characteristics. A kindergarten child might accidentally produce a picture having all the characteristics itemized above—unity, balance, proportion—and still the picture might be utterly devoid of beauty. A Rembrandt painting might lack one or more of these characteristics and still be a thing of undoubted beauty.

Thus, in making judgments of aesthetic value it is, in the last analysis, the presence or absence of beauty itself that determines whether our judgments are true or false. In making such judgments, we may be right or we may be wrong, our judgment may be correct or it may be mistaken. In asserting that something is beautiful, we are asserting that something is the case.

In Support of Intuitionism

In support of this theory of aesthetic judgment, I offer the following considerations. First, I submit that there is an obvious and recognizable difference between the mature work of any artist and the halting efforts of an amateur in the same field, and that virtually any normal observer is able to make the judgment that the work of the former is aesthetically superior to that of the latter. Listen, if you will, to a recording of any composition of Mozart, and compare this with a series of random notes picked out by a child experimenting on the piano. The Mozart, I am saying, is immediately recognizable by anyone who is not tone deaf as being musically superior to—objectively better than—the child's "accidental composition." Or gaze for a few moments at a Rembrandt painting—*any* Rembrandt painting—and compare it with the latest efforts of the entire kindergarten class at the local public school: surely, it is evident that the Rembrandt is infinitely superior *in aesthetic value* to the work of the children—however much we might admire the latter for its innocence, spontaneity, or other nonaesthetic qualities.

Now if it is true that we can and do make judgments of this sort when the contrast in aesthetic value is obvious, as in the examples cited above, it follows that (a) the judgement is, indeed, about an objective fact (is the object in question beautiful, or is it not?), and (b) one should, with effort, be able to develop the capacity to make such judgments to the point where one is able to make them in cases where the contrast is not so obvious. Just as a physician, by learning what to look for and what to pay attention to, can perfect the art of diagnosing illnesses, so the lover of art can with study and practice learn to discern the presence of beauty in the works of art that he or she contemplates.

Second, the very fact that we use words like "beauty" and "beautiful" in reference to objects as diverse as poems, paintings, statues, buildings, symphonies, and sunsets suggests that there is a single quality—beauty—that is present in all of them. Just as the class of red things consists of all the entities in the world that have the quality of redness, and the class of liquid things consists of all the entities in the world having the quality of liquidity, so the class of beautiful things consists of all the entities in the world having the quality of beauty. If this were not so, why would we describe them all as beautiful?

Third, it is to be noted that, over a period of time, those who give themselves most fully to the study of works of art do, in fact, come to substantial agreement regarding the varying degrees of aesthetic value of the various works. Now, to be sure, this agreement is not unanimous. We are dealing here with a matter of judgment, not one of scientific measurement, and in such matters absolute unanimity can rarely be achieved. But there is substantial agreement concerning the aesthetic merit of a large proportion of extant purported works of art. Moreover, such disagreement as there is can be readily explained as the result of (a) varying degrees of skill in making aesthetic judgments (compare the varying skills of physicians in making diagnoses), and (b) varying degrees of care being given by different valuators to particular works or groups of works concerning which they offer a judgment.

Finally, I submit that it is absurd to suppose that all art critics, music critics, and museum curators are merely imposters, self-styled experts who, in fact, have no expertise to justify the judgments that they make. And yet, if aesthetic value—beauty—is not a quality in the object judged to be beautiful, that is just what they are: imposters. For what is the alternative? It is that their alleged opinions about this "priceless" work of art, this "fine" performance, this "excellent" com-

position are nothing more than expressions of their private preferences masquerading as objective judgments. And why should a
museum pay a large sum of money for a picture or a statue that the
curator, for no objective reason, just happens to like? Instead, why does
the museum not round up a few unemployed bartenders and bricklay-
ers, supply them with canvas, paint, and brushes, and let *them* paint
some pictures for the museum? The reason is obvious: because the
trustees of the museum are wise enough to know that there are objective differences in the aesthetic quality of paintings, and that people
trained as curators are, among other things, more expert in judging
such quality than are those who do not have such training. As C. I.
Lewis says,

> "There are those who are especially to be relied upon for judgment,
> because they have a greater breadth of pertinent experience, and per-
> haps some higher degree of the requisite powers of discernment . . . Their
> judgment may stand as against any number of contrary votes gathered
> indiscriminately, because it is something objective which is judged, and
> not something relative to the particular and perhaps undiscerning expe-
> rience."[1]

To sum up: aesthetic value is an objective quality in all works of art.
The quality by virtue of which a work of art has aesthetic value is
beauty. Beauty, however, is a nonempirical quality, a quality that must
be rationally discerned (otherwise it remains unperceived). To say
that a work of art is good is to judge that it possesses the quality of
beauty in an eminent degree. To make such a judgment is to make a
factual assertion, an assertion that is either true or false. To discern
the presence of beauty in a work of art is to acquire knowledge of a
matter of fact, and thus to add to one's total fund of knowledge about
the world. Such is the view of the nature of aesthetic judgment to
which one is led by a careful consideration of the marvelous fact that
we do sometimes speak truly when we say of something, "It is beautiful."

STUDY QUESTIONS

1. Is it correct to say that beauty is the distinguishing characteristic
   of a work of art? Is it beauty, and only beauty, that gives an object
   aesthetic value?
2. "Beauty is that which all beautiful things have in common" (p.
   391). Do you agree? If not, why, in your opinion, do we use the same
   word—beautiful—to describe objects as diverse as paintings, symphonies, and sunsets?

---

[1]C. I. Lewis, *An Analysis of Knowledge and Valuation* (La Salle, Ill.: Open Court
Publishing Co., 1946), p. 460.

3. What do you think of the view that beauty is "a simple, indefinable, nonnatural quality" (p. 391) that can be known only through a direct "intuition"? Why?

4. Intuitionist asks you to call to mind some work of art with which you are familiar, then poses this question: In what does the *beauty* of that work of art consist? How would you answer his question?

5. Summarize and criticize Intuitionist's arguments in support of his theory.

53

AESTHETIC JUDGMENT
AS PRIVATE PREFERENCE

Intuitionist's account of aesthetic judgment, which is neatly summed up in his concluding paragraph, is as mistaken as a theory can be. None of the following assertions is true: (a) that beauty is a quality objectively present in things described as beautiful, (b) that beauty is simple, indefinable, and nonempirical, or (c) that one can add to one's fund of knowledge about the world by discerning the presence of beauty in works of art. I shall argue, on the contrary, that the statement that an object has aesthetic value is nothing more nor less than an expression of the private preference of the person making the statement. Moreover, such statements are, in principle, incapable of being justified by reference to any qualities—observed or unobserved —of the object about which the statement is ostensibly made. Indeed, such statements cannot be justified at all.

Aesthetic Value: A Closer Look

A work of art may be valued in many ways that have nothing to do with its aesthetic value. Much confusion in aesthetic theory results from a failure to distinguish between and among these several kinds of value. Let us identify them in order that we may isolate and thus, hopefully, see more clearly what we are talking about when we say of something that it has *aesthetic* value.

Note, first, that a work of art may be valued for its *antiquity*. This is certainly a part of what we value when we observe and admire, for example, the vases and other artifacts found in the tomb of the Egyptian King Tutankhamen, or the paintings on the walls of ancient caves. Whether or not we judge a given artifact to be beautiful, we feel something akin to reverence for it if we believe it to be the product of the labors of someone who lived many hundred or thousands of years ago. Let us call this "the halo of antiquity" as it affects our judgments concerning works of art.

Second, a work of art may be valued for the evidence that it gives of the skill or patience of the artist in producing it. We may, for example, admire a "life-like" portrait simply for its life-likeness, even though the portrait may be of someone whom we regard as very homely. We may admire the apparent skill with which the artist has painted, say, a cape or a piece of drapery so that it looks like real velvet —whether or not we judge the total painting to be beautiful in any ordinary sense of the word. Let us call this "the halo of the master craftsman."

Third, a work of art may be valued because it was produced by someone who is historically important for reasons unrelated to his or her role as the producer of this or any other work of art. Thus, we might value a painting by Winston Churchill or Dwight Eisenhower, a poem by the young John F. Kennedy, or a piano piece composed by Harry Truman, no matter what we might think of these works on purely aesthetic grounds. Let us call this kind of value "the halo of historical significance."

Fourth, a work of art may be valued because it is believed to have been produced by someone who has acquired a reputation as a "great artist." Such is, undeniably, one of the values adhering to a musical composition attributed to Bach or Mozart, a piece of sculpture believed to have been created by Michelangelo or Rodin, a painting thought to have been done by Raphael or Van Gogh. In each case, it is possible that the attribution to the "great" artist is mistaken, or that the work itself, though genuine, is one that the artist cast aside as an unsuccessful effort. But no matter: in the case that we are now considering, it is the artist whom we are admiring, not the art, and our admiration is likely to continue so long as we continue to regard the work of art as coming from the hand of the master. Let us call this "the halo of the big name."

Fifth, a work of art may be valued because of its economic worth, its "market" value. If we know that an art gallery has recently acquired a certain painting for a price of, say, $1 million, we may be so awed by the *price* of the painting that we are inclined to view it primarily in economic terms. Let us call this "the halo of a million dollars."

Surely, it is clear that the aesthetic value of a work of art does not consist in any of the aforementioned "halo" values. In what, then, does it consist? My answer is that it consists simply and entirely in the fact that the person asserting the aesthetic value finds pleasure in perceiving the object in question. Aesthetic value is relative to the individual perceiver, and an object has aesthetic value for a given perceiver to the extent that the perception of it is experienced as pleasurable by that perceiver. We may value a work of art in a variety of ways, but we value it *aesthetically* only when and to the extent that we value it because of the pleasure that we find in the perception of it.

It is to be noted that the pleasure of which we are now speaking is a very special kind of pleasure, namely, that which results from the perception of an aesthetic object. This kind of pleasure differs from bodily pleasures in that its locus is in the object that we are perceiving, not in the part of the body through which the perception comes to us. The pleasure of a cool shower or of a good wine is plainly physical: the pleasure is experienced as a sensation affecting one's skin or one's palate. With aesthetic pleasure, this is not the case. It is, to be sure, *via* one's eyes and ears that one perceives the aesthetic object, but one's pleasure is in the object, not in the organ through which the object is perceived. This is undoubtedly the reason why the pleasure of aesthetic appreciation is universally regarded as being somehow higher, finer, more "spiritual," than other pleasures.

The reason that beauty cannot be perceived, then, is not that it is a nonempirical quality, but rather that it is not a quality at all. We do not perceive it for the very good reason that it is not there to be perceived.

Critique of Intuitionism

Intuitionist has offered several arguments in support of his view that judgments of aesthetic value are judgments based on the discernment of beauty as a nonempirical quality present in the aesthetic object. Let us review these arguments in the light of the foregoing discussion.

With respect to his first argument, it seems clear that the "obvious and recognizable difference between the mature work of any artist and the halting efforts of an amateur" (p. 392) is to be understood primarily as a difference in *craftsman* skill, not a difference in the aesthetic value of the respective products. People who study painting, sculpting, composition, and the like acquire certain skills that people who have not studied these things do not have. Moreover, it appears to be the case that there are differential aptitudes for acquiring the requisite skills. Thus, it is not surprising that a Mozart, who evidently had exceptional musical ability as well as musical training that began in early childhood, should have produced works reflecting craftmanship skills vastly exceeding those of an untutored amateur. Nor, for comparable reasons, is it surprising that Rembrandt should have exhibited in his paintings skills of craftmanship infinitely greater than someone who had neither his talent nor his training. Intuitionist has mistaken "the halo of the master craftsman," and perhaps also "the halo of the big name," for aesthetic value. If one looks beyond the halos, all that remains is the subjective preference of some individual or individuals for one pattern of sounds or colors rather than another.

If, as I affirm, the assertion that an object is beautiful is to be construed as a report that one finds pleasure in the perception of that object, it is not at all surprising that the word is applied to "objects as diverse as poems, paintings, statues, buildings, symphonies, and sunsets" (p. 393). Indeed, on my theory, one would expect anything and everything that gives pleasure through sight or sound to be so described, and this is precisely what happens. Thus, Intuitionist's second argument is, in actuality, a powerful confirmation of the subjectivist view.

The fact that an approximate consensus concerning the relative merits of various works of art develops over a period of time does not uniquely support the intuitionist view. First, it seems highly likely that the consensus frequently has to do with things other than aesthetic value: the multiple halo effect is undoubtedly at work here as well. Second, insofar as there is a consensus with respect to aesthetic value, it is readily explainable simply as similarity in taste rather than as an objective superiority in the object being judged.

Intuitionist's final argument—that the rejection of intuitionism carries with it the absurd consequence that critics and curators are imposters "who, in fact, have no expertise to justify the judgments that they make"—rests on a misunderstanding of the proper role of both critics and curators. The expertise that one can reasonably expect of a critic or a curator is not expertise in making aesthetic judgments (how could one possibly measure that?), but rather the kind of historical and technical knowledge that can help to direct our attention to features of the works in question that may enhance our understanding and appreciation of them. To be sure, critics and curators do not always acknowledge this limitation. Some of them, I admit, speak and write as if they have some kind of superior insight regarding what is "really good" in the way of art or music. Of such critics it is true to say, as one philosopher has said, that "their equipment in the main consists of what the French call a well-hung tongue,—or pen; and the very ease and abundance of their adjectives hide the fact that what they say is neither important nor authoritative."[1] The subjectivist theory does, indeed, imply that every person's judgment (that is, taste) is as valid as everyone else's, but it does not imply that there is no legitimate role for the critic to play. It implies only that that role cannot be to tell us what works of art we *ought to like.* By directing our attention to certain features of the work that our untutored eye or ear might otherwise fail to note, however, the critic may, in fact, alter our perception of the work in such a way that we find pleasure in it whereas previously we did not. The critic helps us, as we say, to "see it in a different light."

---

[1]C. J. Ducasse, *Philosophy of Art* (New York: Dial Press, 1929), p. 6.

The Case for Subjectivism

The principal and, in my opinion, decisive consideration in favor of the subjectivist view is that when people disagree with respect to a question of aesthetic value there is, in principle, no way to resolve the disagreement. If I like Bach and you prefer the Beatles, there is no referee to whom we can turn to tell us who is "right" and who is "wrong." We have different tastes, different preferences, and that is the end of the matter. In matters of taste there are no experts, and preferences in art are purely and simply matters of taste.

Each of us may find further confirmation of the subjectivist view in the fact that our own tastes tend to change over a period of time. I happen to have a great fondness for classical music, and my tastes today are such that I remember almost with shame that I once preferred Tschaikovsky and Johann Strauss to Vivaldi, Bach, Beethoven, and Mozart. Why "almost with shame"? Because, I suppose, I would like to think that my tastes in music have "improved" or "matured" through the years. Such, however, is not the case. They have simply changed. My current preferences are neither better nor worse than my former ones: they are different, and that is all. And who knows? Perhaps I shall one day abandon my current loves and return to "The Nutcracker Suite" and "Tales of the Vienna Woods."

I want to mention two practical consequences of the subjectivist view, and then I shall conclude. The first is that it is utterly pointless to *argue* about the comparative merits of this or that particular work of art or type of art. In aesthetic matters the ultimate rule is: to each his own. One should, presumably, enjoy one's own preferences in a way that does not impinge unduly on others, but that is a matter of ethics, not of aesthetics. And second, the fact that aesthetic tastes vary so widely suggests the possibility that, with effort, one's own tastes might be broadened to include a much richer variety of works of art than one is able to appreciate at the present time. Most of us, I am afraid, are extremely conservative in the realm of art: we tend to stick with that with which we are already familiar—or, at most, with that which is admired by those whose approval we desire. The subjectivist view of aesthetic judgment, which acknowledges the equal validity of all aesthetic preferences, implicitly encourages the continual expansion of one's tastes as one explores the wonderful variety of sights and sounds that may give pleasure to eye and ear.

STUDY QUESTIONS

1. Subjectivist asserts that "We may value a work of art in a variety of ways" (p. 398). List them. Is he right about this? If so, does this fact count against Intuitionist's view, or in support of Subjectivist's view?

2. Where, exactly, does Subjectivist locate aesthetic value? According to his theory, what does it mean to say that something is beautiful?

3. How does Subjectivist distinguish between "aesthetic" pleasure and "bodily" pleasure? Is this a defensible distinction?
4. Review Intuitionist's arguments in support of intuitionism, and summarize Subjectivist's replies to each argument. Does Subjectivist succeed in refuting all of Intuitionist's argument?
5. Subjectivist claims that there is one "decisive consideration in favor of the subjectivist view" (p. 400). What is this consideration? Is it decisive?
6. What practical consequences does Subjectivist draw from his view? Do these consequences indeed follow from his view regarding the nature of aesthetic judgment?

54

AESTHETIC JUDGMENT
AS CULTIVATED TASTE

Subjectivist has neglected to mention what I think is the most decisive argument against intuitionism in aesthetics, and that is what I shall call the "noncomparability of beauty" argument. If beauty were, indeed, what Intuitionist says it is—a simple, nonempirical quality present in varying degrees in beautiful objects—then it should be possible to make meaningful (albeit not necessarily true) comparisons with respect to beauty between any two objects judged to be beautiful. Thus, it should be meaningful, if not indeed common-place, to make statements like "Mozart's *Jupiter Symphony* is more beautiful than the *Mona Lisa*," or "The Cathedral in Florence is more beautiful than Michelangelo's *David,* but Sibelius's *Swan of Tuonela* is more beautiful than either." Now, we clearly do not make statements of this kind, and the fact that we do not do so seems to me to be absolutely fatal to intuitionism. Beauty is not a single quality present in varying degrees in poems, symphonies, and sunsets.

But neither, I think, has the last word been spoken about aesthetic judgment when it is said that such judgment is, in essence, a report of the pleasure that we experience in the perception of an aesthetic object. Indeed, the "noncomparability of beauty" argument applies with almost equal force against subjectivism, for, according to this view, it should be commonplace to say things like, "I prefer Bach to Rodin, and Van Gogh to T. S. Eliot, but none of them can hold a candle to the sunset I saw last evening." If the assertion that an object is beautiful means only that perception of the object is pleasurable, and if (as I assume that Subjectivist would allow) pleasure varies in degree, such statements should be a part of the normal, everyday language of aesthetic appreciation—but they are not. *Ergo*, aesthetic judgment is not satisfactorily explained simply as a report that one finds pleasure in the perception of the object.

Further Critique of Subjectivism

The proposition that the aesthetic value of a work of art consists in the pleasure that it gives to some perceiver is untenable on other grounds as well.

First, not all pleasure that one may experience in the perception of an object can plausibly be said to be aesthetic appreciation. The pleasure that constitutes aesthetic appreciation, Subjectivist says, is "that which results from the perception of an aesthetic object" (p. 402). But what is an aesthetic object? According to Subjectivist's principles it can only be an object the perception of which gives pleasure of some particular kind. To avoid circularity, Subjectivist needs an independent criterion for the identification of this kind of pleasure, and he attempts to supply this when he says that aesthetic pleasure "differs from bodily pleasures in that its locus is in the object that we are perceiving, not in the part of the body through which the perception comes to us" (p. 398). But this clearly will not do. A given perceiver might find pleasure in a certain landscape, for example, merely because it reminds him of the area in which he spent a happy childhood, and such pleasure—though it fits Subjectivist's definition of aesthetic pleasure—would hardly qualify as aesthetic appreciation. Again, a particular perceiver might find pleasure in looking at pictures or statues of nude bodies because of the sexual fantasies that they arouse, and this—though it appears to fit Subjectivist's definition of aesthetic pleasure—is clearly not a part of what we normally mean by the *aesthetic* appreciation of an object.

On the other hand, there are many instances of undoubted aesthetic appreciation in which the subjective experience of the viewer or listener could hardly be described as one of pleasure. It would be odd, for example, to say that one finds pleasure in looking at a painting depicting the crucifixion of Christ. Yet, we do find aesthetic value in some such paintings—those, for example, of Grünewald and Perugino—and view them with admiration and appreciation. Numerous other examples come to mind: Picasso's *Guernica*, Munch's *The Cry*, Van Gogh's *The Starry Night*, to name but a few.

Where the Issue Stands

Where do these considerations leave us with respect to the issue of the nature of aesthetic judgment? Consider, first, the aesthetic object, that is, the object that is said to have aesthetic value. We rejected the intuitionist account of aesthetic value because, contrary to what we would expect if intuitionism were true, we cannot and do not make comparisons with respect to beauty between aesthetic objects of different types. We do not say that this painting is more or less beautiful than that symphony, that this piece of sculpture is more or less beautiful than that sunset. But we do make such comparisons between aesthetic objects *of the same type*. We say things like, "Yes, this is, indeed, a lovely sunset, but last evening's sunset was even more beautiful," or "The music of Vivaldi certainly is marvelous, but that of Bach is even more so." Now what this clearly suggests is that in some way or other we are comparing the object in question with an ideal standard for objects of that type. We are, so to speak, "grading" the object in question on the basis of how adequately it measures up to the criteria that we deem appropriate for judging objects of that type. We may or may not be able to articulate those criteria—that is another matter entirely —but the very fact that we make comparisons between aesthetic objects of the same type demonstrates that we do, indeed, employ such criteria. That we sometimes give reasons in support of such comparisons (for example, "Note the richness of the bass line in Bach as compared with Vivaldi," or "Compare the eyes in a Rembrandt portrait with those in the portraits of even the best of his contemporaries") further illustrates this important point.

Moreover, it seems clear that the criteria in terms of which we judge various types of aesthetic objects cannot be correctly described simply as criteria of *beauty*. Some aesthetic objects are valued because they are said to be moving, disturbing, or thought-provoking, others because they are humorous, realistic, or true to life. Beauty in its several forms may well be the principal concept in terms of which we judge the aesthetic value of works of art, but it is not the only one.

Turning now to the aesthetic valuator—the person making the aesthetic judgment—our critique of subjectivism has made it clear that aesthetic judgment does not consist simply in a report that one finds a certain kind of pleasure in perceiving the object in question. Just as all works of art having aesthetic value are not beautiful, so also are all experiences of aesthetic appreciation not necessarily experiences of pleasure. There is, it would appear, a range of moods or emotions on the part of the valuator that is as diverse as the objects judged: one may, depending on the object, experience sorrow, revulsion, pity, or any number of things other than pleasure.

It is evident, therefore, that aesthetic judgment is much more complex than either Intuitionist or Subjectivist has comprehended. We are dealing here not with one objective quality but with many, not with one single emotion on the part of the valuator but with a range of emotions. An adequate theory of aesthetic judgment must accommodate this inescapable complexity.

Objective Relativism

The view of aesthetic judgment that I believe is most adequate to the relevant facts is known as *objective relativism*—or, in less technical terms, the cultivated taste theory. I shall attempt, in the balance of this essay, to show how this theory solves the problems that led us to reject the previous two theories.

According to objective relativism, every instance of aesthetic judgment involves both objective and subjective elements. An object must have certain characteristics in order to be a candidate for aesthetic appreciation, and the perception of the object must result in an experience of a specifiable kind in order for the statement "This object has aesthetic value" to be true.

Let us consider first the subjective side of this relationship, that is, the experience of the aesthetic valuator. The inclusive name for this experience is *aesthetic appreciation*. The distinguishing features of aesthetic appreciation—the characteristics that mark it off from every other kind of human experience—are (a) that it involves visual or aural perception, (b) that the perception is valued in and for itself, and (c) that the perception is believed by the percipient to be caused by some entity "out there," namely, the aesthetic object. Whenever we have an experience in which these three characteristics are present, we have an instance of aesthetic appreciation. Wherever any one of them is lacking, what remains is something other than aesthetic appreciation.

What, then, is an aesthetic judgment? It is a statement attributing to an object the power to cause this kind of experience. It is, therefore, a statement *about the object*, not a statement about the experience of the person perceiving the object. If one affirms, for example, that Titian's *The Assumption of the Madonna* is a beautiful painting, one is making a statement about Titian's painting, not about one's experience of the painting. Moreover, one may be able to give reasons for calling it a beautiful painting—its brilliant color, the symmetrical balance created by the placement of the three dominant figures, and so on. An aesthetic judgment, therefore, may also be described as a statement ascribing to some object the qualities by virtue of which it is allegedly capable of producing, in some human percipients, an experience of aesthetic appreciation. This is true, incidentally, even if (as often happens) one is unable to identify the precise features of a painting or other aesthetic object that give it this remarkable power.

Does this account, then, not make aesthetic value relative to human capacity for aesthetic appreciation? Yes. Is it not, then, just another form of subjectivism? No! For human capacity for aesthetic appreciation is, to a large extent, determined by our physiological and psychological makeup—in other words, by human nature. Painters, sculptors, architects, composers, are not merely "expressing themselves" in their work: they are seeking the shapes, the color combinations, the textures, the sounds the perception of which will be experienced as having intrinsic value. The process of artistic creation, to the extent that it is successful, is, at one and the same time, a process of discovery.

It is an important implication of the view here presented that it is possible to have "good taste" or " bad taste" with respect to one's preferences in works of art. The music of Mozart is objectively better than a series of notes picked out at random on the piano, and the reason for its objective superiority is that it is more suited to the human capacity for aesthetic appreciation. The genius of a Mozart, a Rembrandt, a Michelangelo, a Frank Lloyd Wright is that each was able to discern more clearly than his fellows the exact nature of the human capacity for aesthetic appreciation, and to create the works of art—the music, the paintings, the sculpture, the buildings—that correspond thereto.

Who, then, are the people of "good taste" among us, whose lead we presumably ought to follow in aesthetic matters? Unfortunately, it is impossible to say. The only available criterion is the judgment of history: the cumulative judgment of those who care enough about aesthetic value to devote time and effort to the study and enjoyment of works of art. A lover of music is more likely to be a qualified judge of musical quality than a casual listener, a lover of painting a more qualified judge of such works than someone who has never visited an art gallery. Happily, it is the lovers of art in its various forms who, for the most part, determine what is to be preserved for the enjoyment of future generations. One need not hold that they are infallible judges of aesthetic value in order to believe that their selections are more valid than those that would result if the selection were left to chance, or—what might be even worse—if they were made on the basis of a popular referendum.

The assertion that an object has aesthetic value is, then, a kind of prediction—a prediction, namely, that given an opportunity people who care about works of art of this kind will experience aesthetic appreciation in the perception of it. If in general they do not—if concert-goers over a reasonable span of time find a given piece of music trite, uninteresting, unmelodic, unstructured, repetitious, and so on— then the prediction was in that case incorrect, and might well be withdrawn by the person making it. If, in general, people who care do find aesthetic value where it was predicted that they would, then the prediction is verified and the good taste of the person making it is vindicated. Beyond this, I think, one cannot go.

It probably is true that one cannot ultimately resolve disagreements about aesthetic merit, since there is evidently no way to establish that one party to the dispute has "better taste" than another. One's only credentials for making aesthetic judgments are that one cares about the type of object in question, one has attended to the characteristics of many exemplars of works of this type, and one has made one's judgment in terms of the same criteria that one applies to all other works of that type. If people with similar credentials still disagree, the only thing that remains for them to do is to continue to attend to the work of art in question, to continue to test the prediction of those who pronounce it good, and trust that over a period of time a consensus will emerge.

Subjectivist concludes his essay by encouraging "the continual expansion of [our] tastes" as we explore "the wonderful variety of sights and sounds that may give pleasure to eye and ear" (p. 400). Whatever one may think of this advice, it seems to me infinitely more important that we attempt to *refine* and *deepen* our taste rather than simply to expand it. The ultimate reward that awaits us in the realm of aesthetic appreciation is not the series of superficial thrills that we might get by rushing willy-nilly from one object to the next. The ultimate reward is the cultivation of one's taste, the refinement of one's sense of aesthetic value to such a point that one is able to make judgments about such matters with an inner confidence that one's opinion will be substantiated by the judgment of history.

STUDY QUESTIONS

1. What does Objective Relativist (hereafter OR) offer as the "decisive argument against intuitionism in aesthetics" (p. 402)? Is it decisive? How might Intuitionist defend himself against this argument?
2. Summarize OR's arguments against Subjectivism. Can you think of any way that Subjectivist might defend his position against these arguments?
3. Is OR right in his assertion that in making aesthetic judgments we are "grading" the object in question in terms of criteria derived from some ideal standard?
4. Is he right in asserting that criteria of aesthetic value are not always criteria of *beauty*?
5. OR asserts that aesthetic judgment always involves both objective and subjective elements. What are they?
6. "[The] human capacity for aesthetic appreciation is to a large extent determined by our physiological and psychological makeup" (p. 405). What does this mean?
7. What, according to OR, constitute "good taste" and "bad taste" in aesthetics? Can it be determined whether a particular aesthetic judgment represents one or the other? If so, how?
8. OR recommends that we attempt to "refine and deepen our taste" with respect to works of art. What, exactly, does he mean by this? What specific steps might we take to follow his advice?

CORRELATED READINGS[1]

1. Plotinus. "The Essence of Beauty." *The Enneads,* trans. S. Mackenna, First Ennead, Tractate VI, Sections 1–3. Aesthetic intuitionism.
2. Santayana, George. "The Nature of Beauty." *The Sense of Beauty.* New York: Scribner, 1901, pp. 35–52. A subjectivist view.
3. Beardsley, Monroe C. "Can We Dispute About Tastes?" *Swarthmore College Bulletin,* LVI, 2, 1958, 1–5. A move toward objective relativism.
4. Aufhauser, Marcia Cavell. "Critical Dialogue." *The Journal of Philosophy,* Vol. 67 (1970), pp. 339–351. Another move toward objective relativism.

FOR FURTHER READING

Berenson, Bernard. *Aesthetics and History.* New York: Pantheon Books, 1948. See the "Conclusion" for an astonishing statement of the relativist position.

Bosanquet, Bernard. *Three Lectures on Aesthetics.* London: Macmillan, 1915. Includes an interesting discussion of an alleged distinction between "easy" beauty and "difficult" beauty.

Dewey, John. *Art as Experience.* New York: Capricorn Books, 1934. See especially Chap. XIII, "Criticism and Perception."

Diderot, Denis. "The Beautiful," in K. Aschenbrenner, and A. Isenberg (eds.). *Aesthetic Theories: Studies in The Philosophy of Art.* Englewood Cliffs, N.J.: Prentice-Hall, 1965, pp. 129–147. Includes an overview of the aesthetic theories of many writers from Plato to Francis Hutcheson.

Ducasse, C. J. *Philosophy of Art.* New York: Dial Press, 1929. Chap. XV, "Standards of Criticism," gives a subjectivist account of aesthetic value.

Heyl, Bernard. *New Bearings in Esthetic and Art Criticism.* New Haven , Conn.: Yale University Press, 1943, pp. 125–155. A relativist account.

————. "Relativism Again," *Journal of Aesthetics and Art Criticism,* 5 (1946), 54–61. A further elaboration and defense of the relativist position.

Hume, David. *Of the Standard of Taste and Other Essays,* ed. J. W. Lenz. Indianapolis, Ind.: Bobbs-Merrill, 1965. A famous statement of relativism by a philosopher best known for his writings on other subjects (notably epistemology).

Hutcheson, Francis. *An Inquiry Into the Origins of Our Ideas of Beauty and Virtues,* 1725. An early examination of many of the issues still being discussed by writers on aesthetics.

Jeffrey, Francis. "Essay on Beauty," in K. Aschenbrenner and A. Isenberg (eds.). Aesthetic Theories: Studies in the Philosophy of Art. Englewood Ciffs, N.J.: Prentice-Hall, 1965, pp. 277–294. A widely read statement of the subjectivist theory.

Joad, C. E. M. *Matter, Life and Value*. London: Oxford University Press, 1929, pp. 266–283. An intuitionist account that owes much to Plato.

Kant, Immanuel. *The Critique of Judgment*, 1790. An analysis of the beautiful and the sublime. For patient readers only!

Lewis, C. I. *An Analysis of Knowledge and Valuation*. La Salle, Ill.: Open Court Publishing Co., 1946. See Chap. XV, "The Esthetic Judgment." An objectivist view.

Moore, G. E. "The Ideal," in *Principia Ethica*. New York: Cambridge University Press, 1959 (paperbound). A famous and lucid statement of the objectivist view.

Ogden, C.K., I. A. Richards, and J. Wood. *The Foundations of Aesthetics*. London: Allen and Unwin, 1922. Includes a discussion of no less than sixteen definitions of beauty.

Osborne, Harold. *Aesthetics and Criticism*. New York: Philosophical Library, 1955. See Chap. XI, which is concerned with the role of the critic.

Pepper, Stephen C. *The Work of Art*. Bloomington: Indiana University Press, 1955. See Chap. 2, "Can a Judgment of Beauty be True?" The author argues that it can.

Plato. *Greater Hippias*. Many editions. A light-hearted but inconclusive dialogue that seeks an answer to the question, What is beauty?

Plotinus. "Beauty," in *The Enneads*, First Ennead, Tractate VI, trans. Stephen McKenna, rev. B. S. Page. New York: Pantheon Books, 1956, pp. 56–64. *The Enneads* are a collection of treatises written by Plotinus at various times during his life (A. D. 205–270).

Santayana, George. *Reason in Art*. New York: Scribner, 1905. See especially Chap. X, "The Criterion of Taste, " pp. 191–215.

————. "The Nature of Beauty," in *The Sense of Beauty*. New York: Scribner, 1936 (originally published in 1892). An earlier formulation by the same author.

Vivas, Eliseo. "The Objective Basis of Criticism," in *Creation and Discovery*. New York: Noonday Press, 1955, pp. 191–206. Defends a nonintuitionist form of objectivism.

Weitz, Morris. *Philosophy of the Arts*, pp. 191–204. Cambridge, Mass.: Harvard University Press, 1950. A critique of subjectivism from the perspective of what the author calls the "organic" theory.

PART XIII

WORLD VIEWS

55

THE FUNDAMENTAL PROBLEM

When we first set out on this study of philosophy, we observed that the positive goal of the philosopher is to construct a picture of reality in which every element of human knowledge and experience might find its proper place. Philosophy, we said, is humanity's quest for the unity of knowledge: it consists in a perpetual struggle to create the concepts in which the universe can be conceived as a *uni*verse, not a *multi*verse. The history of philosophy, then, is the history of humanity's search for an adequate world view. The problems of philosophy are the problems that arise as we pursue this quest.

We can say, therefore, that the fundamental problem of all philosophy, the one that underlies and ties together all the problems that we have been considering thus far, is the problem of world views. Which "total view" of reality is most adequte to the known facts? What are the foundational truths about reality in relation to which everything else that we can know needs to be understood?

The reader who has worked his or her way through any significant number of the problems dealt with in the preceding pages will surely have become aware of the fact that these problems are interrelated in a variety of ways. The relations that obtain among these various problems are, of course, *logical* relations: if we embrace a given position on one problem, we may be logically prevented from adopting certain positions or logically obliged to adopt a certain position on some other problem. We hope that the positions we hold on various problems are, at least, consistent with each other: that is a minimum requirement that all of us must seek to satisfy. If we look carefully at the various positions that we have taken on the problems considered, we should be able to discern the outlines of a world view that might be called "our philosophy."

How Philosophical Problems are Interrelated

Let us explore by means of a few examples some of the logical interrelationships between and among philosophical problems. Suppose, for example, that on the problem of freedom and authority (Chapters 35–39) I adopt the natural-law theory. Then I cannot—if I am to be consistent—accept empiricism, for this would exclude the possibility of having any knowledge of natural law (in the sense intended by the defenders of the natural-law theory). Hence, I must be a rationalist. And if I am a rationalist, then certain options are open to me on other philosophical problems—intuitionism in metaethics (Chapter 47), a belief in the possibility of proving the existence of God (Chapters 19–21), and so forth—that would not otherwise be open to me. If, on the other hand, I decide that on the rationalist-empiricist question I must take my stand on empiricism, then I am obliged to reject those views on other problems that presuppose a kind of knowledge that as an empiricist I cannot acknowledge to be possible. Every position that we adopt on any particular question implies certain positions and excludes certain positions on countless other questions. This is what is meant when we speak about the systematic character of all philosophical thinking and the multidimensional relevance of all philosophical questions.

To the extent that we engage seriously and honestly in the study of philosophy, we become involved in what might be called a systematic clarification of our world view and a systematic testing of this world view by means of a rigorous evaluation of certain of its elements. There is more at stake in the answer that we give to this or that philosophical problem than the resolution of that particular problem. Indeed, as we remarked earlier, every philosophical problem is a kind of test case for an entire world view. The serious study of philosophy thus requires great intellectual courage.

World Views

At the center of every world view is what might be called the "touchstone proposition" of that world view, a proposition that is held to be *the* fundamental truth about reality and that serves as a criterion to determine which other propositions may or may not count as candidates for belief. If a given proposition p is seen to be inconsistent with the touchstone proposition of one's world view, then so long as one holds that world view, proposition p must be regarded as false.

One important feature of a world view, then, is that it serves as an intellectual framework for all attempts at understanding. So long as one experiences nothing that cannot be satisfactorily accounted for within one's world view, one will presumably continue to hold it without question. If, however, one is confronted with some phenomenon that cannot be thus assimilated—if reality gives the lie to the world view one has espoused—then one has no honest choice but to modify one's world view in such a way as to allow for the troublesome new fact.

Suppose, now, that as the holder of a certain world view one encounters some fact that one cannot incorporate into it, and suppose further that one is unable to think of any way to modify that world view to accommodate the new fact. What are one's options? One may retain that world view and acknowledge that an unresolved problem exists, or one may abandon that world view altogether in favor of another that appears more adequate to the facts as one perceives them.

Alternative World Views

There is, of course, no theoretical limit to the number of world views that might be developed. The world as we experience it is a sufficiently complicated affair to support (with varying degrees of plausibility) a rather wide variety of them. Therefore, we cannot hope to be exhaustive in our classification of alternative world views. At best, we can list the types that are regarded as the major options by most educated and informed people at the present time.

Ethical theism is probably the most widely held world view in the Western world, though it has undoubtedly lost some ground in the modern era. The touchstone proposition of ethical theism might be stated thus: God, who is infinitely good, wise, and powerful, is the creator and sustainer of everything that exists, and human beings are the crown of His creation. One form of this world view is presented in Chapter 56.

In contrast to ethical theism, and in perpetual conflict with it, stands *naturalism*. The touchstone proposition of naturalism might be stated as follows: The primary constituents of reality are material entities whose internal structures and external relations determine absolutely everything that happens in the world. This world view is further elaborated and defended in Chapter 57.

Some philosophers who have wrestled with the problem of world views have found themselves unable to accept either ethical theism or naturalism. They have adopted, instead, a world view called *transcendentalism*. Its touchstone proposition is difficult to state with precision, but a fair approximation would be as follows: There are dimensions of reality that are not a part of this spatiotemporal world that we perceive with our five senses (that is, there are dimensions of reality that "transcend" the natural world), and these transcendent dimensions of reality impinge upon human beings and their world in a variety of ways. A world view of this type is set forth in Chapter 58.

The fourth and last type of world view that we shall consider is *humanism,* which differs from the three world views previously mentioned in that it is, so to speak, less global. The touchstone proposition of humanism might be stated thus: Whatever may be the whole truth about nature, humanity, and God (if He exists), humanity, at least, is unique and not merely a part of nature. Humanism says, in effect, "Whatever view of the whole you choose to adopt, I insist that you preserve the dignity of human beings." Such a view is further elaborated and defended in Chapter 59.

It is evident that these four types of world views cannot be construed as straightforward alternative answers to a single substantive question, since, as a matter of fact, they are not even mutually exclusive. Humanism, for example, could ally itself with any of the other three world views, and has, in fact, done so in the thought of many philosophers. Blaise Pascal could be described as a theistic humanist, Jean Paul Sartre as a naturalistic humanist, and Paul Tillich as a transcendentalistic humanist. World views may be more or less comprehensive and may be worked out in greater or lesser detail: what they have in common is that they are organized around some truth claim that the holders of the respective world views take to be *the* fundamental truth about reality. A world view is a basic intellectual stance, a way of trying to comprehend the totality of things.

Arguments About World Views

How can anyone argue for or against—or even think intelligently about—a world view? What kinds of arguments can reasonably be brought forward to support the claim that this world view is right, or that one wrong? The answer is that in discussing the preceding problems, we have already been arguing for and against various world views. Insofar as a given philosophical problem is logically related to the world views question, any argument that arises in the course of the discussion of that problem is thereby a discussion of world views as well. Indeed, confrontations between the proponents of conflicting world views most commonly occur, not in the direct and overt way that we shall observe in the chapters that follow, but rather as disagreements over subordinate issues on which they find themselves obliged to differ by virtue of their basic philosophical commitments.

If, however, the world views question is explicitly under discussion, several kinds of arguments are open to the disputants. First, advocates of a given world view may appeal to certain facts or alleged facts that in their opinion favor their view. The range of facts to which appeal may be made in the discussion of this question is, of course, extremely broad. Second, participants in this debate may "go on the attack" and attempt to show that the views of their opponents are inadequate. A world view may be attacked in either of two ways: on grounds of *internal inconsistency* or on grounds of *factual error.* And third, holders of a particular world view may present rebuttal arguments (after attack or in recognition of points vulnerable to attack) to show that their view is not internally inconsistent or not guilty of factual error in the ways alleged.

These are the principal ways in which arguments may be employed in discussions about world views. Let us see what kind of case can be made for each of the world views enumerated above.

STUDY QUESTIONS

1. List the philosophical problems that you have studied thus far, and the positions that you have been inclined to take on each. Do you see any inconsistencies in the positions you have taken? Do you see any instances where your position on one problem logically compels you to adopt a certain position on some other problem?
2. List the positions that you have adopted on the problems studied thus far in order of decreasing certainty. (At the top of your list will be the position about which you feel most certain, at the bottom the position about which you feel least certain.) Assume that the position you have listed as "most certain" is correct. What implications does this have for the remaining positions on your list?
3. What exactly is a world view? Does everybody have one?
4. How would you describe the world view that you were given as a child? What, for example, would you say is the touchstone proposition of that world view? How, if at all, has that world view been modified to date?

56

ETHICAL THEISM

Most of my readers are no doubt aware that as an ethical theist I speak for one of the oldest and most widely held world views. Indeed, ethical theism is more than a world view: it is an attitude toward life, a sense of humanity's place in the scheme of things that is felt as well as thought. Many of the values that Western thought prizes most highly —the dignity of human beings, the sacredness of human life, the significance of the individual, the meaningfulness of history—derive from this world view and may be incapable of surviving apart from it. The question of the validity of this world view is, therefore, of great importance.

The Fuller View

Let me begin by sketching in some of the details of this world view. First, God exists: this is the fundamental truth from which all thought about reality should begin. I may or may not be able to prove God's existence—but God exists. My understanding of God's true nature may be ever so fragmentary—but God exists. I may be puzzled about the ontological status of the physical world, or about the nature of the self, or about many other things—but God exists. His existence is the elemental fact, the foundational truth from which thought begins and to which it must return whenever we are driven to inspect once again the foundations of the edifice of truth. God exists.

Everything else that exists—inanimate matter, life in all its forms, consciousness, intelligence, everything—has been created by God and is dependent on Him for its continued existence. I, of course, do not know the manner of God's creation. I do not know, for example, whether the "big bang" that apparently occurred some billions of years ago should be understood as "the moment of creation," or whether it is even correct to think of creation as an event that occurred at some moment in time. My point is simply that everything that we now see existing has its ground and origin in God: if He did not exist, nothing would exist.

God, having created this world that we perceive and of which we are a part, continues to love it and to care for it. The process of evolution, for example, despite the appearance of randomness, is in reality one of the arenas in which the marvelous creative activity of God may be discerned. The course of human history, notwithstanding the suffering and tragedy that are so inextricably a part of it, is not merely the story of humanity's halting efforts to emerge from the jungle and the cave: it is the story of God gently luring His human children toward a future in which His creation will achieve a richness that we cannot yet imagine.

Human beings, moreover, are in some sense the most glorious product of God's creation. That there should be anything at all—that matter should exist—is truly marvelous. That there should be life, organisms capable of nourishing and reproducing themselves, is more marvelous still. And that there should evolve out of these materials organisms that are conscious, organisms that are aware that they are, is a wonder almost beyond comprehension. But beyond even this, consider that among these conscious creatures one has emerged with a capacity for rational thought, speech, science, an appreciation for beauty, and a sense of right and wrong. Whatever may be in store for God's creation beyond this point, surely it is clear that it is through humanity that it will be accomplished.

Philosophical Implications

My theistic commitment provides the basic context within which I approach all philosophical problems. It also gives me a particular bias that makes certain philosophical positions attractive to me because they fit in so nicely with my theistic world view. I make no apology for this, however, since those who hold other world views are equally biased toward the philosophical opinions that favor their world views. We cannot avoid looking at the world through world view-colored glasses.

On the question of freedom and authority, for example, I am persuaded that some form of the natural-law theory is correct. To me, it seems virtually self-evident that if human beings were to rise above the law of the jungle, they had to grasp and cherish the concept of a human community ruled by just and humane laws. It seems altogether natural to me that God should desire the human species to achieve such a community, and that He should have guided human evolution in such a way that people would, at length, begin to discern the outlines of a law (already conceptualized in the mind of God) by which community might be achieved. The question of freedom and authority must, of course, be decided on the merits of the arguments for the alternative answers that may be given. My point is merely that within the context of my world view one of those answers is especially attractive, though I could adopt some other view without in any way violating my basic philosophical commitments.

Since space does not permit me to discuss in detail my position on all the problems raised in preceding sections, I shall have to be content merely to list my preferences. They are as follows:

Philosophical Problem	Preferences of an Ethical Theist
Rationalist-Empiricist Controversy	Rationalism
Problem of Induction	Rationalism
Realist-Phenomenalist Controversy	Direct Realism
Existence of God	Endorse cosmological argument
Problem of Evil	Exoneration of God
Mind-Body Problem	Dualism
Freedom and Determinism	Soft Determinism
Freedom and Authority	Natural Law Theory
The Highest Good	Theological Eudemonism
Language of Morals	Intuitionism
Aesthetic Judgment	Intuitionism

Please note that my theistic world view in no way obligates me to adopt these positions. Indeed, part of the attraction of theism is that it is an extremely "open" world view: a theist could, for example, be a hedonist in ethics, an empiricist in epistemology, and a phenomenalist with regard to the ontological status of the physical world. A naturalist, on the other hand, could not hold many of the views included in my list. Thus, far from shackling thought (as some people seem to think it does), theism actually enables consideration of alternatives that other world views will not allow.

There is, in fact, not a single position among all those surveyed in the preceding pages that I am *compelled* to adopt by virtue of the fact that I am a theist. Furthermore, among all those discussed, the only position that I am *excluded* from adopting, by virtue of the fact that I am a theist, is the one presented in Chapter 22—and that for the obvious reason that it denies the existence of God.

Why I Am a Theist

That theism maximizes a person's philosophical options does not, of course, constitute any kind of a proof that theism is true. What, then, can be said in support of this world view? Why am I a theist?

In dealing with this question, I do not wish to reopen the discussion of proofs for the existence of God. The question before us now concerns not the grounds for believing that God exists but, rather, the broader question of the reasons why we ought to adopt a theistic world view.

I hold, of course, that theism is adequate as a world view in the sense that there are no facts that contradict it, no phenomena that cannot be explained within its context. Thus, when I cite certain facts, I am directing attention to them merely because in my opinion they *uniquely* favor the theistic view. I would urge my readers to look carefully at the accounts that the representatives of other world views are forced to give of these same facts.

Theism provides the most plausible answer to the question, Why is there something and not nothing? That this particular object exists— a chair, let us say— is satisfactorily accounted for by the statement that it was made by a chairmaker. The existence of the wood out of which the chair was made is in turn explained by the laws governing the growth of trees (osmosis, photosynthesis, and so on) until, at length, what began as a tiny acorn has developed into a mature oak. But the elements that became a part of the oak (and eventually a part of the chair)—why should these exist? Or, given the fact that they exist in this moment, why do they not cease to exist in the next? Why does anything at all exist? According to theism, God created it and sustains it in being moment by moment. Only in the belief that God exists do I find an adequate answer to this inescapable question.

Consider next the place of humanity in the scheme of things. When I compare the endowments of human beings with those of any other creature, I cannot avoid the conclusion that we are not merely a species of animal, not merely a part of nature: by virtue of our capacity for rational thought, for language, for morality, and for the appreciation of beauty, we rise above nature. Say, if you will, that we are merely the winners of the grand prize in the evolutionary sweepstakes: I say that this was no accident, and that the aspirations that characterize the spiritual life of human beings point toward a destiny that lies beyond the confines of this life. Theism enables us to believe that these hunches about the nature and destiny of humankind are true, for it depicts us as the favorite of God's creatures, the crown of His creation.

Our intuitive sense of the seriousness of good and evil lends further support to the theistic view. I cannot take absolutely seriously a moral law that is nothing more than an expression of my private tastes, or those of my social subgroup, or of my nation, or even of the majority of humanity. The moral imperative, the injunction to do good and shun evil, is an infinitely serious matter. The seriousness of the moral law is satisfactorily accounted for only on the hypothesis that it is ultimately grounded in the will of God.

Finally, I am convinced that an acceptable philosophy of history cannot be developed apart from a theistic world view. What is the meaning of the struggles, the suffering, the tragedy with which the pages of human history are so distressingly replete? Toward what eventual goal is the story of humanity tending? How can people believe that their lives, their tiny contributions to the common life, have any significance?

Within the context of some world views, the answers to these questions are all too obvious: no meaning, no goal, no significance. Ethical theism, on the contrary, asserts that history is a meaningful process through which God is patiently and lovingly working out His purposes for His creation. Every moment of a person's life, every good or evil thought or word or deed, makes some contribution to the totality of events that constitute human history. Where this history is tending, or what will be the next significant milestone on the path toward that unknown goal, we do not know. But theists believe, nonetheless, that history is moving toward some *tèlos,* and that its progress toward that goal is being guided by God, Who will not abandon the creation that He loves.

There is in the heart of every individual, as Alfred North Whitehead once observed, an "insistent craving that zest for existence be refreshed by the ever-present, unfading importance of our immediate actions."[1] In the views that it enables us to take of humanity, morality, and human history, theism answers to this craving in the hearts of all of us. The facts that most strongly support the theistic world view are the specifically "human" facts—the facts by virtue of which we are able to aspire to a life and a destiny appropriate only for those who are children of God. We are most truly human when we understand ourselves in this way; apart from theism, we are swallowed up in the system of nature and become nothing more than the most fortunate of the beasts.

STUDY QUESTIONS

1. Summarize the basic tenets of ethical theism as expounded in this chapter.
2. Can Ethical Theist consistently hold all the positions he lists on page 420? Is he logically compelled to adopt any of these positions simply by virtue of being a theist?
3. Theist claims that the only position presented in the earlier portions of this book that he is *excluded* from adopting by virtue of being a theist is the "naturalistic rejoinder" of Chapter 22. Is he correct about this?
4. Summarize the arguments offered by Theist in support of his world view. Which do you find most persuasive? Which least persuasive?

---

[1]Alfred North Whitehead, *Process and Reality* (New York: Harper & Row, 1960), p. 533.

57

NATURALISM

A world view, in order to be judged acceptable, must meet three conditions. First, it must be *logically coherent:* it must be free of internal logical inconsistencies. Second, it must be *relevant:* it must provide a plausible interpretive scheme in terms of which at least some facts of our experience can be understood. And third, it must be *adequate to the known facts:* there must be no single fact or realm of facts that cannot be accounted for within the context of the proposed view. Every time a world view is put forward for consideration it is implicitly claimed that the proffered view meets these three conditions.

I admit that it is extraordinarily difficult to develop a view that simultaneously meets all three conditions. Theism, for example, despite its attractive (and, to humanity, highly flattering) account of morality and history, has always had to struggle—unsuccessfully, in my opinion—to maintain some semblance of logical coherence. The most dramatic illustration of this is theism's notorious failure to solve the problem of evil. Anyone who is not an apologist for theism can see that the fact that there is evil in the world is not consistent with the hypothesis that this world is the product of a creator who is perfect in goodness, power, and wisdom (see Chapter 26). Try as they will, the apologists for theism cannot account for the occurrence of evil in a way that is consistent with their world view. All the theodicies that have been written, all the arguments that have been so laboriously woven, have failed to meet the basic issue: if God is perfect in goodness, knowledge, and power, and is the sole creator of this world, then there cannot be evil in the world; if there is evil in the world (and who can deny it?), then this world is not the product of a God who is perfect in goodness, knowledge, and power.

It is not my intention, however, to develop a systematic critique of theism. I want, instead, to describe *naturalism* as an alternative world view and to indicate the most compelling reasons for adopting this view. It has been my observation that on the question of world views people are seldom persuaded by arguments as such: rather, they become bothered by the problem, wrestle with it for a while, perhaps leave it, and one day return to discover that some place along the way they have abandoned one view for another that is more coherent, relevant, and adequate.

A Brief Description

Naturalism asserts, first, that the primary constituents of reality are material entities. By this I do not mean that only material entities exist; I am not denying the reality—the real existence—of such things as hopes, plans, behavior, language, logical inferences, and so on. What I am asserting, however, is that anything that is real is, in the last analysis, explicable as a material entity or as a form or function or action of a material entity. Theism says, "In the beginning, God;" naturalism says, "In the beginning, matter." If the theoretical goal of science—an absolutely exhaustive knowledge of the natural world— were to be achieved, there would remain no reality of any other kind about which we might still be ignorant. The "ultimate realities," according to naturalism, are not the alleged objects of the inquiries of theologians; they are the entities that are the objects of investigation by chemists, physicists, and other scientists. To put the matter very simply: materialism is true.

Naturalism asserts, second, that what happens in the world is theoretically explicable without residue in terms of the internal structures and the external relations of these material entities. The world is, to use an inadequate metaphor, like a gigantic machine whose parts are so numerous and whose processes are so complex that we have, thus far, been able to achieve only a partial and fragmentary understanding of how it works. In principle, however, everything that occurs is ultimately explicable in terms of the properties and relations of the particles of which matter is composed. Once again, the point may be stated simply: determinism is true.

It follows from what I have said that the categories of space and time are categories of great importance of naturalism—are, in fact, ontological categories. If you cannot locate something in space and time, or if you cannot understand it as a form or function of some entity or entities located in space and time, then you simply cannot say anything intelligible about it. *To be is to be some place, some time.*

Naturalism, therefore, denies the existence of any real entities corresponding to such concepts as God, angel, devil, spirit, or soul (as these concepts are usually understood), because they are asserted by those who affirm their existence to be nonmaterial subjects of activities such as deciding, regretting, suffering, and so forth. But from the

point of view of naturalism, any activity must ultimately be understood as a process involving material entities and occurring within
space and time. Since the above concepts cannot be understood in this
way, naturalism must regard them as bogus concepts that purport to
denote some real entities but, in fact, denote nothing at all.

Unacceptable Philosophical Theories

From the point of view of naturalism, several of the philosophical
theories put forward in earlier sections of this book must be judged
unacceptable. This does not mean, of course, that naturalists simply
"rule out" these theories in advance. It means, on the contrary, that
they attend with special care to the arguments put forward in support
of these theories, for they know that their world view is at stake in the
argument. Naturalism is secure as a world hypothesis precisely because it has had to defend itself—and has done so successfully—on
many vital points. Anyone who has grasped the "vision of the whole"
that naturalism espouses will readily understand that a consistent
naturalism must, in the end, reject the following philosophical positions:

Philosophical Problem	Positions Unacceptable to Naturalism
Rationalist-Empiricist Controversy	Rationalism
Problem of Induction	Rationalism
Realist-Phenomenalist Controversy	Direct Realism
Existence of God	Any position implying belief in the existence of God
Problem of Evil	Exoneration of God
Mind-Body Problem	Dualism, panpsychism
Freedom and Determinism	Libertarianism
Freedom and Authority	Natural-Law or Social-Contract Theories
The Highest Good	Theological Eudemonism
Language of Morals	Intuitionism
Aesthetic Judgment	Intuitionism

Anyone who wishes to hold the world view that I represent must be
prepared to refute the arguments put forward in support of these
theories. As a naturalist, I am, of course, convinced that every such
argument can be convincingly refuted.

Why Naturalism?

Naturalists cannot point to certain facts about the world and say,
"These facts *uniquely* favor the naturalist world view." Our claim is

that *all* the known facts support the naturalist account of the world and that no facts warrant our asserting more than this. The evidence justifies our asserting that material entities exist and are involved in numerous processes that together give us the world as we encounter it in ordinary perception and scientific inquiry. But the evidence does not justify the assertion that any entities or processes exist other than material entities and the processes in which they participate. Naturalism is simply the modest claim that a generalized account of the world in terms of material entities and spatiotemporal processes is adequate to the known facts and will be adequate to explain any facts still to be discovered in the future.

Let me illustrate my point with a single example. The question, What causes the noise in the heavens that we call thunder? could lead to any number of explanatory hypotheses. One might be that the gods are angry and are having a fight. Another might be that God is scolding one of His angels. And yet another is that air is expanding rapidly as a result of being heated by a sudden discharge of electricity (lightning). The expansion-of-air hypothesis is, of course, a "naturalistic" explanation. It is more modest than the other two in that it does not require us to posit unobserved entities (God, gods, angels). It is, therefore, the *kind* of explanation that naturalism claims is possible in principle for all phenomena. Naturalism is simply the generalization of this explanatory model. "What can be explained by the assumption of fewer things is vainly explained by the assumption of more things" (William of Ockham).

In order to support the naturalist position, then, it is not necessary to construct independent arguments that supposedly "prove" naturalism to be true. It is necessary only to show that the phenomena that lead some thinkers to posit immaterial entities can be satisfactorily explained in a way that is consistent with naturalism. The only intelligent way to deal with people who make unwarranted assertions is to show that those assertions are indeed unwarranted. Let us look, then, at the considerations that have been advanced in support of a theistic world view.

It is not true that theism has an answer to the question, Why is there something and not nothing? whereas naturalism does not. The truth is that *no* world view is able to answer this question. All that theism does is move the question back one stage. To the question, Why does *God* exist? it has no answer. When we are dealing with the question of ultimate origins, we are forced to acknowledge that we have reached one of the boundaries of human knowledge. The only honest answer that we can give to the question, Why is there something and not nothing? is that we do not know. It adds nothing to our knowledge to pretend that by uttering the word "God" we have answered this unanswerable question.

Nor is it the case that naturalism is in any way demeaning to humanity, as our critics frequently suggest. I am sure that I am no less impressed than is Theist with the marvelous complexity of human beings and with the immeasurable richness of experience that is possible for them by virtue of their capacity for rational thought, language, morality, and the appreciation of beauty. How does asserting that humanity "rises above nature" add to this description? Why must I posit a divine "cheater" at the evolutionary gaming table in order to be properly appreciative of humanity's unique endowments? The evidence warrants the belief that life emerged from lifeless matter on this planet some millions of years ago, and that the various forms of life we now observe have evolved from earlier forms by means of processes that we understand reasonably well. The hypothesis of "God's love" or "God's plan" adds no more to this account than the hypothesis of "God's anger" adds to the account of thunder.

All that the evidence warrants us in asserting about humanity's place in the scheme of things is that human life as we know it is "an episode between two oblivions."[1] *Homo sapiens* emerged as one of the products of natural processes operating upon lifeless matter under conditions that made this emergence possible; there is every reason to believe that some day our species will cease to exist when these conditions no longer obtain. In the meantime, we have the task of making our life together on this planet as rich and meaningful as possible. Although naturalists can offer no divine forgiveness for the acts and omissions born of human frailty, and no future paradise for either the few or the many, we are no less concerned than our nonnaturalist fellows with the quality of life here and now. Indeed, since we know of no paradise apart from such approximations as we are able to achieve by our own efforts, we might even make some claim to being more deeply concerned about the human enterprise than are some who do not share our views. The rejection of a divine plan for humanity, the refusal to acknowledge eternal values in human affairs, in no way prohibits a tender concern for *human* plans, *human* values, and such *human* good as we are able to achieve in a universe that wills us neither good nor ill.

Where, Theist asks, is history tending? The answer is that it is tending ultimately toward the extinction of all life on this planet—not necessarily because of what people may do but because, in the long-range evolution of the cosmos, it appears inevitable that the conditions necessary for life on this planet will eventually cease to exist. For the next several millions of years, however, the history of the human race will be whatever we make it. We are the masters of our fate, the makers of our own history. The meaning of that history will be whatever meaning we give to it. Nothing is added to our understanding of history by positing a God-ordained *tèlos* in which all the problems with which we must contend at present will finally be resolved.

---

[1]Ernest Nagel, *Logic Without Metaphysics* (New York: Free Press of Glencoe, 1956), p. 14.

Human beings are, indeed, to use Theist's phrase, "the winners of the grand prize in the evolutionary sweepstakes." Their unique endowments have enabled them, in a short time relative to the life of the planet, to emerge from a beastlike existence into one that is infinitely rich both in its present qualities and in its potential for further improvement. If some choose to turn their backs upon the challenges and the opportunities of this life in quest of an imaginary kingdom of God, that is their privilege. The available evidence warrants only a belief in the reality of this material world of which we are undeniably a part. The tasks that are set for us by our situation in the world are those inherent in the human enterprise. They are tasks of sufficient magnitude and sufficient difficulty to keep us all occupied for many generations to come, and with this we must be content.

STUDY QUESTIONS

1. Naturalist asserts that an acceptable world view must meet three conditions. What are they? Do you agree that these are appropriate criteria to be used in judging a world view?
2. Is the problem of evil a serious problem for theists? How might a theist defend his or her position against Naturalist's charge that this problem represents an internal inconsistency that is fatal to theism?
3. Summarize the basic tenets of naturalism as they are presented in this chapter.
4. Naturalist presents a rather formidable list of philosophical positions that he says are inconsistent with naturalism. Identify the positions on this list with which you are acquainted, and explain in each case why that position is unacceptable to a naturalist.
5. "In order to support the naturalist position, then, it is not necessary to construct independent arguments that supposedly 'prove' naturalism to be true. It is necessary only to show that the phenomena that lead some thinkers to posit immaterial entities can be satisfactorily explained in a way that is consistent with naturalism." Is this correct? Could the holder of some other world view reasonably make a parallel claim?

58

TRANSCENDENTALISM

Many readers of the preceding two chapters will, I suspect, find themselves in the following dilemma. On the one hand, they cannot honestly embrace the naïve supernaturalism offered by Theist as the key to an adequate world view. On the other hand, they cannot escape the conviction that there is something more to human existence than Naturalist's account will allow. I propose to present an alternative view in which what is valid in both of these views can be retained.

Critique of Naturalism and Supernaturalism

Theist has presented a picture of a two-story universe, one part of which is perceivable by us and the other part of which is not. In the unseen part dwells God, who created the world at some moment in time and who continues to love and care for it. Indeed, He presumably interferes with its orderly operation from time to time (miracles), since He is said to have managed the evolutionary process in such a way that things turned out the way they did, and since He is also said to be guiding history toward some *tèlos* known only to Him. It is also consistent with this world view to hold (as does Theist) that this God has made provision for the eternal happiness of at least some of His human children.

It is apparent from Theist's arguments that he is chiefly concerned about what might be called the dignity of humanity, or better, the seriousness of human life. Theist cannot tolerate the view that human beings are merely "the most fortunate of the beasts," one species among many that have emerged in the evolutionary process. He seeks, therefore, to dignify human beings by making them the favorite children of a divine Creator, and by placing them into a historical process that is being guided toward some good end by this same Creator.

The chief difficulty with this view, however, is that, as Naturalist would say, the evidence does not warrant these beliefs. Natural processes are not interrupted from time to time by divine tinkering, nor is it credible that somewhere out in space—perhaps beyond our solar system—God, like a rich uncle in Australia, is watching the affairs of the world and doing what must be done to ensure that history moves in the desired direction. If we are required to choose between this view and naturalism, then intellectual honesty requires that we choose the naturalist view.

But naturalism is a bitter pill to swallow precisely because it does not take sufficiently seriously the hunger for meaning and the quest for human dignity that theism at least attempts to satisfy. Naturalism depicts human beings merely as exceedingly complex physical organisms, unique animals whose artistic, technological, and cultural creations are as much the products of nature as beaver dams, ant hills, and the nests of birds. The world that Naturalist depicts for us is beautiful in its orderliness and in its potentially perfect intelligibility —but its orderliness and intelligibility are purchased at the high price of banishing from the world those dimensions of reality that give significance to human life. Faced with the human consequences of such a view, we withdraw in horror and consider the possibility that our rejection of theism may have been a bit too hasty.

Nevertheless, no world view could claim the large number of adherents that both theism and naturalism have won if there were not a great quantity of truth in each of these views. Theism incorporates within itself some important and profound insights, some genuine truths about human beings and their world: that is why, despite the onslaught to which it has been subjected in the modern world, it has been able to maintain itself. Naturalism also contains within itself some extremely important elements of truth: that is why, despite the opposition of a firmly entrenched theism (in medieval Europe), it was able to make significant headway. The most important intellectual task of our times is that of creating a new synthesis in which the truth that is implicit in theism and the truth that is implicit in naturalism can be comprehended in one all-embracing vision of the whole. *Transcendentalism* claims to be that synthesis.

The Transcendentalist Vision

The fundamental insight of naturalism, without which no world view can ever be accounted adequate, is that in the attempt to know reality we must be completely honest in the face of the brute facts. The naturalist world view was born in a kind of revolt against what was regarded as the "arid intellectualism" of the prevailing world view (theism). Galileo's opponents could muster all kinds of reasons to show why the world ought to be the way they said it is: Galileo swept these reasons aside not by creating superior *arguments* but by appealing to the *facts*. Respect for the facts has become a part of the mentality of modern man. Insofar as naturalism stands for humility before the facts, it stands for truth.

Where, then, does naturalism go wrong? It goes wrong in assuming —indeed, in defiantly insisting—that these brute facts must be assimilated into a mechanistic, deterministic scheme in which there is no place for values, no place for purposes, and, really, no place for sentience and rationality. Naturalism appears to be haunted by the ghost of the Inquisition: it cannot forget that men who claimed to be God's representatives forced a man (Galileo), who was trying only to be honest before the facts, to say that he had abandoned the beliefs that he was driven by the facts to adopt. But it is not only God and His angels that are banished from the naturalist universe: human consciousness as an agent in the world is banished as well. The scientist who is also a philosophical naturalist is in the position of claiming to know so much about the world that he or she knows that the very act of knowing is merely a complex physical process involving the material entities of which his or her brain happens to be composed—and nothing else.

Transcendentalism affirms, on the contrary, that there is a dimension of *depth* in everything that exists, that the complete reality of the world is not apparent on the surface of things. Consider yourself. You are, of course, a collocation of atoms and molecules—material entities —that are governed by certain laws. Like every physical object, you have a certain weight, a certain size, a certain shape, a certain specific gravity, a certain temperature, and so on. You are also an animal organism: you are capable of nourishing yourself by assimilating nutrients from your environment, you are capable of locomotion, and so on. But you know that you are more than this: you are also a mind, a consciousness. Your being as a physical entity and as an organism is illuminated, so to speak, by the spirit that is within you, by the consciousness that you *are*. Deep within you, at a level of yourself that the objective observer cannot fathom, you are the bearer of hopes, fears, dreams, and aspirations that are as much a part of the reality that is you as are your height, your weight, your blood pressure, and whatever other "surface facts" anyone may care to mention. It is not without reason that the technique by which modern physicians of the soul seek to penetrate this dimension of the self is called "depth psychology."

What is true of us individually is true also of our collective life as a human community. There are, to be sure, "surface" elements in the history of any era: there are natural occurrences, fortuitous events, influential personalities, and numerous other kinds of "historical facts" to which historians of any age can point with good empirical consciences. But there is also a depth to history, a dimension of mean-

ing that lies beneath and behind the simple facts. Surely, it is significant that we commonly use metaphors of deep water when we speak
of history: we speak of the "currents" of history, the "tides" of history.
We know that what appears on the surface is but the troubled water
of a deep and lasting movement beneath the surface, in the depth of
our common life.

Transcendentalism affirms that there is also a dimension of depth
in things, and asks us to consider things with regard to that dimension.
Everything that exists is more than it appears to be, even as we ourselves and the historical events in which we participate are more than
we and they appear to be. Every finite thing points beyond itself to that
which is infinite, unconditioned, inexhaustible. That, in a word, is
what transcendentalism means.

The depth of our life and of our world is the source and ground of
nearly everything that is most meaningful to us. If we believe, for
example, in the true dignity and equality of man, and if we believe
that the struggle toward dignity and equality is one of the deep tides
of the history of our times, then we are affirming convictions that have
been nurtured not on the surface but in the depth of our souls and in
the depth of the history of our times. And if we believe these things
so passionately that we are willing to risk our own convenience and
perhaps our own safety in order to further this goal, and if in the
process we find that our lives are somehow enriched by those very
experiences that externally considered must be described as instances
of inconvenience or suffering, then we are demonstrating—at least to
ourselves—that we are living in the strength of that depth whose very
reality naturalism refuses to acknowledge.

The Truth in Theism

Theism knows that there is a depth in life, in history, and in the world,
but it attempts to give expression to this by means of a conceptual
scheme that has become ludicrous to most of us. "God" is the religious
name for this depth: that is what the word "God" really means. But
since it is impossible to use the term "God" without conjuring up the
image of a celestial superman who oversees the affairs of the world in
some mysterious way, perhaps it is best not to speak of God but to
speak instead of this depth to which theism, in its inner meaning, is
attempting to point the way.

Theism knows, too, of that union of the self with the deeper self that
we experience when we become committed to a cause that transcends
our own selfish interests—when we devote our efforts to the achievement of values that emerge from the depth of our selves and of our
history. The religious term for this union of the self with the deeper
self is "salvation." But since it is impossible to use this term without
suggesting an imagined future blissful existence rather than a quality
of life here and now, perhaps it is better that we also do not speak of

salvation but speak instead about the recovery of meaning, the redis-
covery of our depth, or the wholeness that we experience in the act of
dedicating ourselves to a cause in which we deeply believe.

Some Philosophical Implications

If we take seriously the dimension of depth in human life and in the
world, certain implications follow with respect to a wide variety of
philosophical problems. In the realm of ethics, for example, a transcendentalist holds that moral imperatives emerge from the depths of
our souls and of our common life—that they are, in fact, imperatives
that stand over us as laws only because and insofar as we are estranged from our own depth. The natural law to which natural-law
theorists point and the intuited good to which intuitionists point are
not strange entities floating aimlessly about in a kind of metaphysical
nonspace, waiting to be "intuited" by the discerning mind. They are
the voice of our own depth, the law of our own being, in obedience to
which we find the wholeness that forever eludes us on the surface of
our lives. There are, indeed, many intrinsic goods, but they are all
grounded in that depth without which our lives would be pitifully
shallow.

Space does not permit a detailed review of all the problems discussed in earlier sections or of my reasons for adopting certain positions on those problems. Briefly, then, let me simply state that I am a
libertarian with respect to the problem of freedom and determinism,
a dualist with respect to the mind-body problem, a rationalist in my
epistemology, a direct realist in my view of the ontological status of
the physical world, a "sympathetic appraiser" (Chapter 23) in my view
of the arguments for the existence of God, and an intuitionist in my
view of both moral judgment and aesthetic judgment. I do not say that
consistency *requires* me, as a transcendentalist, to hold these particular views on these problems. I do say, however, that on the basis of an
independent consideration of the arguments I find these to be the most
plausible positions to adopt with respect to these questions. Furthermore, as a transcendentalist, I find these views very attractive. Indeed,
the chief considerations that may be offered in support of the transcendentalist world view are precisely the considerations that tend to
establish the views stated above.

Let me conclude by making a terminological proposal. "Transcendentalism" is a generic term: it denotes not only the world view that
I represent but many others that are more or less similar to mine. In
order to distinguish my view from others that might with equal pro-
priety be called "transcendentalist," I propose calling the world view
I have presented *depth naturalism.* That name represents my position exactly: I want to take absolutely seriously the important truths
for which naturalism stands, but I want also to go beyond this to a
recovery of that infinite depth without which life becomes shallow
and devoid of meaning.

STUDY QUESTIONS

1. What does Transcendentalist find unacceptable about theism? about naturalism? Do you agree with his objections? How might Theist or Naturalist defend their respective positions against these objections?
2. Transcendentalist presents (p. 431) a theory of the self that is, he says, unacceptable to a naturalist. Is it? And, in your view, is this a plausible theory?
3. "But there is also a depth to history, a dimension of meaning that lies beneath and behind the simple facts." What does this mean? What do you think of this claim?
4. Transcendentalist lists a number of philosophical positions (libertarianism, rationalism, dualism, and so forth) that are especially attractive to him as a transcendentalist. What connections, if any, do you see between his commitment to transcendentalism and his espousal of each of these positions?
5. Transcendentalist proposes that his particular version of transcendentalism be called "depth naturalism." Does this seem to you to be an appropriate name for the world view he has described? Defend your answer.

59

HUMANISM

A world view is a way of trying to comprehend in one all-inclusive concept everything that we know and believe about the universe and our place in it. There is a wonderful grandeur in the very concept of a world view. Every such view is a monument to humanity's hunger for knowledge and security. I agree with the sentiment expressed by W. P. Montague:

> The distinctive glory of the human mind is its power to detach itself, not only from the *here* and *now* but from the *there* and *then* of existence, and bathe its tired memories in ideal waters. So it is that the great visions of philosophy, even if considered merely as visions, are precious and imperishable possessions of our culture.[1]

Theism, naturalism, and transcendentalism are some of the intellectual homes that people have constructed, sanctuaries within which they seek to escape the madness of the endless pluralism of experience. To some, they have not proved to be satisfactory. We who are in this situation, and who also have certain positive beliefs in common, call ourselves humanists.

The first thing to understand about humanists is that we are a miscellaneous lot. Some of us find our closest affinities with theists, others with naturalists, and yet others with transcendentalists. What we have in common is a vague dissatisfaction with all such world views, including whichever one each of us individually may happen

---

[1]William Pepperell Montague, *Great Visions of Philosophy* (LaSalle, Ill.: Open Court Publishing Co, 1959), p. 16.

to favor. We also share a firm determination that human values and human potentialities shall not get swallowed up in a system that either takes no account of human beings or that makes of them something less than they truly are. You may recall that Socrates protested when he was on trial for his life, "But the simple truth is, O Athenians, that I have nothing to do with physical speculations."[2] I think Socrates meant that he did not have time to speculate about the "big picture": he was completely absorbed in the effort to understand himself, to understand human existence. That task seemed so important to him that he had to devote his full attention to it.

Socrates' attitude describes rather precisely the situation in which humanists find themselves today. Humanism is not a fourth world view to set alongside the other three. Rather, it is a group of insights that must be incorporated into any world view if that world view is to be regarded as adequate. We stand for the dignity, the rights, and the freedom of human beings, and we are willing to get along with no world view at all rather than allow human beings to be squeezed into the categories of a hypothesis that robs them of that humanity.

A Positive Description

Let me state somewhat more precisely the basic convictions upon which humanists are united in defense of human dignity. First, we believe that human beings are not completely subject to the physical laws that appear to govern material particles. Therefore, we are libertarians on the problem of freedom and determinism, and we are firm and consistent in our opposition to determinism, whether it be offered in a theistic form (as proposed by Jonathan Edwards) or in a naturalistic form (as offered by most modern determinists). Human beings are free in a way that is not compatible with universal determinism.

It follows, therefore, that human beings are more than matter, more than complex physical organisms. "Mind," "soul," and "consciousness" denote real entities that make a difference in the world. Humanists, in spite of the well-known attendant difficulties, are for the most part dualists in their view of humanity (though some are panpsychists). The essential point is that human beings are not *merely* material entities.

Human beings, moreover, are fittingly subject to no moral imperatives other than those they prescribe for themselves. Humanity is answerable to humanity. Any law that people are counseled to obey that is not of their own making enslaves them and robs them of their dignity. For this reason, we reject all versions of the natural-law theory and favor the concept of law advocated by social utilitarianism (Chapter 38).

---

[2]Plato, *Apology,* in *The Dialogues of Plato,* trans. B. Jowett (New York: Random House, 1937), vol. I, p. 403.

It is important to the humanist view to assert that the future is to some extent open and undetermined, notwithstanding the extent to which the future is determined by natural and historical forces beyond human control. Human beings make history, they are not merely its helpless victims. What humanity shall become in the future depends primarily on what humanity choose to make of itself, not on what God or nature may have "programmed" humanity to become. William Ernest Henley (1849–1903) spoke for the entire human race when he said, "I am the master of my fate, I am captain of my soul."[3]

With these convictions clearly in mind, it should not be difficult to see why humanists are unable to fully embrace any of the world views presented thus far. Let us review them briefly.

Theism

From the point of view of humanism, the chief danger of theism is its implicit authoritarianism. If human beings are God's creatures, as theism asserts, then presumably they are as totally subject to the will of the Creator as is a pot to the potter: they have no capacity to stand up to the Power that made them and can, as easily, destroy them. Surely this is the view of the relationship between God and humanity that we find, for example, in the story of the flood:

> When the Lord saw that man had done much evil on earth and that his thoughts and inclinations were always evil, he was sorry that he had made man on earth, and he was grieved at heart. He said, "This race of men whom I have created, I will wipe them off the face of the earth . . . I am sorry that I ever made them."[4]

That there are humanistic elements in theism is, of course, true. Theism in its Judeo-Christian form, for example, speaks of God not only as a wrathful and jealous deity before whom human beings must cower in fear, but also as the loving Father who cares deeply for His children, and as the Good Shepherd who seeks and rescues lost sheep. But these elements, sad to say, have always been subordinate to the authoritarian elements in the theistic view. Historically, the Good Shepherd has been no match for the Grand Inquisitor.

There can be no doubt that theistic authoritarianism is destructive of humanity. In the intellectual sphere, for example, it tends to intimidate people in such a way that they are no longer free to follow an argument wherever it may lead, to seek the truth wherever it may be found. In the moral sphere, theism subjects people to an alien law: it requires ceremonies, rituals, and "good works" of various sorts that may or may not appear to them as morally worthwhile. People are

---

[3]William Ernest Henley, "Invictus," in R. B. Inglis, et al., *Adventures in English Literature* (New York: Harcourt, Brace, 1945), p. 726.

[4]Gen. 6:5–7.

counseled to think of themselves as creatures of little worth, as worms or as nothing. John Calvin expresses this exactly:

> We cannot think of ourselves as we ought to think without utterly despising everything that may be supposed an excellence in us. This humility is unfeigned submission of a mind overwhelmed with a weighty sense of its own misery and poverty; for such is the uniform description of it in the word of God.[5]

In this view people are nothing, God is everything. Any good that people may hope to achieve they must beg from the Celestial Artisan, who in His sovereignty may or may not respond, as He sees fit. "Humility," "sin," "rebellion," "self-abasement"—these are among the most prominent words in the vocabulary of theism. And it is these words that chiefly define how people are taught to think of themselves in the theistic system.

Naturalism

People fare little better in the naturalistic system, however, than in the theistic. As Bertrand Russell wrote in a famous essay: "Brief and powerless is man's life; on him and all his race the slow, sure doom falls pitiless and dark. Blind to good and evil, reckless of destruction, omnipotent matter rolls on its relentless way."[6] In such a world, as Transcendentalist has rightly discerned, it is impossible to find a place for all those things that are most precious to us as human beings. In a world where "omnipotent matter rolls on its relentless way" and where mind is, at best, an impotent epiphenomenon of material processes, the loftiest ideals and the noblest aspirations of the human spirit appear to dissolve into nothingness. What is the status of honor, courage, and the passion for truth in a world where nothing exists but the elemental particles of which matter is composed? How can human beings abide a world that makes a mockery of their conviction that they are, before everything else, conscious agents in the world, beings capable of doing deeds of worth and nobility?

Nor is it only the materialism of the naturalist view that is offensive to humanism: its determinism is equally unacceptable. Whatever difficulties there may be in understanding human freedom in relation to the lawlike regularity with which natural processes seem to occur, humanists will not acquiesce in the view that people are simply a part of nature, their actions as much a product of its workings as the ocean tides and the revolutions of the heavenly bodies. People are free. They can make a difference in the course of events—a difference that is not merely the inevitable product of the physical processes in which

---

[5]John Calvin, *Institutes of the Christian Religion* (Philadelphia: Presbyterian Board of Christian Education, 1928), p. 681.

[6]Bertrand Russell, "A Free Man's Worship," *Mysticism and Logic* (New York: Norton, 1929), p. 58.

"their" atoms will inevitably participate. The future is to a certain extent open and, as yet, undetermined. We have it within our power to put an end to all war—or to terminate all life by unleashing a holocaust that will engulf every living thing. We have it within our power to end poverty—or to perpetuate conditions that make it inevitable that millions of other human beings will live their entire lives as victims of malnutrition and attendant miseries. We have it within our power—*really within our power*—to change the course of history, to make a difference in the way the future unfolds. Naturalism, by virtue of its deterministic element, will not allow this.

Transcendentalism

A humanist's chief concern about transcendentalism is that it seems to be continually in danger of merely substituting the tyranny of the depth for the tyranny of God (theism) or the tyranny of physical laws (naturalism). For too long, people have been intimidated by laws that are not of their own making, laws that hold them in subjection, render them guilty, and stifle their humanity. Moral imperatives that arise "out of the depth," even if the depth is the depth of our own selves, are nonetheless "alien laws" with respect to the empirical self that is supposed to obey them. People in their sovereign freedom have the right not to be subjected to imperatives other than those that they prescribe for themselves. It is only in this way that their full freedom and dignity can be preserved and enhanced.

Conclusion

Where do these considerations leave us with respect to the quest for an adequate world view? They leave us free to continue the search without the fear that we may be seduced into adopting a view that robs us of our human dignity. In the defiant demand that the "big picture" allow full place to those convictions about humanity that we hold dear, we are, in effect, demanding that the whole truth, which at present we do not know, be consistent with the partial truth that even in our present state of knowledge we see clearly. The philosophical quest, whose ultimate goal is the achievement of a comprehensive view in which every element of truth and every aspect of experience shall find its proper place, is one of the most stupendous efforts of which human beings are capable. Humanism's contribution to this quest comes in the last analysis to just this: Those who pursue this quest, being human, should pursue it in such a way that they do not lose sight of humanity.

STUDY QUESTIONS

1. "Humanism is not a fourth world view to be set alongside the other three." Do you agree? Explain.

2. List the propositions that are offered by Humanist as "the basic convictions upon which [all] humanists are united." Are there any with which you disagree? Would Theist disagree with any? Naturalist? Transcendentalist?
3. What does Humanist find objectionable in theism? in naturalism? in transcendentalism? With which of his criticisms do you agree, and with which do you disagree?
4. Does humanism seem to you to have anything to contribute to the quest for an adequate world view? Explain.

CORRELATED READINGS[1]

1. Augustine of Hippo, St. "The Earthly and the Heavenly Cities." *The City of God,* Book XIV, Chaps. 1, 28; Book XIX, Chaps. 13, 17. A beautiful statement of a theistic world view.

2. Nagel, Ernest. "Naturalism Reconsidered." *Proceedings and Addresses of the American Philosophical Association,* Vol. XXVIII (1955), pp. 5–17. A compact summary of the essentials of the naturalist view.

3. Tillich, Paul. "Realism and Faith." *The Protestant Era.* Chicago: University of Chicago Press, 1957, pp. 66–82. An attempt to mediate between theism and naturalism.

4. Sartre, Jean-Paul. "Existentialist Humanism." An outspoken affirmation of one form of humanism by an important twentieth-century philosopher.

FOR FURTHER READING

Boyce Gibson, A. *Theism and Empiricism.* London: SCM Press, 1970.

Britton, Karl. *Philosophy and the Meaning of Life.* Cambridge, Eng.: Cambridge University Press, 1969.

Edman, Irwin. *Four Ways of Philosophy.* New York: Henry Holt, 1947.

Ewing, A. C. *Value and Reality: The Philosophical Case for Theism.* New York: Humanities Press, 1973.

Feigl, Herbert, "Logical Empiricism," in Dagobert D. Runes (ed.). *Twentieth Century Philosophy.* New York: Philosophical Library, 1943. Reviews several philosophical problems from the point of view of a contemporary naturalist.

Flew, Antony. *God and Philosophy.* London: Hutchinson, 1966. Detailed critique of arguments for theism.

Hick, John. *God and the Universe of Faiths: Essays in the Philosophy of Religion.* New York: St. Martin's Press, 1974.

Krikorian, Yervant H. (ed.). *Naturalism and the Human Spirit.* New York: Columbia University Press, 1944.

Kurtz, Paul. *The Fullness of Life.* New York: Horizon Press, 1974. A Humanist reflects on the good life.

Lamprecht, S. P. *The Metaphysics of Naturalism.* New York: Appleton-Century-Crofts, 1967.

Maritain, Jacques. *Existence and the Existent,* trans. by Lewis Galantiere and Gerald B. Phelan. Garden City, N.Y.: Image Books, 1956 (paperbound). See Chap. 5, "Ecce in Pace." Representative of what might be called a "Christian humanist" point of view.

Mitchell, B. *The Justification of Religious Belief.* London: Macmillan, 1973.

---

[1]*Concise Readings in Philosophy,* Part XIII.

Montague, W. P. *The Chances of Surviving Death,* Cambridge, Mass.: Harvard University Press, 1934.

Niebuhr, Reinhold. *Beyond Tragedy.* New York: Scribner, 1937. A collection of essays by a modern theist.

Otto, M. C. *The Human Enterprise.* New York: Appleton-Century-Crofts, 1940.

Pepper, Stephen C. *World Hypotheses.* Berkeley and Los Angeles: University of California Press, 1942. For patient readers only!

Russell, Bertrand. "A Free Man's Worship," *Mysticism and Logic.* New York: Norton, 1929, pp. 46–58. A famous delineation of the naturalist position.

Sorley, W. R. *Moral Values and the Idea of God.* 3rd ed. New York: Macmillan, 1924. See especially Chaps. 18 and 19 for an interesting discussion of some of the problems implicit in the theistic view.

Stace, W. T. "Man Against Darkness." First published in the September 1948 issue of *The Atlantic Monthly* and in several anthologies since. A rather despairing account of the naturalist position.

Whitehead, Alfred North. *Process and Reality.* New York: Harper & Row, 1960 (originally published in 1929). See Part I, Chap. 1, "Speculative Philosophy."

PART XIV

PHILOSOPHIES OF LIFE

60

THE IDEA OF A PHILOSOPHY OF LIFE

Albert Schweitzer (1875–1965) will undoubtedly be remembered for generations to come as one of the most gifted and remarkable men who ever lived. A brilliant student of many disciplines (he did significant work in philosophy, theology, music, and medicine), Schweitzer decided at an early age to give up the pleasures of life in his native Germany in order to serve as a medical missionary at Lambarene in French Equatorial Africa (now Gabon). During the half century that he lived and worked in Lambarene, Schweitzer developed a large hospital and clinic where he attempted to serve the needs of thousands who previously were without medical care. He also continued to write on a variety of subjects that were of interest to him, and he was the recipient of numerous honors (including the 1952 Nobel peace prize) as a result of his humanitarian and scholarly endeavors.

Let us suppose that at some time during his illustrious life we had had an opportunity to put to Dr. Schweitzer the following question: "Sir, what is your *philosophy of life*?" What, exactly, would we have been asking for? What might the eminent doctor have said that would count as an answer to our question? What *is* a philosophy of life?

"I Believe"

It would certainly have been to the point of our question if Dr. Schweitzer had responded by saying, "I believe that all life is sacred, and that every human being has a duty to preserve life, to promote life, to raise to its highest value life which is capable of development . . ."[1] In asking someone for his or her philosophy of life, we are asking that person to state his or her creed, his or her answers to the most fundamental questions that can be asked about human existence.

The distinguishing feature of a belief that belongs to someone's philosophy of life, then, is that it is perceived by its holder to have significant relevance for the way human life ought to be lived. Given his philosophy of life, it made sense for Albert Schweitzer to spend the greater part of his adult life in a foreign land attempting to serve the medical needs of people who otherwise would have been without such care. From the point of view of someone who has a very different philosophy of life, however—one, for example, in which it is maintained that "in this dog-eat-dog world it is everyone for himself"— Schweitzer might well be regarded as a fool who "threw away his life" and received nothing in return. The beliefs that constitute one's philosophy of life are more than propositions to which one gives intellectual assent: they are propositions to which one assents with one's life —that is, by acting in ways that are consistent with those beliefs. One's philosophy of life consists of those beliefs about life that are exhibited in the pattern of one's life.

Let us look more closely at those "fundamental questions" about human life that we spoke of just a moment ago, the answers to which constitute one's philosophy of life.

Humanity's Place in the Universe

One of the questions that a philosophy of life addresses is, What is the nature of humanity? or, What is humanity's place in the universe? Against the background of our recent discussion of world views, we can readily identify some of the answers that might be given. Human beings are children of God, uniquely loved by Him; as such, they are candidates for eternal life (ethical theism). Human beings are products of nature; they are high-level animals whose present endowments are the unplanned result of a blind evolutionary process (naturalism). Human beings are citizens of two worlds—children of nature who, nonetheless, transcend nature (transcendentalism). Human beings are unique; that uniqueness demands that they resist being swallowed up in any system that threatens to deny their freedom and their responsibility for their own destinies (humanism).

This question about the nature of humanity, or about humanity's place in the universe, marks the point where one's philosophy of life is connected to one's world view. Every philosophy of life presupposes a world view that is consistent with the beliefs that are constitutive of

[1]Albert Schweitzer, *Out of My Life and Thought* (New York and Toronto: Mentor Books; originally published 1933), p. 126.

that philosophy of life. Inevitably, therefore, a significant change in one's world view has important implications for one's philosophy of life (and vice versa).

It does not appear to be the case, however, that for any world view there is one and only one philosophy of life that is consistent with that world view. You cannot simply "deduce" all the constitutive elements of a philosophy of life from the beliefs that constitute a given world view. Thus, it is quite possible for two naturalists, for example, who by definition share a common world view (and a common view of the nature of humanity) to hold quite different philosophies of life.

One important element in a philosophy of life, in any case, is a belief about humanity's place in the universe, about "human nature." But this is only the beginning of a philosophy of life.

The Meaning of Life

A second question to which a philosophy of life must provide some kind of answer is the question, Does human life have any meaning, and if so, what is that meaning? Now this is admittedly a puzzling question—we normally ask about the meaning of *terms* or of *propositions*, not about the meaning of life. Yet, it is impossible to escape the feeling that this question is getting at something that is important for us as human beings to understand and to think through to a conclusion. Let us try, at least, to understand the point of the question.

Suppose that a friend comes to us and says, "I've come to say goodbye. Life has no *meaning* for me any more. I'm going to end it all. Tonight." Now under such circumstances, it would be obviously inappropriate for us to quibble with our friend about whether he or she is using the term "meaning" in the proper way. ("End it all? Golly, I'm sorry to hear that. By the way, it seems to me that in what you just said you used the term 'meaning' in an odd way. According to Webster....") No, we clearly have to take our friend seriously at this point, and taking him or her seriously means, in the first instance, trying to understand exactly what he or she means by the statement, "Life has no meaning for me any more."

Our first thought upon hearing these ominous words might well be that something traumatic must have happened to our friend that has momentarily shaken him or her to such an extent that he or she is seriously contemplating suicide. We have all read newspaper accounts of suicides in which it was reported that the victim had been despondent over the loss of a loved one, or worried about mounting debts, or suffering from an incurable illness. Anyone who has ever been subjected to severe emotional stress can, perhaps, understand how another human being might, under certain circumstances, become so distraught or despondent that he or she would consider such an act.

Let us suppose, however, that as we talk with our friend about this momentous decision that he or she has just announced, we learn that none of the usual circumstances surrounding suicide apply in this case. He or she has not been disappointed in love, he or she has no debts, he or she is in excellent health, and so on. "Why, then," we ask our friend "do you want to end your life? What is your reason?" And our friend replies, "I don't have a reason, and I don't really need one. What I need, but have been unable to find, is *a reason to go on living.* We all have the power to choose whether we shall live or die. The living—unjustly, it seems to me—expect those who choose death to explain their choice. I think the burden of proof rests with those who choose life. Why should anyone choose life rather than death? What does life have to offer that is worth the effort? The only thing we can be sure of in this life is that sooner or later each of us must die. Why not sooner rather than later?"

In saying that life has no meaning, our friend is saying that he or she can find no reason to go on living, that nothing that he or she can think of that might occupy his or her time during whatever span of life might remain seems worth the effort. To our friend, the choice seems to be between a meaningless existence and nonexistence—and he or she chooses the latter. Our friend's philosophy of life fails to provide a reason for living.

The view that human existence is totally and irremediably meaningless, that nothing in all the world is really of value, is called *nihilism* (from the Latin word *nihil*, "nothing"), and a philosophy of life that includes such a view is often termed *nihilistic*. Why one who holds such a view should go on living is obviously a critical question for nihilists, and will be discussed in Chapter 62.

Alternatives to Nihilism

With respect to the question whether human life has any meaning, and if so, what that meaning is, the alternatives are really quite limited. In opposition to nihilism there are, at most, three alternative ways of attempting to give an affirmative answer. One is what may be called the theory of *cosmic purpose*, the view that everything that occurs in the world is part of a "grand design," and that every individual human life derives its highest meaning from its participation in the whole (Chapter 61). A second affirmative answer is what we shall call the theory of *immanent purpose*, the view that, notwithstanding the fact that there is no overarching purpose that we can discern, there are purposes that emerge in the course of our lives that demand our allegiance. Life becomes meaningful, according to this view, insofar as we commit ourselves to the purposes that thus claim our attention (Chapter 63). Finally, there is the view that the only purposes that are available to us are those we posit for ourselves—but that these suffice to make human life meaningful. We shall speak of this view as the theory of *temporal purpose* (Chapter 64).

It is evident that each of these views has a certain affinity for one of the world views discussed in the preceding section. Thus, we shall not be surprised to find nihilism allied with naturalism, cosmic purpose with ethical theism, immanent purpose with transcendentalism, and temporal purpose with humanism. Whether we are dealing here with mere affinity or with rigorous logical implication may become clearer as we proceed with our inquiry.

Principles of Action

A third fundamental question to which a philosophy of life must provide some kind of answer is, On what basis ought one to decide what to do with one's life? As long as one lives, one has the inescapable task of deciding how one will spend one's time—twenty-four hours a day, seven days a week, fifty-two weeks a year, n years in a lifetime. How shall one decide? A philosophy of life should provide some kind of an answer. Indeed, a philosophy of life consists, in large part, of a set of *value commitments* that yield some basis for preferring a given way of spending one's time to some other way that may be equally possible for us.

Consider, once again, the case of Albert Schweitzer. In his book *Out of My Life and Thought* Schweitzer provides a brief but fascinating account of the reasoning that led him as a young man to decide to devote his life to the service of other needy human beings. Schweitzer writes:

> While at the university and enjoying the happiness of being able to study and even to produce some results in science and art, I could not help thinking continually of others who were denied that happiness by their material circumstances or their health ... It struck me as incomprehensible that I should be allowed to lead such a happy life, while I saw so many people around me wrestling with care and suffering ... Then one brilliant summer morning ... there came to me, as I awoke, the thought that I must not accept this happiness as a matter of course, but must give something in return for it. Proceeding to think the matter out at once with calm deliberation, ... I settled with myself before I got up, that I would consider myself justified in living till I was thirty for science and art, in order to devote myself from that time forward to the direct service of humanity.[2]

Note that in this account, Schweitzer is stating a number of value commitments: he affirms the value of science (by which he means serious scholarship of all kinds) and art, as well as the value of devoting a significant part of one's time and effort to the service of other human beings. Note further that in the set of values that he articulates in this passage, Schweitzer strikes a definite balance between egoistic and altruistic values: he will spend his time until age thirty principally doing the things he loves and enjoys (but also preparing for his life's work), and the time thereafter principally doing things intended

---

[2]Ibid., p. 70.

to enhance the comfort and the happiness of others. And note, finally, that Schweitzer is affirming these values not merely in the abstract sense of assenting to the propositions that these things are good (though he surely would assent to those propositions), but in the practical sense that he is committing himself to a pattern of life consistent with such assent. The principal evidence of Schweitzer's commitment to these values is not that he articulated them but that he spent his life working for their realization.

So it is with any philosophy of life: it will contain a set of value commitments that enable one who holds that philosophy to choose among alternative ways of spending his or her time (life). It will also provide a basis for answering questions of the sort "Why did you do thus and so?" ("Because I believe such and such").

The number of value commitments that may be a part of a given philosophy of life is indefinitely large, and any statement of a philosophy of life is, therefore, likely to be more or less incomplete. Most of us, if asked to sum up our philosophy of life, would probably identify some few values that seem especially important to us, hoping that our questioner would realize that there is much more that we have left unsaid because at the moment we are not thinking of situations in which values other than those we have mentioned would be more relevant. To adopt a philosophy of life is, among other things, to commit oneself to certain values without being able to say in advance what are all the logical and practical implications of such a commitment.

Moreover, the possible combinations of values to which human beings may commit themselves are so numerous that there is no practical limit to the number of philosophies of life that may be developed. Perhaps we should say that a philosophy of life is, in certain respects, unique to the individual who holds that particular philosophy—though in its main outlines, of course, it will usually be similar to the philosophy of life of many other people whose major value commitments are more or less the same. It is surely evident, in any case, that in the chapters that follow we can expect no more than a few contrasting samples of philosophies of life, since it is impossible in principle to identify and describe all the available variations.

The principal components of a philosophy of life, then, are (a) a view concerning the nature of humanity (that is, humanity's place in the universe), (b) a view concerning the meaning of life, and (c) a set of value commitments consistent with those views. We turn now to a consideration of four representative philosophies of life with which we shall conclude this introduction to philosophy.

STUDY QUESTIONS

1. Assume that each of the following beliefs is held by someone. Which of these beliefs would qualify as a part of that person's philosophy of life?

    a. God has a plan for everyone.

    b. Whatever will be will be.

    c. Human beings have a natural lust for power.

    d. Human nature is perfectible.

    e. Anything that is worth doing is worth doing well.

    f. Human beings will some day colonize other planets.

    g. Solar energy will some day supply all our energy needs.

    h. The best things in life are free.

    i. Every human being who is in need has a legitimate claim on my time and attention.

    j. You only go around once, so you may as well enjoy it while you have the chance.

2. List several theories about "humanity's place in the universe." Does it seem correct to you to assert that any such theory is "the point where one's philosophy of life is connected to one's world view"?

3. Try to rephrase the question, What is the meaning of life? What do you understand to be the point of the question?

4. What is nihilism? What are the alternatives to nihilism listed in this chapter? Can you think of any other alternatives?

5. Write a brief summary of your philosophy of life, giving attention to each of the "principal components of a philosophy of life" identified in this chapter.

61

THE PHILOSOPHY
OF COSMIC PURPOSE

I know of no question that could possibly be more important to a human being than this: Does my life have any enduring meaning? For if one can answer this question in the affirmative, then one can live with confidence and joy no matter what circumstances one may find oneself in at any time. But if one must answer in the negative, it seems to me that even in the midst of comfort and plenty there must be an awful emptiness in life, for when all is said and done, it still does not add up to anything.

Basically, in my opinion, there are only three ways of dealing with this question (notwithstanding what was said in the preceding chapter). You can pronounce the joyful "Yes" of religious faith; you can pronounce the despairing "No" of nihilism; or you can try to avoid thinking about the question. The other philosophies that are sometimes offered as alternatives to nihilism are nothing more than fleeting afterimages left upon the mind of Western civilization by the brilliant light of a profoundly purposeful sense of life upon which our gaze was once securely fixed.

I shall attempt, then, to set forth a philosophy of life that in its main outline is as old as the patriarchs and prophets of the Old Testament. It is a philosophy of life that is shared—with, of course, numerous differences in emphasis and detail—by all who believe that God exists and that He cares about His creation. You may, if you wish, call it the philosophy of cosmic purpose. I prefer to think of it simply as the faith of a believer.

The Nature of Humanity

My philosophy of life is grounded in the world view of ethical theism. I hold, therefore, that everything that exists—the physical universe and life in all its forms—is a product of the creative activity of God. I hold, moreover, that the present forms of life that we find upon this planet are not the merely accidental products of a blind evolutionary process. Rather, they are the exact forms of life that God intended to exist at this particular stage in the development of His creation. I do not mean by this that God had a plan from the beginning of creation that included every last detail of what was to occur at every moment of time for all time to come, for this would imply that there is no freedom in the world and that everything that occurs (notwithstanding the appearance of human freedom) occurs by necessity. I do mean, however, that God had, from the beginning, a plan for His creation that in its main features will be and is being carried out through an evolutionary process that is coterminous with the existence of the cosmos. Human beings appeared in that process at the appointed time, after millions and millions of years of preparation for that event (I am referring to the evolution of our predecessors as well as the development of a suitable planet) and are remarkable, not least of all, for the fact that they are the first creatures (so far as we know) capable of knowing themselves as children of God. Human beings are creatures who are capable of knowing themselves as children of God—that, in my view, is the fundamental truth that must guide our thinking about the nature and destiny of humanity.

As creatures, human beings are naturally akin to every other creature, indeed, to everything that exists. The earth is our home, the destiny of the lesser creatures is in our hands, and the "care of the earth" is our special responsibility.

As children of God, created in His image, human beings are also akin to the Creator of all things. We are destined for fellowship with God, and we find our greatest fulfillment in realizing that destiny. We are most fully human when we perceive ourselves as we really are—finite creatures who are loved by God and are called by Him to play a unique role in the working out of His will for His creation.

The Meaning of Life

If one really believes what I have just said about God and His creation, and about the unique status of human beings in that creation, it follows immediately that the ultimate source of meaning in human life is to be found in the concept of *participation in the divine will.* It was by the will of God that the universe was called into existence out of nothing—*ex nihilo,* as the theologians say. It was by the will of God that this universe that He created was launched on its millenniums-long course toward whatever *tèlos* He has willed for it. It was by the will of God that life was called into existence—first in the sea, then upon land; first in very simple forms, then in species of greater and greater complexity. At every moment, from the beginning of creation to the present and on into the future, the universe was and is filled and moved and lured by the purposes of its Creator. The meaning of the

454 PHILOSOPHIES OF LIFE

life of every creature consists in its tiny but unique contribution to the fulfillment of the divine purpose.

Does it really make any difference in one's view of life—does it give "meaning" to life in any intelligible way—to believe that one is playing a tiny part in the realization of a divine plan whose final outcome is unknown to us? Yes! For it means, in effect, that everything of value that I accomplish in my life is preserved when I am no more, that the universe will forever be different from what it would otherwise have been because of the fact that I have lived. As each vote in an election makes its unique contribution to the final outcome, so each individual life contributes its unique achievement to the realization of the divine plan. Like Abraham of old, who set out to find the land of promise that was not, in fact, to be possessed for many generations, we live our lives in the certainty that the role we have been given to play—though we do not know the entire plot of which it is a part—is unique and important in the eyes of God.

I do not mean to be excessively "homocentric" in my account of the meaning of human existence. It should be apparent from what I have said that I believe that the life of *every* creature has meaning by virtue of its participation in the divine will. Human beings are unique, however, in that they are the creatures who ask whether their lives have meaning, and who are capable of *knowing* that their lives have meaning (and of fearing that they do not). In the history of the universe as it advances through time, God in His infinite love ensures that everything that is achieved by every creature is preserved forever—even the achievements of those creatures that do not know that He exists. Thus, ironically, even the lives of those who despair because they can find no meaning in life are, in fact, meaningful (objectively considered) by virtue of their unique contribution to the evolution of the universe.

Things Worth Living For

As I try to analyze the pattern of life that seems to me to grow naturally out of the views that I have just stated, I find that I have four overarching value commitments that enable me to fill my life with a rich variety of meaningful activities.

First, I believe that life is deepened and enriched if one is consciously grateful to God for all the blessings of life. I believe, therefore, that it is a good thing to provide for moments of solitude when one can deliberately and systematically cultivate a sincere sense of gratitude toward God. I do not mean by this that one should spend one's time thanking God for life's latest trinkets, like a child sending "thank you" letters to Santa Claus at Christmas. I mean, rather, that one should meditate on the great and abiding gifts of God's love: the wondrous variety and beauty of the natural world, the miracle of life, the joy of human friendship and companionship, the opportunity to spend one's energy and one's days doing interesting and worthwhile things. In such moments of meditation, it is as if one were immersing oneself in the stream of the divine will that pervades the universe; one returns to one's daily life renewed and strengthened for the tasks at hand.

Second, I believe that one's dealings with other human beings should be guided by the principle of love, by which I mean a sincere desire for their true welfare. The principle of love requires that I treat other people not as means to serve my ends but as ends in themselves. It requires that I "do unto others as [I] would that others should do unto [me]" (the Golden Rule). It means that I should desire for all human beings those things that I desire for myself, because I believe that they are truly good. Thus, I think it proper in my dealings with other people to attempt to cultivate in them (as in myself) a deeper sense of gratitude to God, a firmer sense of the meaning of life, a clearer understanding of truth, a more sensitive appreciation of beauty, a greater compassion for others. I believe that anything that can be done to alleviate human suffering and to deepen human enjoyment of life is worth doing; and I believe that one of the greatest rewards that can be had from one's daily work consists in the realization that one is enhancing the lives of other people.

The third basic commitment that serves as a guide for the conduct of my daily life is solicitude for all forms of life, and especially for sentient life. I am enough of a realist to know that one cannot live without causing the death of other living things—for example, the plants and animals that we use for food. Nonetheless, I take seriously the view that as the dominant species of life on this planet at this particular time in the history of the universe, human beings have a special responsibility for the care and protection of those other forms of life that also exist. That we must kill to live is a sad fact about human existence—but let us not kill wastefully, or painfully, or unnecessarily. The occurrence of life in all its forms is a miracle of unbelievable proportion, and that miracle is not to be undone except for good and substantial reasons.

Finally, I believe that in the living of our lives it is proper for us to make responsible use of the material resources that are available to us. I believe that the prevailing attitude toward the natural world is exploitative rather than responsible, and I believe that this is wrong. We have known for many years, for example, that there is a finite quantity of petroleum in the earth, but we have been wasting petroleum as if the supply were inexhaustible. We have known for many years that our present practices with respect to waste disposal are seriously polluting the air we breathe and the water we drink, but we continue, year after year, to dump thousands of tons of pollutants into the atmosphere and millions of gallons of raw sewage into our rivers and streams. We are wasting the resources of the earth as if we were Kamikaze pilots out for our final fling. We seem not to remember that these same resources must suffice to serve the needs of our children and our grandchildren for generations to come.

According to the philosophy of cosmic purpose, human beings are on this earth as agents of the divine will and as stewards of the earth. The treasures of the earth are not ours to waste: they are ours to use in ways that will enhance the quality of life, not only now but for all time to come. This philosophy is, therefore, implicitly supportive of the ecological concern that has come to the fore in the recent past, and it provides a deeper rationale for that concern than the considerations of mere expedience that are customarily offered in its support.

A Final Word

You will note that in linking my philosophy of life to a belief in divine purpose, I have at no time claimed to know what that purpose is. It is even possible, so far as I am concerned, that the whole process has no temporal *tèlos*—that what God has wrought in the creation of the world is an evolutionary process of infinite duration in which an infinite succession of *tèloi* are achieved, each succeeding *tèlos* being enriched by the achievements of the beings that preceded it. Be that as it may, the point I wish to make is that the conviction that the evolution of the universe is governed by the divine will not only fills the present moment with meaning but it enables one to face the future with confidence, for one is assured that whatever the future may hold of pain or sorrow or disappointment, it cannot prevent the ultimate realization of the divine will. Thus, one can bear life's adversities with courage and with patience, secure in the knowledge that even one's suffering, bravely endured, will contribute in its own unique way to whatever it is that God in His wisdom is seeking to achieve in the world.

STUDY QUESTIONS

1. Theist argues that there are really only three ways of dealing with the question concerning the meaning of life. What are they? Do you think he is right about this?
2. What does Theist assert to be the "fundamental truth" about the nature and destiny of humanity?
3. What does Theist mean by the phrase "participation in the divine will"? Who "participates" in the divine will, according to Theist?
4. What "overarching value commitments" does Theist profess? Could one reasonably hold some or all these value commitments without sharing Theist's theological views?
5. What does Theist have to say about the final *tèlos* of the divine will?

62

THE PHILOSOPHY OF NIHILISM

Let me begin this account of the philosophy of nihilism by saying that I sincerely wish that human existence could have the kind of meaning that Theist says it has. For there can be no doubt that the beliefs advocated by Theist—that God has a plan for the world, and that every creature plays a role in the realization of that plan—provide the basis for a philosophy of life that is satisfying to one who holds those beliefs. Theist's universe, to put the matter very simply, is inherently and totally *friendly* to human beings: whatever problems or obstacles people may encounter as they make their way through life, the outcome is never in doubt, for the divine will cannot be thwarted. Such a philosophy of life is "fail-safe"—but alas, it presupposes a world view that I and many other people today are unable to accept.

If one finds it necessary to conclude on the basis of the evidence that the universe is accurately depicted by the world view of naturalism, then one's thinking about what one is to make of one's life must be very different from that of a theist. For according to this world view, the emergence of life, including human life, was an incredible accident that came about solely because of the fortuitous occurrence of the conditions that made it possible. It was not intended or planned by God, for God does not exist. It was not intended or planned by anyone: it just happened. That is the premise from which nihilism begins.

Humanity's Place in the Universe

Objectively considered, human beings are highly developed organisms that have evolved out of earlier and simpler forms of life as a result of natural processes working upon the matter of which the universe is composed. These same processes evolved countless other species of life that have long since become extinct, and it seems more than likely that, in due time, the human species, and perhaps all life, will become extinct as well. Nature has no favorites. The evolutionary process is as blind and uncaring as the wind that blows; and the same wind that powers the windmill also wreaks great destruction. The universe is neither friendly nor hostile to humanity: it is indifferent.

Strictly speaking, the above statements apply with equal force to other living things as well as to people. But there is a difference: people are capable of knowing that this is their situation, and of asking how and for what purpose they are to live their lives in such a universe. Thus, in the case of human beings we have to ask what is the subjective meaning of the fact that they know themselves to be an accidental product of a blind process in a universe that neither knows nor cares that they exist.

Subjectively considered, human beings experience their own existence as having no given meaning or purpose. They are "thrown" into existence, and they have to make the best of it. The only thing that they can know for certain about their existence is that one day it will end. In the meantime, they have to decide what to do with their lives—what to work for, what to live for, how to fill the few or many days (they know not which) that may be left to them. That is the true situation of humanity that is revealed once you strip away the mythology and the comforting illusions that for so many centuries have shielded human beings from the truth about themselves.

The Search for Meaning in Life

It is altogether futile to suppose that in a world where God does not exist there is any hope of establishing an enduring meaning for any human life. For to say that my life, or any life, has meaning is to say that it serves some purpose; and in a universe where there are no enduring purposes, there can be no enduring meaning. One must either accept the conclusion that there is no ultimate meaning in life, or one must resurrect the myth of cosmic purpose. Or else, as Theist suggests, one must carefully avoid thinking about the matter.

If we have the courage to think about it, however, and if we also have the intellectual honesty to acknowledge the ultimate meaninglessness of human life, the question posed by the young person to whom reference was made in the introductory chapter (p. 447) is clearly an urgent one: Why should anyone choose to go on living? Does not the view that life has no ultimate meaning imply that life is not worth living? Is not suicide the logical outcome of a nihilistic philosophy of life? Is not nihilism, in the final analysis, a philosophy not of life but of death?

I think it is important that this apparent consequence of nihilism be considered forthrightly, for I think it is clear that the trend of our times is toward the world view of naturalism and the philosophy of nihilism. It would be a strange situation, indeed, if the final wisdom that we could reap from all our efforts to find answers to the profoundest questions about the universe and about humanity were to be the recommendation to pull the trigger and have done with it. We ought to have a better reason for living than the mere fact that "we get into the habit of living before acquiring the habit of thinking."[1]

Does the belief that human life has no enduring meaning imply that life is not worth living? By no means! For to one who clearly perceives the awful truth of the ultimate meaninglessness of human life, holding fast to this truth becomes in itself a reason for living. Never are human beings more noble than when they stand before the uncaring universe, naked and alone, and *refuse to be subdued* by it. Never are they more clear of mind or pure of heart than in that moment when they stare defiantly into the vast emptiness of heaven and from their hearts declare, "We will not be defeated!" The logical outcome of nihilism is not the ultimate submission of suicide, but the ultimate defiance of humanity against the universe. As nihilism rejects that subtle intellectual suicide by which many flee from meaninglessness to a God whose alleged business it is to confer meaning upon our lives, so it also rejects the cowardly flight from life itself that is the inner meaning of an act of suicide. From the point of view of a consistent nihilism it is essential, as Camus says, "to die unreconciled and not of one's own free will."[2]

Moreover, in thus affirming a defiant will to live in a universe that is without meaning, one discovers a marvelous sense of freedom that is quite literally inconceivable in a theistic universe. From the point of view of nihilism it is suddenly clear that in order to secure the prize of meaning, theists have had to pay the terrible price of becoming slaves for all eternity to a master who demands of them all that they have, and to whom they are accountable every moment of their lives *and beyond.* For the nihilist, however, all this is changed. Life has no meaning, but neither has it ultimate accountability to anyone. If God does not exist to confer meaning upon life, neither does He exist to issue commands that must be obeyed. Thus, a nihilist is free to be what he or she wills to be, to do what he or she wills to do, to become what he or she wills to become. To be a nihilist is to be incredibly free.

Further, to be a nihilist is to be totally innocent, as innocent as the prenihilists longed to be as they sought the forgiveness of the God by whose laws they were made to be so terribly guilty. Nihilism, in abolishing all transcendent values, also abolishes all guilt. The burden of

---

[1] Albert Camus, *The Myth of Sisyphus and Other Essays* (New York: Knopf, 1969), p. 8.
[2] *Ibid.,* p. 55.

the law, the burden of the past, the burden of being answerable for one's actions of last year or yesterday or this morning—all are swept away in each moment that one holds fast to the insight that there is no perspective from which anything can finally be declared good or evil. Whatever may be the opinions or the pronouncements of other people, nihilists know in their hearts that they are the most innocent people who ever lived, since for them the prerequisites of guilt simply do not exist.

Finally, to be a nihilist is to savor the present moment (*each* present moment) in a way that is not possible for one who is a slave of cosmic purpose. To be without purpose (which has reference to the future) and without guilt (which has reference to the past) is to be free for the present moment, free to focus the whole of one's attention and passion on the experience of this present moment, which alone is real. A famous spokesman for the philosophy of cosmic purpose once confessed, "We never live, but we hope to live; and, as we are always preparing to be happy, it is inevitable we should never be so."[3] Nihilism says rather, "We hope for nothing, and so we are never disappointed; we care not for the future, but seek to wrest from each passing moment whatever it will yield to one who gives oneself fully to the living of this life."

Freedom, innocence, openness to the present moment: these are the rewards for one who holds fast to the truth that there is no enduring meaning in human life. If nihilism teaches that the quest for meaning must, if we are honest, end in failure, it does not draw from this the melancholy conclusion that life is, therefore, not worth living. On the contrary, it draws from this initially unsettling insight the elements of a philosophy of life that enables one who holds it to live fully and with joy.

Principles of Action

I assume that it is evident to anyone who has followed my reasoning to this point that I cannot derive a list of "things worth living for" from the convictions that I have just stated. Unlike Theist, I have no "overarching value commitments" to tell me what is and what is not worth doing. My convictions about the ultimate meaninglessness of human life yield no blueprint for the living of one's life. I have to improvise as I go along.

Nonetheless, to an outside observer I suspect that my life looks very much like the lives of many other people who do not share my nihilistic views. The truth is that at the level of observable behavior, I am pretty much a conformist: I observe the laws and customs of society, I pay my taxes, I keep my word, and so on. I once even risked my life

---

[3]Blaise Pascal, *Pensées* (New York: Modern Library, 1941), Fragment 172, p. 61.

to save a child from drowning—and was embarrassed beyond words when I was given an award for my "courage" and my "recognition of the infinite value of a single human life." I knew perfectly well that my act was not courageous, and I had no illusions whatsoever about the value of the life of the child who caused all the excitement. It was purely and simply a matter of being there at that moment, and of being open to live that moment through in a way that, at the time, seemed more alluring, more exciting, than the alternative of staying on the beach and letting the child drown. Tomorrow, under identical circumstances, I might do just the opposite.

The principal difference between me and those who do not share my nihilistic convictions, then, lies not so much in the area of outward behavior as in the differing quality of our inner life. I feel no *obligation* to live the way I do, and no *responsibility* for the way I have lived my life to date. As for the past, I would probably do everything differently if I had it to do over again, and as for the future I will simply have to continue to make it up as I go along. I cherish my freedom, and I will be bound neither by my own past nor by the expectations of others.

Another way of expressing the difference between the inner life of other people and my own would be to say that most people seem to me to take life very seriously, whereas I find the whole spectacle of human life rather comical. The comedy consists in the fantastic disproportion between most people's apparent perceptions of themselves ("I'm important in the scheme of things, I'm doing things that make a real difference in the world," and so on) and the reality of their situation as mere blips on the screen of history who will soon be replaced by other blips, and they by yet others—on and on, generation after generation, century after century. The emergence of life out of lifeless matter was an astonishing occurrence for which nature (if it had a mind) might be very proud; but the occurrence of a living being who thinks he or she has a *reason* for living, a being who thinks he or she has a role to play in the fulfillment of some "grand design," is a kind of cosmic joke that nature has played upon itself. Nihilism's counterbalance to the ponderous seriousness with which most people regard the spectacle of human life is a hearty laugh.

Why do I live the way I do rather than some other way? Purely out of habit. Society taught me how to live before it taught me how to think —and lacking any value system in terms of which I might develop a "better" way of life, I simply go along with the crowd. I believe in intellectual honesty; I value my own freedom; I believe in my own innocence; I live for the moment. These fragments of a philosophy of life provide no basis for me to reform the lives of my contemporaries nor to live in an unconventional way myself. You might say that it is simply the law of inertia applied to the sphere of human behavior.

Notwithstanding everything that I have said, however, I want, in conclusion, to state emphatically that the "No" that nihilism pronounces with respect to the question of meaning in life is not a *despairing* "No." It is true that one's initial reaction to the insight that life is without any enduring meaning is a kind of intellectual shock: one wants to say that it cannot be true, or that if it is, one cannot live with such a privation. But this, it must be remembered, is only one's initial reaction. It is the reaction of a child who has just been told that there is no Santa Claus—and who wishes he or she had not asked. But we cannot be children forever, and it cannot be and, in fact, is not the case that the only way to say "Yes" to life is to preserve the illusion of cosmic purpose. Nihilism says "No" to the question of meaning, but it says a joyful "Yes" to life. That is a proper stance for honest people who find themselves in circumstances such as ours.

STUDY QUESTIONS

1. What is Nihilist's account of humanity's place in the universe? Is this account implicit in the world view of naturalism (see Chapter 56)?
2. Nihilist states that in his opinion "it is clear that the trend of our times is toward the world view of naturalism and the philosophy of nihilism" (p. 459). Do you think he is right on this point?
3. Nihilist states that the view that human life has no enduring meaning does not imply that life is not worth living. Summarize his argument on this point.
4. Nihilist argues that a consistent nihilism yields certain "rewards." What are they, and how do they allegedly follow from the fundamental tenets of nihilism?
5. According to Nihilist, how should one who holds a nihilist philosophy of life order his or her daily life? How does a nihilist decide to do this rather than that?

63

THE PHILOSOPHY
OF IMMANENT PURPOSE

As I sit down to write these words, the country is quietly observing another anniversary of the death of President Franklin Delano Roosevelt. The memory of the late FDR in turn calls to mind a number of other people who have left their marks upon the history of our times and are with us no more: Winston Churchill, Dwight D. Eisenhower, John F. Kennedy, Martin Luther King, Jr. Each of these, as we all know, exerted great influence on the thoughts and lives of his contemporaries. Each had a historic role to play, a mission to fulfill. The world is different because of the way they lived, the decisions they made, the goals they set, the things they achieved or failed to achieve.

Nihilism tells me that the conviction that these people made a permanent mark on the experience of humanity is sheer fantasy, that, in fact, their lives and the lives of all people are totally devoid of any enduring meaning. Every human being, according to nihilism, is but "a blip on the screen of history." The blips come and go, year after year, generation after generation; eventually the last blip will vanish from the screen, and the being who fancies that his or her life has meaning will be no more.

Is this the final truth about human existence? Is it possible that a serious commitment to "follow the argument wherever it may lead" must lead us ultimately to the views that life has no meaning, that nothing is really worth doing, that there is no better guide for the living of one's life than mere convention? No! Nihilism cannot be the end of the journey, for nihilism contains within itself a contradiction that requires us to go beyond nihilism. The resolution of that contradiction provides the key through which nihilism can and must be transcended.

Nihilism's Internal Contradiction

Nihilism takes its stand on the proposition that one must be brutally honest about the question of meaning—as honest as one would be if the question did not concern us at all. In the name of intellectual honesty, nihilism accepts the conclusion of philosophical naturalism that life, including human life, is an accidental occurrence in a universe that neither knows nor cares that life exists, and with admirable tenacity it concludes from this that human life is without purpose, and, therefore, without meaning. Nihilist finds, to be sure, some consolation prizes: freedom, innocence, openness to the present moment. But we are left with the lurking suspicion that the "hearty laugh" that Nihilist recommends in view of the "comedy" of the human situation is not so much a counterbalance to an unwarranted seriousness as it is an antidote to an unhealed grief. Bereavement affects us in peculiar ways.

But is it not strange that Nihilist never asks *why* it is so important to be intellectually honest? Intellectual honesty is so important to Nihilist that he finds a reason for living in the alleged "awful truth" that life has no meaning! But how can anything be that important to one who believes that the universe is devoid of meaning, and that nothing is of "overarching" value? Is not Nihilist's assertion equivalent to the claim that there is one ultimate value in human life, namely intellectual honesty? Clearly it is. And then we have to ask how Nihilist knows that this is the case.

The contradiction that lies at the heart of nihilism is this: its assertion that nothing is truly of value is established on the assumption that honesty before the facts is of supreme value. In the name of truth, which it values absolutely, nihilism denies that anything is of absolute value. And in the name of truth, to which it clings notwithstanding the unpalatable consequences to which it seems driven, nihilism eludes the despair that would seem to be its inevitable concomitant.

The Key to Meaning

I fully agree with Nihilist that it is good to be intellectually honest, but what I want to know is how Nihilist is able to assert this conviction. Surely it is evident that on his own premises he cannot know that honesty is good, for he is committed to the proposition that in this universe, where life emerged quite by accident, nothing is really of value. Let me then speak for him: he values intellectual honesty because he recognizes that it is the only pathway to truth, and the intrinsic value of truth is so self-evident to him that in all his talk about the nonreality of values he fails to notice his own valuation of truth. Nihilist is committed to speaking the truth as he sees it—I do not doubt his sincerity—but that very commitment presupposes that he has been so impressed by the value of truth that he cannot do otherwise.

Values certify themselves to us as deserving of our commitment, and when this occurs, we respond with our whole being, without stopping to ask by what right this or that value presumes to bind our behavior. I cannot prove to you by any argument that as a rational being you ought to seek and honor the truth wherever it may be found: if the intrinsic value of truth has not grasped you, claimed you, won your loyalty, there is nothing I can do for you. But if truth has gained your allegiance (as it clearly has in Nihilist's case), then you have but to reflect on the characteristics of that claim to understand something about the nature of value and the important role that values play in human life.

Nihilist's account provides yet another example of the self-certifying character of values. He tells us that on one occasion he saved a child from drowning, and that he was embarrassed when he was given an award for courage and for his "recognition of the infinite value of a single human life." The embarrassment, I feel sure, derives from the fact that, fortunately, his behavior on that occasion was not consistent with his theory. Since, according to Nihilist, the life of that child, like everything else, was without value, it was not reasonable for him to risk his life to save the child from drowning. And just how does he attempt to reconcile his theory with the "embarrassing" fact that he did save the child? "It was purely and simply a matter of being there at that moment," he says, "and of being open to live that moment through in a way that at the time seemed more alluring, more exciting, than the alternative of staying on the beach and letting the child drown." Poppycock! Poor Nihilist cannot admit that this courageous behavior (which it was) grew out of his instinctive awareness that the life of that child *was* indeed of value, that the child's predicament placed an obligation upon him to do everything within his power to preserve that life. His *theory* requires him to say, "Tomorrow, under identical circumstances, I might do just the opposite." I am willing to bet that his practice would be better than his theory.

I say that it is a fact of human existence that values do thrust themselves upon us in this direct and overwhelming way, and that much of our behavior can be understood only on the supposition that it is called forth by the values that are served by that behavior. Very little of our time is spent in fulfilling our basic animal needs, which presumably would have to be met even if we were not value-loving creatures. Most of our waking hours are spent in the service of things we believe in—values—that could, in fact, be different from what they are (that is, we could have different values). During the Middle Ages, for example, people valued contemplation to a degree that it clearly is not valued by most people today. We, on the other hand, value scientific knowledge and technology to a degree that would have seemed utterly strange to our more contemplative forebears. The "overarching value commitments" of a society are evident in the ways that that society deploys its human and material resources. It is not only because of technological progress that in the twentieth century we build superhighways rather than cathedrals.

Every human being is part of a community of human beings—a

society—and to a large extent shares the value commitments of that society, frequently without even being explicitly aware of what those commitments are. Some such commitments are shared by virtually everyone, and form the subject matter of ethics. Others are peculiar to a particular society or social movement at a given time, and constitute what is called an ideology. Yet others may be more or less peculiar to a given individual, and, thus, become a part of that individual's personal philosophy of life.

Life is experienced as meaningful insofar as it is lived in the service of values that impress us as being worthy of our efforts. If one is grasped by the terrible spectacle of human suffering caused by disease, and in response devotes one's life to the prevention and cure of disease and its consequences, one finds meaning in so doing. If one is moved to action by an awareness of the awful human consequences of ignorance, and in response spends one's best efforts in the overcoming of ignorance, one experiences a sense of meaning in the process. The idea that life is without meaning is an idea that could be entertained only by one who is merely contemplating life, not by one who is involved in the actual living of life. To live is to encounter values that cry out for our allegiance. To respond to that cry is to be redeemed.

The Source of Value

What is the source of these values that confront us on the pathway of life, demand our allegiance, and confer meaning upon our lives? And precisely how and why are our lives made meaningful in the service of such values?

Values emerge out of the depth of our lives, out of that dimension of ourselves in which we are in touch with the eternal. The reason that Nihilist is driven to the dreadful view that human life is without meaning is that his starting point is the world view of naturalism. Within that world view, there is no place for the concept of the eternal —nor, as a further consequence, is there any place for transcendent values. Thus, it is only by the contradiction of affirming a value that on his own premises he has no right to affirm that Nihilist is able to find life worth living, notwithstanding the fact that it is without ultimate meaning.

That values claiming our allegiance do emerge in the course of our lives is the best evidence we have that naturalism does not contain the whole truth about the human situation. Nihilist starts from naturalism and finds himself forced to conclude that, when all is said and done, nothing in this world is really of value. I start from the fact that values *do* confront us in the course of our lives, and conclude from this that naturalism is inadequate. If values, which are not temporal entities, emerge in the world of space and time by means of human consciousness, then human beings are more than spatiotemporal beings: they are beings who live in the strength of the eternal, and find their deepest fulfillment in the service of that which is eternal. Human beings are, in short, what they are affirmed to be according to the world view of transcendentalism (see Chapter 58).

The quest for meaning in life is not a search for an answer to the question, What is *the* meaning of life? That is not an intelligible question. The quest for meaning in life is a quest for something worth living for, something that will redeem our lives from the superficiality and pointlessness of mere temporality. That quest is satisfied when we are grasped by the inherent worthwhileness of some task, any task, that engages our efforts and our loyalty. Meaning in life is a dividend that is bestowed upon those who invest some portion of their lives in something they believe to be worthy of that investment.

Things Worth Living For

I noted earlier that in the value commitments of most people it is possible to discern at least three layers of values: those that are shared by virtually everyone, those that are a part of the value system of a given society, and those that are more or less peculiar to a particular individual. In analyzing my own value commitments, I find it instructive to sort them out into these three categories.

With respect to the first of these, it seems to me that the principal values that deserve to be, and to a large extent are, revered by people everywhere are the great triumvirate of truth, beauty, and goodness. I believe that the human mind has a natural hunger to know the truth, and that the experience of coming to know some truth is one of the great "ecstatic" experiences of life—one of the experiences in which one senses a depth and a fulfillment in life. I believe that the human spirit has a natural love for beauty, and that the perception of beauty —in nature, in the visual arts, in music—is as essential to the life of the spirit as is food for the body. And I believe that the human conscience has a natural desire to realize true goodness in human affairs, and that the behavior of most human beings is profoundly influenced by this desire. In professing a love for truth, beauty, and goodness, I feel a kinship with the whole human community, a kinship with literally billions of other human beings from whom I am separated by space, time, and cultural differences. Moreover, I rejoice in the knowledge that we are as one in our commitment to those values without which we would cease to be truly human.

With respect to the second category of values, I must, of course, acknowledge that I am a product of modern Western culture, and that I probably hold a large number of unexamined commitments that are simply a part of the assumed outlook of all or most people who live in this cultural epoch. To the extent that I have been able to identify the value commitments of our culture, however, I find that in the process of incorporating them into my own philosophy of life I have had to modify them in several important ways. For example, I recognize the power of the scientific method to acquire a detailed knowledge of the laws governing the natural world, but—contrary, I think, to the prevailing view of my contemporaries—I do not believe that all legitimate knowledge comes to us by way of the scientific method. I value modern technology as a means of lessening human toil and enhancing the quality of human life, but—again contrary to the dominant view of our time—I do not think that a steadily increasing quantity of the products of technology results in a corresponding increase in human happiness. I acknowledge the success of capitalism in making possible a higher average standard of living than has ever been realized heretofore, but I deplore the injustice, the waste, and the pollution that many of my contemporaries seem willing to accept as part of the price of affluence. I value representative democracy as the best method yet devised to make government responsive, in some measure, to the needs of the governed, but I shudder at the naïvete of those of my contemporaries who think that as long as an elected official is a member of the right political party, that individual can do no wrong. I am, then, both a product and a critic of modern society, and I like to think that, insofar as I find it necessary to be the latter, I am acting in the name of those fundamental commitments that are shared by human beings everywhere.

As far as the third category of commitments is concerned, it is largely a matter of particularizing one's broader commitments in ways that are appropriate to one's interests, skills, and circumstances. None of us can do everything, nor can we make life meaningful merely by revering a set of noble-sounding formulations. It is in the concrete details of our everyday life that we finally must live out our values; otherwise they remain nothing but impotent abstractions. In my own case, for example, several projects have captured my interest: an open-housing campaign in my community, an emergency relief program for famine victims in Africa, a scholarship program for inner-city students. Had I lived in a different community, or at a different time, the particular causes that would have engaged my interest would, no doubt, have been different. Because I have now had the experience of participating in these projects, however, the values that these projects were designed to serve have, undoubtedly, come to occupy a more prominent place in my personal philosophy of life than would otherwise have been the case. We are what we do.

My advice to the young person who announced that he or she was going to commit suicide because he or she could not think of any reason to go on living is this: stop looking for a *reason* to live and try actually *living* for a while. Do whatever you feel *might* be worth doing and see if, in the process, you are not grasped, once again, by values that claim your attention and your allegiance. To one who is merely a spectator, human life may seem pointless and trivial and futile; but to one who enters fully into the living of life, values worth living for well up like springs in the desert. What is needed to find meaning in life is not a better theory but a renewed commitment to life itself. When we think, we should think clearly; and when we live, we should live deeply and well.

STUDY QUESTIONS

1. What is the "internal contradiction" that the writer of this chapter claims to find in nihilism? Is this a real contradiction? How might Nihilist reply to this criticism?
2. "Values certify themselves to us as deserving of our commitment." What does this mean? Is this a plausible description of your own perception of values?
3. How does the writer of this chapter deal with the question concerning the meaning of life? What is your opinion of this position?
4. What view of humanity is held by the writer of this chapter? What is the relationship between this view and his view regarding our apprehension of values?
5. This chapter speaks about "three layers of values." What are they? Does the "three-layer" analysis apply to your own value system?
6. What values are said to be shared by virtually all human beings? Does this strike you as a plausible assertion?
7. What values are identified as the principal value commitments of modern Western culture? At what points do you agree and at what points do you disagree with this analysis?
8. "We are what we do." What does this mean?

64

THE PHILOSOPHY
OF TEMPORAL PURPOSE

The starting point for my reflections regarding the meaning of life and other matters having to do with a philosophy of life is the world view of humanism. As a matter of fact, I normally do not make any distinction in my own thinking between the subject of world views and the subject of philosophies of life. If I am asked, "What is your world view?" my answer is, "I am a humanist." And if I am asked, "What is your philosophy of life?" I again reply, "I am a humanist." I think it is also clear from the preceding discussion that theism, naturalism, and transcendentalism are also both world views and philosophies of life. The theories of cosmic purpose, no purpose (nihilism), and immanent purpose appear to me to be implicit in those other world views, just as the theory of temporal purpose is implicit in the world view of humanism. I shall do my best to show that this last-mentioned theory is more consistent with our experience of life than are any of the theories discussed thus far.

The Myth of Sisyphus

Greek mythology recounts the story of Sisyphus, a legendary king of Corinth whose escapades so offended the gods that he was condemned for all eternity to roll a great boulder to the top of a mountain. According to the myth, the gods had arranged things in such a way that each time Sisyphus neared the top of the mountain the boulder would roll back down to the bottom, and the poor fellow would have to start all over again. Sisyphus's excruciating labor, carried on endlessly and without purpose, is the classic image of pointless human effort. It is instructive to note how various philosophies of life would have to alter the story in order to make it fit their respective readings of the human situation.

Nihilism simply accepts the story as it is: all human activity is as futile as the activity of Sisyphus going up and down the mountain for eternity, with nothing ever being accomplished through all his prodigious effort. Suppose, then, that Sisyphus could thwart the will of the gods by taking his own life. Should he not do so? No, according to nihilism, for in holding fast to the insight that what he is doing is meaningless, Sisyphus finds a strange kind of reason for being. Sisyphus's *consciousness of his own fate* makes his fate endurable. The lesson would appear to be that mankind can find a solace for purposelessness in consciously grasping and accepting the fact that life is without purpose. One is reminded of Pascal:

> Man is but a reed, the most feeble thing in nature; but he is a thinking reed . . . If the universe were to crush him, man would still be more noble than that which killed him, because he knows that he dies and the advantage that the universe has over him; the universe knows nothing of this.[1]

According to theism's reading of the human situation, we must imagine that Sisyphus toils up the mountain with boulders that do not roll back down but are received by the gods to be used in building a beautiful cathedral at the top of the mountain. Sisyphus, to be sure, does not personally set each boulder in place—he never even sees the cathedral—but he is assured that the boulders he brings up one by one are, in fact, being used to build an edifice that will last forever. Thus it behooves him to work quickly and well, for the quality of his work will have definite consequences for the quality of the final product. In theism's reading of the human situation, Sisyphus's efforts unquestionably count for something.

The philosophy of immanent purpose requires an interesting emendation of the myth of Sisyphus. According to this view, Sisyphus rolls his boulder up the mountain not because that is his fate (nihilism), and not in order to contribute to the building of a cathedral at the top of the mountain (theism), but in order to contribute to a series of lesser projects that have impressed him as being worthy of his efforts. We might say that for the cathedral at the top of the mountain this philosophy substitutes a series of chapels on the mountainside, and Sisyphus's life and work acquire meaning by virtue of the fact that each of these projects in turn certifies itself to him as being worthy of his efforts. He is beckoned, as it were, by transcendent values that cry out for realization, and in responding to that cry, his life is filled with meaning.

We will return to Sisyphus later to develop a humanist version of

---

[1]Blaise Pascal, *Pensèes* (New York: Modern Library, 1941), Fragment 347, p. 116.

that ancient and haunting myth. First, however, let us consider directly the problem of meaning and the nature and function of values in human affairs.

Meanings and Values

You will recall from the earlier discussion of humanism as a world view (Chapter 59) that humanism affirms the uniqueness, the dignity, and the essential freedom of human beings. According to humanism, human beings are lonely strangers upon the earth. They stand apart from lifeless matter by virtue of the fact that they live, and they stand apart from all other forms of life by virtue of the very qualities that constitute their humanity: their freedom, their capacity for abstract thought, their power of imagination, their capacity for language, their appreciation of beauty, their capacity for altruistic love. If you imagine the earth existing just as it does now, except that no human beings existed upon it, you must imagine a world without science, without poetry, without art, without love—and without any being who is capable of caring that these things do not exist. However the fact is to be accounted for, it is a remarkable fact that human beings occupy a class all by themselves in the scale of being. It is this radical uniqueness of humanity that humanism feels obligated to defend against every attempt that is made to incorporate humankind into a system that robs us of our distinctness, our humanity.

Consider, once again, the world without human beings. Such a world would also be devoid of value. Why? Because it is human beings who create values by positing future possibilities that they then work to achieve. Human beings are infinitely restless creatures who simply cannot be content to leave the world as they find it. They see the world as it is, and there flashes into their imagination a picture of what it might be: this lump of clay might be formed into a jug, this piece of marble into a statue, these colored stones into a piece of jewelry, these trees into a building to provide shelter from the elements, these sounds into a tune, these words into a poem, these individuals into a nation. Human beings create because it is their nature to create. Were they to cease creating, they would cease to be human beings.

Most human effort is expended in the service of ideals, values, posited by human imagination. Only a tiny fraction of the work that is done by people and machines today would be required if all we aspired to do was to meet our absolutely basic survival requirements. A bit of food, shelter, enough clothing to protect us from the elements, that is about all we would need. But we desire more than this: food that is tasty and varied as well as nourishing, homes that are beautiful as well as functional, clothing that is attractive and comfortable as well as practical, greater mobility than we can get by mere walking, activities more interesting than the gathering of food. And so we create those remarkable monuments to human imagination called *civiliza-*

tions, and we devote most of our efforts to the pursuit of those things that are valued in the civilization whose life we happen to share.

It is by their own imagination, therefore, that human beings are saved from purposelessness. Human beings find meaning in pursuing goals that they have posited as worth pursuing. The building of a civilization is a gigantic game in which any number can play, and almost everybody wins—provided, of course, that the game does not come to an end. When that happens a sense of weariness sets in, and philosophers and poets lament the vanity of all human striving (as in the Book of Ecclesiastes). But ever and again, human imagination comes to the rescue: new ideals are generated, new goals are posited. Filled, once again, with hope and with purpose, people set about the task of building a new and better civilization.

It is quite true that "the glory that was Greece and the grandeur that was Rome" are no more, except in the minds of individuals who study those vanished civilizations and admire the ideals by which the ancient Greeks and Romans lived. As with all things that die, the hopes and the dreams as well as the sorrows and the fears of those noble men and women have vanished forever. The truth is—and perhaps it is a melancholy truth—that nothing in all the world endures forever: on this point, nihilism is correct. But it is also true that individuals find meaning in striving to bring into being the values, the ideals, the visions that they set before themselves. This is the only kind of meaning that is possible for us—but it is enough.

Returning now to the myth of Sisyphus, it is evident that the humanist account of the human situation requires several important changes in the story. First, the humanist Sisyphus is not condemned forever to roll boulders up the mountain: he is free to do whatever he chooses—to play, to make music, to till the soil, to make usable objects from the wood of the trees, to plan a building, to build a city. Second, if he does choose to roll boulders up the mountain, they do not roll back down again: they are used for whatever purpose he intended. Third, he is not alone: the mountainside is populated with human beings like himself who will join their labor to his: together they may accomplish goals that would exceed the capacity of any one of them. Thus Sisyphus, in the humanist view, is happy on his mountain. If his project of yesterday is swaying in the wind and about to come crashing down, do not feel sorry for him: the joy was in the doing, not in the result. He has already moved on to a new and more exciting project, and he will hardly take note when the product of yesterday's efforts has toppled to the earth.

Life as a Work of Art

Each of my predecessors in this debate has concluded his essay with a brief discussion of "things worth living for" or "principles of action" —that is, an account of how he orders his everyday life in a manner consistent with his general outlook. Theist speaks of four overarching values in the service of which his life, he says, is filled with a rich variety of meaningful activity. Nihilist, for obvious reasons, has a bit of trouble at this point, but finally recommends convention as the only available guide for conduct. Transcendentalist tells us he finds several different levels of values (ethical, cultural, personal), and attempts briefly to sort them out for us. And now it is my turn, and my readers no doubt expect that I will offer yet one more set of values for their consideration.

But I will not do so, for there is nothing that I could say at this point that would not be purely and simply autobiographical—and I cannot imagine that an account of my particular pattern of values could be of interest to anyone else. Could it make any possible difference to you whether or not I happen to like music, or art, or literature? Is it any concern of yours whether I am personally involved in this civic project rather than that one? I have my life to live and you have yours. I have my opportunities and you have yours. If I happen to have chosen the rolling of boulders as my principal project in life, that does not mean that you should do the same.

Every human being is an artist, and the life he or she lives is a unique work of art. The artist, to be sure, is limited to some extent by the materials with which he or she has to work. We cannot live at a different time, in a different cultural epoch, or with different natural endowments from those we actually have. But within these limitations, the possibilities for the living of our lives are truly boundless. There are oceans to be crossed, mountains to be climbed, truths to be mastered, dangers to be overcome, civilizations to be built. Each of us must set his or her own goals, and then pursue them with all possible vigor—not because those goals, once achieved, will last forever, but because as artists we take pride in the quality of our art, which is our life. And if in the course of practicing our art we should happen to encounter Sisyphus upon his mountain, let us look carefully into his face. I think we shall discover that as he struggles with his boulder, Sisyphus is smiling—for he is happy.

STUDY QUESTIONS

1. What is Humanist's view of humanity? What are the most important facts about humanity that Humanist urges us to keep in mind as we attempt to develop a philosophy of life?
2. What is Humanist's theory of value? How do values come into being?
3. According to Humanist, how does human life become meaningful? Does this strike you as a plausible suggestion?
4. Humanist does not offer a proposal regarding "things worth living for." Why? What does he offer in its place?
5. Read the Book of Ecclesiastes. Summarize its philosophy of life.
6. Read *The Rubaiyat of Omar Khayyam*. Summarize its philosophy of life.

CORRELATED READINGS[1]

1. Pascal, Blaise. "Thoughts On Nature, Man and God." *Pensées,* Fragments 72, 146, 172, 199, 205, 208-10, 347, 549. Some elements of a theistic philosophy of life by a great Christian philosopher.
2. Nietzsche, Friedrich. "The Advent of Nihilism." *The Gay Science,* Section 283; and *The Will to Power,* Preface and Book One. A powerful statement of nihilism by one who understood it well.
3. Camus, Albert. "The Myth Of Sisyphus." *The Myth of Sisyphus and Other Essays,* trans. J. O'Brien. New York: Knopf, 1955, pp. 88-91. A miniature classic.
4. Nagel, Thomas. "The Absurd." *The Journal of Philosophy,* LXVIII, 20 (1971), 716-727. An analysis of the concept of philosophical absurdity.
5. Taylor, Richard. "The Meaning of Life." *Good and Evil.* New York: Macmillan, 1970, Chap. 18. A humanist account.

FOR FURTHER READING

Bambrough, Renford. *Reason, Truth and God.* New York: Barnes & Noble, 1969. Includes an exhortation to philosophers to concern themselves with philosophies of life.

──────. *Wisdom: Twelve Essays.* Totowa, N.J.: Rowman & Littlefield, 1974.

Capps, Walter H., and Donald E. Capps (eds.). *The Religious Personality.* Belmont, Calif.: Wadsworth, 1970 (paperbound). Centers on the ways religion may orient the personality.

Fried, C. *An Anatomy of Values: Problems of Personal and Social Choice.* Cambridge, Mass.: Harvard University Press, 1970.

Friedman, Maurice. *The Hidden Human Image.* New York: Dell, 1974 (paperbound). Wide-ranging discussion of the condition of contemporary man and woman.

Hoffer, Eric. *Reflections on the Human Condition.* New York: Harper & Row, 1973. A longshoreman's comments.

Joske, W. D. "Philosophy and the Meaning of Life," *Australasian Journal of Philosophy,* 52 (1974), 93–104. Argues that philosophy is relevant to determining whether, and in what sense, life is or is not meaningful.

Kaufmann, Walter. *Without Guilt and Justice: From Decidophobia to Autonomy.* New York: Weyden, 1973. Argues for an emphasis on creative autonomy.

Margolis, Joseph. *Negativities: The Limits of Life.* Columbus, Ohio: Charles E. Merrill, 1975. Discusses death, illness, inequality, and related topics.

Mayeroff, Milton. *On Caring.* New York: Harper & Row, 1971. An analysis of what it means to be human.

---

[1] *Concise Readings in Philosophy,* Part XIV.

Nielsen, Kai. *Ethics Without God.* Buffalo, N.Y.: Prometheus Books, 1973 (paperbound).

Pepper, Stephen C. *The Sources of Value.* Berkeley: University of California Press, 1970.

Peters, Richard S. *Reason and Compassion.* London: Routledge & Kegan Paul, 1973.

Rosen, S. *Nihilism: A Philosophical Essay.* New Haven, Conn.: Yale University Press, 1969. A defense of a rationally ordered life.

Schacht, Richard. *Alienation.* Garden City, N.Y.: Doubleday, 1971 (paperbound). A history of the concept.

Thielicke, Helmut. *Nihilism: Its Origin and Nature—With a Christian Answer,* trans. by John W. Doberstein. New York: Schocken Books, 1969. A sympathetic but critical study.

Weiss, Paul, and John Weiss. *Right and Wrong: A Philosophical Dialogue Between Father and Son.* Carbondale: Southern Illinois University Press, 1974 (paperbound).

White, F. C. "The Meaning of Life," *Australasian Journal of Philosophy,* 53 (1975), 148–150. A critique of Joske's argument (see above).

GLOSSARY
OF
PHILOSOPHICAL TERMS

Controversial issues can be fruitfully discussed only insofar as a neutral language—that is, one acceptable to everyone discussing the controversy and understood in the same sense by all—is available for the discussion. Unfortunately, it is uncommonly difficult in philosophy to formulate neutral definitions of many key philosophical terms. The definitions that follow will indicate the usage observed throughout this book. Moreover, they reflect the usage of a large number of English-speaking philosophers. The reader should be aware, however, that some philosophers have used, and do use, some of these terms in slightly different ways. In reading philosophical materials, therefore, one must be prepared to modify one's understanding of any term that one may encounter being used in some other way.

Aesthetics: the branch of philosophy that asks and attempts to answer theoretical questions concerning the fine arts—questions dealing with the nature of art, the definition of beauty, the nature of aesthetic judgment, and the like.

Aesthetic value: the value, whatever its nature may be, by virtue of which an object is said to be a work of art.

Ambiguous: quality of a term that has different meanings when used in different contexts. (*Ex.:* "line" means one thing to a painter, another to a mathematician, and yet a third to a plumber.)

Analytic: quality of a sentence, statement, or proposition that does not purport to say anything about reality but simply explicates some part of the meaning of one or more of its terms. (*Ex.:* "All circles are round.") Contrasts with *synthetic* (see below).

Anarchism, militant: the view of one committed to the overthrow of existing government without regard to the practical consequences and with no intention of supporting any new government that might be established in its place.

Anarchism, naïve: the view that government actually hinders, rather than enhances, the good of society, and that greater good would result if government simply ceased to exist.

Anarchism, theoretical: the view that the authority of government to restrict the freedom of individuals has no theoretical justification.

A posteriori: completely dependent on, and a product of, experience; mode of knowledge in which experience is the source, as well as the occasion, of knowledge. Contrasts with *a priori* (see below).

A priori: not completely dependent on experience; independent in the sense that experience, although it may be the occasion for one's coming to know, is not the source. Contrasts with *a posteriori* (see above).

Argument: (1) an attempt to show that certain considerations or alleged facts provide evidence in favor of the truth of some proposition; (2) a group of propositions about which it is claimed that the presumed truth of some (the premises) constitutes evidence for the truth of one (the conclusion).

Behaviorism: the view that human beings are constituted in such a way that every detail of their experience and behavior is the inevitable consequence of causes lying outside themselves.

Circumstantial freedom of self-realization: the opportunity to do what one wants to do; a situation in which neither personal limitations nor external restraints prevent one from doing a given thing. (*Ex.:* religious freedom, that is, the opportunity to worship as one wishes.)

Cognition: (1) the act or process of knowing (cognizing); (2) that which is known (cognized).

Common-sense, or direct, realism: the view that the world as it really is does not differ in any important respect from the world as it appears to us.

Consciousness: a center of awareness, feeling, and perception; mind.

Contingent: (1) (in logic) quality of a proposition that is not necessarily true, that is, a proposition the denial of which does not involve a self-contradition; (2) (in metaphysics) quality of a being that does not have the cause of its existence within itself; ontologically dependent. Contrasts with *necessary* (see below).

Contracausal: incompatible with determinism.

Cosmological argument: (1) an argument for the existence of God that takes as its first premise some empirical or quasi-empirical observation about the world; (2) some particular formulation of such an argument.

Cosmology: (1) the study of the origin and general structure of the physical universe; (2) a theory or system regarding the same. Most of the inquiries that once belonged to cosmology have now been taken over by the physical sciences.

Critical realism: any view that affirms that the world as it really is, is in some respects similar to, and in some respects different from, the world as it appears to us.

Cultural relativism: a metaethical theory according to which moral utterances are held to be statements about the approval- and disapproval-tendencies of some social group to whom the person making the utterance has reference.

Deduction: the act of drawing a conclusion from a set of premises; the act of inferring. In the case of a correct deduction, the conclusion (inference) must be true if the premises are true. In this, *deduction* differs from *induction* (see below). Also, that which one deduces from a set of premises.

Defining characteristic: a characteristic that a thing must have in order to be a member of the class of things being defined. (*Ex.:* being unmarried is a defining characteristic of bachelorhood; hence, any person who is to qualify as a bachelor must have the characteristic of being unmarried.)

Determinism: the theory that the universe is constituted in such a way that everything that occurs is the inevitable consequence of antecedent causes; universal determinism; strict determinism. Contrasts with *indeterminism* (see below).

Double-aspect theory: the theory, first advanced by the Dutch philosopher Benedict Spinoza (1632–1677), that mind and body are simply two different aspects of a single underlying reality.

Dualism, mind-body: the theory that body and mind are ontologically distinct, neither being reducible to the other.

Dualism, ontological: the theory that reality consists of two different kinds of being (for example, mind and matter), neither of which is reducible to the other.

Emotivism: a metaethical theory according to which moral utterances are held to be ejaculatory in nature, that is, expressions of the feelings (of approval or disapproval) of the speaker; a form of *noncognitivism* (see below).

Empirical: (1) derived from observation; *a posteriori;* (2) about the real world; capable of being exhibited in sense experience.

Empirical generalization: a general statement about a class of objects made on the basis of observation of some members of that class.

Empiricism: the epistemological theory that all knowledge of reality originates in, and is a product of, sense experience, that is, all knowledge of synthetic truths arises out of experience. Contrasts with *rationalism* (see below).

Epiphenomenalism: the theory that mind or consciousness is a mere by-product ("epiphenomenon") of physiological processes, and that it does not influence those processes in any way; the theory that mind is constituted by physiological processes, and is influenced causally by them, but that it has no causal influence on the body.

Epistemology: (1) a study of the nature and limits of human knowledge; (2) a theory concerning the same. (*Ex.:* "the *epistemology* of Kant.")

Equivocal: quality of a term having different meanings in each of two or more applications.

Ethical pluralism: the view that many things are intrinsically good, and that the highest human good consists in securing a maximum quantity of such goods.

Ethical theism: a world view, the central claim of which is that everything that exists (except God Himself) is the creation of a good, wise, and powerful Creator.

Ethics: see *normative ethics; metaethics.*

Eudemonia: literally, "having a good spirit," from the Greek word *eudaimonia,* usually translated as "happiness."

Existential: of or pertaining to existence, particularly human existence.

Fallacy: an error in reasoning that makes it impossible to establish the conclusion in question on the given premises; a logical mistake. In the case of a deductive argument, the effect of a fallacy is to render the argument *invalid* (see below).

Formalist ethics: a type of ethical theory in which moral obligatoriness is held to be a characteristic of some acts quite apart from any tendency those acts (or acts of that type) may have, or be presumed to have, to produce a good result. Deontological ethics.

Freedom: (1) the opportunity to do what one wants to do; (2) the power to enact any of two or more genuinely open alternatives; free will; (3) the realization of the "ideal" state for human beings, wherein one has become everything that a human being ought to be. (Note: This term is highly ambiguous. It is always important to try to determine the precise sense in which a given writer is using the term.) See also *moral freedom; natural freedom of self-determination; circumstantial freedom of self-realization; free will.*

Free will: power of the self to enact any of two or more genuinely open alternatives; contracausal freedom; natural freedom of self-determination.

Hard determinism: the view that determinism is true, and that it is not compatible with moral freedom, and that human beings are, therefore, not morally responsible.

Hedonism: (1) (analytic form) the theory that "good," in the moral sense, means "pleasurable"; (2) (synthetic form) the theory that pleasure alone is intrinsically good.

Heuristic principle: a principle that is not judged as to its truth or falsity (it is neither affirmed nor denied) but is assumed for the purposes of some particular inquiry because of its demonstrated usefulness in raising fruitful questions.

Humanism: the view that human beings, unlike all other creatures, are, in some respects, not merely a part of nature.

Hypercritical realism: the view that the world as it really is, is highly dissimilar to the world as it appears to us; a radical form of *critical realism* (see above).

Immanent: within; near; not transcendent.

Imperativism: a metaethical theory according to which moral sentences are held to be a species of directive language, that is, implicit commands or recommendations to act in certain ways and not to act in other ways; a form of *noncognitivism* (see below).

Indeterminism: the theory that the universe is constituted in such a way that some events are not the inevitable consequences of antecedent causes.

Induction: the act of affirming a general statement about a class of things on the basis of observation of some members of the class; the act of making an empirical generalization. Also, an empirical generalization affirmed on the basis of observation of some members of the class.

Inference: (1) a proposition that follows as a logical consequence of certain other propositions; that which is inferred; an implication; (2) the act of inferring, that is, of deriving the actual or apparent logical consequences from a set of assumed premises.

Interactionism: the theory that body and mind are ontologically distinct, and that they influence each other causally.

Introspection: the act or process of observing or noting one's own feelings, thoughts, or mental states.

Intuition: according to rationalists, the act whereby the mind discerns nonempirical qualities and grasps a priori truths.

Intuitionism: (1) (in aesthetics) the view that the assertion that something has aesthetic value is a claim that it possesses in some degree the nonnatural quality "beauty"; (2) (in ethics) a metaethical theory according to which "good," in the moral sense, is held to denote a simple, nonnatural quality; nonnaturalistic objectivism; nonnaturalism.

Invalid: quality of a deductive argument whose conclusion may be false even if all its premises are true; not valid.

Legalism: an ethical theory according to which it is held that right and wrong are determined by one's adherence or nonadherence to a set of moral rules (laws) that are applicable at all times, in all places, and under all circumstances.

Libertarianism: the view that free will is a necessary condition of moral responsibility, that human beings have this freedom, and, consequently, that determinism is not the case. Contrasts with *hard determinism* (see above) and *soft determinism* (see below).

Logic: (1) a study of the principles whereby one may distinguish correct from incorrect reasoning; (2) a system or theory regarding the same. (*Ex.:* "The *logic* of John Stuart Mill.")

Materialism: the metaphysical theory that the whole of reality consists of matter and its determinations; a form of *monism* (see below).

Metaethics: a study of the logical structure of ethical reasoning and the logical characteristics of ethical discourse. The main effort of metaethics, to date, has been directed toward the elucidation of the precise meanings of the key terms of moral appraisal ("good," "bad," "right," "wrong," "duty," "ought," and the like).

Metalanguage: a language used for the purpose of talking about language, that is, a language whose terms denote features of language rather than features of nonverbal reality; a language about language. (The language of grammar, for example, constitutes a metalanguage.)

Metaphysics: (1) the study of the nature and structure of being (ontology) and of the origin and general structure of the universe (cosmology); first philosophy; (2) a theory or system concerning the same. (Some philosophers use this term simply as a synonym for ontology, excluding cosmology. Others use it pejoratively as a synonym for "nonsense.")

Monism: the view that the whole of reality consists of various determinations of some one ultimate substance, or kind of "stuff." The principal forms of monism are *materialism* (all is matter), *idealism* (all is mind), and *neutral monism* (all is some substance that is neither mind nor matter but is the ground of both). Monism contrasts with *dualism* (see above) and *pluralism* (see below).

Moral evil: anything generally regarded as evil that occurs as a result of a deliberate act by a human being. Contrasts with *natural evil* (see below).

Moral freedom: the freedom (whatever its nature) that is a necessary condition of moral responsibility; the freedom without which human beings are not, or would not be, morally responsible.

Morally responsible: answerable for one's behavior; a fitting subject of moral appraisal.

Naïve realism: see *common-sense, or direct, realism.*

Natural evil: anything generally regarded as evil that occurs as a result of the ordinary working of the laws of nature. Contrasts with *moral evil* (see above).

Natural freedom of self-determination: the power of the self to enact any one of two or more genuinely open alternatives; contracausal freedom; free will. Libertarians affirm that human beings have such a power, determinists that they do not.

Naturalism: (1) any philosophical system that holds that the whole of reality consists of objects and events occurring in space and time. Contrasts with *transcendentalism* (see below); (2) (in metaethics) the view that "good," in the moral sense, denotes some empirical quality or qualities; naturalistic objectivism.

Naturalistic fallacy: the mistake, according to the intuitionism of G. E. Moore (1873–1958), of attempting to define "good," in the moral sense, particularly in terms of some natural (empirically discernible) quality or qualities.

Naturalistic objectivism: a metaethical theory according to which the key moral predicates are held to denote some empirically verifiable quality or qualities; ethical naturalism. A hedonist who affirms that "good" means "pleasurable," for example, would be affirming one common version of this theory.

Natural law: a fundamental principle of right or justice that, according to some philosophers, human reason can discern merely by attending carefully to the proposition stating that principle.

Necessary: (1) (in logic) quality of a proposition the denial of which involves a self-contradiction; (2) (in metaphysics) quality of a being that has the cause of its existence within itself; not ontologically dependent. Contrasts with *contingent* (see above).

Nihilism: the view that nothing is worth living for, that human existence is without meaning.

Noncognitivism: any metaethical theory that holds that moral sentences are not informative, that is, they assert nothing, and, therefore, are incapable of being either true or false. *Emotivism* and *imperativism* (see above) are examples of this type of theory.

Nonnaturalism: any philosophical system that holds that there are dimensions of reality in addition to objects and events occuring in space and time. Contrasts with *naturalism* (see above).

Nonnaturalistic objectivism: see *intuitionism.*

Non sequitur: an argument containing a fallacy; an argument in which the conclusion does not follow from the premises.

Normative ethics: the quest for general principles of right and wrong; the attempt to determine what things really are good or bad, right or wrong, and to identify the general principles by virtue of which they are so.

Objective relativism: the theory that the assertion that an object has aesthetic value is a claim that the object in question has certain characteristics that people, by virtue of their psychological and physiological makeup, naturally admire; the "cultivated taste" theory of aesthetic judgment.

Occasionalism: the theory that mind and body are ontologically distinct (therefore, a *dualistic* theory), and that each operates according to its own laws, but that they appear to interact because, from time to time, God does whatever is required to keep them synchronized.

Omnipotence: infinite power; an attribute of God whereby He is said to be able to bring to pass whatever He wills.

Omniscience: infinite knowledge; an attribute of God whereby He is said to know everything there is to know; all-knowingness.

Ontological argument: a famous argument for the existence of God, devised by St. Anselm of Canterbury (1033–1106), in which the attempt is made to show that the denial of the proposition "God exists" is self-contradictory.

Ontologically distinct: belonging to different ontological categories, neither of which is reducible to the other.

Ontological status: kind of being. To disclose the ontological status of something is to put it in some ontological category; it is to state in what precise sense it is true to say that a thing is.

Ontology: (1) the study of the nature or structure of being (some philosophers use this term as a synonym for *metaphysics;* others use it as the name for one main branch of metaphysics, the other being *cosmology*); (2) a theory or system put forward as a result of such a study.

Panpsychism: the view that the whole of reality consists of minds ("psyches") of varying degrees of consciousness; one of the classical ways of attempting to overcome ontological dualism.

Paradox: an apparently self-contradictory assertion that is, nonetheless, made on the ground that to eliminate the apparent contradiction would allegedly involve denying some truth.

Parallelism: the view that mind and body are ontologically distinct (therefore, a dualistic theory), and that each operates according to its own laws, the appearance of interaction between the two resulting from the fact that God has established a perfect harmony between them. This view was first advocated by the German philosopher Gottfried Wilhem Leibnitz (1646–1716).

Percept: that which is "before the mind" in the act of perceiving; that which is immediately present to consciousness in perception; sense datum.

Perception: the act or process of taking cognizance of the world by means of the senses.

Phenomenalism; the view that the reality of a material object consists in its being perceived by some perceiver, with the corollary that the physical world does not exist apart from the actual or possible perceptions of some perceiver. See also *subjective idealism.*

Pluralism: the view that reality is not reducible to one ultimate substance, or kind of "stuff," but that, on the contrary, there are several. Contrasts with *monism* and *dualism* (see above).

Premise: a proposition that, in conjunction with one or more other propositions, is alleged to provide evidence for some proposition (the conclusion).

Primary quality: according to the critical realism of John Locke

(1632–1704), a quality that belongs to an object in such a way that no particle of which the object is composed could be conceived to exist without it. Locke gives extension, shape, size, and mobility as examples of such qualities. Contrasts with *secondary quality* (see below).

Private Subjectivism: (1) (in aesthetics) the view that the assertion that something has aesthetic value is merely a statement reporting the personal preference of the person making the assertion; (2) (in ethics) a metaethical theory according to which moral utterances are held to be statements about the personal likes and dislikes of the person making the utterance.

Proposition: that which is affirmed or denied by a declarative sentence; the meaning of a sentence that affirms or denies that something is the case. Propositions (and the sentences in which they are expressed) have the property of being either true or false.

Rational eudemonism: the view that the highest human good consists in "activity according to reason" (Aristotle).

Rationalism: (1) the view that some truths about reality are knowable in a way that is, to some degree, independent of experience, that is, that some synthetic truths may be known a priori; (2) a European philosophical movement represented by René Descartes (1596–1650), Benedict de Spinoza (1632–1677), Gottfried Wilhelm Leibnitz (1646–1716), Christian Wolff (1679–1754), and Immanuel Kant (1724–1804).

Reality: (1) the totality of the real, everything that is; (2) what truly or in actuality is the case, as over against what may appear to be the case. In this sense, reality is often contrasted with appearance.

Reason: (1) a proposition that, in conjunction with some other propositions, supports a conclusion not deducible from the other propositions alone; a premise; (2) a statement that purportedly justifies a belief or act; (3) the faculty of knowledge; (4) the essential nature of the self.

Reasoning: the act or process of drawing conclusions from premises.

Res cogitans: literally, "thinking thing"; that which, according to René Descartes (1596–1650), a person essentially is–in contrast to unthinking, extended being (that is, material objects).

Secondary quality: according to the critical realism of John Locke (1632–1704), the capacity of a material object to produce in a percipient an impression (of color, sound, taste, and so on) unlike anything in the object itself. Such a quality is, thus, said to be "mind-dependent." Contrasts with *primary quality* (see above).

Self: that which one denotes by the pronoun "I"; consciousness; mind. (Its status has long been a matter of philosophical controversy.)

Self-evident: quality of a proposition that can be seen to be true merely by considering the proposition itself, and that, therefore, does not

need to be proven either by deduction from other more evident propositions or by an appeal to factual evidence.

Sense-data: the immediate, uninterpreted objects of sense experience;
the patches of color, geometrical shapes, and so on that one sees
when looking at a material object, the varipitched noises that one
sometimes hears (which may subsequently be interpreted as a melody on a violin), and so on.

Social contract: a voluntary agreement among a group of individuals
whereby, according to some political theorists, the members of society acquire a set of mutual obligations legitimately enforceable by
established authority.

Social utilitarianism: the view that the authority of government is
justifiable in terms of its capacity to secure the greatest good for the
greatest number of people.

Soft determinism: the view that determinism is true, but that the
conditions of moral responsibility are such that human beings are,
nonetheless, morally responsible whenever they have the opportunity to do what they want to do.

Solipsism: the theory that oneself is the only mind or consciousness
that exists, and that everything else exists only as a perception of
this self.

Sound: quality of an argument that is formally valid and contains only
true premises.

Subjective idealism: the view, associated with George Berkeley (1685–
1753), that the being of material objects consists in their being perceived by some perceiver ("esse est percipi"), that they have no
"independent" existence; phenomenalism. Contrasts with all types
of *critical, direct,* and *hypercritical realism* (see above).

Summum bonum: literally, "highest good"; that which is most worthy
of being sought for its own sake.

Synthetic: quality of a sentence, statement, or proposition that purports to say something about reality. (*Ex.:* "Some camels have two
humps.") Contrasts with *analytic* (see above).

System: a comprehensive set of coherent and interdependent propositions in terms of which one attempts to understand and explain the
phenomena within the range of its alleged relevance. An *ethical
system,* for example, purports to provide a context for the understanding and explanation of all ethical phenomena. A *philosophical
system* purports to provide a context for the understanding and
explanation of all phenomena.

Teleological: of or pertaining to ends, goals, purposes (from the Greek
tèlos, meaning "end" or "goal"). *Teleological* explanations (explanations in terms of ends), for example, are often contrasted with
scientific explanations (explanations in terms of causes). The term
is sometimes used to describe a kind of thinking, also to designate
a famous argument for the existence of God (see *teleological argument* below).

Teleological Argument: an argument for the existence of God popularized by William Paley (1743–1805). The argument begins with the allegedly empirical premise that there is order (means subservient to ends) in the universe, and by analogy with human contrivances asserts the necessity of positing a cosmic intelligence to account for this order.

Teleological ethics: a type of ethical theory in which the moral value of any act is held to consist in the tendency of that act (or of acts of that type) to produce a good or bad result.

Tèlos: end or goal; that toward the achievement of which some process or activity is directed. (Plural *tèloi.*)

Theodicy: an attempt to show that the occurrence of evil in the world is consistent with belief in a God who is perfect in knowledge, power, and goodness.

Touchstone proposition: central truth about reality as perceived in some particular worldview.

Transcendent: (1) (Kant's usage) beyond the categories of human experience; (2) (as commonly used in theology and philosophy of religion) beyond the world of space and time; other. Contrasts with *immanent* (see above).

Transcendentalism: a world view that attempts to find some common ground between theism and naturalism.

Utilitarianism: (1) the theory that the goodness or badness of acts consists in their tendency to promote or hinder the realization of that which is intrinsically good; (2) the particular version of this theory advocated by the English philosophers Jeremy Bentham (1749–1832) and John Stuart Mill (1806–1873). This view is more properly called "hedonistic utilitarianism."

Vague: (applied to terms) imprecise in ordinary usage in such a way that any attempt at precise definition would render the term more exact than ordinary usage will allow. (*Ex.:* "warm" is a vague term; it would be inconsistent with ordinary usage to define it precisely in terms of a definite temperature range.)

Verbal: of or pertaining to words. Often applied to a given philosophical controversy to indicate that there is no "real issue" dividing the parties to the dispute, but simply a confusion or disagreement over the meanings of certain terms.

Volition: (1) the act of exercising choice, of choosing among alternatives; (2) the power to exercise choice.

World view: a comprehensive view of reality in terms of which one attempts to understand and "place" everything that comes before one's consciousness.

INDEX

ABOUT THE AUTHOR

WILLIAM H. HALVERSON is Associate Dean of University College and Adjunct Professor of Philosophy at The Ohio State University. He holds degrees from Augsburg College (B.A., 1951), Augsburg Seminary (B.Th., 1955), Princeton Seminary (Th.M., 1957), and Princeton University (M.A., 1959; Ph.D., 1961). He has contributed articles to *Mind*, *The Pacific Philosophy Forum*, and *The Journal of Religion*, and is the compiler and editor of a new anthology, *Concise Readings in Philosophy* (New York: Random House, 1981).